GANDHIANS IN CONTEMPORARY INDIA

GANDHIANS IN CONTEMPORARY INDIA
THE VISION AND THE VISIONARIES

Ishwar C. Harris

The Edwin Mellen Press
Lewiston•Queenston•Lampeter

Library of Congress Cataloging-in-Publication Data

Harris, Ishwar C., 1943-
  Gandhians in contemporary India : the vision and the visionaries /
Ishwar Harris.
      p. cm.
  Includes bibliographical references and index.
  ISBN 0-7734-8352-7
  1. Gandhi, Mahatma, 1869-1948--Political and social views.
  2. Social reformers--India. 3. Sarvodaya movement--India.
  4. India--Social policy. 5. India--Politics and government--20th
century.   I. Title.
DS481.G3H28   1998
954.03' 5' 092--dc21   98-7529
                                                                                        CIP

A CIP catalog record for this book is available from the British Library.

        The Edwin Mellen Press   The Edwin Mellen Press
               Box 450   Box 67
        Lewiston, New York   Queenston, Ontario
        USA 14092-0450   CANADA L0S 1L0

               The Edwin Mellen Press, Ltd.
               Lampeter, Ceredigion, Wales
               UNITED KINGDOM SA48 8LT

        Printed in the United States of America

For

Jyotsna

Meera & Anjali

Contents

Part One
The Vision

Part Two
The Visionaries

Part Three

List of Illustrations

Acknowledgments

The present work would not have been completed without the support of many individuals in the United States and India. It is impossible to list the names of all who have lent their helping hands, and I regret if I have failed to mention any of them.

First and foremost I wish to thank all of the personalities covered in this book. They were generous to grant me multiple interviews, and in many cases, entertained me in their homes, ashrams, and the work place. They opened a world of adventure for me beyond my expectations. I was touched by their generosity, openness, and the willingness to share their stories with me. In many cases they facilitated my entry into the world of Sarvodaya, occupied by the Gandhians whom the world does not know. Beyond the boundaries of this book, I was introduced to numerous Gandhian leaders, scholars, educators, and social workers who shared their views with me.

In particular I wish to thank the late Dr. Radhakrishna, the Secretary of the Gandhi Peace Foundation in New Delhi, who initially discussed the merits of this project and encouraged me to undertake the research. His successor, Mr. Krishnaswamy, was equally helpful in preparing a list of names of the contemporary Gandhians for me to meet and to interview. Thanks are also due to Rajiv Vora, the editor of the journal, Gandhi Marg (Hindi edition), and a research associate at the Gandhi Peace Foundation. His insights on Gandhi and the Gandhians have been very useful to me over the years as I have visited him in India. Equally helpful are the insights of Mr. S.K. De, the present Secretary of the Gandhi Peace Foundation, who over the years has shared with me his knowledge of the Gandhians in India and abroad. I am also indebted to Mr. Ravindra Varma,

vii

the President of the Gandhi Peace Foundation, who invited me to lecture to his students at his Institute of Gandhian Studies in Wardha, Maharashtra, and also asked me to deliver a paper at the conference "Gandhi and the Twenty-First Century," which he organized in 1998. Thanks are also due to Mr. Sadiq Ali, the President of Gandhi Smarak Nidhi, in New Delhi. Mr. Sadiq Ali was gracious enough to grant me an interview at his office and, a few years later, an extended meeting at the Sat Tal Estate in the District of Nainital, where we discussed my project at some length. The Secretary of Gandhi Smarak Nidhi, Mr. Shailesh Bandopadhyay, was also kind enough to discuss the work of contemporary Gandhians with me.

There are numerous leaders within the Gandhian movement who met with me at various times to discuss Gandhism. Due to difficult circumstances, certain individuals could not be included in this book. Nevertheless, their insights were quite valuable in the preparation of this manuscript. They include such personalities as Siddharaj Dhadda, Prem Bhai, Dwarko Sundarani, Manmohan Chaudhury, Homer Jack, and Amarnath Bhai. There are also many members of the Sarvodaya movement who were kind enough to respond to my questionnaire. I thank them for providing me with the necessary information crucial to this book.

I am indebted to Mahendra Kumar, professor of political science at the University of Delhi and also the editor of the journal, Gandhi Marg (English edition), for reading the manuscript and making valuable suggestions. Thanks are also due to professor Paul Mundschenck, of Western Illinois University, for also reading the manuscript and making suggestions for improvements. I am also indebted to professor Wendell Charles Beane, University of Wisconsin Oshkosh, for painstakingly proof-reading the manuscript. Our discussions of certain philosophical, historical, political issues related to Sarvodaya and its adherents were extremely useful in my assessment of the Gandhians covered in this book.

I am especially grateful to Arun Gandhi, a grandson of the Mahatma and the Director of the M.K. Gandhi Institute For Nonviolence in Memphis Tennessee, for graciously agreeing to write the "Foreword" to this work. His comments are insightful and greatly appreciated.

The College of Wooster Leave Program enabled me to make two lengthy trips to India to complete my research. I am thankful to the Henry Luce III Fund for Distinguished Scholarship administered by the College of Wooster for making it financially possible for me to travel the breadth of India in search of the Gandhians covered in this book. My gratitude also goes to Smita Narayan, a native of Bombay and a math major at the College of Wooster, who, along with her computer-expert friend Mustafa Hasham of Tanzania, and a graduate of the College of Wooster spent so many hours assisting me in preparing a camera-ready copy of the manuscript. I thank Smita for sticking with the project from the beginning till the completion.

But most of all, I am indebted to my wife, Jyotsna, and my children, Meera and Anjali, to whom this book is dedicated. I thank them for their courage as I often left them alone, both in America and India, to pursue my research. Without their love, support, and understanding this project would not have been completed.

Foreword

I have always had reservations over the use of the word "**Gandhian**." It implies, to me, the existence of "**Gandhism**" and yet Mohandas Karamchand Gandhi very categorically said: "I wish to leave behind no isms." For very good reasons. First, he did not wish to leave behind a dogma and, second, because he perceived his mission in life to be "*Satyagraha*" -the pursuit of truth with diligence, determination and honesty.

"Truth," Gandhi believed, could only be pursued, not possessed. To possess Truth means attaining salvation since "Truth" is God. Attaining or possessing the truth implies one has merged with the Creator and, therefore, the cycle of life and the search for its meaning must come to an end. For mere mortals to cease the search for Truth is to hold on dogmatically to someone's belief, thought, vision or philosophy.

Gandhi was not only progressive and understanding but also, many felt, painfully inconsistent. His ideas changed and so did his perception. Out of sheer exasperation his followers often asked: "**How can we keep up with you if you change your views everyday?**"

Gandhi replied: "**How can I remain consistent when Truth is ever changing?**" Truth is the most difficult to grasp because it appears differently at different times to different people. The search for Truth requires a great deal of sincerity, honesty, perseverance and humility. More than anything else it requires the magnanimity to embrace Truth even when it appears to be against everything we stand for. Gandhi advised his followers to pursue Truth and develop the ability to recognize it.

xi

So the question arises: If there is no "Gandhism" can there be "Gandhians"? If people followed the teachings of Gandhi to the best of their abilities in their own pursuit of Truth can their successes or failures be labeled as the success or failure of Gandhian philosophy? Oftentimes writers and readers have jumped to such conclusions because the link between an individual's actions and an individual's understanding of Gandhi's philosophy is so intertwined.

For instance, when one speaks of Gandhi's concept of *"Ram Rajya"* - literally meaning the rule of Lord Rama - one could easily conclude Gandhi was supporting the creation of a Hindu State. Some bigoted researchers have even branded Gandhi as a Hindu fundamentalist. Needless to say this is absolutely incorrect.

Gandhi often used Hindu terminology to reach those who were and, unfortunately still are either less educated or less understanding. Gandhi's concept of *Ram Rajya* was a State where absolute honesty, justice and fair play prevailed. Lord Rama believed in absolute justice, even at the expense of self-suffering. What we practice in the name of justice is not justice but revenge. Gandhi sought an ideal State like the one created by Lord Rama. There is, obviously, a great danger of misinterpreting or even distorting Gandhi's philosophy if it is taken literally.

In 1976 when Mrs. Indira Gandhi sought to perpetuate her political career by imposing on India a State of Emergency and suspending the constitution she asked those close to her to endorse what she was doing. Someone close to Mrs. Gandhi at the time was able to persuade the eminent Acharya Vinoba Bhave to support the suspension of liberties.

Vinoba Bhave made a statement commending the emergency and the consequent suspension of civil rights and arrests of political dissenters because, as he put it, it forced the government and the railways to run efficiently. His logic shocked those of us who felt Mrs. Gandhi was wrong. It raised in our minds the obvious question: Was democracy and human rights about efficient working of the Government and the railways? The logic made no sense to most of us.

I sought clarification from Kedar Nathji, an eminent activist and student of Gandhi and the philosophy of Satyagraha. Nathji was a contemporary of Vinoba Bhave and he gave me a profound explanation of the statement. He said: Satyagraha, a combination of two Sanskrit words - Satya = truth and Agraha = determination - can be defined in two ways.

To some it means the pursuit of truth at all costs as Gandhi did. while to others it means holding on to a Truth with consummate determination as Vinoba did. In the total mess resulting from the declaration of emergency Vinoba found truth in the efficient running of the bureaucracy and held on to that.

This book deals with the lives and works of many who lived close to Gandhi and translated his philosophy as best as they could. Prof. Ishwar Harris has evaluated their lives and work diligently and come to his own conclusions and so must the reader since we are all in pursuit of the truth and our success must depend upon how diligent and honest we are.

-Arun Gandhi

M.K. Gandhi Institute for Nonviolence

Memphis, TN

Preface

The years 1997 and 1998 have been crucial for India's self-reflection. They mark the centenary of India's independence from the British as well as the assassination of Mahatma Gandhi, the Father of the nation, respectively. While the nation celebrates its achievements, it is also the time to examine the values upon which the country was founded. The contemporary Gandhians, many of whom shared Gandhi's vision for India's future, are hard at work to convert his dream into reality. They are faced with immense challenges to keep his dream alive while India races to join the twenty-first century. While "globalization" is being embraced, "nationalization" is brought under scrutiny. While the western model of development is accepted, the voices of dissent are also raised.

The present work, Gandhians in Contemporary India, examines the life and work of fifteen leading and exemplary Gandhians who are actively involved in a process to shape the Indian society along certain Gandhian values. It explores how Gandhi's dream has become their dream and what challenges they are facing in actualizing it. The emphasis is put on their respective constructive work programs, something which Gandhi has initiated to turn India into Ram Raj, or the "Kingdom of God." The personalities covered in this book are dedicated Gandhian Lok Sevaks (Servants of the People), who are inspired by Gandhi and his disciples, Vinoba Bhave and Jai Prakash Narayan (J.P.). They are members of the Sarvodaya Movement (Welfare for All), a movement that Gandhi had started, and was expanded by Vinoba and J.P..

In the wake of India's recent nuclear explosion, many have questioned her ability to practice the nonviolence of her native son, Gandhi. They believe that Gandhi has been betrayed in his own country. The contemporary Gandhians have also taken the stance that today the betrayal of Gandhi is an existing phenomenon in India. However, due to the process of modernization, which is rapidly changing India, the Gandhians have argued that Gandhi is all the more relevant today than ever before. Thus they are willing to sacrifice their own comforts to keep the Gandhian vision alive as they work among the poor, the untouchables, the tribals, the laborers, and alike. They firmly believe that the present social, economic, and political injustices need to be challenged in order to establish a Sarvodaya society. Yet their struggle remains a nonviolent struggle in a world filled with violence.

It is my hope that this book will introduce to the reader a family of contemporary Gandhians who are tirelessly engaged in reshaping the future of India against tremendous odds. While Gandhism is on the verge of being ignored in modern India, these men and women have not lost their hope in the gospel of Gandhi. Meeting them, living with them, working with them, and studying with them, has been personally gratifying and a source of inspiration. I trust that the reader will find their stories engaging, fascinating, and revealing.

Ishwar C. Harris, College of Wooster

Introduction

Long before India became an independent nation in 1947, she had to struggle with the question of her cultural identity. For hundreds of years she had absorbed many cultures that entered her boundaries, but the encounter with European civilization produced a unique challenge in the modern era. The question whether modernization meant westernization became the focus of intellectual debate among the makers of modern India. Mahatma Gandhi played a central role in this debate. His fight with the British was not so much over who controlled the territory, but, rather, whose values dominated the culture. For Gandhi this was the issue of survival for India. It is of utmost significance that the issues he raised in this context nearly half a century ago are still being debated by the contemporary Gandhians in India today. As for Gandhi, so for the Gandhians, the survival of the Indian culture is at stake as it moves into the 21st century.

The question of cultural identity is not unique to India. The conflict between tradition and modernity has created a civilizational crisis all over the world. Particularly affected by this crisis are those countries of Asia and Africa that have suffered the onslaught of Western colonialism. Mahatma Gandhi experienced the colonial oppression first hand in South Africa and India. He fought, along with others, for the freedom of his people from the tyranny of the oppressors. However, his fight had two major fronts. The political front and the social front. He is well known for his philosophy of Satyagraha (Truth Force) as a political weapon to fight the British in India. He is not so well known for his social philosophy of Sarvodaya (Welfare for All); which he developed to reconstruct the society, purging it from certain norms impacted by western culture. The Swaraj (self rule) that he envisioned did not entail merely overthrowing the political power, but also overturning the value system that

1

produced and sustained that political power. This was his most difficult battle for it involved fighting the enemy within, e.g., the natives, who were sold to the Western models of governance, economic development, education, etc. It can be debated whether Gandhi was against all Western values, specially when he was educated in the West. Certainly, he cannot be seen as favoring all Indian values. At best, Gandhi represents a synthesis of East and West, although many of his concepts for social development were derived from Indian tradition.

Recovery of the Indian roots and a passion for Western pragmatism to bring about change seem to dominate Gandhian programs of constructive works founded under the movement of Sarvodaya (Welfare for All). Through Sarvodaya he envisioned the establishment of a new society he called Ram Raj (Kingdom of God).[1] An analysis of this concept clearly shows that it forcefully challenges the Western models of political, social, and economic development. A glimpse of his thinking in this area can be ascertained from two important books. First, Hind Swaraj (Indian Home Rule) presents a forceful critique of the 20th century vision of a Western society.[2] Second, Sarvodaya, a paraphrased version of John Ruskin's Unto This Last also challenges the economics of development.[3] Both works enlighten us as to what Gandhi was envisioning as Ram Raj not only for India, but indeed for the whole world. Eventually under Sarvodaya, Gandhi instituted an eighteen point constructive work program for the political, social, economic, and religious development of India.[4] After Gandhi's assassination, his protégé, Vinoba Bhave, further emphasized the foundation of a Sarvodaya Samaj (Society for the welfare of all), bringing several constructive programs together under the organization, Sarva Seva Sangh (Organization for the Service of All). For nearly two decades, Vinoba remained the undisputed leader of the Gandhian organizations, pushing forward a variety of programs for social welfare. In the early 1970s a rift within the organization caused a majority of Lok Sevaks (Servants of the People) to follow Jai Prakash Narayan, a veteran politician who had given up politics to join Vinoba in the 1950s. Now that both Vinoba and Jai Prakash (J. P.) are deceased, there is no charismatic leader to guide the movement. However, Sarva Seva Sangh survives with a majority of its members favoring the ideology of Total Revolution propagated by Jai Prakash Narayan.[5] The ideological differences between Vinoba and J. P. have far reaching consequences for shaping the vision of Ram Raj that Gandhi had initially propounded. Most Gandhians treated in the present work are highly influenced by both Vinoba and J. P., who became their windows to look into the mind of Gandhi.

2

The fight of Gandhi is being fought by contemporary Gandhians in India today. Since India's independence in 1947, it appears that the country has embraced Western models of development. The basic features of such development are: heavy industrialization, consumer based economy, technological advancements, mass production, multi-national corporations, centralization of political power, etc. Most Gandhians seem to agree that the consequences of these developments have created certain crises in India in modern times. They see a correlation between industrialization and the plight of the landless, consumerism and poverty, technology and joblessness, mass production and moral decay, multinational companies and neo-colonialism, centralization of power and corruption. Many observers of India have written extensively about these crises and some have put the blame on India's first prime minister, Pandit Jawaharlal Nehru, who is credited to have been the political lieutenant of Gandhi.[6] It is believed that it was his policies that created the course for modern India, and that they were pushed by his daughter, Indira Gandhi, and his grandson, Rajiv Gandhi, both of whom, as prime ministers, controlled the so called "Nehru Dynasty". They represented the Congress Party, which controlled the power for more years than any of its rivals. Narasimha Rao, who is credited to have revolutionized the Indian economy by inviting the multi-national companies to invest in India, belonged to the same party. The New Economic Policy designed by Rao's finance minister, Manmohan Singh, has been highly praised in the West, but criticized by Gandhians in India. In the 1990s India has taken a giant step toward economic development through liberalizing its economy for powerful domestic and foreign investors. For some it is perceived as a new form of violence against the poor, encouraging exploitation of the have-nots by the fortunate few. "Doesn't this situation call for a renewed Satyagraha and Sarvodaya?" This is one of the major questions that the Gandhians are faced with today.

The crisis has taken many other dimensions. Having traveled in India extensively for the past two decades, this author has witnessed enormous changes that have affected the political, social, religious, economic, and cultural life in India. India has made a great many advances in its nuclear and armaments programs. It claims to have enough grain reserves (due to the Green Revolution) that it could send economic aid to the former Soviet Union.[7] The life expectancy has risen to higher standards. It has improved its computer technology to the extent of exporting computer chips to other countries. Its middle class has risen to approximately 250 million people, which is roughly the population of the United

States of America. In the industrial world it is ranked number seven in comparison with many developed countries. And yet, this is only half of the story. A visitor to India cannot help but also notice a rapid deterioration of the quality of life. The environmental damage caused by industrial waste dumped into India's rivers and lakes is visible everywhere. Its holy rivers, Jamna and Ganga, are so polluted that at places their waters are not fit for bathing let alone drinking. The tragedy of India is that it can provide Pepsi, Coke, Seven Up, and dozens of soft drinks for the consumer to buy, but it cannot provide a clean glass of water for an average citizen to drink. The water-related diseases claim many lives every year throughout India. While India's leaders blame the West for the depletion of the ozone layer, they ignore the damage India is causing to its own environment. Living in Delhi, India's capital, one notices the persistent haze that blankets the city. During the 1970s I was told that the condition was caused by hundreds and thousands of cooking fires at the outskirt of the city. In the 1990s everyone blames the diesel fumes generated by buses and automobiles. Many residents of Delhi have persistent coughing problems that never go away, and a significant number of people suffer from breath related illnesses. The Delhi police advertises and recommends the use of masks for protection. In 1992 I was horrified at the sight of some traffic police directing the traffic at a major intersection in New Delhi with combat masks on. In 1998 the condition seemed worse. Delhi is no exception. Environmental degradation is rampant all over India.

India's large cities are growing at a rapid rate. Virtually all of them are surrounded by a growing number of slums and shanty-towns infested with rotting garbage, open sewers, crime, and all kinds of diseases. Many of its inhabitants are migrants from villages, who move to the city every day in search of jobs. Most are landless laborers with no skills. Their stories are heartbreaking sagas of oppression and exploitation at the hands of their landlords and money lenders, who drive them to bankruptcy and eventual plight toward the city. Some sell their land to pay off a debt, some flee from the torture of bonded labor, some are driven away by powerful forces of village Mafia. The ideal village of Gandhi and Vinoba is their worst nightmare. As victims of hunger, poverty, and threats, they turn to the city for food, shelter, and a better life, only to be trapped in slums. The city cannot provide for them. It does not want them. Anyone traveling by train in India can witness their condition as the train begins to pull near a railway station. The railway tracks are the playing grounds for the children of these slum dwellers outside the city. The sanitary conditions of their dwellings are beyond belief. The

4

humans and animals bathe and drink from the stagnant ponds. During the rainy season, sewage floats on the water at the doorsteps of their makeshift shelters. In a recent seminar on the 'problem of the growing rate of shanty colonies' sponsored by YMCA of New Delhi, Mr. B. K. Singh, Chairman of the Social Concern Extension and Development of YMCA stated, "The social and physical environment in which so many live is a menace to every aspect of their being. The slums are congested, unsanitary, ridden with garbage, filthy water and loitering pigs and dogs. Social and moral values have often broken down, and drug and alcohol abuse are rife. Approximately 98 lac (9,800,000) people live like this everyday.[8]

Conditions like these are a common sight throughout India. The failure of society to make the villages safe and economically attractive is a commentary on India's neglect to heed to Gandhi's advice regarding Gram Swaraj (freedom of the village), and the problem of urbanization.[9]

India is hailed as the world largest democracy, which it is. Politically, it is stable and vibrant. However, there are numerous threats to its stability. After the break up of the Soviet Union and former Yugoslavia, some anticipate a similar fate for India, although many are optimistic about its survival. In Indian politics, regionalism, caste allegiance, ethnic and cultural identities play an important role. The Nehruvian slogan of "unity within variety" is an ideal that India is trying to achieve. However, its unity is constantly being threatened. Take for instance the independence movements in Kashmir, Punjab, and Nagaland. Their demand of cessation from the Union is a constant reminder of the threat of breaking up of the Indian Republic. The conflicts with Pakistan over territory and violence caused by both sides has become a major issue of national security. One often hears of the so called "foreign powers" wanting to destabilize India. The bill board signs promoting "National Integration" are visible in many large cities. Many cultural programs are organized to emphasize national unity, brotherhood, cooperation, and integration. There appears to be a movement to somehow keep the country together. The increasing terrorist activities are common occurrences. All forms of violence pose a constant challenge to Gandhi's non-violent India. The government response to eliminate these conflicts is through the consolidation of power at the center. As a policy, the provinces are deprived of autonomy in many areas. The people perceive that as an infringement of their rights. The consequence is agitation, bandhs (shut downs), riots, disruption of vital services, and in many cases, loss of lives.

In India today there is a growing mistrust in the Central Government's ability to maintain law and order. The Gandhian vision of a <u>Panchayat raj</u> (village council), which calls for the decentralization and handing of power over to the villages, has not been implemented. Socially, communal tension, caste conflicts, the plight of the tribals, the neglect of the <u>dalits</u>,[10] exploitation of children, oppression of women, etc. dominate the national scene. While population continues to increase, the division between the powerful and the powerless is widening. The government's efforts to help the lower castes through a quota system by reserving certain seats in government jobs and university admissions has caused a major upheaval in recent years. The Mandal Commission report,[11] which recommended the uplift of the deprived classes, has been seriously challenged by those who claim to be victims of reverse discrimination. India's Affirmative Action program is seriously undermined when young college students burn themselves alive in protest of the quota system. The government's attempt to grant certain rights to the religious minorities is perceived as granting special privileges in the hope of gaining votes. India's largest minority group, the Muslims, is seen as the nation's enemies by Hindu extremists. In the eastern provinces, where Christians constitute a political force, they are blamed for giving allegiance to vested interests of the Christian West.

Caste conflicts which have religious, political, and economic overtones have produced several militant groups in India among whom the <u>Naxalites</u> are well known.[12] The harassment of non-caste Hindus by the caste Hindus in the Tamil Nadu rice belt has received world wide attention. The case in point is the burning of 44 untouchables by upper caste landlords in the village of Venmani in Tanjore district, Tamil Nadu, in 1968. The human rights organizations have for a long time pointed out the exploitation of children in makeshift factories throughout India. It is only recently that the United States has refused to import such Indian carpets, which are produced by the use of child labor. <u>India Today</u>, a popular English magazine in India, along with others, has periodically published articles on the problem of bonded labor. Many social workers have produced evidence that this practice does exist in India, which Indira Gandhi had once publicly denied. The burning of young brides in the north in the absence of a handsome dowry is one among many atrocities committed against women. These instances are commonly reported in daily newspapers.

Religion is a major part of Indian life. The social fabric of society is intertwined with a variety of diverse religious beliefs, practices, and customs.

Although religious tolerance is supposed to be the trademark of all Indian religions, religious conflicts leading to violent consequences are part of daily life. While religious universalism remains the central motif of the Vedantic Hinduism, religious particularism is on the rise. An example of this development is found in the philosophy of the Hindutva movement. Although claiming to be apolitical, Hindutva has had a great influence on the politics of the Bhartiya Janta Party, which came into power in 1998. The rhetoric that flows through the speeches of the leaders and writings of this party are clear evidence the BJP has had a long historical tie with Hindutva. The destruction of the Babri mosque on December 6, 1992 at the hands of Hindu extremists, which is remembered as the 'Ayodhya Incident', was a direct result of Hindutva's involvement in BJP politics. Following the destruction of the mosque, which brought the Hindu-Muslim conflict at its peek in recent history, it became evident that the Hindu claim of religious tolerance was not part of Hindutva's agenda. Gandhi's dream of Hindu-Muslim unity received a heavy blow at every strike at the walls of the Babri mosque. The carnage that followed not only claimed thousands of lives but was also responsible for the destruction of many temples and mosques in and outside of India. As an eyewitness to the communal rioting, this author, for the first time ever in India, was concerned about the safety of his family. As reports of senseless killings began to surface, it became clear that this was the worst case of communal violence since the partition of India in 1947 and the violence that followed immediately after India's independence and the creation of Pakistan as a separate nation. In the aftermath of communal violence and the subsequent bombings in Bombay in 1993, one wondered about the fate of the religious minorities in India.

The inter-religious conflict in India is not limited to Hindus and Muslims alone. During the Sikh extremists' takeover of the Golden Temple at Amritsar, the Sikh's most sacred shrine, and Operation Blue Star, a Hindu-Sikh conflict surfaced. The assassination of Indira Gandhi at the hands of her Sikh bodyguards subsequently saw a Hindu reprisal against the Sikh community. This author happened to be traveling in India with several American students when this conflict took many Sikh's lives in 1984. As rioting broke out across India, we found a safe haven in the temple town of Vrindavan near Mathura. As Delhi burned, we remained glued to our transistor radio to get every bit of news about conditions all over India. During this tragedy many Sikhs began to claim that they were not Hindus. A rift began to widen between the two communities within India and abroad. In America, England, and Canada many Hindus stopped going to the Sikh temples (which they normally visited) because they felt unwelcomed and, in some cases, threatened. As the Khalistan movement and the demand for a separate Sikh nation gained momentum, the Sikhs and the Hindus alienated each other.[13]

The Christian community in India, though a small minority, has not escaped criticism from the Hindu extremists. As Muslims are viewed as outsiders whose religion originated outside India, Christians are also perceived in the same way. As a Muslim is perceived to be loyal to the Middle East, a Christian is viewed as being loyal to the West. The Christian missionary activity is seen as an attempt to gain converts. While conversion to Hinduism is acceptable, conversions to other religions is seen as betrayal of India.

The crisis of religion in India is not merely a spiritual crisis, but is inter-linked with social, political, economic, and other conflicts. Gandhi used to say that he entered politics to spiritualize it. It seems now religion is being politicized and used for social, economic, and political gains. At the heart of the recent debate in India is the issue whether the Indian nation is secular or religious. The Indian Constitution claims to be secular with equal regards for all religions. The members of minority religions are given certain rights to maintain religious institutions and the freedom to propagate their faith. On the eve of India's Independence, the Congress Party insisted that India would maintain its secular profile while Pakistan opted for a religious identity. The makers of modern India, including Gandhi, believed in religious universalism as propagated by Ramakrishna, Vivekananda, Tagore, and Dr. Radhakrishnan, the well known Indian philosopher. However, their universalism was challenged by such groups as Rashtriya Svaim Sevak Sangha (RSS), which followed the Hindutva line of thinking. For the so called "Sangha Parivar,"[14] India was primarily a Hindu country. They viewed Gandhi and the Congress leaders as a threat to India's cultural identity as they accommodated to the needs of the minorities, particularly Muslims. Gandhi's assassin was linked to those who had strong Hindu nationalistic feelings. The issue of the secular versus the religious was never really fully resolved. The opposition (currently BJP) to Congress challenged the constitutional meaning of "Secularism" as interpreted by Nehru and others. It claimed that in the name of secularism, the ruling party was being partial in favor of religious minorities while suppressing rights of the Hindus. In recent times, the BJP has used this issue to play on the Hindu sentiments to gain popular support. It has even invoked the name of Gandhi to suggest that it is struggling to create a society based on Indian values as Gandhi was attempting. The BJP use (or misuse) of Gandhi is an interesting twist in its politics to justify its actions. One wonders if Gandhi's vision of Ram Raj as a non-violent society has any parallel to what BJP, with the support of Hindutva, is trying to achieve.

If a nation's youth are a guage to measure its future success, India must deal with the unrest, disillusionment, and a sense of hopelessness found among its young people. Much has been written about India's educational system. Many observers have noticed that India is still following the antiquated British educational system in its higher education.[15] Historians often quote the British governor, Macaulay, who founded a system of education in India in order to create a "Babu Class" (Clerk class) who could run the Indian bureaucratic machinery for the British. He saw no value in Indian classical literature or other indigenous systems of learning. He managed to create a certain mindset in the Indian society which favored the Western model of education. Gandhi was well aware of this problem when he instituted "Nai Talim" (New Education) as one of his constructive work programs. It would be unfair to say that India has not moved at all beyond Macaulay's vision for India. Nevertheless, it is fair to say that much of India's higher education system is in trouble as it is caught up in the rut of a system created many years ago by the British. Under the current system, passing exams and obtaining degrees seem to be the major emphasis. Furthermore, it creates a class of students who are elitist in their outlook and lifestyle, but not interested in what Gandhi emphasized as "bread labor". The inability of the nation to provide jobs to university graduates creates anger and frustration often vented in riots, disorderly social conduct, and violence. Many youth wish to escape the lack of opportunity in India by migrating to the West or the Middle East in the hope of finding better jobs. However, not everyone can.

The dilemma of education is not limited to higher education. The pressure to be admitted to a good so called "English Medium School" is felt by younger children. It is not totally unheard of that for admission in the first grade, the young child must sit for an entrance test. Children who should be playing and exploring their universe are subjected to academic pressures. The ordeal of finishing school homework on a daily basis for young children is a parent's nightmare. Staying up late at night to study (mainly to memorize), feeling tired at school, experiencing tension headaches over tests, are common complaints among primary school students. Many of these attend private schools, which is a booming business in Indian cities today. Many parents complain that their social life is non-existent because they have to spend hours coaching their children at home in their schoolwork.[16] And, what is the purpose of this competitive education? It is to memorize facts and regurgitate the same on tests. One wonders what ever happened to Rabindranath Tagore's dream of education for young children or Gandhi's vision of holistic education for India's youth. Under the prevailing norm of education, it is certain that a child's creativity is stifled when it is exposed to intense academic pressures, which ought to be reserved for graduate students. Memorization of facts and accumulation of degrees may be socially prestigious, but does nothing for critical thinking and analytical learning. The criteria for judging an educated person in India today is; "how many degrees?" How these degrees are earned seem not to matter . One hears horror stories of cheating on exams, bribing examiners, and even buying of the higher degrees. This crisis is of a high magnitude that demands serious attention.

The variety of crises mentioned above are merely a sample of the kind of turmoil that the Indian society is faced with in modern time. The concern for its survival is being raised by many experts in the area of politics, economics, education, religion, industry, social work, etc. A student of India is quick to discover that the quality of life in India is rapidly degenerating. The general corruption, bribery, disenchanted youth, terrorism, poverty, and diseases, plague the society.[17] Needless to say that the crises face by India have a global character. Many of the problems discussed here are being tackled elsewhere, particularly in the developing countries. While enormous strides are being made in the area of development, it is questionable whether the quality of life has improved. In a country like India, the effects of development are being felt in every aspect of life. The pressure of "making it" economically and surviving the onslaught of different types of power struggles have made life challenging and difficult.

It is not the intention of this author to be critical of all aspects of Indian life. India is a land of much beauty, charm, and warmth to which I periodically return for my own well being and sustenance. The concern here is not to portray India in a bad light, but to focus on certain issues. It is these issues that the Gandhians in India are most concerned with, and which Gandhi himself had addressed. Though times have changed since Gandhi tackled some of these issues, his legacy is meaningful to those who bear his name in their constructive work programs to alleviate many social ills of the Indian society. During my field studies I came in contact with these Gandhians and was impressed by their dedication and hard work. Many of them can be characterized as having religious zeal, who are motivated by a spiritual concern to help the neighbor, e.g., the poor and the exploited. Some of them see the crisis of India as "moral crisis". To them Gandhi becomes extremely relevant because he too saw the problems of India in moral terms. His protégé, Vinoba Bhave, took the moral issue to a greater depth than Gandhi. Both remained connected to the Indian society though faced with the temptation of retreating to the Himalayas for personal spiritual development and satisfaction. When one studies the lives of the Gandhians in India today, one finds that many of them had spiritual experiences that motivated them to remain connected with society. It is this spiritual dimension in their lives that separates them from a large number of social workers working in India for the poor.

*   *   *

I undertook the task of writing about Gandhians in India for a variety of reasons. The primary reason is to fill a gap that exists in the literature about the treatment of Gandhians in the West. Secondly, over the years, as I have taught a seminar on Gandhi and his thought, my students have increasingly expressed the desire to learn more about the work of Gandhians today. The names of Martin Luther King Jr., Lanzo Del Vasto, Ivan Illich, Caesar Chavez, etc. are known to some. Not much is known about the contemporary Indians who are actively engaged in the Gandhian constructive work. Geoffrey Ostergaad's, The Gentle Anarchists (1971) is an old study and deals primarily with the Sarvodaya movement. Although this work gives valuable information on the makeup of the Sarva Seva Sangha, the working organization for the movement, it does not deal in depth with the personalities involved in the movement. His second work on the movement, Nonviolent Revolution In India (1985), is primarily concerned with Sarvodaya's conflict with Indira Gandhi's government and gives a detailed analysis of the Bihar movement, the rise of J. P. (Jai Prakash Narayan), the emergency years, and the formation of the Janta Party. Ved Mehta's Mahatma Gandhi and His Apostles (1976), deals more with Gandhi's own philosophy than his followers. Nothing is said about the contemporary leaders of the movement. Joanna Macy's Dharma and Development (1983) treats Sarvodaya in Sri Lanka and focuses primarily on its leader, Aryaratna. In the Footsteps of Gandhi (1990), Catherine Ingram deals with individuals who are greatly influenced by Gandhi. However, her focus is primarily on Western thinkers. Furthermore, the individuals treated in the work are not necessarily associated with the Sarvodaya movement in

11

India, neither are they engaged in constructive work programs in India. Mark Shepard's, Gandhi Today (1987), is the only book published in the West that introduces his reader to selected Gandhians that he had interviewed in India. My students' reaction to this book, though positive, is that the work is rather introductory, and furthermore does not deal with such issues as how the Gandhians are living up to the vision of Gandhi, what crises they are facing, and how they are meeting the challenges of modernity. The present work tries to deal with these issues.

Once while teaching a seminar on Gandhian Thought, my students struggled with the question; Who is a Gandhian? In the context of writing this book, the question becomes very important. Unless a parameter is set, this work would have to include everyone who claims to be a Gandhian or exclude many. Since Gandhi himself claimed that he was not a Gandhian, and never wanted a movement created after him, the task of classifying Gandhians becomes more difficult. Ram Manohar Lohiya, the well known Socialist leader of India, once classified the Gandhians in India into these categories: Sarkari Gandhians (Gandhians loyal to the government since they took money from it to support their social work programs), Mathadipadi Gandhians (Gandhians who headed various institutions bearing the name of Gandhi), and Kujat Gandhians (the illegitimate heirs of Gandhi, who were no match for Gandhi and yet used him in their work).[18] Likewise, Geoffrey Ostergaard categorized Gandhians into the following divisions: Political Gandhians (Gandhians who entered politics and used Gandhi's name to their political end), Institutional Gandhians (Gandhians who ran the institution like Gandhi Smarak Nidhi), and Revolutionary Gandhians (Gandhians involved with the Gandhi Peace Foundation).[19] One can classify Gandhians in many ways. During my own field work I came across many types of Gandhians. The list may run like this: University Gandhians (intellectuals who write and teach about Gandhi), Ashram Gandhians (those who control many Gandhian centers all over India), Political Gandhians (who invoke the name of Gandhi in party-politics), Gandhian social workers (those who are insured by certain Gandhian ideals, but are also trained in social work techniques), Gandhians associated with NGOs (Non-government organizations which operate as voluntary organizations), Khadi Gandhians (who insist on weaving the home spun without any affiliation with any organization in a formal way), and Neo-Gandhians (young visionaries who deliberately avoid association with the name

12

of Gandhi due to negative connotations, but are engaged in the work of Gandhi). The list goes on.

For the purpose of giving a definite focus to this project, I have limited my discussion to those followers of Gandhi who seemed to have acted on his "last will and testimony". It is well known that after India's Independence in 1947, Gandhi wanted the Congress Party to dissolve itself and become an organization of constructive workers. This meant leaving politics to others and getting involved at the grassroot level in the rebuilding of the nation. It is at this point that the followers of Gandhi were divided; many remained in politics, some became in charge of certain institutions, some took to Gandhi apparel (Gandhian cap and home spun garments) to make a statement. Others heeded to the call of Vinoba Bhave and joined Sarva Seva Sangha to continue the work of Sarvodaya. By some estimation, these were the real Gandhians, who became the custodians of Gandhi's "last will and testimony". The personalities I have tried to cover in this work have had some connection with the Sarvodaya movement. Although in my research I spoke to all kinds of Gandhians, I have limited the scope of my writing to those primarily involved in the constructive work programs. Consequently, they have been associated with Sarva Seva Sangha at one time or another. Since this organization is facing enormous challenges, and certain ideological differences have divided its leadership, on the national scene, it is still the leading Gandhian organization in India today. Most of the personalities covered in this book were greatly influenced by both Vinoba Bhave (1895-1982) and Jai Prakash Narayan (1902-1979), two leading exponents of the Gandhian vision within the Sarvodaya Movement.

The directory of the Lok Sevaks (servants of the people) engaged in Sarvodaya work published by the Gandhian Smarak Nidhi contains over 500 names. It can easily be read as a who is who? in the Gandhian movement today. While contemplating my project I was determined not to replicate the directory which reads like an encyclopedia. My approach is more phenomenological. It contains my observations and analysis of the movement that I observed over a decade and a half. I am more interested in taking the readers on an intellectual tour of India, acquainting them with the social, political, economic, and religious environment and introducing them to a select group of Sarvodaya Gandhians who have dedicated their lives to a vision. When I first discussed this project with the late Dr. Radhakrishna, the secretary of the Gandhi Peace Foundation in 1989, his reaction was positive. He remarked that Ostergaard had written a profile of the movement in 1971, it was appropriate to profile the personalities in the movement now.

The individuals included in this work are, in a sense, representatives of a team of crisis management. They all feel a sense of urgency to improve the quality of life in India. They are all addressing the crises as they perceive them, taking their strength from the example set up by Gandhi. They have taken to heart the Gandhi "Talisman", which reads:

> Recall the face of the poorest and the most helpless man whom you have seen and ask yourself, if the step you contemplate is going to be of any use to him. Will he be able to gain anything by it? Will it restore him to a control over his life and destiny? In other words, will it lead to Swaraj or self-rule for the hungry and also spiritually starved millions of our countrymen? Then you will find your doubts and your "self" melting away. [20]

Whether the personalities covered in this book have completely molded their lives according to this "talisman" is a difficult question to answer. This book is their story.

My fascination with the Sarvodaya Movement began when I started reading books by Vinoba Bhave and about Vinoba Bhave in preparation for a paper to be presented at the American Academy of Religion in New York. I was so intrigued by the life of Vinoba: the manner in which he had given himself to Gandhi, joined Gandhi's Ashram in Wardha, came to Paunar to regain his health, founded the Brahma Vidya Ashram for women, was declared the first individual Satyagrahi against the British by Gandhi in 1942, the way he brought certain Gandhian organizations together after Gandhi's assassination under Sarva Seva Sangh, his discovery of Bhoodan-Gramdan movement to alleviate the pain of the landless, his association with J. P. who gave his life for Sarvodaya as a Jivandan (gift of life), his attempt to hold the Sarvodaya movement together during the emergency years under Indira Gandhi, his advising J. P. on the matter of "Total Revolution," and his retreat to Paunar in 1972. Thus, I wanted to study this man who was considered to be the embodiment of Gandhian values. I wrote to the Sarvodaya Mandal office in Gopuri, Wardha, and received a reply from Professor Thakurdas Bang. He agreed to meet with me, but felt that my stay at Paunar will not be possible since it was an ashram for women. However, a day visit to Paunar and an audience with Vinoba could be arranged. I was disappointed but not disheartened. The fact that Thakurdas Bang, about whom I had heard through

Rev. Richard Keithahn (an American Gandhian), had responded by letter was encouraging enough.

The year was 1980 and I had been teaching at the Religion Department at Rutgers University in New Jersey. I ran into Professor Charlie Ryerson who had just accepted a position at Princeton Theological Seminary. I learned that Dr. Ryerson had worked in South India and knew Richard Kiethahn and other Sarvodaya leaders in South India. He encouraged me to go to Gandhi Gram (A Gandhian University) outside of Madurai and meet some Gandhians there. In the meantime, I received a letter from a Gandhian scholar, Dr. Vishvanath Tandon, who had read my article on Vinoba Bhave and agreed to meet with me at the Gandhi Smarak Nidhi in New Delhi. The month of June can be miserably hot in New Delhi, especially if the monsoons are late. I arrived in Delhi in June of 1980 in search of Vinoba and his associates. While the heat discouraged me to step outside my residence at the Christ Church in Old Delhi, the adventure to meet the Gandhians encouraged me to ignore the weather. Meeting Dr. Vishvanath Tandon was a pleasure. He was a Gandhian scholar and a gentleman. We discussed various dimensions of the Sarvodaya philosophy over a period of 4 or 5 days at his small living quarter at the Gandhi Smarak Nidhi near Raj Ghat. He told me about the affection he had for Vinoba, and how Vinoba had touched his life. Tandon became my temporary guru. As he described Vinoba's understanding of Sarvodaya, Gandhi became alive for me. We discussed Bhoodan and Tandon's association with Vinoba during those years that all Gandhians look at with nostalgia. On one occasion, while we were discussing the split within Sarvodaya in the 1970s, Narendra Dube walked in the room looking for Dr. Tandon. I had never heard of Dube before. Prof. Tandon, stopped, greeted Narendra Dube, and simply said, "he is the right person to tell you about the split." At that time I did not know that Dube was going to be a valuable resource for my research. Narendra gave me invaluable insights into the relationship between Vinoba and J. P. and the impact they had on the Sarvodaya movement. I was now ready to meet Vinoba, but it was going to be simply a brief audience, or so I thought, since Vinoba had completely lost his hearing and was communicating by written notes.

The Paunar Ashram is located on Wardha-Nagpur road only a few miles from Wardha, Maharashtra. One of the associates of Thakurdas Bang rang up the ashram from Gopuri to inquire if I could come there for a days visit. The response came that I was welcome and could even stay at Vinoba's Ashram. My heart leapt with joy. Subsequently, I ended up staying at Vinoba's Ashram for five days, the days that have vivid memories in my mind. The most memorable event took place one afternoon. I was being seated, along with a few other visitors, in Vinoba's quarter. He was reclined on some pillows in front of us. Suddenly he pointed his finger towards me. His associates asked me to come forward and sit in front of him. When he discovered that my last name was Harris, he laughed and said, "From now on it is "Hari Ish," meaning "Beloved of God." Later I discovered that it was his way to humor people by changing their names. Since it was impossible to carry on a meaningful dialogue with him (due to his hearing problem), I chose to simply be with him and observe him. One day I took his picture while he was playing with the Ashram dog, "Moti". Vinoba chuckled and remarked, "Moti, your picture will go to America." During that week in June of 1980, I had numerous conversations with the women (sisters) who lived in the Ashram. I prayed with them, worked with them, and ate with them. Vinoba had a unique way of communicating with every one of them during his morning walk on the verandah assisted by his male associates. For every one of them he had a special gesture. They would stop whatever they were doing and have a special moment with "Baba." I considered myself fortunate to witness the human side of this great saint of India. The Ashram was full of historical memories. It was here that national and international leaders came to consult Vinoba. It was here that J. P. met with Vinoba on many occasions. It was here that Nirmala Deshpande sat at the feet of Vinoba, and other sisters were trained in "Stri Shakti" (female power). Here I met extraordinary women, including sister Pravina Desai, one of the most articulate exponents of Sarvodaya thinking at this Ashram. My encounter with Paunar was so rewarding in understanding the Gandhian thought that I have returned there on several occasions. The most recent visit took place in February of 1998.

The Paunar experience opened numerous possibilities for me. I was able to meet and interview a variety of Sarvodaya leaders and to understand the Gandhian movement. Contacts were made to travel to South India to visit Gandhi Gram, outside of Madurai. There I met Jagannathan, whom Vinoba called his "Hanuman" (the legendary human monkey of the epic Ramayana who helped Rama). I visited several of his farms where he was experimenting with Gram Swaraj (freedom of the village) under Sarvodaya ideology. Jagannathan was determined to take the experiment of Bhoodan movement forward to realize the dream of Vinoba and Gandhi. I subsequently wrote an article evaluating his work and linking it with Vinoba's Bhoodan-Gramdan movement. The conversations

16

with Dr. Aram, then the vice-chancellor of the Gandhi Gram, proved to be extremely useful in understanding the use of Gandhian philosophy in higher education. Subsequently, I visited several Gandhian centers of learning to fully grasp the relevance of Gandhi in education, particularly in India. Since my first meeting with Jagannathan, I have returned to meet with him on several occasions to learn more about his work with ASSEFA and his Satyagraha against the multinationals in the Tanjore district.[21] Jagannathan's wife, Krishnammal, who was awarded "Padmasiri" by the Indian government, is impressive in her own right for her work with LAFTI.[22] In 1986 I met Krishnammal, an unassuming gentle soul, with Jagannathan at a conference in New Delhi. She handed me a leaflet on LAFTI, but I understood the magnitude of her work only when I did some field work in Tanjore district of Tamil Nadu in 1993 and 1996 with Krishnammal by my side.

I returned to India for the 1984-85 academic year with a dozen of College of Wooster students on a "Wooster in India" academic program. We arrived in India at the height of the Khalistan movement and the end of Operation Blue Star.[23] We got caught in the rioting on route to Mathura from Agra the day Indira Gandhi was assassinated. In the midst of the violence and the subsequent attack on the Sikh community as India burned, Gandhians got busy delivering the message of peace to both the Sikh and the Hindu communities. The Gandhi Peace Foundation and Gandhi Smarak Nidhi in New Delhi organized peace marches, workshops, and talks to defuse the tension. Since I had a research leave to study the Sarvodaya movement, after my students left to return home for Christmas, I found myself at the A. N. Sinha Institute of Social Studies in Patna, Bihar, where I was to spend four productive months studying Sarvodaya. A. N. Sinha Institute had several social scientists who had studied the movement. Through this base I was about to interview many reputable Gandhians. The library research along with field trips to Gandhian projects proved to be most beneficial. I first met Acharya Rammurti at the historical Khadi Gram Ashram in March of 1985.[24] From Patna it is three to four hour run to Jamui by train. From there a horse driven cart to Rammurti's Ashram is a short distance. Rammurti is a friendly, gentle person who gives an astute analysis of Sarvodaya and its place in Indian society. I found him to be the most intellectual of the many Gandhians I met in India. He analyzed the Nehru years with remarkable insight. His conclusion was "that Gandhi has been betrayed in India because the Congress abandoned him." I stayed with the Acharya for four days, listening, dialoguing, and writing. I met

17

him on several occasions during my subsequent trips to India, and found him intellectually stimulating each time.

Bihar is the center of a variety of Gandhian activities. It was here that Gandhi launched his very first Satyagraha, known as the "Champaran Satyagraha." It was here that Vinoba made great strides in his Bhoodan and eventually Bihar Dan movement. It was here that J. P. took to the grassroots level village work in the Mushahri Block and wrote his famous <u>Face to Face</u> that changed the thrust of the Sarvodaya movement in the 1970s. The Bihar Sarvodaya Mandal office, located in the Kadam Kuan area of Patna, proved to be a valuable resource for my research. My daily trips to the Mandal from A. N. Sinha institute for several days put me in touch with a variety of Sarvodaya leaders and lok sevaks (servants of the people). Through these meetings I came in contact with Sachchida Babu, personal secretary of Jai Prakash Narayan during the Bihar movement. He explained to me J. P.'s position and the call for "Total Revolution" which eventually brought a division between Vinoba and J. P.

In April of 1985, while still at the A. N. Sinha Institute, I was invited to attend the annual meeting of the Sarvodaya leadership along with the gathering of the Sarvodaya Samaj.[25] This event was to be held in Jai Prakash Nagar (named after J. P.) near the town of Balia. This was an adventure that left a lasting impression on my mind. I was about to attend the annual meeting of Sarva Seva Sangh, the organization that oversaw the work of Sarvodaya. I was instructed to take a bus from Patna to Chapra, take an auto rikshaw to Khilgan, walk to Sarju River, embark a cargo boat, get down on the other side, and walk a few miles to the village where the three day event was to take place. I could have taken a train from Varanasi to Sumrenpur, and then a truck or bus to Jai Prakash Nagar. Since I was already in Patna, I decided to take the shorter route. I arrived at the banks of Sarju River only to find that there were no boats to take me across the river. My only option was to wade across a portion of the river in waist deep water with luggage on my head in order to board a row boat docked in the main channel of the river. I was not about to give up my chance of meeting the leadership of the Gandhian movement gathered in one place. So, I rolled up my pants, put my bag on my head, said a quick prayer, and started for the river. There were a few scary moments, but the river was calm. I made it across. The boat was there with its cargo and a few passengers. We went across, walked along a while, and made it to the site of the conference. I was escorted to a tent where the delegation from Bihar was staying. I was welcomed with open arms to spread my bedding on the grass

18

floor and rest. There were tents for different states as delegates came from all over India. The site was a mango grove, a few yards from J. P.'s house. The delegates walked around mingling, exchanging greetings, sharing news, and visiting with friends. It was quite evident that this was a gathering of the Sarvodaya family.

The Annual Sarvodaya meeting in Jai Prakash Nagar was my first encounter with the Gandhians in a group that Geoffrey Ostergaard calls the "Gentle Anarchists."[26] The session of Sarva Seva Sangh opened with the brass of the movement gathered on a stage, while the delegates sat on the floor below them. Many pulled out their portable charkhas (spinning wheels) and began spinning while listening to the speakers. The platform party did the same. Speaker after speaker gave reports on their constructive work programs. They interpreted Gandhian philosophy of Sarvodaya, invoked the name of Vinoba and J. P., expressed concern with the problem of national integration, the state of Khadi (home spun), general corruption, non-violent revolution, and the methods of peace. Among the favorite speakers were Narayan Desai, Siddharaj Dhadda, Prem Bhai, Vichitra Narayan Sharma, Acharya Rammurti, R. R. Diwakar, Thakurdas Bang, Ravindra Upadhyaya, and many others. It was here that I ran into Marjorie Sykes and had a fleeting conversation about Sarvodaya. I took a walk with Narayan Desai and taped an interview. I was introduced to Tripurari Saran, who took me aside to an empty tent and spent an hour discussing Gandhian philosophy. While dining, seated on the floor under a huge rent, I intently listened to a man who talked to an American visitor about his work among several villages. I discovered that this was Prem Bhai, who was later to give me a deeper insight into his work when I visited his Ashram in Mirzapur. I made many friends and was invited to visit various constructive work projects throughout India, many of which I later visited. The 1985 Sarvodaya Conference was intense, productive, and informative. One thing was quite clear. It was a gathering of dedicated workers who come together every year to share and learn from each other. They recognize that they are not very influential in Indian politics, and some question whether they should at all be concerned with politics. They realize that they are different, but want to understand Gandhi's vision to improve Indian society.

The year 1992 was a crucial year in Indian politics. The demolition of the Babri mosque in Ayodhya on December 6th at the hands of the Hindu extremists, and the subsequent riots all over India that claimed thousands of lives, seriously challenged the fate of Indian democracy. I had just finished an interview with Vimla Thakar in Mt. Abu, Rajasthan, when the word came that "the mosque was down." I had come to India on an academic leave for 1992-93 to complete a series of interviews with the leading Gandhians. I had a complete list if names that I had prepared with Dr. Radhakrishnan at the Gandhi Peace Foundation in Delhi in 1989. That year I was once again traveling with a group of students from the College of Wooster on a Study Travel Seminar. The Babri mosque issue was alien then, but V. P. Singh had just been elected as the new prime minister; and negotiations were going on with the Bhartiya Janta Party on the issue of the need to build a temple at the site of the mosque. I briefly met with Acharya Rammurti, who had been meeting with V. P. Singh and discussing the vision of Sarvodaya under V. P.'s new government of Janta Dal. Rammurti was getting some heat from other Gandhians who felt that his actions (working with V. P. Singh) were not in the spirit of Gandhi. They felt that he was getting too involved in politics. Rammurti had learned from Jai Prakash Narayan that political involvement was necessary for "Total Revolution". By 1992, V. P. Singh was out of power. Whatever intentions he had to help the cause of Gandhi had no serious consequences.

My work with the Gandhians in 1992-93 involved interviewing most of the leaders of the movement I had intended to meet. I criss-crossed the country several times by every means of transportation available, and even walked to some remote places to meet my interviewees. The experience taught me many things about Gandhians, but one in particular. The Gandhians are humans just like everyone else. They are subject to all human weaknesses. They are diverse in their character, education, vision, and insights. Although most of them cooperated with me on this project, some were unconcerned and took no interest in my study. With some, my personality clashed and the interviews were either cut short or never took place. Sometimes the appointments were set up, but were not honored. And yet, there were many who went out of their way to supply the information I needed. They were hospitable, gentle, and extremely agreeable.

For research purposes, the Gandhi Peace Foundation in New Delhi proved to be most beneficial. I was to stay there while not on the road visiting various projects and meeting contacts. Since many Gandhians stay there while passing through Delhi, it was easy to make contacts and conduct interviews. Through G. P. F., I also had easy access to Gandhi Smarak Nidhi, an institution created to coordinate the constructive programs conducted by various Gandhians. In North India these two institutions provide invaluable resources to establish contacts with their workers. From my headquarters at G. P. F., I made several trips to Uttar

Pradesh, Rajasthan, Gujarat, Bihar, Orissa, Maharashtra, Andhra Pradesh, Bengal, Tamil Nadu, and Sri Lanka to do my field studies. During these field trips, I visited a variety of constructive work projects, attended conferences, listened to lectures, gave talks, interviewed Lok Sevaks, and conducted library research. Although much of this work deals with the Gandhians involved in the constructive work, I had the opportunity to converse with many intellectuals, politicians, social scientists, and other Gandhians outside the movement to get a thorough insight into the challenges faced by Gandhians in India today. Although there are many personalities who could not be included in this work due to a variety of reasons, their input is reflected in the writing of this project.

Subsequent to my research in the academic year of 1992-93, I returned to India briefly in 1996 and for four months in 1998. My goal was not only to complete all interviews but also to study the current socio-political situation in India. The trip made in 1998 was very useful since India was celebrating its 50th Golden Jubilee year of India's Independence (1947), and Gandhi's assassination (1948). I was able to attend several useful programs related to Gandhi, including an international conference on 'Gandhi and the 21st Century.' My participation in the conference helped my research tremendously. Perhaps the most valuable aspect of the 1998 visit was to meet the individuals covered in this book in an attempt to bring their stories up to date.

          *   *   *

The book is divided into Three Parts. The first part, entitled The Vision, primarily deals with the vision of Mahatma Gandhi, and his conception of Sarvodaya for the uplift of the masses in India. It also includes a survey of the contributions made by Vinoba Bhave and Jai Prakash Narayan, two outstanding leaders who followed in the footsteps of Gandhi. Part Two, the heart of the book, is entitled The Visionaries. Here I have given a brief biographical sketch of 15 well known Sarvodaya Gandhians in India today, along with a description of their activities as well as their thoughts. An important aspect of this section is to discuss how these Gandhians hope to live up to the challenges posed by many crises faced by modern India. The Third Part, I have chosen to call The Assessment. In this section I take up certain critical issues involved in assessing the work of Gandhians. In spite of my objective stance to look critically at the work of individuals covered in this book, I have great admiration for their

21

dedication and commitment to the cause of Gandhi. I invite the reader to share their excitement by indulging in reading the pages that follow. In the appendix, I have included the addresses of the people discussed in this book to facilitate a dialogue between the reader and the Gandhians in contemporary India. I trust that this attempt will prove to be useful.

Endnotes: Introduction

[1] For a Comprehensive analysis of the Gandhian vision of Ram Raj, see chapter on Gandhi.

[2] Gandhi wrote Hind Swaraj in 1909, and defended its basic thesis until the end of his life.

[3] About the book Unto This Last, Gandhi said the following in his autobiography, "That book marked the turning point in my life." (Part IV, Ch. 18, p. 250)

[4] See Chapter One for the details on 18 point program.

[5] A detailed analysis of Total Revolution is given in Chapter Three on Jai Prakash Narayan.

[6] See the writings of J. D. Sethi and Rajni Kothari.

[7] Green Revolution refers to India's advances made in the production of a new variety of wheat in the 70s, which made India self-sufficient in food.

[8] Reported in the Delhi Newspaper, 'The Pioneer', Friday March 20, 1998, New Delhi.

[9] See the article, "India : State of the Nation," India Today, Aug. 18, 1997, p.24.

[10] Dalit is the term now used to describe the "deprived class" in society. According to the Dalit Movement, this term should replace the term Harijans, which Gandhi used to describe the untouchable, and which is perceived as derogatory by the leaders of the Dalit Movement.

[11] Mandal Commission was set up by the Prime Minister V. P. Singh to look into the issue of the Affirmative Action.

[12] Naxalites named after the Naxalbadi village in Bengal. They constitute a militant group that believes in using force to punish the oppressors of the poor, particularly the landlords.

[13] Khalistan (land of the pure) is a movement to create an independent nation of the Sikhs in the western province of Punjab.

[14] 'Sangha Parivar' (The Sangh Family) refers to several organizations that support the Hindutva ideology and are linked with RSS

[15] See the writings of Rajni Kothari

[16] This information was attained during interviews with several Indian families in North India in 1998.

[17] See the article, "India : State of the Nation," India Today, Aug. 18, 1997.

[18] Information provided by Mr. S. K. De, a veteran Gandhian in India.

[19] Geoffrey Ostergaard, The Gentle Anarchists, (Delhi : Gandhi Peace Foundation, 1985), p.6.

[20] Credited to Gandhi, this statement repeatedly appears in Sarvodaya literature.

[21] See the chapter on Jagannathan for details on his Satyagraha against the multi-national companies in India.

[22] See the chapter on Krishnammal for details on her life and thought.

[23] Operation Blue Star was the code for the attack on the Golden Temple of the Sikhs in Amritsar by the Indian military under the order given by Indira Gandhi.

[24] See the chapter on Acharya Rammurti for details.

[25] 'Sarvodaya Samaj' refers to a larger family of Sarvodaya to which anyone who favors the Gandhian philosophy of welfare for all can belong.

[26] See the book The Gentle Anarchists by Geoffrey Ostergaard.

Part One

The Vision

I

Mahatma Gandhi and Ram Raj

"What I want to achieve - what I have been striving and pinning to achieve these thirty years - is self-realization, to see God face to face, to attain Moksha... I live and move and have my being in pursuit of this goal. All that I do by way of speaking and writing, all my ventures in the political field are directed to this same end."
                                                                                        - Mahatma Gandhi

There is hardly a Gandhian who disputes that Gandhi was a religious man. There may be disagreements on how he manifested his spirituality in the public domain, but most agree that his concern with religious values guided his actions. While discussing this issue with the sisters at Vinoba's Ashram at Paunar, they agreed with the analogy that Gandhi's life was like a train that was headed for a final destination of "self-realization." On the way, it stopped at many stations, and his involvement with India's independence was one of such stations.[1] Thus, when we speak of Gandhi's vision, we inevitably need to look at his spiritual quest or the "Ultimate Concern" which guided his "Proximate Concerns." It would be short sighted to say that Gandhi's dealings with economics, politics, society, religion etc. were merely incidental. On the contrary, his deliberate involvement with socio-economic and political spheres was an integral part of his holistic view of life in which spirituality was the guiding principle.

During my association with many Gandhians, the term Ram Raj has become the central topic of conversation. It appears that one way to explain Gandhi's vision is to invoke the imagery of Ram Raj, which he also called the Kingdom of God. At the heart of this concept is Gandhi's concern with the individual as well as society. On a personal level, he followed the yogic model of self-realization advocated by the Vedantic Hindu philosophers. On a social level,

27

he attempted to create a society based on certain universal spiritual values. Both Gandhian concepts of <u>Satyagraha</u> and <u>Sarvodaya</u> were grounded in his spiritual values. Vinoba and J. P., along with many contemporary Gandhians, have attempted to decipher what Gandhi meant by Ram Raj, and how it can be implemented today.

In the context of the existing crisis of Ayodhya and Ram Janmabhoomi affairs, it is important to understand what Gandhi meant by Ram Raj. During his lifetime, Gandhi was aware that both Hindus and Muslims could misunderstand his use of the notion. The possibility of such a misunderstanding still exists today, particularly when the followers of Hindutva have invoked the same imagery to justify their attempt to build a temple of Rama at a site which they claim to be the birth place of the Hindu deity, Rama, and where the Babri Mosque once stood. On the other hand, for many Muslims, Gandhi's reference to Rama and Ram Raj as given in the Hindu texts did increase the fear that perhaps Gandhi was looking for a Hindu state for independent India. Of course, many Hindus would have liked this to be the case. However, Gandhi made it clear that his Rama was not the Rama of the Hindu epic, Ramayana, and neither was Ram Raj a Hindu Raj. In 1929 in one of his speeches given in Bhopal, he stated, "I warn my Mussalman (Muslim) friends against misunderstanding me in my use of the word 'Ramrajya'. By 'Ramrajya' I do not mean Hindu Raj. I mean by 'Ramrajya' Divine raj, the Kingdom of God. For me Rama and Rahim are one and the same deity. I acknowledge no other God but the one God of Truth and Righteousness".[2] He even used Urdu language (spoken by most Muslims in India) to equate Ram Raj with <u>Khudarajya</u> (Kingdom of Khuda (God)).[3] At the heart of Ram Raj is Gandhi's concern with Dharma as the universal truth. It also translates into the concern for justice, both on the individual and social levels. He used Rama as a symbol of Justice because the populace understood the epic Ramayana and were familiar with the basic religious idealism as applied to family, society, and state. During my field work in India during 1992-93 I included a question on Ram Raj in a survey which was filled out by thirty-five Gandhian workers. The question stated; What do you think Gandhi meant by Ram Raj? The answers were quite telling. The majority confirmed that Ram Raj was not a Hindu Raj, rather a kingdom of peace and harmony where love prevailed over injustice, and power was shared with the people.

Throughout his life, Gandhi utilized the concept of Ram Raj in different contexts. Ultimately it boiled down to the creation of an ideal state where the

28

rulers would look out for the welfare of all, disregarding any social, economic, religious, and political distinctions. He wrote, "We call a state Ramrajya when both ruler and subjects are straightforward, when both are pure in heart, when both are inclined towards self-sacrifice, when both exercise restraint and self-control while enjoying worldly pleasures, and when the relationship between the two is as good as that between a father and a son."[4] The ideal state for Gandhi was a federation of self-sufficient villages which practiced Panchayat Raj (the rule of five elders in a village). He stated, "Such a state must be based on truth and non-violence and must consist of progressive, happy and self-contained villages and village communities."[5] Panchayat was crucial for Gandhi because he did not believe that public opinion could be established by a mere showing of hands, as practiced in a democracy. When speaking of Ram Raj, once Gandhi went as far as to equate the panch (five members of the panchayat) with divinity. In 1931 he wrote, "Rama means Panch; the Panch implies God, implies public opinion. When public opinion is not artificially created, it is pure. A government founded on public opinion is Ramrajya for that particular place."[6] When speaking of Ram Raj, Gandhi's idealism went beyond the confines of India. At the time of India's independence in 1947, Gandhi said, "The establishment of such a Rajya would not only mean the welfare of the whole of the Indian people but of the whole world."[7]

Much can be learned about Gandhi's personal piety from his autobiography, My Experiments with Truth. It is clear that such religious principles as belief in a personal god, self-control, prayer, fasting, control of senses, yoga, non-stealing, brahmacharya, asceticism, speaking truth, non-violence, vegetarianism, and respect for all religions, guided his life. Many of his beliefs and practices have been subject to religious, philosophical, and psychological scrutiny.[8] Gandhi would recommend a pious life as a participant in Ram Raj. However, for the purpose of this study, I intend to focus more on the social side of the vision. Much of Gandhi's life was given to social action. He may have had the desire to retreat to the Himalayas and work on his "self-realization" like many saints. However, his vision of Moksha entailed not a retreat, but a total involvement in society. This earned him the title of a "Karmayogi."[9]

In Gandhi the two paradigms, Satyagraha and Sarvodaya, provide the fundamental core for what developed to be the blue print for his Ram Raj. These were his philosophies which also took the form of two movements. They were inter-linked with a variety of concepts leading towards a holistic vision of a

29

utopian society. He often quoted the medieval Indian poet <u>Tulsidas</u>, who had narrated the idealistic vision of the kingdom of Rama in his poetry, and who still remains alive in the hearts and minds of many Indians today.[10] Gandhi wanted the post-independent India to transform itself into a Kingdom of God. However, he was conscious of the fact that this dream will not come true until the whole society, through Satyagraha and Sarvodaya, made conscious efforts to translate the vision into a concrete reality.

The birth of <u>Satyagraha</u> (Truth Force) is an event that made Gandhi an international figure. Having been thrown off the train in 1893 in South Africa by a white man who refused to share a railway compartment with him, brought Gandhi face to face with the prejudice and the injustice against blacks and Indians in a white society. Gandhi was determined to fight the system, but needed a weapon. In his autobiography he states how he used the term "Civil Resistance" and then "Passive Resistance" but rejected both as unsuitable labels for his movement. Even rejecting the term "Sadgraha" (firmness in a good cause), which was proposed by Maganlal Gandhi, and initially liked by Gandhi, he coined his own term <u>Satyagraha</u>. Recalling the incident he writes, "I liked the word (sadagrah) but it did not fully represent the whole idea I wished it to connote. I therefore corrected it to "Satyagraha". Truth (Satya) implies love, and Firmness (Agraha) engenders (strength) and therefore serves as synonym for force... that is to say, that Force which is born of Truth and Love or non-violence."[11] Analyzing the concept Satyagraha, Joan Bondurant, a well-known political scientist, rightly suggests that Satyagraha is made up of three major concepts, Truth, Non-violence, and Self-Suffering. These three concepts constitute the fundamentals of Gandhian philosophy. The application of Satyagraha in resolving a conflict then means, first, to identify the Truth of the matter and then act. Gandhi admitted that Absolute Truth is difficult to ascertain, therefore one must act with relative truth, which appears to be absolute at the time. Second, since both the oppressor and the oppressed are dealing with relative truth, they must remain non-violent toward each other. Since no one is absolutely right (in the Knowledge of Truth), none has the right to use force to persuade the other. This analysis gives Ahimsa (non-violence) a philosophical rationale in Gandhian philosophy. Third, the notion of self-suffering brings into focus Gandhi's attitude toward love as a religious principle. In the context of Satyagraha, self-suffering means willingness to bear pain and loss for the sake of a higher goal, i.e., conflict resolution.[12]

30

Gandhi constantly refined his philosophy of Satyagraha as he applied it to socio-political action in South Africa and India. For him it was not merely a technique but required spiritual preparation. It would be more appropriate to say that for Gandhi Satyagraha became a theological concept because it included not only metaphysics and ethics but a strong belief in God. When it took the form of a movement, it became essential to train Satyagrahis, who properly understood the religious nature of their actions. The code of discipline he laid out for the participants in Satyagraha is telling of the nature of the discipline to which they were subjected. The following points were emphasized:

1. Harbor no anger but suffer the anger of the opponent. Refuse to return the assaults of the opponent.
2. Do not submit to any order given in anger, even though severe punishment is threatened for disobeying.
3. Refrain from insults and swearing.
4. Protect opponents from insults, or attack, even at the risk of life.
5. Do not resist arrest nor the attachment of property, unless holding property as a trustee.
6. Refuse to surrender any property held in trust at the risk of life.
7. If taken prisoner, behave in an exemplary manner.
8. As a member of a Satyagraha unit, obey the orders of Satyagraha leaders, and resign from the unit in the event of serious disagreement.
9. Do not expect guarantee for maintenance of dependents.[13]

The list presented above well indicates that Gandhi took Satyagraha's preparation very seriously. He was concerned that as a movement, Satyagraha should not become a form of agitation and protest which merely utilized strikes, fasts, boycotts, sit-ins etc. to achieve the desired results. Such activities were prevalent before Gandhi ever came on the scene, and many have continued since Gandhi, using the name of Satyagraha. In the context of Ram Raj, Satyagraha cannot be perceived simply as a technique of conflict resolution, but, rather, a method of preparing individuals, and preparing them to establish a peaceful society. As long as Ram Raj is to be established on earth, it cannot be free from conflicts. What is significant is how an individual is prepared to deal with the conflict. In his lifetime Gandhi led several satyagrahas, but none is more famous than the Salt Satyagraha of 1930-31. In the manner Gandhi prepared the Satyagrahis and mobilized the masses became exemplary of a non-violent movement. The independence of India, though attributed to many causes, was a

31

direct result of the Gandhian approach to fight the British in a non-violent way. The consequence was that the British did not leave as enemies, and India willingly joined other nations of the Commonwealth. In this effort Gandhi was able to put into practice what he conceived as a theory. The legacy of Gandhi is that wherever injustice prevails, Satyagraha will present itself as an option to challenge the source of that injustice. It will seek justice, not as a short term goal by defeating the opponent, but by showing the opponent the wisdom of Satyagraha in creating a peaceful society.

Much has been written about religion as the basis of Satyagraha in Gandhi. One can trace his notion, Truth as God, to the Advaita Vedanta of Shankara, and his belief in a personal God to the Vishistadvaita of Ramanuja. The influence of Jainism through his mother may have been the source of "Ahimsa", which became central to his thought. The notion of self-suffering (tapasya) is traced to the Gita, which Gandhi loved and admired. However, the concrete model of self-suffering was seen in Jesus, who in forgiving love, embraced crucifixion. Thus Gandhi was inspired by a universal spirituality rather than a particular religious tradition. He said, "By religion, I do not mean formal religion or customary religion, but that religion which underlines all religions, which brings us face to face with our Maker... This religion transcends Hinduism, Islam, Christianity, etc. It does not supersede them. It harmonizes them and gives them reality."[14]

Since Gandhi believed in Sanatana Dharma (universal religion), he did not present any new religious concepts, but revised the old. He himself stated, "I have presented no new principles, but have tried to restate old principles."[15] In the words of S. Radhakrishnan, Gandhi's religion was "religion not in the sense of subscription to dogmas or conformity to ritual, but religion in the sense of an abiding faith in the absolute values of truth, love and justice and persistent endeavor to realize them on earth." [16] Gandhi's religion culminates in his belief in right action. He is perceived as a karma yogi because it was the application of spirituality to concrete situations that dominated his life. His vow to celibacy at the age of thirty-five, his vegetarianism, his fasts, his experiments in nature cure, his observance of silence, his prayers, etc. were all directed towards self-purification and self-improvement in order to be fit for the Kingdom of God. Inherent in the life of this karma yogi was a positive view of history. It has been viewed as the "non-violent interpretation of history."[17] Under this view history was evolving toward a state of non-violence which was inherent in Reality. This

32

is linked with his understanding of human nature as basically good. Consequently he believed in the human potential to create the Kingdom of God on earth.

Ram Raj cannot be established unless the individual as well as the society take up certain concrete programs. This is the basis of Sarvodaya in Gandhi. Sarvodaya (welfare for all) was Gandhi's blue print for social welfare. Like Satyagraha it also originated as a philosophy, but turned into a movement. If Ram Raj was Gandhi's goal, Sarvodaya was its content, and Satyagraha a means to arrive at the goal. It has been suggested that the term Sarvodaya had already been used by the Jains in India.[18] Nevertheless, it was Gandhi who turned it into a movement. The genesis of Sarvodaya goes back to 1904 when Gandhi read John Ruskin's Unto This Last on a train from Johannesburg to Durban in South Africa. In retrospect Gandhi made a remark, "that book marked the turning point in my life."[19] It is interesting to note that Ruskin based the title of his book on Jesus' teachings regarding helping the least of all human kind and justice for the poor. Ruskin was reacting against the evils of the Industrial Revolution and its impact on the 19th century England. Although an artist by profession, he had the foresight to analyze the economic theory that influenced the policy makers in the English society. The impact of the economics of consumption was devastating. He witnessed the rise of slums, exploitation of children by factories, inhumane working conditions of the laborers, and the rise in alcoholism and crime. On top of that there was inequality in wages whereby the rich were getting richer and poor poorer. The system driven by the capitalist approach to profit-making was robbing the poor. Ruskin appealed to the economists by quoting proverbs from the Hebrew Scriptures. In particular, he called their attention to Proverbs 22: 22-23, which states, "Rob not the poor because he is poor; neither oppress the afflicted in the place of business. For God shall spoil the soul of those that spoiled them."[20] Thus, the call of Ruskin was the call for justice. It was also a call for a changed life style in which there was an equitable distribution of wealth for all. In many ways Ruskin's thought was similar to that of Tolstoy in that both believed that "the reformation of the social order cannot be brought about from without."[21] They called for an integral change in the value systems adopted by an individual. For Ruskin the key to this change was "social affections" translated as love. Gandhi was so impressed with Ruskin's analysis that he translated (in a paraphrased version) Unto This Last in Gujarati as Sarvodaya. He later wrote that he understood the messages of Unto This Last to be:

1. That the good of the individual is contained in the good of all.

2. That a lawyer's work has the same value as the barber's, inasmuch as all have the same right of earning their livelihoods for their work.
3. That a life of labor --- the life of the tiller of the soil and the craftsman --- is the life worth living.

Referring to these points Gandhi confessed that he already knew the importance of the first point, and the second he has some understanding of; but the third was new to him.[22] He decided to practice these ideals in his life, and the Sarvodaya movement was born. Gandhi decided to give up his comfortable living, gathered like-minded people, and began the experiment of Sarvodaya at Phoenix Farm in Johannesburg. Later the Tolstoy Farm was started for similar activities. Thus, Satyagraha and Sarvodaya came together to form the basic tenants of Gandhi's revolutionary thought.

Armed with Satyagraha and Sarvodaya, Gandhi entered the Indian political scene in 1915, upon his return from South Africa. As he gradually launched himself into the freedom struggle, he realized that Satyagraha against the British was not enough. India needed to create a new socio-political, economic, and religious order to improve the lot of its people. Thus, as he proclaimed Satyagrahas on various fronts, simultaneously he initiated several programs for the reconstruction of the society under the banner of Sarvodaya. These programs came to be known as the "Constructive Work Programs". He wrote, "Readers, whether workers or volunteers or not, should definitely realize that the constructive work programme is the truthful and non-violent way of winning Poorna Swaraj (complete freedom)."[23] It should be noted that by, "winning Poorna Swaraj," Gandhi did not mean that such a freedom already existed and was waiting to be captured. Rather, such a freedom needed to be created through hard work and perseverance. Ram Raj symbolized a state of complete freedom in every sphere of life, and the constructive work program became the means of realizing such a state.

Initially Gandhi included eighteen projects under his program. These were:
1. Communal Unity
2. Removal of Untouchability
3. Prohibition
4. Khadi
5. Other Village Industries
6. Village Sanitation

7. New or Basic Education
8. Education
9. Women
10. Health and Hygiene
11. Provincial Languages
12. National language
13. Economic Equality
14. Kisans (cultivators)
15. Labor
16. Adivasis (tribals)
17. Lepers
18. Students

Gradually Gandhi began to attract individuals who had similar concerns. However, none of them had the talents to succeed in all of the programs. Consequently, while progress was made in certain areas, other areas suffered neglect.

Inherent in the constructive work programs was Gandhi's vision for a different India than the one controlled by the British. When Gandhi wrote the Hind Swaraj, he was convinced that the British had no interest in improving the condition of the Colonies, but to continue to exploit their resources. While he came to India, he continued to defend what he had said in the controversial booklet. Written in 1909, the booklet was a severe condemnation of "modern civilization." Based on his experiences in India Gandhi said of his earlier work, "my conviction is deeper today than ever. I feel that if India will discard "modern civilization," she can only gain by doing so."[24] His constructive work programs were a response to modern civilization, which was perceived as the gift of the Industrial Revolution. The growth in machinery, money economy, consumerism, city culture, mobility (as in trains), etc., which were being welcomed with open arms, were highly problematic for Gandhi. For in order to maintain the new technocratic society, a new socio-political, and economic order was needed. He did not see any evidence that the British government was working for the welfare of all people. It is in this context that he made the remarks against the British parliament stating, "That which you consider to be the mother of parliament is like a sterile woman and a prostitute - that Parliament has not yet, of its own accord, done a single good thing... It's like a prostitute because it is under the control of ministers who change from time to time."[25] Although at the request of a

British lady, Gandhi dropped the word "prostitute," since it was considered degrading to women, he did not rescind the rest of the content.

Due to <u>Hind Swaraj</u>, which he defended till the end, Gandhi has been often misunderstood. The critics are quick to point out that Gandhi was anti-modern and therefore anti-technology. Thus, by attacking modernization he was attacking development and progress. Ram Raj then could be nothing more than a return to the past to a primitive society. This is far from the truth. Gandhi's attack on machinery as a symbol of technological advancement is to be seen in the context of colonial suppression. Machinery was not inherently evil, but was being used to create a civilization in which the rich reaped the rewards of production by exploiting the poor. For Gandhi this was a moral issue. Any civilization that did not uphold moral values was not a civilization to be sustained. Therefore, Gandhi wrote, "this civilization takes note neither of morality nor of religion. Its votaries calmly state that their business is not to teach religion. Some even consider it to be a superstitious growth."[26] He defined civilization as "that mode of conduct which points out to man the path of duty. Performance of duty and observance of morality are convertible terms... The Gujarati equivalent for civilization means "good conduct."[27] Gandhi's analysis of civilization in religious terms brought him in ideological conflict with European civilization and its impact on India. In the name of modernization it perpetuated slavery, exploitation, and dehumanization. Gandhi was concerned with the creation of a new civilization based on the Indian ideals of self-control, self-sacrifice, and what Ruskin termed as "social affection." He could not have been anti-technology if he sought the improvement of the Charkha (the spinning wheel) to save the people from the drudgery of monotony in spinning the traditional way. In fact, it is well known that he praised the inventor of the Singer sewing machine because it had improved the lot of the poor people. Gandhi favored technology with a "human face." Furthermore, if Gandhi detested technology he would not have brought the best Indian scientists of his time to form All India Village Industries Association in Wardha. Today it thrives as a research institution for rural technology. For Gandhi, Sarvodaya was not anti-science and technology. True Sarvodaya was a humanization process through constructive work programs. That Independent India did not see the wisdom of this insight is disheartening to many contemporary Gandhians.

Gandhi did not equate modernization with Westernization. On the contrary he set out to challenge the popular acceptance of the equation of these two notions. His vision of Ram Raj in this respect was not an antiquated concept to glorify the past, rather to create a bright future for the welfare of all. While the Western model sought the centralization of power to safeguard the interests of the rulers, in Ram Raj there were to be the decentralization of power to safeguard the interests of all. Hence Gandhi emphasized the Panchayat Raj.[28] The focus of Panchayat Raj for Gandhi was the village, not urban cities. He had realized that villages had been long exploited by the rulers of India whose primary interest was to collect revenues. They paid no attention to village development programs as long as their own needs were met. Consequently, due to neglect, the villages suffered from lack of proper education, hygiene, nutrition, etc. With the rise of a centralized power structure, they also lost the right of self-governance and self-determination. Gandhi's vision for India was to return to the villages the right to plan their own future. He wrote, "Independence must begin at the bottom. Thus, every village will be a Republic or Panchayat having full powers. It follows, therefore, that every village had to be self-sustained and capable of managing its affairs even to the extent of defending itself against the whole world."[29] Gandhi knew that India was far from reaching this goal at the time of her independence and therefore challenged the country toward obtaining this goal in the future. He advocated that when Panchayat Raj. in its true character, is realized then Ram Raj will occur.

In the absence of Ram Raj, economic power within the society was controlled by the powerful elite. In pre-independent India this power rested in the hands of the colonial rulers and their rich Indian allies. With the rise of the Industrial Revolution, there also came a proliferation of big companies which began controlling national resources. Gandhi was concerned that unless economic power rested in the hands of the masses, true independence shall not prevail. Thus, he advocated the ideal of Swadeshi.[30] This concept had far reaching consequences that went beyond economic concerns. It gave the natives a psychological and moral boost towards self-determination. It empowered them to control their own destiny regardless of their failure or success. Ultimately it gave them a sense of freedom from foreign dominance. Economically, it sought to stop the drainage of local resources by outsiders. It stressed the health of the village economy by utilizing local resources, by the people, and for the people. Ram Raj was an expression given to such an economic independence.

Gandhi was realistic to realize that the rich in India were not going to disappear, neither were they going to give up all of their possessions for the sake of national development. It is a well known fact that Gandhi often relied on his

37

rich friends to support his movement. For him, the issue was how to convince the rich to keep their riches and yet support the welfare of all. He was aware that the Marxist Revolution had declared a war on the rich and that they were not hesitant to use violent methods to bring the rich to their knees. Since Gandhi advocated a non-violent solution for the equitable distribution of wealth, he propagated the theory of Trusteeship.[31] According to this concept, the rich were to become the trustees of the resources they possessed, but encouraged to use them for the benefit of all. His theory of Trusteeship was based on his religious conviction that wealth belonged to God, and the individual had the right to only "honourable livelihood".[32] Gandhi found the source of this idea in the Bhagavad Gita, but must have also learned from the Biblical notion of 'stewardship' from his Christian friends. According to the Biblical notion, the world belonged to God, but was entrusted in the care of Adam and Eve. Gandhi truly believed that if the rich practice the theory of Trusteeship, it will create a harmonious society. On the one hand, the rich who are often the source of envy and contempt by the poor will be accepted by them. On the other hand their riches will be utilized for the welfare of the poor. When questioned about the practicality of his idealism, Gandhi admitted that Trusteeship was not easy to implement, but defended the wisdom of the theory.

It is difficult to prioritize the Eighteen Point Constructive Work Programs that Gandhi instituted in the name of Sarvodaya, which he linked to his notion of Ram Raj. While they were all important, particular emphasis was put on Charkha (spinning), Nai Talim (Basic Education), Stri Jagaran (awakening of the women), and the uplift of the Harijans (untouchables).

As far as the Charkha is concerned, it became a symbol of economic self-sufficiency. Gandhi is reported to have said, "God comes to the poor in the form of bread." Thus, Ram Raj had no meaning for the hungry. As a symbol of protest against British made clothes, Charkha also became the symbol for all forms of cottage industries. The call for Swadeshi was Gandhi's call to liberate the masses from big industries and to preserve and promote native small scale industries. In his view, before the advent of the British, Indian villages were thriving in spinning and other forms of cottage industries that made them self-sufficient. When he formed Charkha Sangha (spinner's association), his goal was to encourage people to realize the economic as well as the cultural significance of native crafts. Thus, Charkha became a medium of holding on to certain moral and ethical values that were necessary to preserve Indian civilization. When Gandhi proclaimed that he would win the Swaraj through Charkha, he had more than India's independence in mind. He was thinking about reclaiming an important aspect of the Indian culture which might suffer the fate of extinction if not preserved.

Nai Talim (The New Education) was also a revolutionary idea to protect Indian civilization. The key to Nai Talim was making the educational process relevant to the needs of the people. As early as 1921 Gandhi wrote the following in his magazine, Young India, "Whatever may be true of other countries, in India at any rate where more than eighty percent of the population is agricultural and another ten percent industrial, it is crime to make education mere literacy, and to unfit boys and girls for manual work in after-life."[33] He elaborated the concept of Nai Talim throughout his active life to make it practical and suitable to India's needs. Although educated in England, he remained critical of the British model of education for India since it promoted elitism. Nai Talim was an attempt to promote Indian cultural values as it emphasized knowledge of agriculture, handicrafts, and manual labor. He wrote, "My plan to impart Primary Education through the medium of village handicrafts like spinning and carding, etc. is thus conceived as the spearhead of a silent social revolution fraught with the most far-reaching consequences."[34] It is quite evident that through education Gandhi wanted to preserve and maintain a system of development which challenged the values of an industrial society. He was convinced that "industrialization on a mass scale will necessarily lead to passive or active exploitation of the villagers as the problems of competition and marketing come in."[35]

Women had been the focus of Gandhi's attention ever since he began his Satyagraha movement in South Africa. There is no doubt that he brought women out of their homes and made them full participants in the active life of his movement. Despite criticisms of his treatment of his wife, his encouraging of motherhood as the primary duty for women, and discouraging women to participate in the industrial corporate life, Gandhi maintained equality of women with men on religious and moral grounds. He was convinced that, "a woman is the companion of man, gifted with equal mental abilities. She has the right to participate in every minute detail in the activities of man and she has an equal right of freedom and liberty with him."[36] He recognized, nevertheless, that women had been subjected to all forms of oppressions by men in the Indian society. Thus, he made the uplift of women a major concern in his constructive work programs. Needless to say that he attracted many notable women from both

39

East and West, who fought beside him in India's freedom struggle. As far as such social concerns as marriage, divorce, dowry, veiling, widowhood are concerned, Gandhi gave his utmost attention in speaking out against the cultural norms that disadvantaged women. It is easy to surmise that there will be no Ram Raj in which the rights of women are violated and they are deprived of their equal status with men.

Gandhi accepted the caste system, but disapproved the discrimination perpetuated in the name of the caste. No man in the history of modern India has fought more against the evil of untouchability than Gandhi. Even Dr. Ambedkar, who became the undisputed leader of the untouchables (as an untouchable), did not question Gandhi's dedication to fight against injustices committed against those he called harijans (People of God). The disagreement between Gandhi and Ambedkar was more on the issue of the nature of political participation of the untouchable class. Despite the fact that Gandhi received ample criticism from the upper caste for his association with the untouchables, he did not deter from his conviction that caste discrimination was a social evil and must be eradicated. He believed, "Untouchability as it is practiced in Hinduism today is, in my opinion, a sin against God and Man and is, therefore, like a poison slowly eating into the very vitals of Hinduism."[37] It is unfortunate that with the rise of the Dalit Movement today, Gandhi is being scandalized by those who have failed to understand the true intentionality of his love and concern for the deprived classes in the Indian society. The task of vindicating him of unwarranted criticisms rests on the shoulders of the contemporary Gandhians.

In sum, Gandhi's constructive work programs under the banner of Sarvodaya were a blue print for the establishment of a just society for the welfare of all. This is what he meant by Ram Raj or the Kingdom of God. Injustices were to be fought on all possible fronts (social, economic, political, etc.). However, the fight was to be won following the principle of Ahimsa. In this sense his vision of Ram Raj is similar to the vision of the Old Testament prophet, Isaiah, who dreamed of a society in which peace and harmony prevailed. It is similar to the vision of Jesus, who envisioned the kingdom of God based on love. The responsibility of shaping such a kingdom rests in the hands of the committed.

Endnotes: Chapter I

1 The Paunar Ashram is located near Wardha, Maharashtra. Also known as Brahma Vidya Mandir, it was started by Vinoba Bhave to educate and train women in spirituality and Gandhian thought.

2 The Govt. Of India Publication, Collected Works of Gandhi (Ahmedabad : Navajivan Trust, 1970) vol.41, p.374 (1966).

3 Ibid., (1966) vol.20, p.167, also vol.80. p.374.

4 _____., (1969) vol.35, p.489.

5 _____., (1980) vol.80, p.300.

6 _____., (1971) vol.45, p.327.

7 _____., (1983) vol.87, p.23.

8 For a psychological understanding of Gandhi's development, see Erik Eikson, Gandhi's Truth.

9 A Karma Yogi is one who follows Karma Yoga (yoga of action) as described in the Bhagavad Gita.

10 According to Hoshiyari Bahin (a nutritionist at Gandhi's Nature Cure Center in Urlikanchan, near Pune), Gandhi loved to hear Tulsidas' Ramayana as Hoshiyari recited the couplets to him regularly.

11 Louis Fischer, ed., The Essential Gandhi (New York : Vintage Books, 1962), p.87.

12 Joan Bondurant, Conquest of Violence (Berkeley : University of California Press, 1969), pp. 16-29.

13 Ibid., p.39.

14 M. K. Gandhi, My Religion (Ahmedabad : Navajivan Publishing House, 1955), p.3.

15 N. K. Bose, ed. Selections from Gandhi (Ahmedabad : Navjivan Pub. House, 1957), p. IX.

16 S. Radhakrishnan, ed., Mahatma Gandhi (London : Allen and Unwin), p.259.

17 Vishwanath Tandon, Sarvodaya After Gandhi, (Varanasi : Sarva Seva Sangh Prakashan, 1965), p.16.

18 T. S. Devadoss, Sarvodaya and the Problem of Political Sovereignty, (Madras : University of Madras, 1974), p. 109.

19 Louis Fischer, op. cit., p.68.

20 Lloyd J. Hubeka, ed.; Unto This Last (Lincoln : University of Nebraska Press, 1967), p.44.

21 Ibid., p.XI.

22 Gandhi in Louis Fischer, Ibid., p.68.

23 M. K. Gandhi, Constructive Programme It's Meaning and Place (Ahmedabad : Navajivan Publishing House, 1941) p.3.

24 M. K. Gandhi, Hind Swaraj (Ahmedabad : Navajivan Publishing House, 1938), p.16.

25 Ibid., p.31.

26 Ibid., p.37.

27 Ibid., p.61.

28 Panchayat refers to an ancient Indian Judiciary system according to which the village elected a group of Five (Panch) elders to settle their disputes. The system allowed the power to rest with the local Panchayat rather than the State.

29 M. K. Gandhi, Panchayat Raj (Ahmedabad : Navajivan Publishing House, 1959), p.8.

30 'Swadeshi', literally meaning 'one's own' refers to a movement Gandhi started to promote India's own production of goods.

31 'Trusteeship' (See the chapter on Govind Rao Deshpande), refers to a notion according to which the rich become the trustees of their wealth, but use it for the benefit of all.

[32] M. K. Gandhi, India Of My Dreams (Ahmedabad: Navajivan Publishing House, 1947), p.66.
[33] Ibid., p.184.
[34] Ibid., p.187.
[35] Ibid., p.31.
[36] Ibid., p.225.
[37] Ibid., p.252.

II

Vinoba Bhave and Gram Swaraj

"But when Swaraj becomes a reality in each individual village, we
call it Gramraj. When all the people of a village have reached
maturity of judgment, and there is never any need to coerce anyone,
that is Ram Raj."

- Vinoba Bhave

Gandhi's vision of Ram Raj finds a unique expression in the life and work
of Vinoba Bhave (1895-1982). Today, Vinoba Niwas (Vinoba's Cottage) in his
Paunar Ashram near Wardha is quiet and serene. The silence is occasionally
interrupted by the arrival of some visitors, who wish to offer a flower or two at his
samadhi, quietly ponder on his life, and move on to their mundane activities. For
decades, after the assassination of Gandhi, Vinoba Niwas was the center of
attraction. It was here that Sarvodaya leaders, politicians, intellectuals, and
peasants gathered to seek his guidance. It was from here that he sought to find an
answer to India's land problem and to bring about Gram Swaraj (freedom of the
village), which he perceived to be the key to Ram Raj.

In accordance with Gandhi's "last will and testimony", which called for
leaders of the Congress Party to resign and get busy with constructive work
programs for the real independence, Vinoba Bhave called a meeting in Wardha to
lay the foundations of a Sarvodaya Samaj (Sarvodaya society). Interested people
were asked to take a pledge to become lok-sevaks (servants of the people), and an
organization in the name of Sarva Seva Sangh was established to oversee the
work of Sarvodaya.[1] As an architect of Sarva Seva Sangh, Vinoba became the
recognized spokesperson for the Gandhian cause. He had joined Gandhi's Ashram
in 1916, and had dedicated his life to the constructive work programs that Gandhi
had initiated. Gandhi had taken a personal interest in Vinayak, giving him the
affectionate name of Vinoba. He grilled him into the philosophies of Satyagraha

and Sarvodaya, while working together in Sabarmati Ashram kitchen, cleaning latrines, attending prayer meetings, scavenging, and taking walks.

It was at Gandhi's suggestion that Vinoba moved to an ashram in Wardha, and later to Paunar. It was a unique bond between the two that led Gandhi to once remark, "your (Vinoba) love and faith fill my eyes with tears of joy. I may or may not deserve them, but they are sure to do you infinite good. You will be an instrument of great service."[2] Vinoba returned the compliment throughout his life as evidenced in such comments as; "whatever I am today I owe to Bapu. He turned an uncouth person like me into a servant of the people,"[3] again, "--- it was Bapu who initiated me into the philosophy of karma-yoga. True, it is explained in the Gita, but I saw its application only in Bapu's life. It was here that the karma-yoga of the Gita was most clearly illustrated,"[4] also, "I always have the feeling of Gandhiji's presence before me behind me and above me. I have never been influenced by anyone the way I was by Bapu."[5] The relationship between Gandhi and Vinoba went beyond the stereotypical relationship between a guru and a disciple. It was more like a relationship between father and son. In 1940, two years before he launched the "Quit-India" slogan, Gandhi choose Vinoba to be his first individual Satyagrahi against the British. At that occasion he introduced Vinoba to India, and indeed to the world, by writing an article, "Who is Vinoba Bhave?" in his magazine, Harijan. In his description of Vinoba, Gandhi flaunted him for his knowledge of Sanskrit and Arabic, his ability to attract "an army of disciples", his skills in spinning, his devotion to the cause of the poor, and for his practice of non-violence.[6] Having such credentials, Vinoba stepped into Gandhi's shoes after his death in 1948.

For Vinoba Bhave, the Sarvodaya movement became a medium to express his spirituality. He plunged into the constructive work programs outlined by Gandhi, adding his own vision of Gram Swaraj as the immediate goal. To this end he took to a pad yatra (journey on foot) to visit hundreds and thousands of India's villages. His major disagreement with Prime Minister Nehru's government came in 1951 when he was invited to attend meetings of India's Planning Commission to discuss development of India's future.[7] Vinoba chose to walk to Delhi. His disagreement with Nehru over the need for industrialization in India shows his unprecedented concern for India's villagers. While members of the Planning Commission planned their strategies to bring heavy industries to India and push development along the western model of development, Vinoba left the meetings to continue his pad yatra. It was clear to him that there was no place for

Sarvodaya in Nehru's vision. He felt that Gandhi had been betrayed. It has been reported that during the last stages of his life, Nehru regretted having followed the scheme of industrialization because it did not bring the economic equality he had hoped for. He regrettably muttered that perhaps he should have listened to Gandhi.[8] Upon hearing Nehru's remarked, Vinoba reportedly quipped, "now he (Nehru) is really discovering India."[9] For Vinoba, as for Gandhi, the real India was in the villages. Industrialization meant the loss of a culture that had survived the onslaught of many invasions for thousands of years. The independent India was planning the demise of a culture at its own hands, something that the foreign invaders did not do. Vinoba could not tolerate this destruction and began preparing for its preservation and reconstruction.

Vinoba Bhave's finest hour came in his discovery of the <u>Bhoodan</u>.[10] It was a discovery because when he arrived in Telangana in Hyderabad in 1951, he had no solution for the non-violence instigated by the communists against the land lords. Ramachandra Reddy's offer of a portion of his land to the peasants at their request started a movement which even surprised Vinoba. Vinoba rose to the occasion and realized the potential of a simple dan (gift) of a piece of land. As an astute mathematician, he concluded that he needed 50 million acres of land in donation to solve the problem of the landless in India. For nearly two decades he walked all over India to collect land. He was able to collect only about 4 million acres before he returned to his ashram in Paunar. For Vinoba, Bhoodan became a way to realize Sarvodaya. Although Gandhi was well aware of the problem of land and the atrocities committed by the landlords against the villagers, he did not find a solution. Through Bhoodan, Vinoba seemed to have discovered a <u>mantra</u> to end the problem of the disequitable distribution of land. For the Sarvodaya movement Bhoodan became the primary constructive work program. Most lok sevaks followed Vinoba's leadership and took to <u>Pad yatras</u> to collect land. Vinoba's determination to bring Gram Swaraj through Bhoodan is evidenced by the oath he took in 1957 at <u>Kanyakumari</u> when he pledged, "as long as <u>Gram Swaraj</u> is not established in India. I shall continue my yatra (journey) and ceaselessly carry on the efforts in that direction. May God give me strength for achieving this goal."[11]

Bhoodan could have not been born without Vinoba's understanding of Sarvodaya as a spiritual movement. He stated, "In Bhoodan, distribution of land is not the only question. It aims at the moral regeneration of the whole nation."[12] When his critics charged that he was fragmenting land through Bhoodan, he responded by insisting that he was uniting hearts. Gradually he gave a new dimension to the movement by adding such concepts as Premdan (gift of love), Buddhidan (gift of wisdom), Shramdan (gift of labor) and Sampatidan (gift of property). The concept of dan was used by him as a moral imperative to touch the conscience of people in favor of giving and sharing. He viewed the incorporation of various dans into the Bhoodan movement as a mission of "Dharma-Chakra-Pravartana" -- establishment of a righteous order.[13] The highest form of dan was Jivandan (gift of life), which meant a complete surrender of one's life to Sarvodaya. Through these processes, Vinoba was able to attract many dedicated souls for the Gandhian cause. Bhoodan movement became a catalyst for empowering poor villagers. Gram Sabhas (village assemblies) were created to settle disputes and to oversee other problems. The goal was idealistic and it is questionable whether it really brought freedom to the villagers. Nonetheless, those within the movement tried to reconstruct the village for Gram Swaraj.

Soon after Bhoodan was taken up by Sarva Seva Sangh as a constructive work program under Sarvodaya, Vinoba added another dimension to the movement by introducing the concept of Gramdan (village gift) in 1952. Hence the movement was labeled as the Bhoodan - Gramdan movement. This step was taken to foster a change in the power structure within a village and to create a just social order. In a Gramdan village, land was to be owned collectively and not individually. The entire land of the village was to be handed over (and legally transferred) to the village assembly (Gram Sabha), which was made up of village adults. Under its guidance, the assembly had the power to redistribute 1/20 of the total land among landless farmers. The Gram Sabha also instituted a Gram Kosh (village chest), where farmers were asked to deposit one day's income per month. While gram kosh kept the money, Sarvodaya Patra (Pot) kept donated food to meet the needs of the poor. This was a system designated for the people helping people within a community. In order that the system may work smoothly, Vinoba initiated certain steps to complete the task. These steps are identified as Prapti (signing of the land to village assemblies), Pushti (transferring the land through legal channels), Nirman (developing the process), retention of 19/20 of the land by the owner with the right to sell or mortgage the land without permission of the gram sabha, and Arohan (to ascend through stages towards the desired goal of bringing harmony in the lives of the villagers).[14] If we look at the list of objectives that Vinoba put forward, it is clear that he was seeking freedom of the village along Sarvodaya lines. The sevenfold objectives were stated as follows:

1. Elimination of poverty.
2. Awakening the feeling of love and affection of landlords.
3. Strengthening the society by eliminating divisions.
4. To revive the Indian value of Yagna (sacrifice), dana (giving), and tapas (renunciation).
5. Building a new social order on the basis of voluntary bodily labor, non possession, cooperation and self-reliance.
6. Presenting a common platform for all political parties.
7. Helping world peace.[15]

The sequence of events that followed succeeding the launching of Gramdan is a testimony to Vinoba's dedication to work for Ram Raj as he understood it. In 1953, while in his pad yatra in Bihar, Vinoba emphasized a need for Shramdan (gift of labor) in his movement. The mantra for Shramdan was, "Bhai Kudali chalate chalo, mitti ka sona banate chalo" (brother keep on lifting the blade and turn the soil into gold).[16] An event that gave a boost to Vinoba's movement was the conversion of a well known politician and a socialist leader, Jai Prakash Narayan to Sarvodaya in 1953. Jai Prakash (J. P.) was an ardent Marxist-socialist leader, who was not convinced by the Gandhian philosophy of welfare for all. However, Vinoba's speeches and interpretation of Sarvodaya changed his mind, and he offered his life for this work. In this manner, the concept of Jivandan (gift of life) was brought into the movement. Impressed by J. P.'s dedication, Vinoba also made a renewed pledge which stated, "I dedicate my life to the non-violent revolution, based on Bhoodan-Yagna, and village industry oriented programs."[17]

The Bhoodan-Gramdan movement did not have a smooth sailing. In 1956 a major outbreak of violence in Bihar distressed Vinoba immensely. He had hoped that the Sarvodaya ideals and Bhoodan-Gramdan activities would bring peace and harmony among the peasants and the landlords. However, the movement had the least effect on rioting villagers. In distress Vinoba stated, "I declare I have not achieved success and I accept my defeat. People might say that I got lacs of acres in Bhoodan and hundreds of villages in Gramdan. It has given immense hope to the people but I confess that I am in a terrible agony."[18] Vinoba revived the concept of Shanti Sena (Peace Brigade) given by Gandhi, and asked the villagers to support Shanti Sainiks (Peace soldiers) by keeping a Sarvodaya Patra (Pot) in their homes. This pot was to contain grains to feed the peace keepers as they volunteered for this task.

In 1962, on one of his Bhoodan-Gramdan marches, Vinoba came to the defamed Chambal Valley occupied by decoits. The government had failed to bring law and order here having spent a large amount of financial resources. At Vinoba's initial request twenty-one decoits surrendered. In subsequent years many others surrendered their arms to Vinoba. The same year as the Indo-China war broke out, Vinoba continued to emphasize the importance of Gram-Swaraj. He continued his march to promote internal solidarity and to preach self-reliance in food in the villages. In 1963, he introduced the notion of Sulabhadan (easy gift) to his movement. This was an attempt to make Gramdan easier. The principles used were 1) Ownership of the land was to be transferred to the Gram Sabha. 2) The landholders were to donate 1/20th of their land for the landless. 3) 1/40th of the annual income in money or kind was to be submitted to the village chest. 4) From each family in the village an adult was to become the member of Gram Sabha.[19] Soon after, Vinoba announced the scheme of Prakhandadan (block gift), according to which 85% of the villages in a block were to follow Gramdan pattern. Vinoba received most of his success in this program in the state of Bihar. Thus, in 1969 while a large number of villages had accepted Gramdan, Vinoba declared, Bihardan. It was his hope that the rest of the states in the country will follow suite. However, this was too good to be true. Having celebrated Bihardan, Vinoba returned to his ashram in Paunar in 1969, thus ending his personal march for Bhoodan. The task of continuing the efforts of Bhoodan fell in the laps of Sarva Seva Sangh leaders. With their efforts, the government helped create Bhoodan Boards, a legal body to oversee distribution of land in many states.

Vinoba's return to Paunar and his decision to cease walking for Bhoodan-Gramdan remain a mystery, perhaps known only to his close associates. Several speculations have been made. Perhaps he was physically exhausted and by the time he turned 74 it was difficult for him to keep up with his pad yatras. He had been nursing an ulcer which also hampered his physical movements. As some of his associates have suggested, he was entering a new phase of spiritual development which required him to practice detachment to enhance spiritual powers.[20] There is also a view that perhaps he realized that a new leadership was needed to take over the work of Gram Swaraj. The time had come for Vinoba to recede in the background and let others guide the movement. Since he believed in developing lok-shati (people's power), he though it was necessary that the real grass roots level work must be done by the lok-sevaks with the help of the villagers. There is also a view that Bihardan was a quick move to celebrate the

48

success of Bhoodan-Gramdan too soon. Actually, the movement was failing in the sense that not many Gram Sabhas were functioning, the land was slow to be distributed, and the workers were not adequately trained to deal with the variety of problems involved in community development. Vinoba retreated to Paunar to rethink the entire process. Finally, there is also a view that by the time Vinoba returned to Paunar, India entered an era of new political crisis which shook the entire nation, and subsequently also effected the fate of the movement in the years to come. Whatever the reason for Vinoba's retreat to Paunar, with the dawn of 1970s, the Gandhian movement in India took a unique turn. It brought into the lime light Mr. Jai Prakash Narayan, a veteran politician turned Sarvodayaite, who is the focus of the next chapter.

In assessing Vinoba Bhave's contribution to Sarvodaya, it is important to understand his spiritual development. In this respect there is a remarkable similarity between Gandhi and Vinoba. Like Gandhi, Vinoba was also concerned with his Moksha. To this end he relentlessly carried out his own experiments with Truth. Both were deeply affected by the ideas of the Bhagavad Gita. And both can be truly classified as karma-yogis. While Gandhi's last phase of spiritual development was interrupted by the assassin's bullet, Vinoba was able to carry out his experiments till he died at the age of 77 in 1982. By some estimations, Vinoba went beyond Gandhi in his personal quest for Moksha. As a Brahmachari (celibate) who never entered the Grahasta Ashrama (household life), he led an extremely austere life of a monk. His discipline in yogic practices, meditation, fasting, prayer, etc. went far beyond Gandhi. Thus, Vinoba brought a yogic dimension to Sarvodaya which was perhaps not truly appreciated by its leadership all the time. His disagreement with J. P. on the direction the movement ought to take during Indira Gandhi's regime, which subsequently split the movement, has, at the center of controversy, his spiritual concerns. Either J. P. and his followers (a majority of whom belong to Sarva Seva Sangh) did not understand Vinoba's spirituality, or they understood him too well to continue to follow his line of thinking.

How did Vinoba Bhave apply his spirituality to Sarvodaya? A detailed analysis of this issue has been provided elsewhere.[21] Here I wish to present a summary to contextualize the life and work of Vinoba Bhave along Gandhian lines.

Vinoba's attraction to Sarvodaya is directly linked with the worldview provided by the Vedantic form of Hinduism. In this worldview the Divine is perceived as an ultimate Reality that manifests in many forms. Based on the Upandishadic dictum it affirms that "Reality is One but the sages speak of it in many ways." Like Ramakrishna and Vivekananda, Vinoba viewed religion as a universal phenomenon and not limited to a particular creed or dogma. Consequently all religions contained truth as the divine described by them was One. For Vinoba the One (God) had many qualities whom Jesus saw as "loving," Upandishadic sages as "true" and Mohammed as "compassionate and merciful."[22] The true meaning of Vedanta for Vinoba was the end of the Vedas. He suggested that as the word Vedanta means the end of the Vedas, it should encourage the end of religious orthodoxy based exclusively on the Vedas. He even coined new words like Biblanta, Quranta, and Purananta to demand an end to the blind attachment to scriptures and their exclusive theologies in various religions. Behind this analysis was Vinoba's understanding of religion as Sanatana Dharma (universal religion) which was the guiding force behind Sarvodaya. As such, it was tolerant of all faiths, castes, and creeds. To give an expression to this universal religion, Vinoba instituted a universal prayer to be sung at his ashrams. He also explicated the truths of the Gita in the manner to show its insistence on the Sanatana Dharma.

Belief in God as an Absolute Power and the conviction that Absolute resides in each individual, forms the fundamental basis of Vinoba's philosophy. Welfare for all (Sarvodaya) was seen as a necessity because all humanity was united together with Brahman (tat tvam asi). Therefore, when Sarvodaya preached equality of all, it was motivated by the religious philosophy expressed in Vinoba's Vedanta. When the Bhoodan-Gramdan movement was born, Vinoba used the Vedantic notion of the Absolute to emphasize that the land actually belonged to God, humans were merely its caretakers. Thus, the notion of stewardship was linked with the Gandhian ideal of Trusteeship to achieve equality. Furthermore, like Gandhi, Vinoba's Satyagrahas against the harijans' entry into the caste dominated temples under his movement was also motivated by his deep conviction that all humans were created equal. If Gandhi called the untouchables of India as harijans, Vinoba gave the poor the title of daridra-narayana (God manifested in the poor). Behind this thinking was the vision of Gandhi as expressed in his well known Talisman:

> Recall the face of the poorest and most helpless person whom you may have seen and ask yourself if the step you contemplate is going to be any use to him, Will he be able to gain anything by it? Will it restore him to control over his life and destiny? In other

50

> words, will it lead to Swaraj, self-rule for the hungry and also the
> spiritually starved millions of our countrymen? Then you will find
> your doubts and yourself melting away.

Through Sarvodaya's constructive work programs, Vinoba was trying to listen to the voice of Gandhi.

The fact that the Bhoodan-Gramdan movement was spiritually motivated is quite clear from Vinoba's speeches and writings. Reflecting on the birth of the movement in Telangana he once said, "I at once realized that the universal force wants to execute something new (through Bhoodan)."[23] He called the work of Bhoodan as the mission of "Dharma-Chakra-Pravartana," which is best translated as the wheel of Dharma rolling to establish a new righteous order. It has been recognized by interpreters of Vinoba that, in Bhoodan, he applied the philosophy of the Gita. In this context the three spiritual principles of Yagna (sacrifice), Dana (giving), and tapas (self-sacrifice) are crucial. The application of these ideals meant the ability to sacrifice by sharing with others. Bhoodan was born in the spirit of self-sacrifice and sharing. Vinoba called it a new mantra of Sarvodaya which was going to change the hearts of the people.

Through Sarvodaya, Vinoba was attempting to establish what he called a "Samyayogi society." He explained, "To the society which we seek to build up I have given the name "Samyayogi society." I struck at this word from the Gita which teaches us to do unto others as we do unto ourselves."[24] Furthermore, "Samya-yoga means 'leveling' the field. That we have to do. Ours (our goal) is not to merely distribute land, but to level up the mental values of the entire society. With this mental approach you go from village to village and explain the idea."[25] This is precisely what Vinoba attempted to do during his two decades of Pad Yatras. He dialogued with Marxists, who had a different vision of leveling up the society through class struggles which involved violence. He called Marx a maha muni (great saint), but disagreed with the communists who wanted to use force to bring social equality. Vinoba's vision of a samyogi society included the practice of lokniti (politics of the people) rather than Rajniti (politics of the government). Such a society was to be established by increasing lok shakti (people power) and eliminating Dand Shakti (power of the punishment). The Samyagoi society is nothing but a Gandhian vision of Ram Raj. For Vinoba, before Ram Raj becomes an actuality, Gramraj needs to be achieved, and Gramraj cannot be established without a Samyogi society. It is interesting to note that while Gandhi invoked the name Rama to speak of Ram Raj, Vinoba invoked the name of Krishna and his

51

abode in Gokula in <u>Vrindavan</u>. Vinoba believed that true democracy existed in Gokula because people willingly cared for each other. It was his belief that such a society can emerge through the efforts of Sarvodaya. It should begin with the individual and society, and then transform the world. From here comes Vinoba's slogan of <u>Jai Jagat</u> - victory to the world.[26] Such is Vinoba's humanism guided by spiritual principles.

Vinoba's spiritual concerns are further reflected in his involvement with J. P. during the seventies when he had retired at Paunar. His vow of silence which he undertook for a year, his emphasis on Acharyakul,[27] cow protection as constructive work programs, and, indeed the manner in which he chose to die at the very end, are testimonies of his spirituality. Since some of these events are intertwined with the life and work of Jai Prakash Narayan, it is best to take them up in the context of the next chapter.

Endnotes: Chapter II

[1] For detailed description of the founding of Sarva Seva Sangh, see Geoffrey Ostergaard, Nonviolent Revolution In India (New Delhi : Gandhi Peace Foundation, 1985), p.4.

[2] Daniel P. Hoffman, India's Social Miracle (California : Nature graph Co., 1961) p.41.

[3] Kanti Shah, Vinoba on Gandhi (Varanasi : Sarva Seva Sangha Prakashan, 1973) p.4.

[4] Ibid., p.4.

[5] Ibid., p.3.

[6] Vasant Nargolkar, The Creed of Saint Vinoba (Bombay : Bharatiya Vidya Bhavan, 1963) pp. 29-30.

[7] Ibid., p.191.

[8] Jai Prakash Narayan, Meri Vichar Yatra (Varanasi : Sarva Seva Sangh Prakashan, 1974) p.57.

[9] The pun refers to Nehru's book, Discovery of India.

[10] Bhoodan (Bhoo = land, dan = gift), the land gift movement through which Vinoba asked the rich to donate their land for the poor. Although the movement was most successful in the 1950s and 60s, some Gandhians are still seeking donations of land for free distribution.

[11] Suresh Ram, Vinoba and His Mission (Kashi : Akhil Bharat Sarva Seva Sangh, 1954), p.194.

[12] Vinoba Bhave, The Principle and Philosophy of the Bhoodan Yagna (Tanjore : Sarvodaya Prachuralaya, 1995), p.15.

[13] Vinoba Bhave, Democratic Values (Kashi : Sarva Seva Sangh Prakashan, 1962), p.126.

[14] S. Dasgupta, A Great Society of Small Communities (Varanasi : Sarva Seva Sangh Prakashan, 1968), Ch. II.

[15] Daniel P. Hoffman, India's Social Miracle, California : Nature graph Company, 1961), p.56.

[16] Suresh Ram, Ibid., p.97.

[17] Kanti Shah, Vinoba : Life and Mission (Varanasi : Sarva Seva Sangh Prakashan, 1979), p.55. Bhoodan-Yagna means looking at land gift as a sacrifice.

[18] Suresh Ram, op. cit ., p.163.

[19] Information received from Sri Narendra Dube, a lok sevak in the Sarvodaya Movement.

[20] Information received from interview conducted with several sisters at Paunar Ashram in 1980.

[21] Ishwar Harris, 'The Spiritual Dimensions of Vinoba's Thought' in Vinoba the Spiritual Revolutionary (New Delhi : Gandhi Peace Foundation, 1974), p.37.

[22] T. N. Atreya (ed.) Dharma Samanvya (New Delhi : Gandhi Peace Foundation, 1974), p.37.

[23] Daniel P. Hoffman, op. cit., p.51.

[24] Vinoba Bhave, The Principles and Philosophy of the Bhoodan Yagna (Tanjore : Sarvodaya Prachuralaya, 1955), p.1.

[25] Ibid., p.5.

[26] Vasant Nargolkar, The Creed of Saint Vinoba, (Bombay: Bharatiya Vidya Bhavan, 1963) p.218.

[27] By Acharyakul (a federation of intellectuals), Vinoba meant to create a fellowship of concerned intellectuals who were interested in propagating the ideas of Sarvodaya. Today this organization still exists under the leadership of Balvijaya, Vinoba's secretary. The local chapters are found in different states. Some tend to be more active than others.

III

Jai Prakash Narayan and Total Revolution

"...Once a Gandhian conceptual framework is accepted, it became
quite clear that any Gandhian approach or model is one of a
continuous revolution which I have called Total Revolution.
Satyagraha, or non-violent struggle, is the essence of this
revolution."

- Jai Prakash Narayan

Jai Prakash Narayan (1902-1979) can be viewed as the "St. Paul" of
Sarvodaya. In his youth he was a Marxist who did not fully understand Gandhi's
non-violent struggle against the British.[1] Born of a modest farmer, he refused to
study at Banares Hindu University on the grounds that it was supported by
government grants. He worked his way through higher education in America,
receiving a Master's degree in sociology from the University of Wisconsin. He
contemplated studying in Russia, but instead returned home in 1929 after seven
years of sojourn in America. Upon his return to India he joined the Communist
Party of India. However, since the Communists were denouncing Mahatma
Gandhi as "a lackey of Indian bourgeoisie", which Jai Prakash (affectionately
known as J. P.) could not accept, Narayan joined the Congress Party. By 1934 he
started the Congress Socialist Party. During the "Quit India" movement, J. P.
plunged into India's struggle for freedom. He was jailed, but escaped, and
organized underground resistance for which he was again arrested in 1943.
Gradually his passion for freedom, his activities, his intellect, and political
movement in Indian affairs made him a national hero. Disenchanted with
democratic socialism for its inability to create a classless society, J. P. began to
slide toward Gandhian philosophy. By some estimations, he could have been the
next prime minister of India after Nehru, but J. P. had a different calling. Little did
he know, at the time of India's independence, that he was to become one of the

greatest leaders of Sarvodaya next to Vinoba Bhave. Convinced by Gandhian alternatives to solve India's social problems under Sarvodaya, the Bhoodan activity made perfect sense to him. In 1952 he met Vinoba, and by 1954 he was surrendering his life in Jivandan (gift of life) for the work of Sarvodaya. At this time, as the nation was captivated by the Bhoodan movement, J. P. began his Pad yatra and started collecting land in the name of Vinoba. Thus an avowed Marxist became a confirmed Gandhian.

During the height of the Bhoodan-Grandan movement, J. P. accepted Vinoba's leadership as an exponent of Gandhian values. In light of India's socio-economic problems he became convinced of Gandhi's vision of Ram Raj and Vinoba's assistance on reaching Ram Raj through Gram Swaraj. J. P. not only worked for Bhoodan, but donated much of his family land to poor peasants. He took to a simple lifestyle dedicating his time and energies to the Sarvodaya movement. He refused Nehru's invitation to join his cabinet on the grounds that the Nehruvian vision for India's economic development was contradictory to Sarvodaya's vision of welfare of all. In J. P.'s view, Nehru might have understood the Gandhian philosophy of life, but he did not adopt it for India. Nehru bypassed Sarvodaya on the pretext that it was a lofty ideal and that the Indian government was not worthy of it. In his mind, all energies needed to be directed toward socialism.[2] To J. P.'s disappointment Nehru went after the western model of economic development being followed all over the world. He tried to develop the country on the basis of state controlled law-and-order and capital investment. Millions were spent, laws were created, but Nehru's wishes were not fulfilled.[3] In his criticism of Nehru and his policies regarding his imitation of the West, J. P.'s analysis was similar to that Gandhi and Vinoba. The difference is that while Gandhi, knowing Nehru's mind, still chose him to be his political successor, J. P. stayed away from Nehru's government. He remained convinced of the Gandhi-Vinoba ideology of social welfare during the 1950s and 1960s. Along with the work of land distribution, creation of lok sabhas (people's assemblies), supervising shanti sena, he was highly instrumental in the surrender of hundreds of decoits. Though unconvinced of Gandhian non-violent methods in his youth, in his middle years non-violence became his creed.

J. P.'s Jivandan (giving one's life) for Sarvodaya was a remarkable act of surrender to Vinoba's Bhoodan-Gramdan program. However, J. P. will be mostly remembered for his call for "Total Revolution" which he gave to the nation on June 5, 1974.[4] Inherent in this call was J. P.'s critique of the Bhoodan-Gramdan movement, his disenchantment with Vinoba's current policies, his disillusionment with Indira Gandhi's Congress Party and her dictatorial rule, his dedication to the youth of India who wanted change, and his vision to bring Sarvodaya to new heights to create the India of his dream. The chain of events that followed after the call for "Total Revolution" ultimately created a serious rift within the Sarva Seva Sangh, shifted the direction of Sarvodaya, defeated Indira Gandhi as the Prime Minister, and brought about a new government under the leadership of the Janta Party.[5] It was due to this call that he was given the title of Lok Nayak (guide of the people) by his followers. His actions during the years 1974-1979 were so profound that he was seen as a national threat to the survival of democracy, was beaten, jailed, and died a mysterious death.[6] Through all of these personal trials and tribulations, J. P. remained convinced that he was doing the work of Sarvodaya along Gandhian lines and that "Total Revolution" was merely an extension of Sarvodaya. Whether or not his "Total Revolution" can be equated with Sarvodaya can only be judged on the basis of his involvement within the movement and an analysis of his thinking that led to Total Revolution.

A crucial turn in the life of J. P. came in the year 1970. He had been actively engaged in the Bhoodan-Gramdan work when violence erupted in Bihar and some landlords were killed by the communist Naxalites in reprisal for atrocities committed by the landlords against the peasants. While traveling in the Himalayas, J. P. got the word that the lives of Sarvodaya workers in Bihar were also threatened. J. P. postponed his travel plans and immediately returned to Bihar. It was during his visit to the violence torn areas in Bihar that J. P. came to a momentous conclusion. He attributed the cause of violence to the inhumane condition of the peasants in the villages and their exploitation by the rich land owners. What was happening in Bihar was symptomatic of a general socio-economic malaise prevalent around the country. J. P. concluded that among the masses there was a discontent against rising high prices, corruption, exploitation, moral degradation of political leaders, problems with law and order, and a general mistrust in the ability of the government to properly govern the nation. Convinced by the belief that Sarvodaya had the answer, J. P. decided to launch a major experiment with Gram Swaraj in the Mushahri block in Muzzafarpur district in Bihar. J. P. and his co-workers set up a camp in Mushahri from which they planned to travel to different villages, continuing the work of Bhoodan-Gramdan in the hope of creating Lok Shakti (people's power) along the Gandhi-Vinoba thinking. During the course of this work, J. P. wrote a booklet evaluating his work, which has acquired a unique place in Sarvodaya literature. Entitled, Face to Face, the booklet holds the key to what transpired in J. P.'s life which led to his call for "Total Revolution".

In Mushahri, J. P. came face to face with the naked truth and stark reality of the Bhoodan work in Bihar villages. He discovered that in spite of the slogan of Sulabhdan (dan made easy), the ugly reality was that, in fact, nothing had changed in the Mushahri block. J. P. had to confront reality and admit to the truth that the Bhoodan-Gramdan had failed. If this was true in Bihar then what about the rest of the nation? Determined to make Gram Swaraj a success, J. P. accepted the challenge and got down to work. He denied the claim of the press that he had come to Mushahri to fight the communist backed Naxalites.[7] He wrote, "Naxalism was primarily a social, economic, political, and administrative problem, and only secondarily a law-and-order question."[8] He came to Mushahri to initiate "a peaceful and constructive social revolution." In accordance with the Bhoodan-Gramdan movement he began with the work of establishing Gram Sabhas, distributing the land, setting up village community chest (Gram Kosh) and organizing Shanti Sena (Peace brigade). He gave particular attention to properly registering the land in the names of the farmers to which it belonged. He discovered that a great deal of injustice was done to many peasants whose land had been taken away from them by rich farmers. In many cases the Bhoodan land donated to the poor in previous years had been illegally confiscated by others. There was fear among the peasants to the point that their lives were threatened if they opened up to J. P. and told him the extent to which the exploitation was effecting them.[9] J. P., through his conversations and meetings with many inhabitants in various hamlets, saw the actual living conditions of the exploited. Reflecting on all of the problems, J. P. wrote, "I must confess that it would appear on a close examination that socio-economic reality in the village is ugly and distressing in the extreme."[10] He further stated, "It is clear that if something is not done soon to pull the villages out of this morass, they will sink deeper into it, dragging the whole country down with them, as it seems happening already to this state (reference to Bihar)."[11] It is obvious from his reflections that J. P. was putting Bhoodan-Gramdan under severe scrutiny in a manner that Vinoba had never done. Not only that, he was also questioning the efficacy of government supported land reforms, developmental schemes, and laws created to help poor farmers. None of these attempts were producing desired results. In assessing the entire situation as J. P. saw it, his own words are quite telling:

My first reaction on coming face to face with this reality was to realize how remote and unreal were the brave pronouncements of Delhi and Patna (capital of Bihar) from the actuality at the ground level. High-standing words, grandiose plans, reform galore. But somehow they all, or most of them, remain suspended somewhere in mid-air... What meets the eye is utter poverty, misery, inequality, exploitation, backwardness, stagnation, frustration, and loss of hope.[12]

That both the government and Sarvodaya had failed in their missions was disheartening to J. P. Nevertheless, he decided to buckle down and work for Sarvodaya. During his one year stay in Mushahri, he made Gram Swaraj his goal to be achieved.[13] To this end he reports that through his efforts, in fourteen out of the forty three villages, the conditions for Gramdan were fulfilled, and in ten of them Gram Sabhas were formed.[14] He managed to distribute some Bhoodan land and discussed the problem of land distribution with various Panchayats (the village governing body). He also looked into the problem of evicting poor peasants by the rich from their lands. He reported of looking into 675 cases where the papers of legal ownership (Parchas) had never been issued to peasants. He was able to rectify that problem in most cases.[15] J. P. admitted that although progress was slow, he received reports from various sources that Gramdan and Sarvodaya had replaced Naxalism, and were major topics of discussion among the villages.[16] Though pleased with such reports, J. P. was not satisfied with the progress he was making. Based on his analysis of corruption prevalent in the area, he concluded that neither the handful of Sarvodaya workers nor the government agencies could solve the problem. "...the main responsibility will have to be borne by the village communities themselves. If that fails to happen, Gramdan and Gram Swaraj would also join the limbo of history together with Community Development and Panchayat Raj."[17] J. P. ended his report on Mushahri with a nationwide appeal for help and emphasized that the problem was not limited to Bihar, but was prevalent all over India.

Why did J. P. leave Mushahri after a year's experimentation with the work of Sarvodaya? A variety of answers have been given. The most accepted answer among his close associates is that his experience in Mushahri made him realize that the nature of corruption he confronted there was so profound that it could not be tackled on the village level alone. Furthermore, the source of corruption was at the top with the administration in New Delhi (for India) and in Patna (for Bihar). Likewise, the entire nation was in the grips of corruption that flowed from the nation's capital as well as from state capitals. J. P. realized that problems of such magnitude needed to be fought at all levels. Thus, the notion of "Total Revolution" was born even though the name was not proclaimed until 1974.[18] How could J. P. attack such a problem without challenging the national and provincial governments? How could he do it without support of the people? J. P. had to struggle with these questions before he could put forward the idea of "Total Revolution" before the nation. The three years which elapsed since J. P. left Mushahri and made a call for Total Revolution were crucial.

In 1971 the Bangladesh crisis erupted and millions of refugees were pouring into India. J. P. went on a world tour in 1971 explaining the need for freedom in Bangladesh and its creation as a new nation. During this tour he also observed the workings of the youth movement in Europe. He realized that there was a general discontent among the youth around the world, and India was no exception. After his return, J. P. wished to take a year off due to his poor health.[19] During the period of 1972-73 there was a growing discontent among the youth in India related to many issues that effected their education and joblessness. Furthermore, criticisms were also surfacing of Indira Gandhi's government, and the manner in which the Congress Party had won general elections in 1971. The first state to erupt in 1973 was Gujarat where students called for the dissolution of the state assembly. The next state to follow was Bihar. J. P. found himself at the center stage in what came to be known as the Bihar Movement. Along with J. P. the entire Sarvodaya Movement, including Vinoba, once again came into the limelight since the Bhoodan-Gramdan days of 1950s and 1960s.

The Bihar Movement produced a crisis situation for the Sarvodaya Movement. In Bihar, Sarvodaya leaders were tested for their understanding of Gandhi, their loyalty to Vinoba or J. P., their commitment to constructive work programs, and their vision for Ram Raj. The impact of the movement was so profound that it split the Sarva Seva Sangh into Vinoba and J. P. camps. The effects of this split are still felt in the lives and works of contemporary Gandhians in India today.

J. P.'s involvement as the leader of the Bihar Movement was crucial to his call of Total Revolution on June 5, 1974. The events that led to the declaration are skillfully presented in detail by Geoffrey Ostergaard in his book, Non-Violent Revolution in India (1985). Here I will present a brief account to set the context. Since J. P. reached the conclusion that the Bhoodan-Gramdan Movement had failed, he was looking for an alternative for Ram Raj.[20] In 1973, he suddenly had the insight to call upon the youth of India to help him. Soon he sent an appeal under the title of "Youth For Democracy." The appeal was sent to the Prime Minister, Indira Gandhi, which outlined the youth dissatisfaction around the world, with particular reference to India. In a nutshell, J. P. was calling for the end of a variety of corruptions that were plaguing Indian society. His primary focus was on saving democracy and making it a people's democracy. He also suggested that youth were looking for a new revolution to end poverty, politicization of students, exploitation of poor, beaurocratic oppression, etc.[21] Consequently, the Gujarat Movement of 1973 and the Bihar movement of 1974 were led by students. Like in Gujarat, in Bihar the target was the state assembly. The students had charged that most elected M. L. A.s (Members of Legislative Assembly) were corrupt. While Bihar was in the grips of poverty, land related violence, rising inflation, hunger, and disease, the state assembly was useless and no longer represented the interest of the people. It was rendered ineffective to solve people's problems. There was also a serious problem with higher education in terms of curriculum, admissions, governance, and examination system. The failure of the government to respond to students' demands and its determination to forcefully suppress the Movement led to student led strikes, marches, and a call to shut down Bihar. In response Indira Gandhi declared a state of emergency in 1975 which lasted until 1977. The emergency suspended freedom of the press. J. P., along with many students and Sarvodaya leaders, were jailed, and Indira Gandhi emerged more dictatorial than ever before.[22] For J. P. this was the end of democracy in India.

First and foremost, for J. P., "Total Revolution" was an extension of Sarvodaya. He admitted that during the Bihar crisis, in a speech he delivered to a large crowd in Patna, he suddenly and unexpectedly used the words "Total Revolution".[23] What he was doing before and did during the Bihar Movement was the work of Gandhi. Throughout his many writings and speeches there is ample evidence that J. P. meant what he said. At one occasion he wrote that Gandhi wanted Antyodaya (uplift from the bottom) and equated it with Sarvodaya (welfare for all). For J. P. this is what "Total Revolution" was after. He went as far as to say that when there is a total revolution then there will be Sarvodaya.[24] Like Gandhi, who wanted to develop lok shakti (people's power), J. P., through his call for Total Revolution, was also doing that. Surely the context was different. Gandhi was fighting with a foreign power in order to return power to the people. In J. P.'s mind, he was fighting a domestic power (Indira's government) to return

61

power to the people. He viewed his task as an attempt to complete the unfinished work of Gandhi. J. P. often referred to Gandhi's last will and testament, which was a call for the Congress Party to dissolve itself and become Lok Sevaks (servants of the people) after India's Independence. Since it did not happen, J. P. was carrying out the dream of Gandhi by calling on people to join his Total Revolution. In this movement, J. P. saw himself as a soldier of Gandhi to complete the fight of real independence.[25]

J. P. also viewed his Total Revolution as a moral revolution. Here again he viewed himself as following the path of Gandhi. Like Gandhi had raised his voice against corruption in all spheres of life, J. P. spoke up against corruption. Here Gandhi, Vinoba, and J. P. were on the same wave length. While J. P. did not consider himself to be a spiritual person in the same vein as Vinoba, he believed that a civilization cannot survive in the absence of a moral force. He did not see the state providing any guidance in the area. This force needed to be awakened in the lives of people. Thus, his movement against the immoral acts of the government was motivated by his desire to cleanse the entire society. While during the Bihar Movement, J. P.'s attention was concentrated on state based corruption, he was concerned about many social evils such as caste prejudice, the practice of dowry, child marriages, bonded labor, etc. Thus, his Total Revolution was a moral war against all fronts.[26] It had the appeal of a Gandhian Satyagraha to achieve a long term goal of Ram Raj. In the context of the Bihar Movement, J. P. invoked the imagery of Ram Raj, but hastened to add that the people of India were witnessing "Indira Raj" instead.[27] Naturally he saw fit to raise his voice against it.

It can be asserted that Gandhi's Satyagraha against the British was a temporary hurdle that needed to be overcome in order to reach the higher dream, likewise, J. P.'s Satyagraha against Indira Gandhi's policies during the Bihar Movement was a temporary obstacle that needed to be dealt with in order to pursue higher goals. Therefore, he admitted that the complete picture of "Total Revolution" cannot be realized in the present. It will manifest itself gradually as people progressed toward their goal.[28] He often recalled that Gandhi used to insist that taking the "first step" was enough. In those days, J. P. and his young friends wondered what "the old man" was saying. They wanted the complete picture. However, J. P. admits that his experience has shown that Gandhi was right. Referring to his "Total Revolution," J. P. saw it as a step toward many revolutions to come. He also quoted Vinoba, who used to compare a vision with climbing a mountain peak. Once you reached one peak, then you saw the higher peak beyond the first one, and so one.[29] Thus, J. P. had a longtime goal. However, for the present he stated, "Total Revolution is a combination of seven revolutions -- 1. Social, 2. Economic, 3. Political, 4. Cultural, 5. Ideological or Intellectual, 6. Educational, 7. Spiritual."[30] Needless to say that this is what Gandhi and Vinoba wanted through their constructive work programs.

Since J. P. belonged to Sarva Seva Sangh, it was only fitting that Sarvodaya would respond to Total Revolution. It should be remembered that Vinoba Bhave had retired in Paunar Ashram in 1969, and was monitoring developments from there. J. P. had thought it necessary to seek his blessings for the Bihar Movement and the "Total Revolution." He was disappointed. Vinoba's hesitation to bless "Total Revolution" stemmed form a variety of reasons. Along with several (but minority) members of the Sarva Seva Sangh, Vinoba took the position that J. P. was "politicizing Sarvodaya," which was against Sarvodaya ideology. Since J. P. was attacking both state and central governments, this was viewed as interfering in political matters. Vinoba was content with Sarvodaya's involvement in Bhoodan-Gramdan activities. During the early stages of Bihar Movement, Vinoba told J. P. that he understood J. P.'s vision of struggle, and even promised to lend a helping hand. However, he asked J. P. to give up the notion of struggle against the government.[31] Vinoba was concerned that during this period the United States was arming Pakistan, which was also receiving support from China. Under these circumstances, J. P.'s fight against his own government will make the nation weak. J. P. regretted that if he did not help save the Indian democracy, there would be no nation left to save from foreign aggression. Vinoba could not be convinced.[32] In Vinoba's view, J. P's struggle against Indira Gandhi's government was a form of "Negative Satyagraha." It could not be compared with the "Positive Satyagraha" of Gandhi against a foreign power.

The relationship between Vinoba and J. P. was further strained during Indira Gandhi's call for National Emergency in 1975. Vinoba did not oppose the emergency but called it a time of <u>Anushasan Parva</u> (era of discipline).[33] Subsequently, Indira Gandhi herself visited Vinoba on September 7, 1975, and later participated in his birth celebrations in New Delhi, emphasizing in her speech the importance of Bhoodan work of Vinoba. She promised to lend her support to Vinoba's work, and asked the nation to follow his teachings. That would make the nation strong.[34] It appeared as if Vinoba was blessing the emergency and not Total Revolution. J. P. and his followers within the Sarva Seva

Sangh (the majority members) were totally disenchanted with Vinoba's actions. Some began referring to Vinoba as Sarkari Sant (government saint). Despite Vinoba's disagreement with J. P., he never lost his love and respect for Vinoba. Reflecting on his relationship with Vinoba, J. P. later stated that there was no serious diversion between him and Vinoba on certain "fundamental questions" regarding Sarvodaya. The difference existed on "the approach." While Vinoba was more concerned with spiritual issues, J. P. was more interested on social values.[35] During the Bihar Movement, J. P. found one area of serious disagreement. The question was whether Sarvodaya workers should take part in nation's political life or not. While Vinoba said "No", J. P.'s answer was an emphatic "Yes."[36]

Jai Prakash Narayan was quite pleased when during the early stages of Sarva Seva Sangh's involvement in the Bihar Movement, Vinoba had presented a solution. Vinoba wanted Sarvodaya workers to work on both fronts of Gram Swaraj and Bihar Movement as long as the principles of truth, non-violence, and disciples were maintained. He equated both with the two rivers Ganges and Brahmaputra (both essential for India).[37] However, it was J. P.'s reading that certain followers of Vinoba, within the movement, wanted to create a rift between the two. Thus, Sarva Seva Sangh got divided into "two wings." A final solution was reached when J. P., who had contemplated resigning from Sarva Seva Sangh, along with some other influential leaders within Sarvodaya, took a leave of absence in order to plunge into the Bihar Movement. Consequently, Sarva Seva Sangh was split into two camps. While the majority of Sarvodaya leaders went with J. P., a group of dissenters remained with Vinoba. They left Sarva Seva Sangh and issued a statement ("Statement of 54 Lok Sevaks") which in part read, "...We took the decision to leave Sarva Seva Sangh only to preserve its basic ideology. Truth, non-violence, restraint, keeping aloof from party and power politics, unanimity and consensus are the basic principles of the Sarvodaya thought."[38]

As the Bihar Movement caught momentum, student led strikes and marches intensified, leading to the infamous police firing on April 12, 1974 in which several students lost their lives. J. P. rendered his full support to the cause of Bihar students and called for the dissolution of the state assembly. By November 18, 1974, an angry Indira Gandhi challenged J. P. to a national general election, a challenge he accepted.[39] Since the movement was spreading to other states and assumed the stature of a national crisis, Indira declared a State of

Emergency in June of 1975, which was to last for roughly nineteen months. During the emergency, many Gandhians were arrested, their institutions investigated, some of their publications banned. Despite the emergency, the political activities of the opposition parties did not cease. They approached J. P. to help them unite against Indira Gandhi. The coalition of several opposition parties gave birth to the Janta Party, which ultimately won the general election in 1977. Indira Gandhi had to resign as Prime Minister and a new chapter in Indian history commenced. There is some controversy over the fact whether or not the leaders of the Janta Party used J. P. and his Total Revolution to their advantage. There is some evidence that he was disillusioned with the Janta Party's agenda to seize power. J. P. wondered if the Janta leaders were really committed to Gram Swaraj which was J. P.'s primary concern. By the time he died in 1979, no significant changes in the socio-economic and political life of India had taken place. In fact the Janta Party became victimized by its own short comings and power struggle. Consequently Indira returned to power in 1980.

That J. P. was genuinely concerned with reforming the Indian society cannot be doubted. That he tried to follow Gandhi in his approach to Satyagraha also cannot be doubted. His disagreement with Vinoba needs to be understood in light of the differences between the two personalities. Temperamentally Vinoba leaned toward things spiritual. This is not only evidenced by his writings, his monastic life-style, his experiments with Kanchan-Mukti (freedom from material things), but also by the manner he voluntarily ended his life.[40] He looked at the Bihar Movement and Total Revolution from an entirely different perspective than J. P. As J. P. himself admitted, Vinoba's and Gandhi's spirituality made them think in terms of "the search for truth" that had universal implications. On the other hand, J. P. thought in terms of social concerns and his interests were more national than international.[41] Also, J. P. was trained as a Marxist-Socialist. Even though he converted to Sarvodaya, he kept his Marxist zeal for change and pragmatism. Furthermore, he was a man of his own vision and character. He rejected all forms of "Gandhism' and "Vinobaism." During his involvement with "Total Revolution" he wrote a letter to Kusum (his sister at Vinoba's Ashram in Paunar) in which he expressed his dissatisfaction over the fact that some followers of Sarvodaya were creating a Vinoba-cult. J. P. did not want to follow a "sectarian mentality" but to go beyond Vinoba, like Vinoba had gone beyond Gandhi. In response to the letter, Kusum told J. P. that Vinoba agreed with J. P.'s ideas and was in total agreement with him.[42] It is clear that J. P. wanted to take the revolution started by Gandhi to a new height, even if it meant disagreement with Vinoba. He repeatedly affirmed that this fight was not with Indira Gandhi. He was not a part of the conspiracy that demanded "Indira Hathao" (Remove Indira). Rather he was against the autocratic policies of Indira which smothered Indian democracy.[43] He was not power hungry to claim a place for himself within the Janta Party. His loyalty to Sarvodaya was unmistakingly his prime concern.

Endnotes: Chapter III

[1] Jai Prakash Narayan, Meri Vichar Yatra, Vol. 1, (Varanasi : Sarva Seva Sangh Prakashan, 1974), p.28.

[2] Ibid., p.57.

[3] Ibid., p.57.

[4] Jai Prakash Narayan, Sampoorn Kranti (Varanasi : Sarva Seva Sangh Prakashan, 1984), p.5.

[5] The Janta Party came into existence in 1977 after Indira's Congress lost the elections. However, Janta Party's rule under Morarji Desai as its Prime Minister was short lived.

[6] There is a view that while under treatment for his kidney ailment, J. P. was poisoned.

[7] Jai Prakash Narayan, Face To Face (Varanasi : Navachetna Prakashan, 1970), p.6.

[8] Ibid., p.8.

[9] Based on a conversation the author had with a lok sevak (servant of the people) when the author revisited Mushahri to converse with the peasants in 1993.

[10] Jai Prakash Narayan, Face to Face, p.11.

[11] Ibid., p.23.

[12] Ibid., p.11.

[13] Pradhan Prasad, "The Economic Perspective" in Sarvodaya and Development (Patna : A. N. S. Institute of Social Studies, 1976), p.83.

[14] Jai Prakash Narayan, Face to Face, p.25.

[15] Ibid., p.26.

[16] Ibid., p.26.

[17] Ibid., p.28.

[18] This information was attained during a conversation with Acharya Rammurti, a close associate of Narayan

[19] Geoffrey Ostergaard, Nonviolent Revolution in India, pp. 57-58.

[20] Narayan, Meri Vichar Yatra vol. II, p.11.

[21] Ibid., pp. 13-15.

[22] Based on a conversation with a Lok Sevak in Bihar. The view may be considered one sided as far as his sentiments towards Indira Gandhi are concerned.

[23] Narayan, Sampoorn Kranti, p.5.

[24] Ibid., p.16.

[25] Ibid., p.7.

[26] Ibid., p.21.

[27] Narayan, Meri Vichar Yatra, vol. I, p. 94.

[28] Narayan, Sampoorn Kranti, p.39.

[29] Ibid., p.39.

[30] Acharya Rammurti, Total Revolution For All (Varanasi : Sarva Seva Sangh Prakashan, 1978), p.VI.

[31] Narayan, Meri Vichar Yatra, vol. II, p. 51.

[32] Ibid., p.51.

[33] Geoffrey Ostergaard, Ibid., p.221.

[34] Ibid., p.221.

[35] Narayan, Meri Vichar Yatra, vol. II, p. 133.

[36] Ibid., p.133.

[37] Ibid., p.131.

[38] Geoffrey Ostergaard, Ibid., p.175.

[39] Ibid., p.175.

[40] Towards the end of his life he refused taking any food or water and died.

[41] Narayan, Meri Vichar Yatra, vol. II, p. 127.

[42] Ibid., p.128.

[43] Ibid., p.131.

IV

Sarvodaya After J. P. and Vinoba

By the time Vinoba Bhave died in 1982, the Sarvodaya Samaj (society), the extended family of Sarvodaya, had gone through a great turmoil. "Total Revolution" was turning into "Total Disaster." The leadership within Sarva Seva Sangh was bitterly divided over the goal of Sarvodaya. The Janta Party had crumbled under its own weight, and its promise to continue to work for Gram Swaraj remained an unfulfilled dream. Due to Sarva Seva Sangh's inability to unite itself over a variety of issues, different factions began to surface. Generally speaking, four distinct groups claimed Sarvodaya affinity. First, there was Vinoba's group. Second, there was J. P.'s group which constituted the majority of Sarva Seva Sangh's leadership. Third, a group that followed Nirmala Deshpande, who had been a supporter of Vinoba Bhave, gradually drifted to the side of Indira Gandhi, when she joined her personal staff.[1] She became a separate leader, first joining with Narendra Dube, and finally branching out on her own.[2] Fourth, several Sarvodaya workers, who did not participate in the J. P. - Vinoba conflict, continued to work for Sarvodaya independently.

Due to the division within the leadership, constructive work programs were given different emphases. Vinoba Bhave's group still considered the work of Bhoodan-Gramdan very important. However, after Bihardan, since Vinoba had stopped his pad yatras, the movement had lost momentum. It was decided that attention would be given to the distribution of land which had already been received, rather than seeking more donations. Although small donations kept coming, Bhoodan-Gramdan was not in the limelight. Since, during the emergency, Vinoba had called for the protection of cows, and had gone as far as to fast until death, "Cow Protection" became the focus of attention as a constructive work program for many followers of Vinoba. Vinoba had established a Go-Seva Sangh, which had taken a 5-point program as its goal. It included: monthly prayer meetings, popularization of cow milk, animal husbandry, the provision for a cow house in every village, and Go-grass, provision by each family to protect cows.[3] How Gram Swaraj is possible through the protection of cows is a leading question. For Vinoba and his followers, it was the question of village economy, self-sufficiency, and preservation of cultural values. The cow was considered central to preserving village economy.[4] Since hundreds and thousands of cows were being slaughtered to export meat abroad, a Satyagraha against such practices was deemed necessary.

Vinoba had given a call to all teachers to collectively join and create a force to fight against social malpractice, corruption, and political oppression. Thus, the foundation of <u>Acharyakul</u> (family of teachers) was organized in 1968. Later it was expanded to include social workers, literary figures, lawyers, doctors, students, and others.[5] During the emergency, Vinoba revived its emphasis, and it acquired an important place on the list of Vinoba-oriented constructive work programs. His supporters accepted it as an important work of Sarvodaya, and made attempts to enlarge its membership. Several conferences were called to outline its goals and means to achieve its objectives. Along with <u>Acharyakul</u>, the work of Shanti Sena (peace brigade) was also re-emphasized. Shanti-Sena was an old concept given by Gandhi. It had been experimented by Vinoba, J. P., and subsequently by many Sarvodaya leaders. For the followers of Vinoba, it remained an important vehicle to maintain peace and order in the villages. Not only that, an international peace brigade had been formed to resolve the Cyprus crisis, and during the Indo-China war, the famous Peking March was organized by Sarvodaya leaders.[6] Consequently, for Vinoba's followers, it remained a major activity in their work toward Gram Swaraj.

Since Vinoba, along Gandhian lines, had worked for women's liberation, much emphasis within Sarvodaya was laid upon the uplift of women. Vinoba had founded Brahma Vidya Mandir for the purpose of training women to become a force within Indian society. It was only fitting that "female power" became an important aspect of his constructive work program. His followers continued to work for the independence of women making it an important part of Sarvodaya activity. Many prominent Sarvodaya women workers were trained by Vinoba. After his death, the work of women's liberation along Gandhian values continued to be of high priority. It should be noted that Nirmala Deshpande, who played a highly significant role during the Bihar movement, was a product of Vinoba's Brahma

Vidya Mandir. She was one among many who became a prominent leader of Sarvodaya. For the sisters of Vinoba's Ashram, the work of hygiene, community development, and female power in the villages remained important. However, they intensified their work on propagating the values of the Bhagavad Gita. In addition to that, publication of the magazine, Maitri (Friendship) in order to preach Sarvodaya ideals, remained in their hands as well.

Since the "J. P. Wing" did not favor dissolution of Sarva Seva Sangh, and the majority of its leaders remained within the Sangh, they also took up their own constructive work programs. During the Janta regime (1977-1979), along with J. P., many leading Sarvodaya leaders had anticipated that India would make considerable progress toward the uplift of villagers and other weaker sections of the society. The most dramatic step taken by the Janta cabinet in this direction was to assemble at Gandhi's samadhi to take a solemn oath to work for the Gandhian ideals of Gram Swaraj. Many Sarvodaya leaders were present at this occasion and were enthusiastic about the prospects of the Janta government turning the nation around from a line of Nehruvian policies of industrial development. When the Janta coalition collapsed and Indira's congress came back into power, the "J. P.'s wing of Sarvodaya" decided to become the conscience of the people. Thus, their main emphasis became to continue to criticize Indira Gandhi's government for its autocratic policies. Indira responded by setting up the famous "Kudal Commission" to investigate several Gandhian institutions like the Gandhi Peace Foundation, Gandhi Smarak Nidhi, and AVARD (Association of Voluntary Agencies for Rural Development). Her main accusation against these organizations was twofold. First, these organizations had become centers of political activities and were no longer following the ideals of Mahatma Gandhi. Second, these organizations were receiving money from foreign donor agencies and as such were being used to finance anti-government campaigns. The Kudal Commission took a long time to give its report, which was forthcoming in bits and pieces. No serious actions were taken against these institutions, and they are still functioning without any serious governmental control.[7] Since returning to power, Indira Gandhi began propagandizing her own "Twenty-point Programs" for national development. Many items of her program such as elimination of poverty, good education, and development of villages were similar to those preached by the Sarvodaya movement. This may have been a technique used to diffuse the popularity of J. P.'s Revolution and to regain support of the people.

The "J. P. wing" Sarvodaya response to Indira Gandhi's "Twenty-point" program was to intensify their efforts to create "people's power." It included organizing Lok Sabhas (people's gatherings), Lok Samitis (people's committees), and putting up Lok Umeedvars (people's candidates). The rationale for creating people's power was that Indian democracy was in deep trouble. People had become hostage to the policies of the elected officials whose loyalty was not to the people but to vested interest groups. Power was centralized in the hands of a few who made decisions for the majority but not by the majority. An example of such a consolidation of power was the existing Congress government of Indira Gandhi.[8] The "people's power" movement was seen as an extension of the ideas of Gandhi, Vinoba, and J. P. The key to the movement was decentralization of power. It was Gandhi's vision to see India as a republic of many villages where a village itself would be seen as a republic.[9] The government of each of these republics was to be determined by "consensus," and not by a majority vote. It was agreed that "there was a general consensus (within Sarva Seva Sangh)...that the hour had arrived to begin the struggle to achieve complete independence for the people living in the villages."[10] A program was launched to create people's committees all over India. According to one report, by February of 1980, there were 5,000 primary people's committees in the country, and by August the number had doubled.[11] By this time, a National People's Committee had been created to oversee the work of people's committees. Likewise, state committees were also created. The activities of Sarva Seva Sangh, which emphasized the creation of "people's committee," eventually led to the formation of "Swaraj Sangam" (national collective).[12] Its goal was to guide and supervise decentralization of power, work for the Harijans and Adivasis (tribals), look after the landless and the poor, and be ready to participate in non-violent Satyagrahas to achieve their goals.

Throughout the 1980s, the Sarva Seva Sangh published many small booklets by such veteran Gandhians as Sidharaj Dhadda, Thakurdas Bang, Acharya Rammurti and others, publicizing the rationale as well as the rights and duties of the "people's committees."[13] One salient issue taken up by these leaders was the issue of 'people's candidates' as an alternative to party candidates. It was decided that for Lok Swaraj, Lok Umeedvars were necessary. These candidates were to be selected by various people's committees. The following are some of the conditions set by leaders of the movement for these candidates. The candidate:

1. Must not be a member of a political party.
2. Must not be a proven case of corruption.

3. Must believe in freedom, freedom of the press, law and order.
4. Must not accept caste, religion, and denominational loyalties, and must not favor untouchability and gender differences.
5. Must accept prohibition.
6. Must not have a collective income of the family members in the excess of 5,000 rupees.
7. Must be responsible to his/her constituency and keep in touch with the people.
8. Must give full account of the income to auditors periodically.

The list is exhaustive and gives a minimum of 14 conditions, which could be multiplied into many.[14] One wonders if it is at all possible to locate such perfect candidates.

It could be surmised that the goal of the Sarvodaya Movement, through this emphasis on people's committees and people's candidates, was to set up a kind of "parallel government." To what extent it succeeded to achieve this goal remains dubious. In fact, the attempt to put up such candidates has been a failure. As desired not many people's committees are functioning. Post J. P. Sarvodaya is sometimes referred to as "Radical Sarvodaya" because it was no longer interested in working with the existing government, but seeking a "non-party alternative."[15] However, it appears that it has not succeeded in convincing the people of India that their welfare resides in such an alternative.

Although, under the impact of Total Revolution, the followers of J. P. emphasized the work of people's committees, they continued to work on other fronts as Khadi, Shanti-Sena, Cottage Industry, uplift of the harijans and adivasis, etc. Since the work of Khadi is heavily subsidized by the government, there is an ongoing discussion whether the movement of Gram Swaraj is possible under the Khadi Commission.[16] Some Sarvodaya workers are experimenting with what has been termed as "Asarkari Khadi" (non-governmental Khadi).[17] The goal of this movement is not to accept any subsidies from the government, but to make spinners self-sufficient through there own efforts. This requires educating the public, who needs to accept this idea by paying higher prices.[18] Those involved in this effort feel that true Gram Swaraj must begin by learning to be self-sufficient within the village. However, Asarkari Khadi is merely in an experimental stage. Though the concept of freeing Khadi from government control is appealing, in reality, it is a difficult proposition economically. Another constructive work program undertaken by the J. P. group is Shanti-Sena. J. P. led youth peace brigade is no longer

73

effective. It, however, helped a lot to maintain peace and order during the Bihar Movement. Presently, Narayan Desai and Acharya Rammurti are committed to this work. Narayan Desai, through his 'Institute of Total Revolution' at Vidchi, Gujarat, continues to train young men and women in the ideology of Shanti-Sena.[19] At the same time Rammurti, through his Khadi Gram, attempts to involve people in Shanti-Sena. Due to the efforts of men like these, Shanti-Sena is very much a platform for the work of Sarva Seva Sangh. Other Sarvodaya leaders accept its importance and, in principle, support its activities. In fact, all Sarvodaya groups consider it a Gandhian activity to promote non-violence.

During Rajiv Gandhi's years (1984-1989), Sarvodaya was faced with another challenge. Rajiv's promise to India was to "carry it into the 21st Century." Once again, the Nehruvian vision of modernization and industrialization was reaffirmed. Since Rajiv had immense popular support of the people, Sarvodaya adopted a "wait and see" approach toward his government. Soon it was clear that, like his grandfather and mother, Rajiv wanted to modernize India at a rapid pace. He opened the door for multi-national companies to invest in India. He insisted on computerizing various government departments, improve the transportation system, and invest in heavy industries. The reaction from the Sarvodaya side was predictable. It did not see any promise in Rajiv's policies for the development of villages. In fact, his goals to take India to the 21st century were viewed as anti-Gandhian, and detrimental to the long term development of India. The usual rhetoric of "building from the bottom up" as the Sarvodaya vision was projected as the only alternative. Sizing up the situation, eleven years after the dawn of J. P's "Total Revolution" (1977-1988), one leading Sarvodaya leader summarized the situation in the following manner: "In the last eleven years, the powers of capital (money) and government have joined forces. That is the foremost dangerous aspect of the present crisis. From the village to the capital of the nation (Delhi), no aspect of life is devoid of the influence of this merger. In reality, the government is sold out to money."[20] This indictment on Rajiv Gandhi's years in power simply reflects the Sarvodaya sentiment that corruption had reached to the highest level. There was no Ram Raj in sight.

In 1989, Rajiv Gandhi's Congress Party was defeated, and V. P. Singh, as the leader of Janta Dal in coalition with other opposition parties, was asked by the president to form a new government. It appeared that the days of persecution for Sarvodaya were over. V. P. Singh seemed sympathetic to the notion of Panchayat Raj in the villages. He also favored the cause of the Harijans, and promised to

74

develop the agriculture sector rather than the industrial. During his short stay in power, a major controversy gripped the Sarvodaya movement. V. P. Singh came in close contact with several Sarvodaya leaders, particularly Acharya Rammurti. It was believed that the Acharya was his guru "so to speak." Many of his colleagues saw this as his entering into politics.[21] In some Sarvodaya circles, Acharya Rammurti was proclaimed "non-Gandhian." The controversy became so overwhelming that Rammurti attempted to explain himself in his talks and writings. In one booklet he compared his situation with that of J. P. As J. P had responded to a national crisis by advising Janta leaders, Rammurti was doing the same. He did not see his actions as entering into politics, but those of a disciple of Gandhi responding to the current political situation. He explained himself by stating that his association with V. P Singh was an experiment which he was conducting as a citizen. He concluded by stating that he was a lok sevak (servant of the people), but a citizen first.[22] V. P. Singh's tenure as the prime minister was short lived. Due to his policy of enforcing a "quota system" in favor of the harijans and the "scheduled castes," many upper caste Hindu's turned against him. The Congress Party returned to power in 1990 with Narasimha Rao as Prime Minister.

While "Radical" Sarvodaya adopted the policy of non-cooperation with the government, leaders like Nirmala Deshpande believed in cooperation with the government, while maintaining Sarvodaya's apolitical stance. As we have already discussed, during the period of Sarvodaya's split, Nirmala had sided with Vinoba Bhave. Later she joined Indira Gandhi's personal staff. Since she had withdrawn from Sarva Seva Sangh, she had no formal connections with it. However, she was the elected president of the Harijan Sevak Sangh (Society for the Service of the Untouchables), an organization started by Gandhi. This was an independent institution which, like the Kasturba Trust, never joined Sarva Seva Sangh. Thus, Nirmala still remained a committed lok sevak under the larger Sarvodaya, but stayed away from the radical Sarvodaya group. Through Harijan Sevak Sangh, she gradually formed her own constructive work organization. According to some observers, through her organization she pushed the same constructive works as emphasized by the Indira Twenty Point Programs.[23] During my first interview with Nirmala in 1984, she expressed sadness over the fact that J. P. had dragged Sarvodaya into politics. She claimed that her relationship with Indira Gandhi was on a "personal friendship" level. She was not interested in Indira's politics. Of course, others have a different view of this issue.[24]

By the time Nirmala founded Akhil Bharat Rachnatmak Karyakarta Samaj (All India Society of Constructive Workers), she had strayed away from Paunar and Vinoba Bhave's direct influence. In her mind she represented true Sarvodaya. Through her constructive work organization, she took up similar works as those taken by Vinoba's followers. It included programs on Acharyakul, female power, cow protection, Shanti-Sena, Bhoodan, and national integration. While Harijan Sevak Sangh, which she headed, received grants from the Home Ministry of the Central Government, Nirmala claimed that she received no money from the Indian Government or foreign donors for her work through All India Society of Constructive Workers. She set up a gigantic network of constructive work organizations solely on people's donations. She accused "Radical" Sarvodaya of accepting money both from the government and foreign donor agencies, and regretted that Lok Shakti cannot be built on foreign funds. Along these lines she was in total agreement with Vinoba. During the Punjab Crisis, which led to the "Operation Blue Star," Nirmala took several pad yatras through Punjab for national integration.[25] Her work was highly praised by the government as an example of non-violent activity of Shanti-Sena. In 1992, she held an all-India conference of his constructive work organization, which was attended by roughly 5,000 delegates. The chief guest at the conference was none other than Prime Minister Narasimha Rao. Nirmala maintains that she is not interested in politics, but cooperates with the government on the uplift of the have-nots.

In the post J. P. and Vinoba years, there has been a crisis of leadership within the movement. There is no single leader who commands enough respect from all others to lead the movement. Consequently, there are many independent constructive workers who seem to be doing "their own thing" in their respective geographical areas. On the issue of leadership a variety of answers has been given. First, if there had not been a split within the movement, perhaps a successor of Vinoba might have merged. Second, since Vinoba believed in creating Lok Shakti (people's power), philosophically there was a deliberate downplay on creating a succession of leaders. Therefore, people should be the leaders exercising their power to bring Swaraj. Third, leaders are generally born out of a crisis situation when they respond to their calling. Perhaps a future leader will arise when the timing is right. Fourth, for some lay members within the movement, the crisis of leadership is attributed to the lack of cooperation among the existing leaders.[26] According to this observation, many leaders have become so independent and often "self-centered" that their egos will not allow the rise of a single leader. As one lok sevak put it, "Gandhi taught his associates to be independent and free in their thinking, but the current leaders are entirely too independent."[27] In the absence of a single leader, Sarvodaya is surviving on the basis of "Samoohik Sadhana" (a collective quest).

In the 1990s, Sarvodaya is not so much attached to Sarva Seva Sangh as it once was during the J. P. and Vinoba years. The annual Sammelan (meeting) attracts fewer and fewer people. Many leaders who used to take an active part in its affairs have stopped coming. Granted that from the very beginning Sarva Seva Sangh was a loose federation of many constructive work organizations, currently its affiliation with many Gandhian activities has become even more relaxed. As one lok sevak put it, "no one takes Sarva Seva Sangh seriously any more."[28] However it does not mean that the Gandhians involved in Sarvodaya work take their involvement lightly. It means that the emphasis seems to have shifted from a central organization to local activities. More and more, Sarvodaya is becoming "issue centered," which are many. The following are on top of the list:

1. The New Economic Policy
2. Arrival of multinationals in India
3. Involvement with World Bank, IMF, and GATT
4. The rise of Hindu fundamentalism
5. National Integration
6. Narmada Dam issue
7. Environmental issues
8. Deforestation and Chipko Movement
9. Harijans
10. Minorities
11. Tribals
12. Landless
13. Prohibition
14. Female Power
15. Khadi and Cottage Industries

Since all of these issues cannot be tackled by a single leader, many leaders have emerged on the basis of the problems they are trying to solve. To some extent, "constructive works" are being viewed as "projects." Consequently, a new debate over the difference between "development" on the one hand, and "service" on the other has emerged. The notion of "development" is generally tied with economic progress, urbanization, industrialization, etc. The question is being raised whether

Gandhians should be involved in the development of the nation along these lines. Most Gandhians directly involved with Sarva Seva Sangh reject this view. They wish to see their work as "service" to the community in freeing the people from a variety of oppressions. The critics claim that by assuming the role of NGOs (Non Governmental Organizations), many Gandhian organizations have unconsciously been involved in development work. Like many non-Gandhian NGOs, they receive money from the government and from many foreign donor agencies. These agencies are not necessarily interested in promoting Gandhian values, neither do they have a vision of Ram Raj along Gandhian lines. They measure their success in terms of "progress" with all of its modern connotations. There is also the issue of how these agencies raise money in their own countries. A charge has been made that some agencies utilize immoral means and fool their people when raising money for developing countries. Should Gandhians be associated with such well wishers? Questions like these are at the center of discussion among various Gandhians.

Since Gandhi used the imagery of Ram Raj to put forward his vision of the future of India, many changes have accrued globally and locally in India. Besides dealing with economic, political, social, and religious realities of our times, the Gandhians have to struggle with the questions like: What would Gandhi have done? What did he mean by such and such? or would he have changed his mind on issues? The attempt to answer these questions has produced diversity among Gandhians. However, along with diversity, there exists a continuity in their mission to understand and practice Sarvodaya.

The men and women discussed in the next section of the book are certainly diverse, but they are united in their mission to serve the poor and the neglected. In spite of the differences that exist in their approach to tackle particular problems, they are committed to Gandhi in the manner they best know "how." Their motivation to change India can be encapsulated by the two often used terms among them; first, Sankat (crisis), and second, Vikalpa (alternative). For them, India is beset by many crises, and Gandhi is the alternative. It is their belief that in light of such developments as the environment problem, corruption, casteism, heavy industrialization, rise in poverty, nuclear proliferation, religious fundamentalism, exploitation of women and the poor, etc., Gandhi has become all the more relevant for Indians than ever before.

Endnotes: Chapter IV

[1] Geoffrey Ostergaard, Non-violent Revolution in India, p.298. In a personal interview with the author, Nirmala Deshpande denied she had ever joined Indira Gandhi's personal staff. She claimed that Ostergaard got his facts mixed up.

[2] Narendra Dube, an articulate spokesperson for Sarvodaya has been a critic of J. P.s Total Revolution. Currently he has been behind the Go-Raksha (Protection of the Cow) Satyagraha led by Achyut Deshpande, a protégé of Vinoba Bhave.

[3] Geoffrey Ostergaard, Nonviolent Revolution in India (New Delhi : Gandhi Peace Foundation, 1985), p.255.

[4] It was Vinoba's belief that in an agricultural society like India, cow products such as; calves, milk, curd, butter, skin, dung, bones etc.) as well as its energy to drive ploughs, carts etc. were intrinsically related to the sustenance of the village economy.

[5] Vinoba Bhave, Acharyon Ka Anushasan (Varanasi : Sarva Seva Sangh Prakashan, 1981), p.3.

[6] The Peking March remained unsuccessful as China refused the entry permits to the participants.

[7] Nirmala Deshpande, a Sarvodaya leader, who grew closer to Indira Gandhi, mentioned to the author that the Kudal Commission was not a serious commission. If Indira really wanted to punish the leaders of the Total Revolution upon her return to power, she could have easily done so. However, revenge was not Indira's motive behind the Kudal Commission. No wonder its investigation dragged on for years.

[8] Acharya Rammurti, Sampoorn Kranti : Tab Aur Ab (Patna : Bihar Sarvodaya Mandal, 1989), p.15.

[9] Rajniti Men Lokniti Ka Pravesh (Author Unknown); Varanasi : Sarva Seva Sangh Prakashan, 1984, p.XIV.

[10] Geoffrey Ostergaard, Ibid., p.341.

[11] Ibid., p.331.

[12] Ibid., p.345.

[13] Most of these are published by the Sarvodaya office at Rajghat, Varanasi, U.P., India

[14] Rajniti Men Loknitit Ka Pravesh, op. cit., p.10.

[15] Geoffrey Ostergaard, op. cit., p.367.

[16] Khadi Commission with its headquarters in Bombay is a government organization to co-ordinate the production of Khadi in India.

[17] A leading Sarvodaya leader in the 'Asarkari Khadi' movement is Devendra Upadhyaya in the state of Assam.

[18] The government supported Khadi promotes a rebate system through which the khadi material is sold on discount to the customers. This is made possible due to the government subsidies given to the Khadi program. The leaders of the Asarkari Khadi question the wisdom of subsidies to promote self-sufficiency for Gram Swaraj.

[19] See the chapter on Narayan Desai.

[20] Acharya Rammurti, op.c.t., p.15.

[21] Acharya Rammurti (see the chapter on him) was reported to have actively campaigned for V. P. Singh's candidacy.

[22] Acharya Rammurti, Vartaman Rashtriya Paristhiti Aur Meri Bhoomika (Patna: Bihar Sarvodaya Mandal, 1992), p.18.

[23] This is the view of Pravina Desai, an articulate lok sevak and a sister at Vinoba's Paunar Ashram. The conversation with Desai took place in an interview in 1985.

[24] Several Sarvodaya leaders, who belong to the J. P. wing disagree with Nirmala Deshpande and hold her partially responsible for the split between J. P. and Vinoba.

[25] By Punjab Crisis I mean the rise of the Khalistan Movement which asked for the creation of a separate nation of the Sikhs. The Operation Blue Star was the code name for the military action

through which Indira Gandhi attempted to suppress the movement by bombing the Sikh's Golden Temple in Amritsar, Punjab in 1984.

[26] This view was given in a survey I conducted with several lok sevaks of the movement in 1993.

[27] The comment made by Mahadev Vidrohi, a young Sarvodaya lok sevak from Gujarat, in an interview in 1993

[28] Personal interview with a lok sevak from Bihar in 1993.

Part Two

The Visionaries

1. Mahatma Gandhi
Photo Courtesy of Gandhi Museum, New Delhi

2. Vinoba Bhave
Photo Courtesy of Gandhi Museum, New Delhi

3. Jai Prakash Narayan
Photo Courtesy of Gandhi Museum, New Delhi

4. Acharya Rammurti

5. Achyut Deshpande

6. Chunibhai Vaidya

7. Devendra Kumar

8. Govind Rao Deshpande 9. Harivallabh Parikh

10. Jagannathan 11. Krishnammal

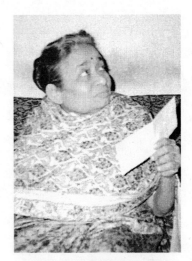

12. Narayan Desai   13. Nirmala Deshpande

14. V. Ramachandran   15. Shobhana Ranade

16. Subba Rao   17. Sunderlal Bahuguna

18. Thakurdas Bang

V

Struggling For National Reconstruction
Acharya Rammurti

The Gandhian ideologues have to struggle constantly to define for the Indian people the kind of government Gandhi had envisioned for India. The task becomes difficult when Gandhian philosophy seems to have been defeated and his ideas are betrayed in the formation of the Indian nation. Since India's independence in 1947, national reconstruction has been based on the theory that India is a 'Nation-State'. However the concept of 'Nation-State' is defined in terms of the central government which controls power. Many Gandhians feel that in this scheme, national policies are designed by the elite for the elite. The elite are the educated rich who live in the handful of India's big cities. Clearly, for Gandhi, 'Nation-State,' defined in terms of a centralized power structure, was not the goal. He had envisioned India as a republic of many 'village-states' with a decentralized power structure. Since India, against the wishes of Gandhi, adopted the blue-print of a 'nation-state,' many Gandhians feel that it has taken on an approach of 'welfareism' towards the poor masses who inhabit India's thousands of villages. In national reconstruction, 'welfareism' is viewed by them as neglect of the poor. It is viewed as a policy of 'handout' for those who are left out of the mainstream of national life. The critics point out that there is a big difference between 'Sarvodaya' on one hand and 'welfareism' on the other. Sarvodaya accepts the poorest person as the basic unit of the Indian Republic. Thus, it preaches a philosophy of 'uplift' not of 'handout' for all. National reconstruction, therefore, must involve the least of humanity, not just the fortunate few.

Among the contemporary Gandhians in India today, those who are well versed in articulating Gandhi's views on national reconstruction, the name of Acharya Rammurti stands out. He is not merely a theoretician of Gandhian thought,

83

but a dedicated <u>Lok Sevak</u> (servant of the people) within the Sarvodaya Movement. As a constructive social worker he has spent his entire life in the Gandhian movement for the uplift of the people. A close associate of Vinoba and J. P., Rammurti is among the few intellectual Gandhians who understand the successes and the failures of the Sarvodaya movement. He does not hesitate to point out the mistakes the movement has made. He carefully scrutinizes the Indian national scene to pronounce a negative judgment on how India has implemented the Gandhian philosophy in its policies of national reconstruction. An author of many monographs and pamphlets on Gandhian thought, he is widely accepted as a 'clear thinker' of the Sarvodaya philosophy. In recent years he became a center of controversy when he supported V. P. Singh as Prime Minister of India. Some of his fellow Gandhians accused him of "entering politics." In response, his thoughts on the issue were published by Bihar Sarvodaya Mandal in a short booklet to vindicate him.[1] Rammurti explained how he was following the Gandhian line of thinking through his actions. During my interview with a Gandhian mystic, <u>Vimla Thakar</u>, I was encouraged to meet Rammurti whom she called, "a real gem."

I first met Acharya Rammurti in 1984 when I was staying at the A. N. Sinha Institute of Social Studies in Patna, Bihar. I arrived at Jamui railway station from Patna by train, only to discover that there was no one there to meet me. My disappointment turned into encouragement when I discovered that every rickshaw puller knew the ashram where Rammurti resided. <u>Shramabharati</u> ashram, popularly known as <u>Khadigram</u> (Khadi Village), is located on the main road in Mellahpur, a few kilometers from Jamui railway station, and can easily be reached by local transportation. The place is filled with history and memories of the past, since the ashram was started at the wishes of Gandhi for the experiment of national reconstruction. His trusted associate, <u>Dheerendra Majumdar</u> had first come to the village to start the work of Khadi and other related Sarvodaya programs. It was he who invited Acharya Rammurti to take charge of the ashram in 1954. Since then Rammurti has made Khadigram his abode from where he carries out his constructive work activities.

Life:

Acharya Rammurti was born in 1913 in Uttar Pradesh (Northern Province) in a well to do family. His father was a police officer in the British Raj. Educated at Ewing Christian College and later at Allahabad University, he received his M. A. degree in History with a gold medal for outstanding scholarship. As a student of history he became aware of the colonial expansion in India, and was attracted to freedom fighters who wanted to break the chain of slavery. During his student career he met Gandhi at two occasions, but these meetings were entirely too brief. He remembers, "I can recall two short meetings with Gandhiji, one in 1936 when he visited Lucknow for an annual conference of the Indian National Congress. I was then a student at Lucknow University. The other was in 1938 at Allahabad. On both occasions my interest lay more in watching Gandhiji at close quarters than having a conversation with him." What he observed about Gandhi made a lasting impression on young Rammurti, and he decided to begin corresponding with him. He recalls, "Gandhiji seemed to me a passionate person who had a vision for the future of India. He appeared determined and dedicated to the cause of India's independence. He was polite and yet firm, straightforward but gentle. He made a favorable impression on me, and I thought I must know him better." Rammurti did not think that Gandhi would pay much attention to his letter. However, when a reply came from him, Rammurti was touched. Thus began the communication between the two that lasted for a long time.

Rammurti began his professional life as a teacher of history at Queen's College in Varanasi, a post he held from 1943 to 1953. It was during this period that he began to reflect seriously on Gandhian non-violent revolution. Like many young people of his time, he was concerned about the freedom of India, but more so about the future reconstruction of Indian democracy. He was particularly impressed by the Russian Revolution and what Marxism had been able to achieve in the Soviet Union. He was attracted to Marxist socialism and wondered if it had any role to play in India's development. He read Karl Marx and was deeply moved by his devotion to create a just society. He understood Marx's critique of capitalism and cherished his vision to end exploitation of the proletariats at the hands of the bourgeoises. He found many parallels between feudalism of Russia and the situation in India. As he heard the so called "success stories" of the Russian Revolution and the reconstruction of the Soviet Union, he realized that Indian leaders like Jai Prakash Narayan were impressed with what Russia had achieved. Although his association with J. P. did not occur until much later, Rammurti was aware of J. P.'s studies of Marxism and his visits to Russia. In spite of his attraction to communism, Rammurti turned to Gandhi. The decisive factor was the issue of the use of violence in creating a just society. The Marxist justification for violence to free the poor was unacceptable to young Rammurti.

During the 1940's, Acharya remained a silent observer of the Gandhian struggle for India's freedom. While Gandhi sent a call to the youth of India to quit their education and join the freedom struggle, Rammurti remained schooled preparing for a career in teaching. Nevertheless, the environment of the city of Allahabad was quietly influencing his mind. Allahabad was home to the Nehrus. Since the Nehru family was close to Gandhi, many political leaders frequently visited Allahabad. Gandhi himself came to town to stay with Motilal Nehru, the father of Jawaharlal Nehru. Thus, the atmosphere in Allahabad was charged with emotions in favor of the freedom struggle. In an unseen manner it affected the mind of young Rammurti. By the time he moved to Varanasi as a teacher, Marx and Gandhi became his mental companions. At Varanasi, he came in contact with Dheerendra Majumdar, an associate of Gandhi. When Gandhi established <u>Charkha Sangh</u> (Spinners Organization), Dheerendra was his right hand man. After Gandhi's assassination, he assumed the leadership of Charkha Sangh, inspiring many youth for national reconstruction. Rammurti responded to his challenge and entered the Gandhian movement.

In 1952, under the auspices of Charkha Sangh, an ashram was started as <u>Shramabharati</u> near Jamui in Bihar. It was meant to be a training center for young men, who were willing to train in Gandhian constructive social work for the uplift of the poor. Rammurti joined the center in 1954 having left his teaching position at Queen's College forever. It was Gandhi's vision that a program of national reconstruction through Khadi could be initiated all over India. Thus, the khadi centers were not merely to promote spinning, but take up a variety of constructive work programs that Gandhi has initiated under Sarvodaya. Rammurti recalls, "when we came to Khadi Gram, where Shramabharati is located, the place was a jungle. It was inhabited by the tribals and a few farmers who cultivated nearby fields. With our bare hands we set out to build the ashram." Gradually the ashram began to attract the youth from all over India, who were trained in Gandhian thought and other skills. As an astute teacher, Rammurti assumed full responsibilities for the training program at the ashram after Dheerendra Majumdar passed away. His trainees began working among the tribals in the surrounding villages, emphasizing hygiene, education, spinning, and promoting various cottage industries. The ashram became a resource center where villagers were taught skills in better farming, spinning, animal husbandry, education and other cottage industries. Rammurti insists, "in line with the Gandhian way of thinking, our goal was not 'development', but 'reconstruction.' We were not interested in developing big industries for large production. Rather we encouraged self-sufficiency and freedom from exploitation at the hands of the landlords." This scheme of 'building from below' was viewed essential for reconstruction of the country.

By the time Acharya Rammurti came to Khadi Gram, the Bhoodan Movement was beginning to gain momentum around the nation. Since Dheerendra Majumdar was taking an active part in the movement, Rammurti also joined the Bhoodan. Shramabharati became an active center for training of the Bhoodan workers. Vinoba Bhave began taking interest in the ashram since many of his workers received their training here. During the Bhoodan years, Rammurti took to padyatras (journey on foot) in Bihar and elsewhere with Vinoba in search of land donations. His goal became to explain the goal of gram swaraj (freedom of the village) as a means of national reconstruction to the villagers. He felt extreme disappointment when in early 1950s, the First Planning Commission of India launched its First Five year Plan. The plan did not emphasize rural sufficiency, rather supported the development of big industries. It was clear that the government of India was making policies contrary to the philosophy of the Bhoodan/Gramdan movement. Rammurti recalls, "Vinoba called the First Five Year Plan, 'a scheme of exploitation'." Rammurti agreed with Vinoba that the rulers of independent India were bent on developing big cities and neglecting the villages. Nonetheless, for eighteen years, Rammurti worked with Vinoba in solving the land problem through the Bhoodan/Gramdan movement. He was instrumental in creating hundreds of gram sabhas (village assemblies) in the villages where gramdan had occurred. The goal of these assemblies was freedom from the big government and taking charge of their own affairs. "We were convinced that we were doing Gandhi's work," says Rammurti, "and we were seeing the good results."

By the time Vinoba returned to Paunar Ashram, Rammurti was drawing closer to J. P. and his vision of national reconstruction. As we have already seen, J. P. was growing impatient with the dictatorial tendencies of Indira Gandhi's regime. In the early 1970's students in Gujarat and later in Bihar were protesting against all forms of corruption, unemployment, bribery, and police brutality. When J. P. assumed the leadership of the Bihar Movement, Rammurti became his right hand man. Both recognized that the Bhoodan had reached a stalemate and a new strategy of national reconstruction was needed. Rammurti recalls, "J. P.'s restlessness which he felt after his Mushahri experiment[2] was beginning to be felt by many Sarvodaya leaders." Thus, Rammurti joined J. P.'s 'Total Revolution.' A confrontation with the central government was inevitable as J. P. analyzed the national scene and found that the source of corruption was the Central Government. An analysis of the nature of corruption has been presented elsewhere.[3] Here it would suffice to say that Rammurti was disillusioned by his years of efforts in the area of Gandhian constructive work when the very existence of the democratic principles were being violated by Indira Gandhi, Prime Minister of India. Therefore, the primary goal of Total Revolution became to first save the Indian democracy and then focus on the Gandhian program of reconstruction of the nation. The rest is history. With the efforts of J. P. as the central figure, the Janta Party won the general elections and for the first time Indira's Congress was defeated. Rammurti was impressed that the new cabinet of the Janta Party gathered at the grave site of Mahatma Gandhi in New Delhi and took a solemn oath to make Gandhi's vision a reality for India. The dream was alive again.

During the years when Janta Party lost power and Indira's Congress returned at the Center, Rammurti stayed at Khadi Gram to continue constructive work. However, he continued to travel all over India to promote Sarvodaya activities. During Indira Gandhi's rule, his main activities centered around two major issues. First, he launched a prolonged struggle against landlords in Bihar, who tried to eject the Musahar families (a tribal landless untouchable caste) from the Bhoodan land which had been allotted to them. Second, he continued to take an active part in J. P.'s Total Revolution. During the emergency when many national Sarvodaya leaders were put into prison, Rammurti went underground preparing Sarvodaya literature and expounding J. P.'s philosophy of national reconstruction. Gradually, he was emerging as a national leader himself.

After Indira Gandhi's assassination in 1984 and Rajiv Gandhi's appointment as the prime minister, Acharya Rammurti continued his Sarvodaya activities, particularly writing for and editing the weekly 'Sarvodaya Jagat' (The World of Sarvodaya). During this period of his life, he came to realize that the Sarvodaya movement was ineffective in meeting the needs of people. He felt that for Total Revolution that J. P. had started, there needed to be a closer relationship between Sarvodaya workers and political activists. They must share the common concerns and work together. However, he maintained that Sarvodaya should concentrate on building people's power and not run after state power. He was motivated by his conviction that "politics without constructive work leads nowhere; similarly constructive work divorced from democratic politics remain ineffective."

In 1983 Acharya Rammurti, with the help of some close associates, started a systematic reorganization of Shanti Sena (peace brigade) in Bihar. A five day conference was hosted by khadi gram. Among those who attended were such prominent Gandhians as Ramnarayan, Narayan Desai, Manmohan Chowdhury, Rammurti, and Vimla Thakar. It was agreed upon that in the villages of Bihar, the problem of violence had reached its apex. This violence was precipitated by a complete breakdown of the machinery of law and order. In some villages on both sides of the Ganges river, the problem was so bad that even the police seemed helpless in maintaining peace. Rammurti felt that the violence which took the lives of many people and generated fear among the villagers was a symptom of the failure of the state government. Since the Bihar movement of 1974 nothing had changed for the common people. In many villages Mafia-like dons controlled the lives of the people. Robberies, murders, burning of homes and destroying crops had become everyday affairs. Reflecting on the situation Rammurti states, "I was concerned that what was happening in the villages of Bihar, was also happening in other states all over India. However, Bihar was an extreme case, and we needed to do something about it. It seems logical that we, as Sarvodaya workers, must give priority to the work of peace brigade." It was estimated that since there were 66,000 villages in Bihar, approximately 100,000 volunteer peace keeping soldiers were needed to work in these villages.[4]

Rammurti intensified the work of training <u>Shanti Sainik</u> (peace soldiers) through his ashram at Khadi Gram. Priority was given to holding camps in various violence-torn districts where the youth responded to his call. It was emphasized that the Shanti Sainiks be local people, who will work through local village assemblies to solve the law and order problem. Rammurti recalls, "This was very difficult work because the communities were divided along class and caste lines. They were not willing to listen to each other let alone accept the decision that the peace soldiers were to give on various conflicts." With intense effort, the Gandhian approach to conflict resolution was taken to several villages where Shanti Sena received a positive response. In many cases, people were more open to the Gandhians than the local police. Rammurti was amazed that several criminal-minded youth surrendered themselves to him rather than to the police. Some accepted imprisonment for the crimes they had committed. As the peace keeping work intensified, it was deemed necessary to work on other fronts as well. People were educated to form village assemblies in order to solve their own problems. They were told that by settling their disputes through these assemblies they will avoid trips to the police stations and the courts. Often these agencies were sources of exploitation as they sought bribes and extortion money from villages. Also, they were instructed to set up lok

89

umeedvars (people's candidates) for elections, and not vote for candidates supported by various political parties active in the villages. In this manner an approach of 'building from below' was used for the purpose of Gram Swaraj.

Rammurti accepted Sarva Seva Sangh's decision to promote three programs which were passed by the executive body of the Sangh in 1985.[5] It was decided that Sarva Seva Sangh will support the formation of voter's councils, village assemblies, and shanti sena on the national level. The lok sevaks (servants of the people), who belonged to the Sarvodaya family, were encouraged to choose an area of their work and plunge into the constructive work. At this time approximately 5,000 lok sevaks were estimated to be active in the movement. Rammurti was one of the keynote speakers at the 1985 Sarvodaya meeting. His remarks were quite telling as to how he felt about the national scene during this period. He challenged the audience to carefully examine what he called 'the line of Nehru, Indira, and Rajiv,' and compare it with 'the line (of thinking) of Gandhi, Vinoba and J. P.' He expressed doubts whether Rajiv's government would be able to deliver to the poor what Gandhians could do through village uplift. He believed that Rajiv was following Nehru's scheme of industrial development which only benefited the elite, and not the villagers.

Acharya Rammurti became the talk of the Sarvodaya world when he supported V. P. Singh as Janta Dal's candidate for Prime Minister in the next general election. When Congress was defeated, V. P. Singh did become Prime Minister in 1989. Rammurti mentioned to this author that he had several meetings with V. P. Singh prior to his election as Prime Minister. He was convinced that V. P. wanted gram swaraj and would promote the uplift of the villagers if given the people's mandate to govern the country. He also agreed to promote the concept of 'Panchayat Raj' (governance of the five elders) for the villages. During his tenure a law was passed to initiate Panchayati Raj. While Rammurti received severe criticism from some of his colleagues for supporting V. P. Singh, he insisted that he was not seeking any political power for himself. The charge that he was entering into politics was unfounded since his actions were no different from J. P.'s who had supported the formation of the Janta Party without seeking political office for himself.

In 1990, during V. P. Singh's tenure as Prime Minister, Rammurti was appointed as chairman of a committee to recrew the progress of the New Education policy introduced by Rajiv Gandhi in 1986. Under the leadership of Rammurti, his committee deliberated for six months and prepared a report entitled, 'For an

Enlightened and Humane Society.' This report was submitted to the government in 1992. Commenting on this report, Rammurti states, "For the first time in educational history an attempt was made to integrate productive work (on the lines of Gandhian Basic Education) and liberal courses in one stream and produce a scheme for total education from the primary stage to the university." He feels discouraged that this report has been shelved as the government changed hands.

In 1992 when Bhartiya Janta Party supported the cause of Hindutva which resulted in the destruction of the Babri mosque in Ayodhya at the hands of Hindu extremists, Rammurti took to a pad yatra to promote communal harmony between the Hindus and the Muslims. He traveled throughout the state of Bihar in the riot-torn areas with his Shanti Sainiks to promote peace and harmony. At the same time he initiated a dialogue between the Marxists and the Gandhians to come to an understanding on their platforms - to serve the poor - a goal common to both groups. To this end he organized several meetings with the leaders of both groups and also wrote position papers on the possibility of a dialogue between the two movements.[6]

Currently, Acharya Rammurti, along with his close associates, is whole-heartedly involved in what he calls 'The Democracy Movement.' In his view, during Narasimha Rao's prime-ministership in 1995, a very important amendment was made to the Indian constitution. This amendment added a third tier to the existing two tier (federal and state) administrative structure. The third tier is that of the Panchayati Raj, which itself has three tiers of functioning on the levels of village, block, and district. The constitutional amendment stipulates that the Panchayati Raj should function as a unit of self-rule without state and federal interference. Rammurti believes, "This important step strengthens democracy as well as it takes it beyond party lines. My own feeling is that here is an opportunity, provided by the Constitution itself, for building from below. It has the great potential of building up an organized and self-managed civil society. It leaves a very limited space for centralized administration in the state and national capitals." Thus, for the past three years (1995-1998) he has been devoting his time to work out the many dimensions of this constitutionally guaranteed grass-roots democracy. He feels that democracy was Gandhi's first concern after independence. It is also the most valuable legacy that J. P. also left behind.

Thought:

Acharya Rammurti is one of the most astute thinkers in the Sarvodaya movement. His thought is marked with a clear understanding of Gandhi, criticism of the Indian political system, analysis of the Sarvodaya constructive work programs, and a vision for the future. He is the author of numerous articles and monographs that are sold and circulated throughout India as part of Sarvodaya literature. An ardent supporter of J. P., he has been actively involved in an attempt to take the goals of J. P.'s 'Total Revolution' to their fruition.

One of the outstanding features of Acharya Rammurti's thought is his ability to critically evaluate the impact of the Gandhian thought and action on the Indian culture. In the process he is not afraid to pronounce judgment on the Indian political leadership as well as the leadership of the Sarvodaya movement on the issue of how they have propagated and utilized the wisdom of Gandhi in transforming India into a Ram Raj. As a committed Gandhian he identifies numerous failures since the formation of post-independent India that have defeated the cause of Gandhi in India. He calls them different 'betrayals.' His own efforts through his thought and action have been to face challenges posed by these betrayals and to bring Gandhian thought back into the mainstream of Indian life.

For Rammurti, the first 'betrayal' is the betrayal of Jawaharlal Nehru, India's first Prime Minister. He is critical of the fact that Nehru, contrary to the wishes of Gandhi, took to a policy of national reconstruction which was based on the western model of development. For Rammurti, Nehru was attracted to the West because he was educated in the West. Furthermore, soon after the independence in 1947, America had poured a considerable amount of economic aid into India both in money and kind (primarily wheat). Perhaps Nehru felt obligated to the West in showing that India can achieve economic self-sufficiency by following a capitalist model of industrial development and market economy. At the same time Nehru was attracted to the socialist system of the Soviet Union. He attempted to combine both, but failed in succeeding well in either of them. Consequently it produced a "non-committed policy of national reconstruction which proved to be disastrous for India."[7] For Rammurti, the basic problem for India was land reform, not industrial development. Nehru committed his government's resources more toward industrial development and less toward solving the land problem. Since the agricultural sector did not receive the primary attention, the villages suffered the most. Rammurti believes that Nehru had all the good intentions of India's development, but his priorities were misplaced due to his faith in the Western approach to development. For Rammurti, this was "a tragedy of good intentions self-defeated."

The second betrayal occurred during the Bhoodan-Gramdan movement and the blame goes to none other than Vinoba Bhave. Rammurti had been a great supporter of Vinoba during the Bhoodan movement. He recalls, "I gave eighteen years of my life to Vinoba's movement, the years that would be considered the 'prime years' of one's life." He was in the movement because "Vinoba had it right" believes Rammurti; "He dared to tackle the land problem for Gram Swaraj." Since 1951 till 1969, the movement had been a great success. Rammurti himself had been responsible for receiving, processing, and distributing thousands of acres of land. He roamed the countryside to preach Sarvodaya philosophy and establishing village assemblies for gram-swaraj. He recalls, "There was a great enthusiasm among the field workers that the uplift of the villagers was taking place. The landlord class was being completely demoralized and they themselves used to approach us to donate land." This process continued until Bihar-dan was proclaimed in 1969 with a great fanfare. However, the glory was short lived. In the midst of a great success, Vinoba withdrew from Bihar and retired at Paunar. To this day, Rammurti believes that this was Vinoba's mistake. He states, "It was as if the commander-in-chief had deserted his soldiers when the fight was about to be won." He accepts the explanation that Vinoba was now engaged in a spiritual experiment and needed to withdraw from the movement, however he holds that Vinoba's timing was wrong. Many Sarvodaya leaders, along with Rammurti, perceived Vinoba's actions as 'the betrayal' of the Bhoodan-Gramdan movement. For Rammurti, this was again, "a tragedy of good intention self-defeated." Since 1969, the Bhoodan rapidly declined never to regain its lost glory.

The third betrayal is that of the Bihar government during the hey-day of the Bhoodan movement. The abolition of the <u>Zamindari</u> system[8] coincided with the rise of the Bhoodan movement. In both cases, the government passed laws to limit ownership of the land in large amounts. At Vinoba's efforts, a Bhoodan-Act was instituted according to which land was being transferred to local gram sabhas. Thus in those villages which had been declared as <u>Gramdan villages</u>, the landlords could no longer own land. The ownership went to the village assemblies who were to supervise the distribution for cultivation. However, many of the laws passed were never implemented. Rammurti puts the partial blame on Vinoba's withdrawal to Paunar ashram. His retreat was viewed as lack of interest on the part of the Sarvodaya leadership in the process of the Bhoodan-Gramdan movement. More

93

than that, Rammurti blames the government of Bihar for betraying the people. In his thinking, "if such radical laws were passed by the state, the government should have implemented them." The other problem was that, with the creation of the 'Bhoodan Boards', the matter of receiving land and distributing land went into the hands of the government. Now, often the Sarvodaya workers had to deal with government workers to get anything done. "The government beaurocracy is so corrupt," holds Rammurti, "that the laws are passed, but nothing is done about them." Once again, he calls it, "the tragedy of good intention self-defeated."

The fourth betrayal came with the Janta Party, which took office in 1977. After the Bihar movement of 1974, there were high hopes among Sarvodaya leaders that the new government will take up the work of gram-swaraj as its major political platform. As we have seen, its first cabinet took the oath at the gravesite of Mahatma Gandhi in New Delhi to hold true to the vision of Gandhi for India. J. P. who was the architect behind the leadership of the Janta Party asked his Sarvodaya associates to co-operate with the new government. Rammurti gave his full support to the newly formed government. He recalls, "there was a renewed enthusiasm among us, and we hoped that new changes will occur." However, the success turned into a failure. Soon the coalition which formed the party got involved in an internal power struggle. The factionalism caused the demise of the party and once again the hope to make Gandhi relevant through government supported programs was lost. What could Rammurti call it except, "the tragedy of good intention self-defeated?"

In his thinking, Rammurti has been greatly influenced by Jai Prakash Narayan. In many of his essays and speeches he draws upon J. P.'s thinking to clarify Sarvodaya ideology and the future plan of action. He refutes the argument that by challenging Indira Gandhi's government, J. P. was entering into politics. Like Gandhi, J. P. was saving Lok Tantra (people's democracy). He perceived of himself as a lok sevak (servant of the people) whose task was to build people's power rather than to seek power. For Rammurti, the pivotal point in J. P.'s life was his Mushahri Experiment of 1970.[9] He believes that what J. P. learned as a Sarvodaya worker in Mushahri was of great use for the movement. He identifies three major 'lessons' that came out of that experiment. First, corruption in Indian society had reached to such a high scale that no local solution to the national problem seemed possible. J. P. reached this conclusion after he tried to solve the problems of the villagers in Mushahri through a constructive work program. Ultimately, he decided to tackle the central government itself. Second, he realized that for the Sarvodaya movement to succeed in the uplift of the masses a sympathetic government was necessary. Third, creation of people's power was necessary for self-governance. Based on these insights, J. P. took the leadership of the Bihar movement in 1974 which popularized the slogan of 'Total Revolution'. For Rammurti, the lessons learned from Mushahri have far reaching consequences for national reconstruction.

Now that J. P. is no more and the Janta Party experiment ended in a disaster, Rammurti has launched his own plan for national reconstruction. He has become a promoter of what J. P. termed as 'Radical Sarvodaya' incorporating the lessons learned from the Mushahri experiment. Radical Sarvodaya envisages to work on two fronts. On the local level it works to create lok shakti through the organization of village assemblies. On the national level it seeks to promote the establishment of a sympathetic government. It was in this line of thinking that Rammurti gave his energies to the creation of village assemblies in many villages of Bihar. His work of Shanti Sena on the local level was also motivated by this ideology. On the national level, his support of V. P. Singh in 1989 as Prime Minister of India was also an act under the vision of 'Radical Sarvodaya'. His recent attempts to bring the Marxists and the Gandhians together can also be seen as an effort along the same line of thinking.

Acharya Rammurti readily admits that no significant results can be seen either on the local level or the national level that can be attributed to the success of Sarvodaya today. On the local level, the masses seem to identify the constructive work programs as the plan of the government. The tendency, therefore, is to expect that the government should do everything for the people. Consequently, any effort to ask people to take control of their own destinies often falls on muted ears. In the expectation that the government should take care of the people, the people shy away from volunteerism. Rammurti marvels at Gandhi's ability to mobilize people, but adds, "If Gandhi had full support of the people, the gram-swaraj would have occurred in his own life time. Of course, it did not." Thus, he reaches the conclusion that generating lok shakti is not an easy affair. On the national level, V. P. Singh's own frustration on the impossibility of moving the political system in favor of certain Sarvodaya goals is a testimony that the political machinery even renders a prime minister helpless.[10]

Why is Sarvodaya not able to make progress? Rammurti concludes that no progress is possible until the entire political structure of India is changed. He deeply regrets, "Although the British left India, the British political and economic structure

95

did not leave with them." National reconstruction of Independent India began with the British system well in place. Gandhi, Vinoba, and J. P. were quite aware of the problem and proposed 'the building from below'. Rammurti remembers what J. P. used to tell his students during the Bihar movement of 1974. He would say to them that they were seeking reforms in education, politics, economics, etc., but they should not be disillusioned if these reforms do not change much. J. P. insisted that the problem was with the entire structure of the Indian institutions (based on the western model) which needed to be redesigned to fit the Indian way of life. Rammurti adds his own wisdom to this line of thinking by stating, "We keep saying to our students, 'be punctual', but 'punctuality' will not change the education system which is at fault."[11] J. P.'s 'Total Revolution' was a revolution to shake the foundations of the structure of Indian institutions. Rammurti wants to rekindle the spirit of that revolution.

For Acharya Rammurti, "Sarvodaya today is going through a period of survival." He is convinced that the Gandhian approach of national reconstruction is the right alternative for India. He believes, "the capitalist and the communist systems are based on violence of all shapes and forms. The Gandhian system promotes the non-violent foundation at the very base of the society." In national reconstruction, non-violence must be the prime consideration to create a peaceful society. For Rammurti, gram-swaraj is the right step in this direction. And it will come when the Panchayatiraj is fully implemented all over India. Such a raj will move India from a 'nation state' to a 'civil society.' Despite all odds, he remains committed to it.

Endnotes: Chapter V

[1] The book, <u>Vartman Rashtriya Parasthiti Aur Meri Bhoomika</u> (The Current National Situation and my Approach) was published in 1992 by Bihar Sarvodaya Mandal in Patna.

[2] Mushahri experiment conducted by J. P. in the village of Mushahri which he describes in his book <u>Face to Face</u>.

[3] See the chapter on J. P.

[4] In 1985 when I interviewed Rammurti at Khadi gram, I was told that about 5,000 peace soldiers were working in about 12 districts. More work needed to be done. The goal of 100,000 was never reached.

[5] This author attended the 1985 Sarvodaya annual conference in Jai Prakash Nagar where the three resolutions were passed.

[6] See his <u>Marx and Gandhi</u> (1992).

[7] Rammurti in a private conversation with the author in 1985.

[8] Zamindari system was introduced by the British through which the landlords were allowed to hold a great portion of land as long as they paid revenue to the government.

[9] See footnote number 2.

[10] Evidently V. P. Singh described this situation to Rammurti, who shared the conversation with the author.

[11] Rammurti has been an exponent of 'Nai Talim' which has not been able to make any headway in the Indian education system.

VI

Protecting The Cow
Achyut Deshpande

A few miles outside of the metropolis of Bombay is the city of Deonar. It is a bustling suburb and thousands of commuters pass through its railway station to and from Bombay. Not too far from the railway station, hidden behind the high walls and barbed wired fences, is Asia's largest slaughter house.[1] Spread over a large area, and equipped with modern technology to slaughter animals, it has the capacity to kill 11,000 animals per day.[2] Started under the third five year plan by the government of India, the facility was completed under the fourth five year plan. It employs approximately 3,000 workers, whose job is to manage the enterprise of buying and selling the animals, shipment of the meat abroad, and supervising other related industries. On a given day, truck loads of cows, bulls, buffaloes, goats, pigs, etc. can be seen lined up at various gates of the slaughter house. At another end refrigerated trucks load the meat to be delivered to the Bombay shipyard, from where it finds its way to foreign countries. Amidst the hustle and bustle of traders haggling over the prices of meat, skin and bones, one can hear the faint cry of the animals being led to their final destination. Outside the main gate there is a small shelter with a few small benches. This is the outpost of a few Gandhians, who have been leading a Satyagraha against this particular slaughterhouse since 1982. They stop the entering and departing trucks, get arrested by the police, are released after a few hours, while a new batch of volunteers take their place.

The man in charge of the Deonar Satyagraha is none other than Achyut Deshpande, a close associate of Vinoba Bhave, who was instructed to undertake the monumental task after Vinoba's own efforts had failed to stop the cow slaughter in India. I had heard about the Deonar Satyagraha and the dedicated work of Achyut Deshpande, who is affectionately called Kaka (uncle), and longed to witness his activities. My memories of him were limited to the one visit I had with him at the Paunar Ashram in 1980. At that time I was more interested in learning about Vinoba Bhave, and Kaka had given me some insight into Vinoba's thinking. He was reluctant to talk about himself, but it was well known that he had been a close associate of Vinoba during the Bhoodan years. More importantly he was an Urdu and Arabic scholar who had advised Vinoba on his work on the Essence Of The Quran. When I had climbed to his room at the tallest portion of a building at Paunar Ashram, he had been reading the Quran. During my subsequent visits Kaka had already moved to Ghatkopar (near Bombay) to lead the Deonar Satyagraha. I finally caught up with him in the winter of 1995, when he invited me to observe the Satyagraha. At the age of 83, Kaka seemed alert and full of energy. Fifteen years had passed since our first meeting, but I found him to be the same in his demeanor; kind, gentle and friendly. Presently, he and his associates (some with their families) occupy a building at the Nature Cure Hospital in the town of Ghatkopar, a suburb of Bombay. This is headquarters from where the movement to protect the cow is supervised. It is from here that I accompanied Satyagrahis to witness their protest at the slaughter house in Deonar.

Life:

Achyut Deshpande was born in 1912 in the village of Rajini in the state of Maharashtra. Coming from a family of landholders, he had a close affinity with land, farming, and being with nature. Having completed his early education in Aurangabad and Hyderabad, Achyut found himself being pulled towards the Gandhian movement at an early age. By the time Gandhi launched his famous Salt Satyagraha in 1930, Kaka was being hailed as a khadi wala (man of homespun) by his peers. He left his college to fully dedicate his life for the independence of India from the British. Even though he were not to meet Gandhi until much later, Gandhian ideals of wearing khadi, spinning, Swadeshi, etc. began to catch his imagination. What attracted him most was the concept of Satyagraha as a non-violent movement against the British. In 1929 he moved to Bombay in search of a Satyagraha in which he could participate and eventually be jailed. Having not found "the action," he plunged himself into the work of khadi with his friends.

The search for Satyagraha took him to such towns as Ratnagiri and Kohlapur, but to no avail. By the time he reached Kohlapur, he learned that the Satyagraha there had been stopped. Disappointed, he continued to preach Satyagraha ideology, settle village disputes and teach spinning in the surrounding villages. Now that the salt march had taken place, Achyut thought of ways to make salt. His thought was that he would be arrested and sent to prison. Somehow this was a romantic ideal for him as he heard stories of many Gandhians who were being arrested all over the country. He felt that imprisonment was the true mark of a Satyagrahi. So he publicly started distilling sea water to make salt with his young friends. "As my luck would have it", he recalls, "soon the Irwin-Gandhi pact was reached (on the salt issue) and making salt was no longer viewed as breaking the law. So I was again not arrested and I was very unhappy." Some Gandhian friends decided to go to the town of Deogarh, where the issue of 'anti-alcoholism' was being taken up. Achyut followed them and for two months began picketing British owned liquor shops, explaining the need for prohibition to the people, and organizing the villagers for the movement. In 1931, a veteran Gandhian, Appa Sahib Patwardhan, held a camp to protest against the British-made clothes. Achyut, with some of his friends, started living with Appa Sahib. They picketed the stores that sold the British-made clothes, confiscated many clothes, and burned them. Many stores were closed as the agitation spread. Finally Achyut was arrested and sentenced to prison. His dream finally came true and he felt like a confirmed Gandhian.

After his first experience of being imprisoned for the cause of Gandhi, Kaka became even more enthusiastic about Gandhi's call to build the nation. "Gandhiji was advising not to do Satyagraha against the states controlled by Maharajas and the Nizam. Since I was from Hyderabad (under a Muslim Nizam), I decided to move away to other towns to do Satyagraha and engage in the constructive work," remembers Kaka. He found himself in the vicinity of Nasik with several Gandhian friends. Together they took up the task of Gram Seva (service to the village). Achyut understood Gandhi's call to 'build the nation' as an invitation to go to the villages and improve condition of the masses. So he took up the constructive work of scavenging, hygiene, spinning, and anti-liquor activities. Kaka moved from village to village teaching Gandhian thought to people and working with them to change their suffering lot. It was during this period that Achyut participated in several Satyagrahas and suffered imprisonment. On one such imprisonment he landed in Dhulia jail. It was here that he came in contact with a fellow prisoner, who was to transform his life forever. It was Vinoba Bhave. He recalls, "Vinoba used to visit our prison cells and encourage us to remain strong and steadfast. We attended many of his talks on the Gita. He used to give lectures on the Gita for two hours every day. They was so very much inspiring." Many of these talks were later published as <u>Gita Pravachana</u>.

After his release from the Dhulia Jail, Kaka followed Vinoba to his ashram in Wardha. His goal was to learn spinning from Vinoba and become an expert. Vinoba taught him with much affection and interest. For the next several years, Kaka made khadi and scavenging central to his life's work. He recalls, "We started picking up the night soil and filth of the people. On one occasion I cleaned the outdoor bathrooms of 800 people. The people were defecating in front of their houses, and my job was to clean it." The readers will recall that 'hygiene' was one of Gandhi's constructive work programs, and Vinoba also had taken up scavenging as a part of his social work activity. Kaka took up the task of educating people in the hygienic methods of disposing their feces. He taught them how to construct native bathrooms, proper use of water to wash themselves, and to keep their yards clean. The education was taken into the schools and the children were rewarded upon cultivating good hygiene habits. Kaka was not afraid of hard labor. "I had worked in a Chakki (grinding machine used manually to turn wheat into flour) in the prison," he recalls, " Scavenging was nothing compared to that hard labor done as a punishment." For three and a half years Kaka served the villages near Wardha through the Gandhian constructive work. For him this was the real task of nation building.

Finally the time came when Achyut met Gandhi in 1938 and grew closer to him as he participated in his programs. The initial occasion came when Gandhi sent a call to do Satyagraha in Hyderabad which he had opposed earlier as it was a separate state under Nizam's control. Kaka responded to the call as an 'individual Satyagrahi', which was a designation ascribed by Gandhi himself. Kaka's main task was to explain the philosophy of Satyagraha to people. Here he had to deal with the Muslim population which was suspicious of Hyderabad's annexation to India after independence. Furthermore, the work of Hindu Maha Sabha, which was perceived by the Muslims as a fundamentalist Hindu organization, was not appreciated by the Muslim community in Hyderabad. As tensions grew between the Hindus, Muslims, and the Gandhians, Gandhi called off the Satyagraha, only for it to be relaunched a few years later. Kaka recalls that during this period he came closer to Gandhi. At the request of Jamnalal Bajaj, he got involved in formulating <u>Gandhi Seva Sangh</u>, which became the main body to oversee Gandhian constructive work programs.

Achyut Deshpande was with Gandhi in 1940 in Bengal, when a meeting was called to reflect upon the state of the nation.[3] He remembers how Gandhi was attacked verbally by the followers of Subhash Chandra Bose, the architect of the Forward Block that stood in opposition to the Indian National Congress. During this period, Kaka came in contact with such prominent national leaders as Nehru, Sardar Patel, Rajendra Prasad, Rajgopalachari and others. Gandhi's attitude toward the followers of Netaji Bose was conciliatory. He decided to disband Gandhi Seva Sangh, only for it to be revived by Vinoba Bhave as Sarva Seva Sangh after Gandhi's death. Kaka watched the developments of 1942 as Gandhi launched the Quit-India movement. His main work initially remained in Hyderabad where Gandhi had re-opened the work of Satyagraha. Gandhi wanted only those volunteers for Hyderabad who could spin. This was his way to make a statement that a Satyagraha was intrinsically linked with the constructive work program. Since Kaka was well known for his spinning capabilities, he was among the five selected for this Satyagraha. He remembers how his task remained to assure the Muslim community that the Gandhians were there to protect the Muslims and to pray for them. These were Gandhi's instructions to his Satyagrahis in Hyderabad. Gandhi was totally against dividing people along religious lines. He insisted that his was a nationalist movement which needed the support of the Hindus and the Muslims alike. When Gandhi was arrested in Bombay, Achyut was also arrested. By now he had spent approximately nine years in British jails.

Achyut Deshpande was overjoyed by the independence of India in 1947, but his heart was troubled by the situation in the state of Hyderabad. The Nizam of Hyderabad declared his own independence and refused annexation with India. Immediately, Kaka joined the Satyagraha against the Nizam and demanded that Hyderabad must become a part of India. As a reaction, the Nizam began persecution of the Hindu population, and Kaka found himself in a struggle to liberate his motherland. How the Nizam was persuaded to join the Indian Republic has a long history. It satisfied Kaka immensely that Hyderabad eventually became an integral part of India. However, the violence that followed kept Achyut in Hyderabad as he traveled from village to village to maintain peace. The assassination of Gandhi in 1948 greatly saddened Kaka, but he found solace in the company of Vinoba Bhave. Under his inspiration and with a conviction of his own, he worked among the Muslim communities to assure them that they would be safe as Hyderabad became part of India. He recalls, "I pulled many Hindus out of the trucks who were organizing to hurt the Muslims." Due to his efforts he was asked to supervise the Muslim communities. With the help of many fellow Satyagrahis, Kaka convinced many Hindus not to persecute Muslims, and in many cases, persuaded Hindus to return illegally occupied land to the Muslims.

During the Telangana Crisis,[4] Achyut witnessed the birth of Bhoodan as Vinoba tried to settle violent disputes between the peasants and the landlords, which had taken many lives. For Kaka, this was one major crisis for India where Gandhian principles were to be tested. How Vinoba came to Telangana and the story of how Bhoodan was born need not be repeated here. Kaka narrates that even though Ram Chandra Reddy gave 100 acres of land to Vinoba, which launched the Bhoodan movement, there were other donations of land which had already taken place before Vinoba arrived there. The genius of Vinoba was that he seized the occasion and created a movement. Another insight that Kaka offers about Reddy's donation is that upon speaking with him, Kaka discovered that Ram Chandra Reddy's father, who was a communist, had already put 100 acres of land aside to be distributed among the poor. He had entrusted it to his son Ram Chandra and then passed away. According to Kaka, Ram Chandra was in search of an opportune time when he might distribute the land. When he met Vinoba, he thought that a saint like him might have a better scheme of distributing the land to the poor. Hence, when Vinoba asked for 80 acres, Ram Chandra offered the 100 he had been saving. Kaka's suggestion to Vinoba was that through Bhoodan a steady stream of Jan Shakti (people's power) can be created. Thus, during the Bhoodan/Gramdan phase of the movement, Achyut worked among the villagers, creating gram sabhas (people's committees), and mobilizing them for nation building. An interesting phase of his life began when Kaka left Vinoba for three years and became a farmer. During this period he single-handedly ploughed and tilled the land, sowed the seeds and harvested the crops. Kaka explains this action as "my need for identifying with the labor class and to get my hands and feet in the soil."

While working for Bhoodan near the town of Aurangabad, Achyut came in closer contact with another associate of Vinoba, Nirmala Deshpande. She had been working with Bhoodan and walking with Vinoba for quite some time. She was studying the Quran since her plans were to go to Kashmir and work for Bhoodan among the Muslims. She inspired Kaka to study the Quran as well. Little did he know then that the study of the Quran and learning Arabic would bring him the notoriety of a scholar. He learned Arabic and soon found himself engaged in translating and proof-reading Vinoba's work on the Essence Of The Quran. He moved to Paunbar and commenced his work with Vinoba. Throughout the 1960's Kaka's main preoccupation became the study of the Quran and Arabic. He became the unchallenged advisor to Vinoba on matters related to Arabic, the Quran, and the

104

Muslims. In this capacity he prepared several manuscripts for Vinoba, some of which were published.

During the period when Vinoba returned to Paunar, Kaka also found a home in Paunar Ashram. He became privy to numerous discussions among Sarvodaya workers and Vinoba Bhave. In the crucial years when a rift became inevitable between the followers of J. P. and Vinoba, Achyut remained a silent observer. He lamented that Sarvodaya movement was splitting and factionalism was taking hold of the workers. He supported Vinoba's belief that the members of the Sarva Seva Sangh should not get involved in politics. Thus, his ideas came in conflict with the actions of J. P. Kaka held a deep regard for J. P., but regrets that he could not follow his vision of 'Total Revolution'. His understanding of the relationship between Vinoba and J. P. is that both respected each other's viewpoint, and never felt alienated from each other. However, it were the followers of both who made a larger issue out of the differences that existed between the two. For Kaka, one thing was certain. He believes, "Vinoba was a spiritual being. He was more interested in the issues of Moksha and <u>Sadhana</u> (spiritual quest) than in politics." During the Emergency (1975), Kaka remained with Vinoba at Paunar ashram. He witnessed the sadness of Vinoba over the turn of events as they unfolded. However, he also witnessed Vinoba's strength as he deepened his spiritual quest. Kaka remarks, "Vinoba was truly a saint."

1976 was a momentous year that was to change the direction of Achyut Deshpande's life. Although Vinoba had been working a long time for the cow protection movement, in 1976 he declared that if all the states of India do not pass the law to protect the cow, he would 'fast unto death.' Indira Gandhi, then the prime minister of India, responded by assuring Vinoba that by Dec. 31, 1976 all the states (except Bengal and Kerala), with the help of the supreme court, would pass laws to disban the slaughter of cows. She requested him not to undertake the fast. Vinoba agreed but no changes occurred. Disheartened Vinoba again declared that he would commence his fast on April 22, 1979. Now the current prime minister, Morarji Desai intervened and promised that the cow slaughter will be stopped all over India. After five days of 'fast unto death,' Vinoba agreed to stop the fast. However, Morarji's government did not last long and 1980 saw the return of Indira Gandhi into power. Once again Sarvodaya workers approached Indira Gandhi and reminded her of her previous promises. The prime minister once again repeated the promises, but no changes were seen forthcoming. During this period other Gandhians also fasted for the cause, but were not heard. In 1982, Vinoba asked his followers to launch a major Satyagraha. His instructions were to stop the slaughter of all cows and bulls, no matter of what age. Thus, the Deonar Satyagraha was launched, and Achyut Kaka was given the responsibility of organizing the work. Since 1982, he has made Ghatkopar, near Bombay, his Go Raksha (save the cow) office. Every day volunteers are dispatched to the slaughter house to stop the trucks full of animals from entering the premises. The Satyagrahis are arrested and released after a few hours. When I asked Kaka if he had achieved any results through the years of struggle, he replied, "Our task is to raise consciousness of the people about this terrible act. Our success will be measured by the future generation when they study and analyze what we stood for."

Thought:

During my conversation with Achyut Kaka, he posed a question; When Vinoba explained Gandhi's concept of Ram Raj as Gram Swaraj, what did he mean? He answered his own question by elucidating that the freedom of the village meant that the people like us, who claim to be the Lok Sevaks (servants of the people), must serve the people. "For me it has meant moving from village to village to find out how I could serve them the best," he added. When I look at Kaka's life, 'serving the people' seems to be the motivating factor behind his thought and action. In this process, he was greatly influenced by the thought of Vinoba Bhave. Achyut Kaka is among those Sarvodaya workers who stayed away from J. P.'s 'Total Revolution,' and followed Vinoba's long term vision to bring Gram Swaraj. When I was speaking with Narendra Dube, a nationally known Sarvodaya worker and a supporter of Vinoba, he insisted that after Vinoba, Achyut Deshpande should be recognized as the protégé of Vinoba. Dube (who supports Go Raksha movement) also expressed sadness over the fact that Achyut Kaka had not been appointed as the president of the Sarva Seva Sangh, and recognized as a leading Sarvodaya personality today. For Dube, Kaka is that person who can bring the J. P. and the Vinoba factions together and reunite the Sarvodaya family.[5]

In Kaka's thinking, Satyagraha plays an important role in serving people. He feels that the poor and the underprivileged population of India have always been exploited at the hands of the rich and the powerful. First, they were victimized by the colonial power, and now by those who control the power. Therefore, Satyagraha must be launched wherever the subjugation of the have-nots exists. Achyut is disheartened by the misuse of Satyagraha by many organizations today. He regrets that many people justify break-ins, riots, looting and lawlessness in the

106

name of Satyagraha. For Kaka, Satyagraha requires spiritual preparation, discipline, and non-violent actions as Gandhi and Vinoba taught them. Kaka had to learn Satyagraha through a life-long involvement with the Gandhian movement. In his youth, he wanted to participate in Satyagraha at any cost as long as it landed him in prison. Gradually he came to realize that according to the Sarvodaya philosophy, Satyagraha was not a means for self-gratification, but service for others. Since his aim was nation building, he found Satyagraha to be an effective tool to raise the consciousness of people about their rights, educate opponents, and work for desired goals. And if the Satyagrahis intentions are pure, they can bring about a non-violent peaceful resolution to the problems, and contribute toward Gram Swaraj.

Achyut Deshpande's thought is highly influenced by the Vedantic vision of Religious Universalism. He is a believer in the tradition of Sanatana Dharma which upholds that all religions are equally valid in their quest for truth. Thus, there should be the practice of religious tolerance among various religious groups. No doubt, Kaka received support for his convictions in this regard from Gandhi and Vinoba. Vinoba's book, <u>Dharma Samanvya</u> (unity of religions), played a significant role in formulating his thinking. Kaka's involvement with the Muslim community in Hyderabad has already been discussed. What is impressive is that he not only accepted Muslims as his brothers, but dedicated a good portion of his life to the study of the Quran. Moreover, at the risk of endangering his own life, he worked for saving the lives and property of many Muslims during the period when Hyderabad was annexed into India. Today, he is concerned about the rise of religious extremism all over the world, but particularly in India. He is critical of religious fundamentalism within Hinduism and Islam. However, he believes that the religions themselves do not propagate religious exclusivism that breeds violence. He attributes religious intolerance to the actions of those who are either politically motivated or are being manipulated by those who have selfish desires to ascertain power. He also recognizes that economic, social, and political reasons are some of the contributing factors to the rise of religious fundamentalism. He is encouraged by the work of those Sarvodaya leaders who are working for communal harmony.

Kaka believes that he must fight to preserve the ancient culture of India. By that he means the preservation of values that have sustained the agricultural society, meaning the village culture. This belief brings him in conflict with the values of the industrial society, meaning the city culture. At the center of the controversy are

107

issues related to family, education, economy, politics, etc. For him, the rise of the industrial civilization in India has brought havoc to the village culture. Like Gandhi, he mentions a variety of problems. For example, the movement to the city has affected the joint family structure, alienation from nature, loss of agricultural activity, and formation of slums around the city. Industrial development has produced crowded cities, environmental degradation, unemployment, and crime. As a consequence, the economic structure is changed to feed the cities at the cost of manipulating the farmer. Also, political power is in the hands of the elite, who govern the masses living in the village. In education, the emphasis is laid on producing "white collar" workers, who detest working with the land. And, under the 'new economic policy,' India is increasingly becoming hostage to multinational companies. Like Gandhi, Vinoba, J. P., and many other Sarvodaya workers, Kaka is disturbed over this situation. His Go-Raksha Satyagraha is an attempt to fight these developments and preserve the integrity of the ancient Indian culture.

Since presently Achyut Kaka is focused on the Cow Protection campaign, he views this as a serious agenda of Gandhian constructive work, and believes that if the cow is saved, India will be saved. In a small booklet on <u>Go Raksha Satyagraha</u>, he explains his views on the tension between the agricultural and the industrial developments in India. He links the agricultural sector with animal husbandry and feels that approximately 75% of the population in India depends on agriculture-animal husbandry for its livelihood. Furthermore, he regrets that the industrial sector can provide jobs only for 15% to 20% of the population. Not only that, agriculture-husbandry provides self-employment for which the government has to provide neither the capital nor the management. Based on this analysis, he feels that a great many thinkers in India have opposed the slaughter of the animals, particularly the cows and the oxen. He cites evidence to show how these animals have provided food, fuel, labor and other useful commodities for the Indian civilization. And today, animal dung has being used to produce bio-gas to supply energy needs as well. He presents astounding statistics to show that, while in 1974 at Deonar Slaughter house, 66,786 bulls were slaughtered. In 1988, the number had reached to 120,553. Since then it has been steadily increasing. One can only imagine what will be the fate of livestock in India at this rate. What is astonishing for Kaka is that since Indian independence in 1947, the Constitution of the Republic made provisions to protect the cow family. In 1958, the Supreme Court even set the guidelines. Accordingly, no young bulls, cows, and milk producing buffaloes could be slaughtered. Gandhi's efforts to protect the cow are well known. Since his death, there has been an accelerated effort by many organizations to stop the killings. However, these efforts have not produced any significant results. Kaka concludes; it is clear that meat brings hefty revenue for the government. Therefore, the government only gives lip service to the promises it makes to ban the killings. Thus, Vinoba went on a hunger strike, and Kaka is involved in a lifelong Satyagraha.[6]

Endnotes: Chapter VI

[1] The actual railway station is named Govandi and can be easily accessed from Bombay.

[2] Achutya Deshpande, <u>Goraksha Satyagraha Ki Prishtabhoomi,</u> p.35.

[3] This event is known as the Bangal Sammelan of 1940.

[4] Telangana Crisis: refers to a violent conflict between the peasants and the landlords, which caused Nehru to send the Indian military to the region of Telangana to settle their disputes.

[5] Since the majority of the leadership of Sarva Seva Sangha is in the hands of J.P. supporters, the likelihood that Achyut Deshpande will be elected president of this body is remote. Achyut himself had stayed away from Sarva Seva Sangh

[6] Much of this information on cow slaughter and its effects on Indian civilization is found in <u>Go Raksha Satyagraha Ki Prishtabhoomi</u> by Achyut Deshpande, published by Parmdham Prakashan, Paunar (no date given)

VII

Crusading For People's Power
Chunibhai Vaidya

Nothing is more crucial to the survival of Northern Gujarat than water. One failing monsoon and drought is imminent. The Sardar Sarovar Project, commonly known as the Narmada Dam Project, is a dream turned nightmare.[1] Conceived soon after independence, the gigantic project is marred with controversies and numerous court battles. In the midst of uncertainties, what are the farmers to do? Who will mobilize them to put pressure on the state government to provide them with an adequate supply of water for their crops? There are smaller dams on the Banas river that flows through the districts of Banaskantha and Mahesana. However, the water is diverted to the farms of rich farmers and politically influential people. Left to cope with the water shortage are hundreds of villages whose rights to claim the water have been violated. There is an urgent need to generate people's power through community organizations and fight the establishment -- the state government. On another front, hidden in the remote corner of Northern Gujarat, where even electricity and modern means of transportation are scarce, who will venture out to serve the people?

The challenge is taken up by a veteran Gandhian, <u>Chunibhai Vaidya</u>, affectionately known as <u>Kaka</u> (uncle), throughout the region. He has given his entire life, mostly in Gujarat, to the work of creating <u>Lok Samitis</u> (people's organizations) according to Gandhian principles.

"A lone fighter," that is how Chuni Kaka described himself to me when I met him recently for the third time at his residence across from Gandhi's famous Sabarmati Ashram in Ahmedabad. "Why a lone fighter?", I asked. The energetic man suddenly became pensive. With a reflective mood he replied, "because most often I have been alone in my fight for justice for the people. Sometimes my

111

colleagues think that it is a misadventure on my part and sometimes they find some differences of opinion, but I think we lack a leadership that can command the respect of all. Though we learnt the doctrine of collective leadership from Acharya Vinoba Bhave, we have yet to learn to practice it in our lives and activities."

I first met Chunibhai in 1992. On Dec. 7, 1992 I arrived in Ahmedabad with my wife and two daughters. The old city was burning and Hindu-Muslim riots had broken out due to the destruction of the Babri mosque in Ayodhya the day before. Concerned with the safety of my family, we managed to make it to the Sabarmati Ashram and from there to Chunibhai. Since all transportation was suspended for days, Kaka played host to us for several memorable days. It was through him that I was to travel in Gujarat and meet with many famous Gandhians like Manubhai Pancholi, Narayan Desai, Hariballabh Parikh, Kanti Shah, Ramlal Parekh and many others. For the first time in all of my travels throughout India, I felt that Gujarat had a flavor of Gandhian culture. It was through Chuni Kaka that I was able to taste some of it. Impressed by his hospitality, I made several subsequent trips to him. The most recent one was in 1998.

Life:

Chunibhai Vaidya was born some time around 1917 in the Mahesana district in Northern Gujarat in a poor family. He remembers the days when the family had very little food. It was in 1930 he first saw Mahatma Gandhi from the terrace of his residence leading the world-famous Dandi Salt March.[2] He recalls, "Young children were climbing trees, people were on top of buildings, mobs were lined up along the streets, as Gandhi briskly passed through the crowd. I knew then that here was a leader." During this period the whole country was with the feeling of revolt against the British government. The young Chuni was no exception. Having finished his high school studies and thereafter, in response to Gandhi's call to give up formal studies, he left the school. He wandered here and there doing small jobs, but all the time continued to listen to Gandhi's speeches. He felt that a strong bond between Gandhi and himself was developing even though he had no contact with him. During his stay in the city of Surat, he happened to read Mahatma Gandhi's autobiography, My Experiments with Truth. He states, "The book impressed me deeply. I felt that here was a common man's messiah with nothing extraordinary about him and yet on the strength of Truth he rose to the heights of Mahatma (great soul)." Not knowing what to do with his life Chunibhai took up some jobs, but all the while he was charged with the fervor of the movement of independence. Now

112

as a young man something was moving him toward Gandhian thought. For a few more years he studied accounting and worked in Karnataka and Kerala. It was in Kerala that he came in contact with some Gandhians who took him under their wing. These "friends from Kerala" were to deeply affect his life later.

In 1942 when Gandhi launched the Quit-India movement, Chunibhai found himself distributing revolutionary literature on the streets. As the police came after him, he ran from the city of Surat. For the next 4 to 6 months he went into hiding from place to place. He wanted to fight the British all the more and kept a knife in his pocket all the time. Recalling those days, he remarks, "The knife was nothing but a small piece, but it shows my resilience to fight. I couldn't fight if I were in jail so I ran." After a few months, Chunibhai surfaced again but decided to settle in a village. For a while he split wood for a living, but then became a teacher at a school. He joined an Anglo-vernacular school as an assistant teacher but soon became its headmaster. He greatly enjoyed working with his students in whom he could impart the fervor of social and political reform. As a teacher he gained popularity and respect. He excelled in literature and became a successful short story writer. Finally the pressure came to finish college if he wanted to continue teaching. Reluctant to further his education he made a case that he was an excellent teacher. However, when promotion was denied, he knew it was time to move on. His "friends from Kerala" provided an option. They invited him to come to Delhi and work with them for Gandhian activities. This was indeed a turning point in young Chuni's life.

Chunibhai Vaidya was called to Delhi to document some 33,000 letters that Gandhi had either written or received in his life.[3] This was a monumental task. Recalling the impact of this work on his life, Kaka states, "this was my real encounter with Gandhi. I had read his autobiography, yes, but I knew the real Gandhi through his letters. I came to realize that this man 'said what he meant, and meant what he said,' and that was impressive to me." Again it was Gandhi's commitment to truth that impacted Vaidya. In the 1950's when Vinoba Bhave launched his Bhoodan movement, Chunibhai returned to Gujarat. Narayan Desai was to arrange Vinoba's pad yatra throughout Gujarat. He solicited Chunibhai's aid, and Kaka became an ardent supporter of Vinoba. Although he walked with Vinoba for Bhoodan, his main focus was to write about the movement. He became responsible for publishing a regular column, 'Vinoba ki Vani' (the Voice of Vinoba). Through the column, Chunibhai gave a push to the Bhoodan movement. During these years he firmly believed that Bhoodan will bring a revolution in India.

113

Now he was trenched with Gandhian thought through Vinoba. Soon he became involved with the publication of 'Bhoomi Putra' (Son of the Land), Gujarat's most popular Sarvodaya magazine. Through Bhoomi Putra, the Sarvodaya world came to learn about Chunibhai Vaidya. As he got more involved with Vinoba's revolution, he was asked to leave his Rs. 275/- per month job for Rs 75/- per month job for the Bhoodan. Kaka gladly accepted the challenge. He became a believer in 'voluntary poverty' as Gandhi had advocated it for his social workers.

Under Vinoba's direction, Chunibhai undertook the work of Sootanjali (yarn offering). Basically it was the work of Khadi that Vinoba was trying to push along with Bhoodan. A quota of home spun gundi (spool) was set for each state of the union. Gujarat was expected to produce 5,000 gundis. The responsibility of overseeing this work was assigned to Kaka. He coordinated this effort with such an enthusiasm that instead of 5,000 allotted gundis, he produced 13,000. When Dada Sahib Maulankar, a respected Gandhian came to inaugurate the function where gundis were to be presented, he paid a laudatory tribute to Chunibhai. Recalling the event, Kaka with a gleam in his eyes speaks, "Tears came to my eyes when I received the praise. I realized that it was not I, but God who had done this." From this event he drew two lessons for his life. First, that he was an instrument of God. Second, he must do everything to remove poverty. In 1958, after a long and dedicated work under the Bhoodan movement, Vaidya left for Varanasi. Little did he realize that he was needed in Assam, where he ended up staying for 12 years of his life.

In Assam there was a need to establish the publishing work for Sarvodaya literature. Chunibhai decided to learn the Assami language and commence publication. Soon he realized that he had to assume various responsibilities. Gradually he became the official spokesperson for Sarvodaya, giving talks, entertaining the press, writing essays, and dealing with government officials. Soon he became very famous throughout the state and many honors were bestowed upon him. In Assamis, people began addressing him as 'Sunni Kaka'. When Vinoba was to come to Assam on his pad yatra, Chunibhai was one of the key individuals to facilitate his visit. He oversaw the numerous details pertaining to the Bhoodan work. One of his foremost tasks was the creation of several Lok Samitis (people's organizations) in the villages of Assam. Here he got the first hand experience of generating people's power. He worked with the farmers, artisans and merchants alike to mobilize them and acquaint them with their rights. The work in Assam

114

turned Vaidya into a seasoned Gandhian. By now he had truly embraced the Gandhian ideals of voluntary poverty, Satyagraha, and Sarvodaya.

While in Assam, Chunibhai visited Nagaland and Manipur states where he was successful in creating Sarvodaya publication committees which published books in the local languages. He wanted to leave Assam soon after Vinoba's departure from the state but had to prolong his stay at Vinoba's insistence who foresaw the conflict between India and China on the Assamese border. Chuni Kaka was reluctant in the beginning but the Sino-Indian conflict was imminent. The Chinese army, after capturing the Indian out-posts on the border, rushed to the foothills of Assam.[4] He remembers, "At the face of the armed conflict the people panicked and refugees started pouring in from remote villages creating a chaotic situation." Chunibhai resolved to stay with the Assamese people even if it meant living in the territories captured by the Chinese. He went on preaching the message of non-violence and non-aggression as he visited thousands of Assamese villages. He created many lok samitis (people's committees) for political and social awareness along Sarvodaya lines. This activity brought him in direct conflict with many local politicians who disliked his activities. "For me," states Kaka, "this was a true experiment in Gandhian philosophy. My steadfastness was being tested, but I did not mind it."

In the 1970s, Chuni Kaka found himself back in Gujarat and assuming the editorship of Bhoomi Putra magazine. Readers will recall that during early 1970's the Sarvodaya movement was faced with many controversies. Jai Prakash Narayan was coming into the limelight and Vinoba had taken a self-imposed retirement at Paunar. The rift between Vinoba and J. P was becoming pronounced, and Indira Gandhi had declared a state of emergency.[5] Under emergency a strong censorship was imposed on all forms of media. The most affected were newspapers and magazines. During the period, Chunibhai took the bold step to criticize the emergency, and to cover J. P.'s Total Revolution. The tool to criticize Indira Gandhi's policies was Bhoomi Putra. Kaka recalls, "There was fear everywhere, people were being put into jail, publications were being ceased, and presses closed." Chunibhai published 6,000 copies of Bhoomi Putra under difficult circumstances and distributed them all over India. He managed to bring three different editions of the publication, before the government sealed the press. The censorship board forfeited Bhoomi Putra's license to publish and imposed a Rs. 1,000/- fine in the form of security money. Chuni Kaka sent the appeal for money to the people. "People were eager to send money even though we had collected Rs.

10,500/-. Finally I had to request them to stop sending money," recalls Kaka. His opposition to the emergency landed him in prison for seven months. Chunibhai was hailed as a hero and his fame spread throughout Gujarat. Not only that, the state of Maharashtra adorned him with the "Fearless Journalism Award" (Nirbhaya Patrakarita Sane Guruji Award) for his deeds.

After his release from prison, Chunibhai launched his Lok Samiti work in Ahmedabad. He traveled all over Northern Gujarat, reaching small villages and assessing their problems. The main work centered around creating people's power through mobilization of human resources. To this end, Kaka had to hold numerous meetings with the villagers, and train leaders who could work with the people on a regular basis. The work had to be carried out at various levels, which included education, assessment of needs, negotiations with the powerful landlords, meeting government officials, and planning Satyagrahas. In 1980, Chunibhai led a major Satyagraha against the state controlled liquor shop in Ratanpur. The problem was serious since this liquor center was attracting poor farmers and youth, who were wasting their hard earned money and precious time getting intoxicated. As always, the addiction was destroying family relations, increasing crime and violence, decreasing productivity, and adding to the general poverty in the area. The state was not about to close the shop since it was a source of revenue. Chunibhai took up the non-violent fight and lead a Satyagraha against the state. Through his work with Lok Samiti, he organized the villagers against the state owned liquor industry. The fight took time but at the end the state government had to close the shop. Reflecting on the success story, Vaidya states, "I was a 'lone fighter' in this struggle. No leading Gandhian in Gujarat except the district workers came to my support. Some of them, keeping at a distance, watched my struggle with amusement." However, his bold actions brought him, among others, the 'Darshak Award' which carries a citation as well as a sum of Rs. 100,000. This is all the more remarkable because the award is called 'Darshak' to honor one of the great literary figures of Gujarat, Manubhai Pancholi. As an exponent of Gandhian thought, Pancholi himself has been the recipient of two all-India literary awards, and whom this author had the good fortune of meeting and interviewing through Chunibhai.

In Gujarat, Chunibhai organized a number of movements for the rights of the poor. On one occasion, he led a Satyagraha against the scheme of life-long pension plan for the members of the legislative assembly of the state of Gujarat. His plea was based on the argument that if the government could not offer security to ordinary citizens, farmers, and laborers, how could they offer it to those who serve only for the limited years under the best of conditions? He protested against the policy of the legislators voting on their own benefits. In the face of the state-wide protest, the legislation, though passed, had to be shelved. Meanwhile, he also launched movements against state-wide corruption, the multi-national companies, and communal riots. In all of these, he remained a 'lone fighter.'

Chuni Kaka's longest struggle with the state government of Gujarat is on the issue of water. As stated earlier, to harness water from the rivers and to catch the monsoon rain are the two biggest issues for the farmers of Gujarat, and for India as a whole. Chunibhai had concentrated his efforts in the northern region of Gujarat, since he knows that area best. Also, through the Lok Samiti work, he was able to identify that water conservation was the most serious problem for the inhabitants of this area. This is the most drought prone region that affects roughly 75 villages with thousands of people. The problem is simply this; the farmers have been periodically assured that when the Narmada Dam project is completed, there will be no water shortages. In the meantime two dams on the Banas and Sipu rivers respectively, which flow through the region, are not serving the deprived people. Their water is diverted upstream to influential rich farmers. The villages settled along downstream are largely affected by the state government policy. Their crops are failing and often they are unable to grow even one successful crop. Chunibhai discovered that in 1929 the Bombay High Court had given a decision in favor of the villagers in a similar case. The entire case rested on a law which states that the people living in the close proximity of the river have the first right to its water. Thus having diverted the waters from the Banas and Sipu rivers, the state government was violating the law. For Kaka this was a situation that demanded generating people's power to fight the government.

Chunibhai Vaidya devised a two pronged program to deal with the water conservation program. First, he experimented with his own methods of harnessing the water. Second, he launched a Satyagraha against the state government and persuaded them to find a solution to the problem. The struggle began in 1987.

As far as his own method of water conservation is concerned, Chunibhai was successful in raising the flow of the Sipu river (the flow was low because of the dam upstream) downstream by constructing what he called a Gupt Bandh (hidden dam). The method requires digging the riverbed at several places and spreading large plastic sheets underneath the sand. As a consequence seepage to the ground is minimized and the water level is raised. This process inundates the banks and the water reaches the fields. The experiment worked and the farmers praised

117

Chunibhai's effort. However, Kaka realized that Gupt Bandh will not solve the larger problem of bringing water to the areas away from the river. Thus, a Satyagraha was necessary. As the Lok Samitis, under the guidance of Kaka launched the movement, it came to be known as 'Sipu Agitation'. The village of Radhanpur became Kaka's center as the Satyagraha began. He demanded that the construction of the Sipu dam be stopped, the locks of the constructed dam should not be opened to divert the water, and no canals be dug to carry the water to other areas. After a long and hard struggle, an agreement was reached in 1992, which was signed by the state government and by Chunibhai as the people's representative. According to the agreement, Chuni Kaka asked the government to take three main steps. First, construct several temporary mud dams for the affected area. Second, construct more Gupt bandhs as Kaka had experimented with. Third, release some water periodically in order that the river have water in its last stretch of approximately 130 kilometer area. On his own initiative, he cleared some old water tanks that had been covered with sand and brush to collect rain water.

Feb. 4, 1993 was a sad day for Kaka. He discovered that the irrigation department had broken the agreement, and the water was continually being diverted to other areas. At this point he sent an ultimatum to the Chief Minister of Gujarat that he was to commence a 'fast unto death' in protest of government's underhanded actions. The Chief Minister (at the time, Chimanbhai Patel) responded and promised a new agreement. He pleaded with Kaka not to undertake his 'fast unto death'. Under the new agreement, Kaka agreed to the construction of the Sipu dam since the government had borrowed a large amount from the World Bank. On his part the Chief Minister ordered to stop the diversion of the water. He also agreed that until the big Narmada dam is completed, the state will release the overflow of the Sipu dam for the affected areas. Also, the government agreed to compensate the rest of the water from Banas river dam. Chunibhai realizes that even though not all the people's demands have been met, they have achieved some success. He is proud of the fact that he fought a non-violent fight according to Gandhian principles. While many attempts were made to discredit him in the press that he was disturbing the progress of Gujarat by opposing the building of the Sipu dam, Kaka defended the rights of the people. For his devoted struggles he was publicly recognized by one of Gujarat's literary figures, Manubhai Pancholi. His Darshak Foundation awarded him the sum of Rs. 100,000/- as a gift.

In 1995, while inspecting a dam near the village of Badarpur, Chunibhai fell off a tractor and seriously injured himself. The recovery took a long time, but he continued to work for the people from his bed. Today he continues to find solutions to Gujarat's water problems. His goal is to survey as many rivers of Northern Gujarat and Kuchchh, and build Gupta bandhs on them. This task can only be achieved through people's power.

Recently, Chunibhai has been involved in a bitter dispute with the environmentalists on one hand and the state government of Gujarat on the other over the completion of the Narmada river dam project known as the Sardar Sarovar Project. Having invested millions of dollars for its completion, the work halted in 1995 as environmentalists opposed its construction on many grounds. The case has reached the Supreme Court of India where it stays bogged down in legalities while construction has been suspended. Bitterly opposed to its completion, the Narmada Bachao Andolan (Save Narmada Movement) headed by the world renown environmentalist, Ms. Medha Patkar, has succeeded in stopping the construction on the grounds that no adequate arrangements have been made to resettle thousands of villagers whose homes would be submerged under water if the dam stops the flow of the Narmada river. Chunibhai opposed Medha Patkar and believes that the Narmada Dam is a necessity for the people of Gujarat, a state which is prone to famine year after year. He feels that the Dam will provide much needed water for millions of people. He also feels that the charges that no adequate provisions have been made to resettle the villagers are totally false. In his opinion, the resettlement package that the state had offered to the affected people is the best ever offered anywhere in the world where the mega dams have been built.[6]

In 1997, Chuni Kaka decided to challenge the environmentalists by filing a writ in the Supreme Court on behalf of the millions of people who will be disadvantaged if the dam is not completed. To his amazement the writ was accepted and the Supreme Court has to reevaluate the entire situation. Naturally, the Save Narmada Movement appealed to the court that Kaka's writ should not be accepted. Now the legal fight has taken a different turn as the Chief Justice is willing to listen to Kaka's point of view. Kaka is hopeful that the case will go in favor of the people who are in a dire need of water. He has spent countless hours working with many lok samitis, mobilizing them in the cause of Narmada Dam. He feels disheartened that the leading Gandhians in India are divided in their views over the completion of the dam. Therefore, the Sarvodaya Movement has been unable to take a united stand on this issue. Once again, Chunibhai finds himself alone in the fight.

In Gujarat, Chunibhai is the leading Gandhian social worker who has opposed the presence of multi-national companies in India. Through his Gram

Swaraj work he had launched a Satyagraha against several multi-national companies which are buying up the much needed land for cattle ranchers. He feels that in Gujarat alone, thousands of cattle keepers are in search of grazing land for their herds. Before the arrival of the big companies, the land was plentiful where cattle used to roam for food and naturally fertilize it for better farming. Now, the cattle owners find themselves in a difficult situation as the fertile land is used to build big factories and high-rise apartments. Due to Kaka's organized protest, selling of the land has been stopped in many parts of Gujarat and in some cases the multi-nationals "have been chased out." Before the 1998 general elections, Kaka sent a letter to 18,000 villages of Gujarat to vote only for the candidates who support the Gram Swaraj movement. He also insisted that people support his plea that grazing land should be sold for other purposes only if the 2/3 majority of the Gram Sabha (the village assembly) supports such move. He insists, "India is an agricultural country, and we should not let the multi-nationals spoil it."

Thought:

Like many thinkers, Chunibhai believes that thought and action should not be separated. This is the gift of Gandhi and Vinoba to him. He marvels at Gandhi's determination to know the truth and to know it through experimentation. This is what attracted Kaka to Gandhi after he read his autobiography, and later worked on cataloging 33,000 of Gandhi's letters. As for Gandhi, the quest for truth turned into a fight for truth, so for Chunibhai fighting for truth became a central feature of his life.

Chunibhai believes that a sense of freedom in one's life is connected with the knowledge of truth. And freedom generates 'fearlessness'. As a 'lone fighter' he has remained fearless in facing his opposition. With fearlessness one gains power which can be directed to solve problems. This is the principle behind Lok Shakti (people's power). Through his lok samiti work, he had intended to empower the people. Through empowerment, people brought change in their own lives as evidenced by the Satyagraha he fought for the people.

Chunibhai has wrestled with the basic philosophical question; What is the aim of life? He is aware that the traditional Hindu answer to this question has been given in the classical idioms of Artha, Kama, Dharma, and Moksha. However, Kaka's personal answer has been 'service of society' (Samaj Seva). He understood the importance of Samaj Seva from Gandhi, but from Vinoba he learnt the practical application of the ideal. He recalls, "Vinoba sent us to the people, to identify with the people and serve the people." Chunibhai got his training of public service through the Bhoodan movement. That is how he turned to the work of building lok samitis. To this date, he has established 400 lok simitis in Northern Gujarat. He admits that most of the samitis are not functioning as well as they should due to many problems. There are no regular meetings and no formal membership. Nevertheless, he is hopeful that people will come together if presented with a valid cause. The cause of water conservation discussed earlier brought many samitis together and Lok Shakti was generated which produced some positive results. For Kaka, Samaj Seva (service of society) is central to the success of Sarvodaya.

Central to Chunibhai's thinking is the issue of 'conflict resolution'. He believes that in a fearless fight under Satyagraha, one must come to a truthful resolution. In this process, for him, the spirit of 'compromise' is very important. He reminds the lok sevaks (servants of the people) that a stubborn persistence to win your own way should not be the goal of Satyagraha. During his 'Sipu Agitation', Kaka often compromised with the state officials. Out of his anger he demanded that the Sipu dam should be torn down, but when the Chief Minister explained his own commitment to the World Bank, Kaka backed off and settled on a lesser demand. He told this writer that the goal in this struggle was not to defeat his opponent, but to come to an amicable agreement that was satisfactory to both parties. Thus, for Chunibhai, 'conflict resolution' should exercise the principle of love. He learned this principle from Gandhi. It is not an accident that he continues to be friendly with many state officials in Gujarat that he has been in conflict with. He has earned their respect, even though at times they have been the recipient of his anger as well.

Many of Chunibhai's actions give us an insight into his thinking. He agrees that "power corrupts and absolute power corrupts absolutely." He also believes that as a Gandhian he must oppose corrupt power. It was on this basis that he sided with J. P. and left the Vinoba camp in the 1970's. He felt that J. P. was right in challenging Indira Gandhi's power since it had become oppressive. So when J. P. gave the call for 'Total Revolution', Chunibhai joined him. He states, "I had to join J. P. in order to save Vinoba." I find this statement insightful. What Chunibhai means is that when Indira declared the State of Emergency, whatever Vinoba stood for was at stake. The entire Sarvodaya philosophy faced the challenge of being discredited and ridiculed. When J. P. gave the call to face oppression of a political power, Kaka had to respond. The call was to fight oppression and not to accept it. Chunibhai has no regrets that he suffered imprisonment for his involvement in

'Total Revolution'. This was a "test of the philosophy of Satyagraha and Sarvodaya as Gandhi taught us." Kaka's siding with J. P. did not mean discrediting Vinoba's philosophy. Chunibhai is greatly indebted to Vinoba for teaching him spirituality and showing him the dynamics of people's power.

For Chunibhai, the meaning of Satyagraha and Sarvodaya is deeply rooted in the Indian notion of 'Dharma'. It is this glue that has held the Indian society together. For Kaka, Dharma does not mean 'religion' in the conventional sense of belief in God. Rather, he likes to use the phrase 'Dharma Samskara' to mean "those virtuous deeds that have held the Indian society together for generations." These deeds are the deeds of love, non-violence, and tolerance toward all creatures. And, if a religion teaches these virtues, it is spiritual. Vinoba held this belief when he taught the notion of Sarva Dharma Samabhava (respect for all dharmas). This is the basis for Chunibhai's respect for all faiths, and his work for communal harmony. He has fearlessly visited the riot-torn areas of Ahmedabad to bring peace among Hindus and Muslims. This writer participated in a march for peace that Kaka led in Ahmedabad after the destruction of the Babri mosque in Ayodhya. When the atmosphere was so tense and the police had warned the participants about possible sniper shooting, Chunibhai was in the front line leading the march. He was exemplifying his thought through his actions.

Chunibhai believes that globally we must think seriously about the divisive factors that are destroying the very fabric of humanity. According to him the main factors are; economics, politics and religion.

On the economic issue he believes, "Limitless growth or development is detrimental to the growth of a real human being. Limitless affluence is suicidal. Humans have no right to recklessly exploit nature for wallowing in their unsatiable desires." As an exponent of Sarvodaya philosophy he wants remuneration for intellectual and physical labor to be equal. He advocates globalization but condemns the interpretation of globalization as advocated by the multi-national companies. He states, "To us (Sarvodaya family), globalization -- Vasudhaiva Kutumbakam -- the whole world is one family; to multi-nationals it is a market where one goes with the sole objective of looting and amassing money and wealth without any consideration of the welfare of others or of the whole society." He advocates that under globalization, India is prepared to open its borders for investment of capital by the big companies, but the capitalist countries should also open their borders to India's capital i.e. multitude of human beings. He says, "Our farmers, our laborers should

122

be freely allowed to go to any country in the world to earn a bread of sweat. There should be the economics of non-violence."

On the political front, as a committed Gandhian, Chunibhai propagates the decentralization of political power. He quotes Gandhi when he states, "That government is the best that rules the least." For Chuni Kaka, "Any organization party of association on the basis of narrow-minded appeals like nationalism, regionalism, linguism, etc. is wholly undesirable and should go."

His views on religion have already been presented earlier. Here it would suffice to say that Chunibhai follows Gandhi and Vinoba in advocating religious universalism. He is fond of quoting Vinoba who states, "The days of politics and religions are gone, now are the days of science and spirituality." In the end Chuni Kaka sums up his beliefs by once again quoting Vinoba Bhave:

> We don't nurture any sense of pride of attachment to any particular country. We don't insist on a particular religion. We do not belong to any sect or community. Our field of study is to soar in the region of noble thoughts all over the world. To assimilate noble thoughts is our social duty.[7]

Endnotes: Chapter VII

[1] Started in 1947, Narmada Dam Project was perceived to be the biggest irrigation and hydro-electric project in Asia. Partially funded by the World Bank, its construction came to a stand-still in 1995 due to some legal problems.

[2] Dandi Salt March is Gandhi's most famous Satyagraha against the British which he undertook in 1930. He marched from his Sabarmati Ashram to Dandi covering over 250 miles to defy the British monopoly over making salt. People all over India began making and selling salt in defiance of the British law.

[3] The invitation was extended to him by the Gujarat Mahatma Gandhi Memorial Trust.

[4] This was India's war with China in 1962 over a border dispute which India lost. To this day China occupies India's territory in the north which it claims to be China's.

[5] Declared in 1975, the Emergency was Indira Gandhi's ploy to take power in her hands and suspend civil liberties and the freedom of the press on the pretext that India was under a threat of insurgency perpetuated by J. P.'s case for the Total Revolution.

[6] This author visited several resettlement projects in Gujarat headed by Harivallabh Parikh. The work is impressive and quite generous in terms of providing land, housing and cattle to those who had to leave the Narmada valley to resettle elsewhere. All families seem happy and satisfied with the resettlement packages they had been offered by the Sarvodaya leadership.

[7] This quote from Vinoba was cited by Chuni Kaka in a document he sent to the author. It carries no exact reference to the text attributed to Vinoba.

124

VIII

Striving for Appropriate Development
Devendra Kumar

Generally speaking, in our post-modern world, when social scientists describe the dilemmas of the so-called 'developing countries,' they usually employ the western model of development as a norm to which the others should comply. Here, development is measured against industrial economic growth, urban city planning, high-tech achievements, etc. collectively proclaimed as measures of modernization. In the Indian context, Gandhi was among the very few who challenged this definition of modernity. As we have seen, he tried to show that urbanization, industrialization, and uncontrolled technological advancement were exploitative of the poor and the have-nots of society. From Sir John Ruskin's Unto This Last, he learned of the evils of post-World War I Industrialization of Europe and the havoc it created for the common folk. For Gandhi, 'development' implied the application of a different set of values than materialistic advancement and economic growth. Since the Gandhian vision was challenged in the post-independent India, the issue of development has posed a serious problem for the contemporary Gandhians.

If one travels in India, one cannot miss the signs of the Western type of development everywhere throughout the breadth of the land. Industrial complexes, high-rise apartments, national highways, automobiles, factories, urban centers, and fast means to telecommunications are visible everywhere. However, equally visible are various forms of pollutions: environmental degradation, slums, heaps of garbage, and traffic jams. While economic progress is being measured through uncontrolled consumerism, poverty is on the increase. There is hardly a news media which does not report the plight of those who are not victimized in the name of progress. While seminars and panel discussions are organized to discuss the merits and demerits of this form of 'development,' the present Indian government is sold on the notion of economic boom which, it feels, will come only through heavy industrialization and technological advancement. While many institutes for the advancement of rural (as opposed to industrial) development are flourishing, their goal seems to be bringing the rural sector on par with the urban sector through the application of the current model of development. However, among the contemporary Gandhians, many have questioned this process, and are working on an alternate model of development. Dr. Devendra Kumar is one such Gandhian, who heads the Center of Science for Villages, spread of several campuses near Wardha, Maharashtra. A believer in 'Appropriate Development,' he is involved in many projects which he feels are suitable to the Indian context. From Maganwadi in Wardha, where Gandhi founded the All India Village Industries Association, Devendra Kumar launched an organization in 1976 whose work is being recognized all over India as well as abroad.

Life:

Born in 1925 in the state of Uttar Pradesh, Devendra Kumar was exposed to Gandhian thought during his student days. He recalls, "Gandhi was a familiar name in our household. In fact, my father left his studies for two years (1920-22) in order to join Gandhi." As a young man, Devendra was encouraged to study a degree in engineering. Educated at Ewing Christian College, Allahabad, and later in Lucknow, he found himself at the Indian Institute of Technology at Kanpur. The turning point in his life came when, while on an educational tour from his engineering college, he reached Wardha. Here he met the famous Indian economist, Dr. J. C. Kumarappa, who was intensely involved in applying Gandhi's thought for the development of rural economy.[1] Captivated by Kumarappa's dedication to Gandhi, and his vision for appropriate development of India, Devendra began questioning his own education in the traditional forms of engineering. During his brief visit to Kumarappa's center in Wardha, he was asked by his guru-to-be "to study the village industries that Kumarappa was working in and offer any suggestions for improvements." This initial contact turned into a long relationship which eventually changed the course of Devendra's life. From Wardha, Devendra went to Calcutta where Gandhi was working. There he merely saw him, but no meeting took place. However, he made up his mind that after completing his education he would join Gandhi's Sarvodaya.

In 1946, Devendra Kumar joined Kumarappa at Wardha at an institution which was founded by Gandhi in 1935. As a young engineer, he began training under the tutelage of Kumarappa. He discovered that Kumarappa was a dedicated Christian who was highly influenced by his mother, a saintly figure. In his desire to practice the Christian ideal of 'helping others,' Kumarappa found an expression of this ideology in the Sarvodaya movement. Thus he joined Gandhi at the All India Village Industries Association to work for the villagers in search for alternate forms of development. During my conversations with Dr. Devendra Kumar I discovered that he never got tired of praising J. C. Kumarappa for his vision of rural development. He stated, "Kumarappa's thinking was original. He lived a disciplined life according to Christian and Gandhian ideals. However, he was a scientist, and looked for scientific methods of appropriate technology for appropriate development suitable for the conditions in India." According to Dr. Devendra Kumar, J. C. Kumarappa was among the few economists who began discussing the scarcity of natural resources. He made it known that the world had two kinds of resources, renewable and non-renewable. The non-renewable like minerals and fossil fuels were not replenishable. Therefore, he questioned the modern industrial development which was bent on exploiting non-renewable resources. Kumarappa's research led him to find ways in which renewable resources could be used, and he wished to bring this knowledge to the villagers and encourage rural development.

When Devendra Kumar joined the Wardha Center, he was encouraged by the fact that Kumarappa believed in employing scientific methods to improve human condition. It was because Gandhi himself encouraged scientific research. Devendra states, "Gandhi was very much in favor of using scientific knowledge. Therefore, he chose great scientists like Raman, Bose, and Ray to be involved in his All India Village Industries Association. He asked them to relate their scientific knowledge to the grass-roots level of development." When Devendra joined Kumarappa, Gandhi himself was experimenting with food resource, looking to find ways to eliminate protein deficiencies. Devendra worked out a way to use the ground nut, mixing it with the wheat flour to bake the common Indian bread (roti). He wrote two articles on the subject which Gandhi published in his magazine, <u>The Harijan</u>. When I asked him if he tried to meet Gandhi in those years, he responded, "No. I did not. I discovered that Kumarappa discouraged meeting with Gandhi. He held the view, 'Why bother the old man', and when I saw that my own guru did not press on meeting Gandhi, I figured why should I." However, both mentally and spiritually they remained connected to Gandhi. Devendra recalls, "When Gandhi was assassinated, Kumarappa fell ill for three months and could not get up from his bed." The bond between Gandhi, Kumarappa and Devendra remained firm. As an expert in oil technology, Devendra continued his research to extract oil from various trees that proved to be useful for rural economy. He felt he was doing Gandhi's work.

A few years after India's independence in 1947, India began a program of opening big national laboratories for scientific advancement. Such cities as Bombay, Nagpur, Lucknow and Delhi were chosen as sites of this activity. Devendra Kumar recalls, "I started going to these laboratories in order to see what they could do for our center in the area of rural development." He felt that this dialogue with great centers of scientific learning was important for two reasons. First, it kept the national policy makers informed about the need for giving attention to rural development as they were more focused on urban development. Second, it gave Dr. Devendra Kumar an opportunity to apply the latest scientific knowledge in his work for the uplift of the villages. As his work intensified, he realized that he needed to move to a village to really understand all aspects of village life if he were to help them. Thus, having worked at the research laboratory of the All India Village Industries Association for six years, he shifted to a small village of Machala near Indore in the state of Madhya Pradesh for eight years. Recalling this experience, Devendra Kumar narrates, "I shifted to a small village with approximately 60 families, who were cut off from the urban life. I realized that the majority of Indian villages lived in a situation like this. This was the most precious period of my life because I learned about village life from my first hand experience. It was spiritually crucial because I was in close proximity to nature as well as human beings. There was something authentic about it which I have not experienced in the urban setting."

Dr. Devendra Kumar's move to settle in a village was highly inspired by his contact with Vinoba Bhave in 1952. Vinoba had a keen interest in the work of Kumarappa at Wardha and had met Devendra Kumar in that context. As the Bhoodan Movement was launched by Vinoba, he was increasingly drawn towards the villages. He had equated Ram Raj with Gram Swaraj and was working to free the villages from poverty and exploitation. He encouraged Devendra to study the problems of the villages and try to find solutions to these problems. His work in the village of Machala was not limited to appropriate technology schemes, rather, it focused on the multi-dimensional problems of the landless people. He recalls, "We had most success in forming cooperative farms in order to save the farmer from the exploitation of the landlords and the middle men who used to buy their produce for less and sell for higher prices. Through the cooperation we made the poor farmer owners and sellers of their own products." About eight years later, in 1960 Vinoba's Bhoodan party came to Devendra's village. He was now instructed by Vinoba to move out of the village and to go and experience the problems of city life. When Devendra questioned Vinoba, he replied, "I don't want you to stagnate and I don't want the villagers to become dependent on you. It is time for you to move on."

At Vinoba's behest, Devendra Kumar moved to the city of Indore. The city problems were different in nature. He plunged into the work of sanitation, devising ways and means to improve the conditions of the city. He worked among the beggars to improve their lot. He also worked for the lepers, trying to find suitable treatment for them. In addition he started several secondary schools for children and institutions for the uplift of women. He recalls, "I became a social worker and tried to solve whatever problems I could. All the while working in the city I thought of the welfare of the weaker sections of out society. After all that is what Gandhi and Vinoba wanted to do under Sarvodaya." While in Indore, Devendra also interacted with various political parties. His goal was to enter into a dialogue with various political leaders on the issue of nation building with particular reference to the role of the poor. He also conversed with them on communal problems that led to riots and social chaos. He wanted to encourage various religious leaders to work for peace and non-violence. To this end, he also kept in touch with many national and international organizations interested in peace making. He became particularly interested in the work of the War Resister's International and kept in close touch with that body.

In 1965 Devendra Kumar was to experience yet another change in his life. He was called by Gandhi Smarak Nidhi (an organization that coordinated Sarvodaya constructive work programs) in New Delhi to become its secretary. A committee was formed at Nidhi to commence planning celebrations for Gandhi's centenary in 1969. It was deemed necessary to involve Devendra in this process. Once again, Vinoba played an essential role in encouraging Devendra Kumar to accept the position in Delhi, but return to Wardha in due time. Devendra did exactly that. For eleven years he became the secretary of the Gandhi Smarak Nidhi, a position that carried great responsibilities. He traveled throughout the country working at the grass-roots level for the uplift of the villages. It involved meeting with local as well as national Sarvodaya leadership as it planned its Gandhian

129

activities throughout the country. Since various committees were being formed throughout the world to plan for Gandhi's centenary in 1969, as a secretary of Gandhi Smarak Nidhi and in charge of the celebrations, Devendra Kumar traveled to many countries in Europe to discuss how the centenary would be celebrated. His main job was to inform various groups what others were planning to do to make 1969 a successful year. He remembers, "So much effort was being put on Gandhi's centenary. I wanted this to be an occasion to present Gandhi to the world and to focus on his ideas of peace and non-violence. I think we succeeded in doing that by organizing exhibitions, lectures, films, rallies, workshops, etc. for this purpose."

During his tenure in Delhi, Devendra Kumar also came closer to Jai Prakash Narayan as he worked with him on various projects. Although he had met J. P. when Devendra was 25 years old and had responded to his call for a rally to support his Land Army Movement, it was during the 1960s and 1970s that he became his confidant. When the Nagaland[2] problem erupted, Devendra met the Nagaland leaders in London to negotiate a settlement. While J. P. presided over the negotiations, Devendra was his assistant. Soon after the Indo-China war of 1962, when J. P. became the president of the Himalaya Seva Sangh, Devendra was its secretary. Together they toured the Himalayan regions that were threatened by Chinese occupation. Not only did they encourage people to remain non-violent, but assured them of a variety of support. He also accompanied J. P. during the surrendering of the decoits in the infamous Chambal Valley.[3] During this period in his life, Dr. Devendra Kumar met the Prime Minister and various members of the cabinet on a regular basis. As the secretary of Gandhi Smarak Nidhi, his opinion was sought by government officials on various matters. He states, "At least once a month I had a meeting with the Prime Minister, and often with other ministers. I regret that this privilege no longer exists. In recent years the Gandhian institutions have lost their prestigious position in the eyes of the government, and are no longer influential in the government's decision making process."

Devendra Kumar's work with Gandhi Smarak Nidhi brought him to a closer relationship with Sarva Seva Sangh in the early mid-1970s. Since the Nidhi was the administrative wing of the Sarvodaya and Sarva Seva Sangha concerned itself with the actual constructive work programs in the field, Devendra Kumar constantly interacted with the Sarvodaya leadership both on the planning and the implementation stages of their work. By virtue of being in charge of the Gandhi centenary, he was also in touch with Indira Gandhi, then the Prime Minister of

India. It is in this context that he played a significant role in mediating between Vinoba and J. P. on the one hand, and Indira Gandhi and J. P. on the other, as the tensions began to rise among them during J. P.'s 'Total Revolution' movement.[4] Despite his close relationship with J. P., Devendra disagreed with him on the issue of 'Total Revolution.' He states, "When J. P. started a movement against corruption in the state of Bihar, I agreed with him. However, when he turned it into a national movement, I disagreed with him. J. P. understood my position and asked me to follow my own conscience in this regard. That was the Gandhian thing to do." Disagreement with J. P. did not necessarily mean that Devendra Kumar joined the Vinoba camp. He remained neutral as the rift between Vinoba and J. P. began to grow which ultimately split the Sarvodaya movement. He remembers, "J. P. wanted me to become a link between him and Vinoba in order that their relationship may not stray too far." He wanted Vinoba to bless his Total Revolution, which Vinoba never did. When J. P. challenged Indira and proposed for a new general election, Vinoba remained firm that Sarvodaya should not participate in the elections. He conveyed the message to Devendra and through him to J. P.

In the triangular relationship among J. P., Vinoba and Indira Gandhi, Devendra also mediated between J. P. and Indira Gandhi. He had access to Indira Gandhi because of his work with the Gandhi centenary celebrations in which the government also took a keen interest. During his meetings with Indira Gandhi, the subject of J. P.'s 'Total Revolution' inevitably came up. Indira Gandhi was extremely concerned that the Gandhian organization like Sarva Seva Sangha was taking such an active role in Indian politics by opposing her government. She knew that key players of the movement like Vinoba, J. P. and their supporters were instrumental in swaying public opinion. Since Total Revolution had become a national movement, she saw it as a threat to her power. Devendra Kumar remembers, "When J. P. was arrested by Indira Gandhi along with several other Sarvodaya leaders, Indira Gandhi called me and asked me why J. P. was so much against her. I told her that J. P. was not against anyone rather he was raising issues of national interest." When Devendra conveyed Indira's sentiments toward J. P. to him, J. P. was greatly distressed, "Because," says Devendra, "J. P. was a friend of Nehru and considered Indira as his daughter." On another occasion, Indira's anger toward J. P. was softened when Devendra Kumar told her that J. P. had respect for Indira but disagreed with her politics. Devendra Kumar believes that because of his dialogue with Indira, J. P. was released from prison even though during the period of Emergency, Indira never called Devendra back to discuss Sarva Seva Sangh's

131

involvement in politics. Looking back at those years, he feels that his role was that of a peace maker.

In 1976, Devendra Kumar returned to Wardha to recommence his work with rural development. In the absence of J. C. Kumarappa, his mentor, based on his application of Gandhian ideals, he founded the Center of Science for Villages. He has been with this organization ever since.

According to Dr. Devendra Kumar, his center is following seven progressive steps as goals leading toward its work of evolving new rural technologies that are ecologically sound and will lead to social justice. These are listed as:

1. Identification of Focus Action Areas:

   Under this goal the Center identifies critical problems that require scientific and technological solutions. It focuses on the local resources and finds ways to optimize traditional knowledge and skill to solve the problem.

2. Search out for Options:

   The Center contacts other science and technology based institutions that are engaged in research and development in order to identify available solutions and their alternatives.

3. Research Project:

   Based on the information received, the Center undertakes research projects to make appropriate technologies available that are suitable under village conditions.

4. Extension:

   The technology is tried out in a number of villages to construct a viable model.

5. Publication:

   The results are published for general use.

6. Training:

   The program of training personnel of various voluntary organizations is undertaken to spread the use of technologies involved.

7. Influencing State Policies and Programs:

   An attempt is made to convince the government that it should include the solutions provided by the Center in its plans and policies.[5]

Currently, the Center of Science of Villages works through several of its campuses in the Wardha area. Its team consists of engineers, social scientists, artisans, and apprentice rural youths. Presently, it is focusing its activities on the following areas:

1. Renewable Energy:

The main focus of this activity has been the development of bio-gas plants, red clay segments and bamboo bio-gas plants, and the construction of smokeless chulhas (hearths). In order to implement the technology that the Center has developed in these areas, it has conducted numerous camps throughout the state of Maharashtra. Until 1997, the Center had conducted 175 bio-gas mason training camps and trained 3,000 masons in bio-gas technology. It had installed approximately 4,000 bio-gas plants in the state. In order to reduce the cost of a bio-gas plant, it has developed clay segments and bamboo-cretes. The red-clay burners are used to replace expensive steel burners. In order to increase fuel efficiency, the Center has installed 10,000 smokeless hearths that it developed in its laboratories. Approximately 1,900 rural women have been trained in the construction of these cooking devices. All of these activities have shown the villagers how to save energy and become self-sufficient in fuel.

2. Agriculture and Environment:

One of the Center's main concerns has been the development of organic farming in order to deal with the environmental hazards created by the use of chemical fertilizers and pesticides. Various types of bio-fertilizers using animal dung have been developed for farming use. The methods of composting via 'vermipit' have been developed for the farmers' use. In addition, the technology for the use of indigenous earthworms has been developed to enhance organic farming. Various methods of irrigation, goat repellent (use of urine) as pesticide, and other natural methods to develop herbal pesticides are being used in the field. These are deemed environmentally friendly and less harmful to nature. The technologies to collect natural honey, raise bees, and collection of gum without harming the trees, have been developed to aid poor farmers and tribals engaged in this work.

3. Rural Housing and Sanitation:

In light of the depletion of building resources like timber, bamboo, and cement, which have become costly, the Center has developed a model of building mud houses, now known as "Wardha Houses." Several engineers from Pakistan, Bangladesh, Sri Lanka, Nepal and France have been trained in this technology. These houses are proven to be stronger, safer, comfortable in all types of weather, and cheaper. In the area of sanitation, which remains a big problem for the majority

133

of Indian cities, the technicians have developed "Wardha Latrines" that are being widely used. Over the years, the Center has trained many masons in the art of building these cost effective homes and latrines.

4. Tools and Equipment:

While mechanized agriculture has received tremendous support from the government, the poor farmers have not benefited from these advancements in India. Recognizing the problem, the Center has developed many farming tools that could be used by an ordinary farmer and yet increase productivity. These tools include bullock driven cultivators, hand weeders, heavy duty wheeled cultivators, improved seed drills, and improved sickles. In addition, various forms of wheels to be used by potters, carpenters, and blacksmiths have also been invented and are in use.

5. New Industries and Crafts:

The Center of Science for Villages has been a great promoter of various forms of cottage industries to raise the standard of living for thousands of artisans. It has trained people in manufacturing new products like suitcases, carry-bags, lamp shades, soap-cases, hangers, pens, hair-pins, rocks, furniture, etc. In the area of pottery, bio-gas burners, roofing tiles, irrigation pipes, chimneys, lavatory seats, clay water filters, etc. are among the many innovative products that the Center has produced. Various forms of popers by using fibers from banana leaves, coconut, saw dust, and cotton are also in production.

6. Women Technologies:

Based on a survey conducted by the Center of Science for Villages, it identified as many as 200 technologies that could be developed to aid the work of women in the villages. It developed several items and had them made available to hundreds of institutions. Some of these technologies include such innovative tools as a ball bearing pulley which could be easily used by women to fetch water from the wells. It also has a ball bearing chakki (grinding machine) which easily grinds food grains at home. Known as a poor man's refrigerator, the Center has marketed Sheetal-pots (cool clay pots) with a system of evaporation that keeps water cool. In addition such items as water filters, solar baskets, and various types of crockers are produced to aid women in their chores.

7. Science Popularization and Awareness Development:

In order to educate the people about scientific methods and appropriate technologies, the Center has initiated many programs. The most significant is <u>Jana Vigyan Jatha</u> (People's Science Group). Through this organization, in about 3,453 villages in 30 districts programs like art shows, slide shows, street plays, songs, demonstrations, etc. on subjects like water, health, environment, scientific awareness, appropriate technologies, etc. are organized. In addition there is also a Rural Technology Center in place, where short term courses on various skillful technologies are offered. The Center has trained more than 400 trainees in different voluntary organizations all over the country.[6]

This has been a very brief account of the activities that Dr. Devendra Kumar has been involved in since the inception of his center in both the government and various volunteer agencies. Within the Sarvodaya family his work is unique and highly praise-worthy. Due to his achievements in rural development, many foreigners from European and Asian countries are frequently visiting his center and training there to bring the methods of appropriate developments to their respective countries.

Thought:

As a committed Gandhian, Dr. Devendra Kumar believes in the establishment of a classless and casteless society. In order to achieve this goal he believes on focusing on the individual as well as the society. He argues that many religions as well as Marxism have tried to create a classless society, but have failed. In his opinion, "While religion focuses on changing the individual, Marxism wants to change the society. Both have been in conflict with each other, and have failed. Gandhi, on the other hand, focused on the individual as well as the society. In my rural technology, this is what I am trying to do -- change the attitude as well circumstances -- for the creation of a new social order. Call it Ram Raj or Gram Swaraj, the goal is the same."

Devendra Kumar is critical of those Gandhian constructive workers who tend to focus primarily on the village, neglecting the urban centers. In his view, the reality of the urban life is very much here and is not likely to disappear in the near future. He reflects, "The differences between the urban and the rural will disappear when you work on both ends. Often the problems of the rural and the urban centers are the same. They need to be educated to address these problems." His Center of

135

Science for Villages provides an important link between the villagers and the city dwellers, bringing them together to solve some of their problems through appropriate development. He jokingly remarks, "Since I am the middleman trying to bring the two diverse groups together, sometimes I am disliked by both. And yet, I live with the poor and work with the rich and poor alike." He believes that a non-violent and non-exploitative society can emerge when peoples of all economic levels work together.

As a constructive worker, Devendra Kumar has a keen insight into the current problems faced by contemporary Gandhians. He maintains that the present constructive work programs suffer because Gandhians have failed to understand Gandhi's approach to his programs. For him, Gandhi worked on two levels. First, his immediate concern was to fight for the rights of the have-nots. Second, his ultimate concern was to establish a classless society. Vinoba followed the same line of thinking. For example, through Bhoodan-Gramdan, he fought for the rights of the people, but his ultimate goal was to work for the establishment of equality. Devendra Kumar states, "We Gandhians are trapped on the first level of fighting for the rights of the people. The second level seems so remote and far away. Thus Ram Raj eludes us. We have not even begun the work for it. We are not very clear about it. We are struggling with the 'rights' issue." When I asked him whether the Gandhians will ever be successful in realizing the goal of Ram Raj, he pensively responded, "The journey of a thousand miles begins with the first step. We are struggling to take that step." In this context, Devendra Kumar upholds that the true meaning of Satyagraha (a favorite of Gandhians) is not agitation for people's rights but educating them for dynamic change. This is central to his work as he works for Sarvodaya.

In his commentary on the present condition of Gandhian social work, Devendra Kumar is fond of using the analogy of making the curd.[7] He states, "To make the curd you need milk, you need yeast, and you need churning. The milk is the people, the yeast is the Gandhian thought, but the churning requires the active involvement of the people." He regrets that active involvement of the people is not there because Gandhians do not have the support of the masses. Both Gandhi and Vinoba were able to muster people's support for the success of their movements. Contemporary Gandhians do not have that support. This is the problem of credibility that concerns Dr. Devendra Kumar to a great extent. In his opinion, "People have lost faith in Gandhians today because they do not see a united group. They see conflicts, inner fights, and tensions within the leadership. Unless we come together as a joint family, we will not attract people." Dr. Devendra Kumar's sentiments are shared by many Gandhians, but there seems to be no real effort to consolidate the leadership. Most Gandhians are involved in their own projects of development. It is to his credit that Devendra Kumar tried to mediate between Vinoba and J. P. in order to safeguard the split within Sarvodaya. He feels, "Vinoba and J. P. were not against each other. They understood each other. It is the followers of both that exaggerated their differences and exploited them for their own needs."

Devendra Kumar also regrets that Sarvodaya today has lost the support of the media as well as the intellectuals, something that both Gandhi and Vinoba had. He reflects, "Maybe this situation exists because they don't trust each other. The Gandhians feel that the intellectuals and the media have no commitment to the Gandhian vision. The media and the intellectuals, on the other hand, feel that Gandhians are non-progressive and orthodox." As a concerned Gandhian, Devendra Kumar has taken certain positive steps to solve this problem. He has always been in touch with the intellectual community by holding a visiting lecturer's position at the Gandhi Gram University near Madurai, South India. He constantly visits reputable centers of science and technology to keep abreast with the latest technological advancements. At the same time he remains in touch with the Sarvodaya leadership in planning for the future. He serves on various committees that deal with the enhancement of Gandhian constructive works. He considers himself an important link between the Gandhians and the scientific community at large. Many of his technological innovations in the area of rural development are promoted by the Gandhians in the field. His center also serves as a resource center for many constructive workers.

As an exponent of appropriate development, Dr. Devendra Kumar is critical of India's development policies since independence from the British. He feels that India's industrial development, which is based on the western model of economic growth, is not suited for India's needs. He also recognizes that in opposition to this model many have advocated a 'small is beautiful' ideology. During my discussions with him on this issue, Dr. Devendra Kumar stated that his experiments in appropriate technology "are not a reaction or a protest to the other forms of technology." It is meant to be "a correction of the direction in which technology is taking in India." When I probed further, he remarked, "We are interested in helping technology to get on the right path. Therefore, I am not anti-technology. I am scientific and logical and want to 'correct' rather then 'react' to the current mode of

137

technology. For this purpose, I believe I should be in touch with even atomic scientists." As he continues to develop rural technologies, he remains active in organizing and participating in national and international seminars related to the issues of science and technology. When I asked if he were being successful in changing the direction of technology in India, he responded, "I believe the change is brought about by working on a small level. That is the dynamics of change. I am working on a small level, the level of the village, in the hope of making a difference."

On the issue whether the Gandhians should participate in politics or not, Devendra Kumar has his own views. He feels, "To vote or not to vote is an individual choice, and it is up to one's conscience in this matter." Regardless of this personal choice, he believes that politics, politicians, and the political institutions will remain with us. With the Gandhian emphasis on 'decentralization of power,' institutions will change but will not disappear. Thus, Devendra Kumar believes that Sarvodaya should be in dialogue with all levels of political institutions. He states, "I believe that we should establish links with political parties, the parliament, as well as the United Nations. Our goal should be to bring the people together and not to isolate them. I am involved in this process and feel good about it."

In Devendra Kumar we meet a progressive intellectual Gandhian who is beyond the party-politics of Sarvodaya. As a peace-maker within the family of Sarvodaya and outside, he can be viewed as a neo-Gandhian, who defies the image of a stereotypical Gandhian wedded to an orthodox system of Gandhian values. Although he counts himself among the "older generation of Gandhians," he remains young in his thought and action. He is an inspiration for the younger generation who wish to follow in his footsteps.

Endnotes: Chapter VIII

[1] J. C. Kumarappa was an associate of Gandhi, who helped Gandhi in thinking through the process of development and its consequences for India. He attracted many scientists who agreed with the notion of 'appropriate technology' and helped him to design tools for an appropriate rural development.

[2] Nagaland, now a state in Eastern India, sought its statehood in the 1960s after much violent struggle.

[3] For a detailed description of Chambal Valley problem see the chapters on Jai Prakash Narayan and Subba Rao.

[4] For a fuller understanding of the Total Revolution, see the chapter on Jai Prakash Narayan.

[5] Based on the booklet entitled Center of Science for Villages published by Magan Sangrahalaya, Wardha, Maharashtra (no date given).

[6] Ibid., pp. 5-30.

[7] Curd or yogurt.

IX

Experimenting With Trusteeship
Govind Rao Deshpande

In the West, some environmentalists have linked the present ecological crisis to the Biblical injunction of Genesis 1:28 through which God proclaimed Man's dominion over all of creation. Others have pointed out that the issue in the book of Genesis is not of 'dominion' but of 'stewardship.' God established the lordship of Adam over creation as a 'caretaker' of something that belonged to God, not to Adam. Thus, the Bible teaches human responsibility to take care of God's creation rather than to exploit it. The Gandhian concept of 'trusteeship' is like the concept of 'stewardship' through which Gandhi wanted to challenge the capitalistic economic system. He wanted the rich of India not to become sole owners of the capital, but trustees of the capital which could be shared with the poor. The fundamental principle of trusteeship for Gandhi was that the capital belongs to God, humans are given the responsibility to be caretakers for this resource for the benefit of all. The man with whom I was discussing this Gandhian thought was Govind Rao Deshpande, a well known Gandhian in India today, who is experimenting with the concept of trusteeship. "Look around India today," he said, "What do you see?" I let him answer his own question. "The rich are getting richer and the poor are getting poorer. There is exploitation of natural resources, degradation of the environment, and suppression of the have-nots. Does anyone care for the weaker sections of our society?" We both sat in silence for a while.

In 1989 when I was conducting a study-travel seminar for College of Wooster students in India, I went to the Gandhi Peace Foundation in New Delhi to discuss the basic structure of this book with Dr. Radhakrishna, then the secretary of the foundation. During our conversation he pointed to another gentleman sitting quietly across the table, clad in khadi (home spun) clothes. "Why don't you speak

141

with him? He is a veteran Gandhian." For the first time I met <u>Govind Rao Deshpande</u>, who greeted me with a polite '<u>Namaste</u>' and a gentle smile. I had heard about him from various Gandhians but never expected to run into him in Delhi at Radhakrishna's office. It so happened that in 1989 I never got to talk to Govind Rao. He had meetings to attend, and I was busy teaching. In 1992 I returned to the Gandhi Peace Foundation with the intention of staying there for a year, which I did. One day while walking in the hallway of the hostel, where I had occupied a room, I glanced at a room with its door wide open. Seated on the bed, reading a news paper was Govind Rao Deshpande. He had forgotten me, but was willing to grant me an interview. Since we were staying in the same hostel, we met several times to converse over a variety of issues related to Gandhi and his thought. He was most friendly and willing to share his life's experiences. I was impressed by his openness, and what I learned about his life and work was even more impressive. Our subsequent visits followed in 1996 and most recently in 1998.

Life:

Govind Rao Deshpande was born in 1922 in the state of Maharashtra in a family of freedom fighters. His father, who was a lawyer, failed in his law practice because he refused to address the British Judge as "Me Lord." Inspired by the revolutionary thought of B. G. Tilak, a leading nationalist, Rao's father joined the revolutionaries in agitating against the British occupation of India. For the act he was fined heavily (RS. 17,000/-) by the British. He joined the Gandhian movement in 1930, and soon found himself jailed. By the time Govind Rao was in 3rd grade, both his older brother and father were in jail and the family lost all of its property which was confiscated by the authorities. Recalling those years, Govind Rao remembers that "these were difficult years for all of us." He missed his father while he was in jail and spent days longing for the deprived love and affection. "Anyway, that's how Gandhi came into my life, and I began shouting '<u>Gandhiji Ki Jai</u>' (long live Gandhi) in public marches," he recalled. Upon their release from jail, his brother began circulating 'Satyagraha bulletins' hiding them in a yoga magazine he was editing from home. Govind Rao secretly began posting these bulletins here and there around town. He recalled that once, while in school, the director of education who was an Englishman asked him, "What would you do with a million rupees if given to you?" He immediately responded, "I will give one half to Tagore and the other half to Gandhi." The director was taken aback, but his school teachers praised

Rao for his answer. Perhaps this was the beginning of a child's understanding of Gandhi.

In 1934, Govind Rao first met Gandhi at the tender age of 12. He heard that Gandhi was passing through Yeotmal near Wardha on his march to help the harijans. The meeting inspired him to learn more about Satyagraha and the non-violent approach to the freedom struggle. At the age of 15 he read 3 volumes of a book by Pandit Sunder Lal, Bharat Mein Angrezon Ka Raj (The English rule in India). This book, which was eventually banned by the British, influenced Govind Rao's thinking tremendously. He began to lean toward Gandhi even more, and began thinking about the oppression of his country. While in high school, he was instrumental in forming a student union and organizing marches in support of the freedom struggle. By the time he entered Nagpur Christian College, he had instincts toward being a leader. During college years he became interested in history and English. He read the English newspaper, The Times of India, translating the news into the vernacular language for students. He followed events of the war in Europe closely and figured it out that the British were going to be defeated. As he organized strikes and marches, he earned the title of 'College Gandhi' from his teachers.

Govind Rao recalls a momentous meeting he had with the legendary leader, Subhash Chandra Bose, generally known as Netaji (honorable leader). As a zealous young man, he asked Netaji, "What should the students do?" Bose responded, "Read more and study." Rao was particularly impressed by Bose's affectionate nature and kind demeanor. He recalls Netaji's words when he said to the audience, "Aap ki kripa hoti hai jab aap log ate hain" (it is your generosity that you come (to see him))." As a student Rao heeded to Bose's advice and read the works of Tolstoy, Gandhi, and the communist literature. Eventually he walked for eight days to join Gandhi at his ashram at Seva Gram near Wardha in the state of Maharashtra.

"The 1940s were challenging years," recalls Govind Rao. Gandhi had launched the 'Quit-India' movement. Many youths were attracted to Gandhi and came into the movement. There were eruptions of violence here and there, but Gandhi remained firm in his non-violent approach to Satyagraha. As Gandhi organized marches, Govind Rao participated in them, ever remaining fascinated by the Gandhian techniques. However, it was not so much his technique that attracted young Rao, it was Gandhi's insights and his life style. "Gandhi was amazing in practicing what he preached," remembers Govind Rao. He attracted the young and the old alike. They were willing to give up their lives for the cause Gandhi was fighting for. Govind Rao became part of an underground movement to avoid attention of the authorities. However, he was captured and jailed. "In those days so many people were being arrested that going to jail was becoming a lifestyle for some," remarked Govind Rao. He willingly went to jail because he was fighting for swaraj. He was not sure if he understood the deeper meaning of Ram Raj that Gandhi spoke of, but he knew that freedom was the Indians' birth right, and Rao was willing to pay a price for it. "The arrest of Gandhi, and his fasts, had enormous impact on people" remembers Rao. He was amazed how the "illiterate people" were attracted to Gandhi's concerns and responded to him.

In 1944 Govind Rao Deshpande joined the Nai Talim program at Seva Gram Ashram. He was offered RS. 60/- ($2.00) per month, but he insisted that RS. 40/- would be sufficient. "I did not need much money. I wanted to change my lifestyle and continue to practice self-discipline and sacrifice," said Rao, something he still continues to do when he talks about trusteeship. He still wears the homespun (khadi) and continues to work on controlling his desires. His simplicity and gentle but firm persona attracted many youth. He became a leader in Rashtriya Yuvak Sangh (National Youth Organization). This movement was influenced by Gandhian thought, particularly to the idea of 'non-violent resistance.' The youth pledged their support to Gandhi, but also to the nation. Through the life of discipline, courage, and self-sacrifice, the members of this organization mobilized many youth of India for the cause of independence. During this period Govind Rao came in contact with many leaders who were close to Gandhi. He learned a lot from these individuals, but none was so influential as Dada Dharmadhikari. When Rao mentioned Dada's name, I was most curious to hear about him. Anyone studying the Sarvodaya movement cannot escape reading about Dada Dharmadhikari. He was a veteran Gandhian, whose writings, particularly the book, Sarvodaya Darshan (the Sarvodaya Vision), is a classic study on the philosophy of Sarvodaya. At Seva Gram, Govind Rao befriended Dada, who became his mentor. "He was more like a father to me," remarks Rao as his eyes gleam with affection. "He helped me to understand Gandhian thought," said Rao in a tone that revealed respect and reverence.

During the 1940s Govind Rao had several encounters with Gandhi, but one in particular he will never forget. While at Seva Gram, Gandhi once came to the hostel where Rao was the warden. He toured the hostel but stopped at the toilet facilities. He complained that the toilet should be cleaned more thoroughly. He called Govind Rao and wanted to know why the students didn't wash their hands at the roots of the trees. Rao was baffled and remarked to Gandhi, "What will a

144

glass of water do." Gandhi was quick to remark, "Have you ever been to Rajasthan? There, in the desert, for this much water a person risks his life." Govind Rao was speechless. Reflecting on this incident he marveled at how much Gandhi was "One with Reality." When I probed further, he smiled and said, "You see Gandhi did not just care for people, but the whole environment. For him everything was connected, and he wanted us to develop the same attitude." Rao further told me how Gandhi was concerned about conserving our resources. For example, he saved every bit of the pieces of paper to write on or take notes on. He would use old letters and used memo pads to write on so the paper was not wasted. He reminded people that somewhere there was one less tree which had been cut down to make the paper he was writing on. There was another incident. Gandhi once asked Meera Bahin (Madeline Slade) to get him a twig from a Neem tree to chew and use it as a tooth brush. Meera evidently broke a small branch and brought it to Gandhi. Gandhi was polite but upset. He gently reprimanded Meera for wasting a whole branch for a small twig. Incidents like these are reminiscent of Gandhi's attitude toward human responsibility to be stewards of natural resources. The notion of trusteeship emerged out of such concerns.

After having been at Seva Gram Ashram for two years, Govind Rao returned to Nagpur to take care of his ailing brother, who was suffering from tuberculosis. For five to six years he went from one sanitarium to the other nursing his brother. He saw the dawn of independence in 1947. While many youth felt that the work of Gandhi was over as they succeeded in getting independence, Rao realized this was not an end to the journey. He heeded Gandhi's call to continue to struggle for complete swaraj. "He wanted us to work for Gram Swaraj and ultimately Ram Raj," Rao remarked and went on to explain how on the independence day Gandhi was not even in New Delhi to participate in the celebrations. He was walking from village to village in Bengal for communal harmony. It was then that Rao realized that the constructive work program must go on. At the behest of Vinoba Bhave, Govind Rao took to scavenging in the town of Wardha to teach the people about cleanliness. This is something Vinoba wanted to experiment with, and Rao joined in. He recalls how from 6 a.m. till 11:30 a.m. every morning a team of volunteers will go out in the outskirts of Wardha and pick up garbage, including human waste. He grieved over the poverty, unsanitary living conditions, joblessness, and many other problems faced by the masses of India. He realized the magnitude of the problem and the need for a lifetime of dedication to undertake the constructive work programs that Gandhi had proposed. "Through the exercise of scavenging I developed mentally and spiritually," he remembered. He remained optimistic and energetic, believing in the mantra that "someday we shall overcome." He still holds to this motto.

During the initial years of the Bhoodan movement, Govind Rao was not attracted to it. He felt that the movement for land distribution was unnecessary since land was being divided and distributed automatically as it passed from grandfather to the grandchildren and so on. Even though he had known Vinoba and worked with him, he was not convinced that this was a course worth taking. However, his mentor, Dada Dharmadhikari explained to him that Bhoodan was not about dividing land only but about 'joining hearts.' It was about sharing of the ownership of the wealth. He explained to Rao the spiritual significance of Vinoba's movement and its implications for Gram Swaraj and ultimately Ram Raj. In retrospect, Govind Rao is thankful to Dada Dharmadhikari for revealing to him the truth about Bhoodan. Rao not only joined the movement, but became an active participant in Vinoba's pad yatras. He also became a leading member of the Sarva Seva Sangh, the national body to oversee the work of Sarvodaya. When Vinoba came to Maharashtra on his Gramdan march, it was Rao who laid the ground work for Vinoba's activities and marched along with him. "There was a lot of enthusiasm as we walked with Vinoba," recalls Rao, "We really thought that an important revolution was in the making, and the movement was going to bring equality in the masses of India." So, Rao wholeheartedly participated in various pad yatras in Maharashtra, Rajasthan, and Gujarat. He convinced his father, "a man attached to land," to donate a portion of his ancestral land for Bhoodan. Besides working with Vinoba, on his own initiative, he helped in collecting 100,000 acres of land through individual pad yatra. However, towards the end of the movement, when Bihar Dan had been declared and Vinoba retired at Paunar, Rao became party to a controversy within Sarva Seva Sangh regarding the Bhoodan-Gramdan movement. He sided with those leaders who favored dropping Bhoodan-Gramdan from the Sangh's platform. He took this step because he came to the conclusion that the movement was not helping in the cause of Gram Swaraj. The readers will recall that Sarva Seva Sangh did drop this activity from their agenda at the cost of displeasing other members who supported it.

When Sarva Seva Sangh decided to take up the work of Shanti Sena (peace brigade), Govind Rao became an active supporter of the move. The concept of Shanti Sena was given by Gandhi and championed by Vinoba Bhave. Rao, along with other Sarvodaya leaders, began recruiting youth for the work. Their primary focus was the village. As gram sabhas (village assemblies) were being created, the work of Shanti Sena was being encouraged at the same time. The main function of Shanti Sena was to maintain peace and harmony in the villages, and promote non-violence as a method of conflict resolution. During the China-India border dispute in early 1960s, Rao became instrumental in formulating an international wing of the Sena. Along with such veteran Gandhians as Shankar Rao Deo, Narayan Desai, and others, Rao participated in the famous 'Delhi-Peking Freedom March' in 1962. For fourteen months a group of Gandhians marched from Delhi with the intention of reaching Peking and convincing the Chinese to resolve the conflict through peaceful means. Although this struggle failed and the Chinese refused the marchers an entry into China, for Rao, "It was a moral statement, regardless. We made a statement in favor of people to people diplomacy, not government to government diplomacy."

During the Bihar Movement, Govind Rao Deshpande was one of those leaders within the Sarvodaya movement, who sided with Jai Prakash Narayan. Recalling his involvement with J. P's 'Total Revolution', Rao states, "J. P. was a person of deep insight. He understood the importance of saving democracy in India while the prime minister, Indira Gandhi, was suspending civil liberties." Rao himself realized that there can be no Gram Swaraj if democracy is lost. He regrets that Vinoba could not directly participate in J. P.'s movement. He respected Vinoba but felt that "Vinoba was losing touch with the situation on the ground." Rao was among those Sarvodaya leaders who supported J. P. whole-heartedly. On his own volition, Rao in 1970-71 organized Bihar Jan Sanghrsh Sahayata Simiti (Bihar People's Movement Aid Committee). The function of this committee was to mobilize people to support J. P.'s "Bihar Movement." He remembers that he educated "thousands of people" for this task. He would not have done so if he did not agree with the logic of J. P. For Rao, "J. P. realized that the sources of corruption that his Total Revolution was committed to fight was flowing from the center (Delhi) to the bottom (village level). Therefore he opposed Indira Gandhi." When the 'Emergency' was proclaimed, Rao was jailed for fourteen months.

Among the contemporary Gandhians today, Govind Rao Deshpande is well known for his work in the area of promoting the Gandhian concept of 'Trusteeship.' In 1973 he founded 'Trusteeship Foundation,' which was registered as a non-profit organization in 1974. He explains that the goal of the foundation is fourfold:

147

1) It propagates the message of trusteeship. 2) It publishes literature on the subject. 3) It seeks to change the laws on the basis of which various profit making companies are allowed to be formed. 4) It promotes experiments in the practice of trusteeship. He admits that the most difficult challenge for his foundation is convincing the government to change the laws in favor of the trusteeship ideal. "Presently only those companies are allowed to be formed that have ample capital and can show a margin of profit," explains Govind Rao. These laws in India are patterned after British laws. Several efforts to change the law have been a failure. Rao hopes that a time will come when the Indian government will see the wisdom in promoting the concept of trusteeship in business and industry.

When I asked Govind Rao about the experiments that have been done to supplement the notion of trusteeship in business, he cited the examples of those in Europe and one of his own with which he is currently involved with. As far as Eastern Europe is concerned, Rao believes that former Yugoslavia had taken a courageous effort to introduce the concept of 'common ownership' in several industries. According to this concept, which is the same in trusteeship, the owners of the company and the workers were put on the same footing. They became 'partners' in a common enterprise and shared the loss and the profit equally. However, after the break-up of Yugoslavia, one wonders how the innovation is faring. The second example is that of 'Scott Bader Commonwealth Limited' which was founded in 1951 in England. It appears that as a Quaker, Scott was impressed by Gandhi's ideas of non-violence as applied to economics through trusteeship. He was directed to Vinoba and other Gandhians to learn more about trusteeship. Upon his return to England he founded the Commonwealth Co. A detailed report on this venture is given in the book, Humanized Society through Trusteeship, which Govind Rao published in 1973 through his foundation. In a nutshell, the Bader experiment was based on the ideal that capital (resources) belongs to the community and therefore investment of the capital for profit should be managed by the community. In Scott Bader Commonwealth Limited, " Ninety percent of the shares owned by the Commonwealth have been held corporately by the members of the commonwealth. No individual member owns a share and no individual can personally benefit from a sale of the share. They are truly communal shares and if ever the company should be sold, the receipts must go for some charitable purpose."[1] The members agreed to three basic conditions; "(i) To give at least eight hours of voluntary service each year, (ii) not to enter into dual employment, and (iii) to share losses as well as profits."[2] According to Rao, presently there are

148

numerous companies in England which are part of a Common Ownership Movement, spearheaded by Scott Bader's experiment.[3]

Govind Rao's own experiment in India has set an example for companies to follow. In collaboration with the dairy industry of the state of Gujarat, Rao founded People's Trusteeship Packaging Co. It is located near the city of Ahmedabad in Mahesana district. The company has successfully produced quality packaging boxes for Amul Butter, a nationally known company. Despite warnings that his experiment will fail within two years, Rao is proud to say that it has lasted for eight years, and still doing well. He has tried to apply the principles of Trusteeship with remarkable success. For example, the company is based on the fundamental belief that there is no 'ownership' but 'partnership.' There are no bosses, but equal participants in the enterprise. The company adheres to bylaws which allow one vote to one person, not one vote per share. Rao explains that most companies that are founded on the capitalist system allocate voting power based on the amount of shares a person holds. This creates an imbalance of power and affects the decision making process. As a consequence, the self interest of the powerful is guarded at the cost of the powerless. Under Trusteeship, power must be shared equally and everyone involved must feel responsible as a community. "The key to the success of Trusteeship," says Rao, "is the people's participation and a sense of belonging." So far his experiment is working and is proving to be just, non-violent, and profitable.

Govind Rao remains active as a member of the executive board of the Sarva Seva Sangh. In 1995 he was elected as a convener of the National Affairs Committee to study such issues as the state of the Indian nation, the global situation, the political and economic situation, etc. The purpose of the Committee is to advise and better inform the Sarva Seva Sangh for proper action. It is on the recommendation of this committee that in recent years Sarva Seva Sangh has chosen such issues as protest against the multinational companies, protest against the New Economic Policy, and working for Gram Swaraj, as its platform for action. Independent of Sarva Seva Sangh, it has been one of Rao's dreams to establish a Sarvodaya Research Center for the benefit of the lok sevaks. He feels that Sarvodaya workers today have no place to study, refresh their minds, and learn about the latest developments around the world. He had discussed the idea of a study center with Vinoba Bhave, who had blessed the idea. The work for such a center has begun near Pune in the state of Maharashtra. However, due to lack of funds the program has been slow. It is Rao's hope that eventually he would have a

Sarvodaya center equipped with a research library, lodging and boarding facilities, where like minded people will be able to come together periodically to study and to share their knowledge.

As recent as 1998, Rao has taken a keen interest in the water conservation problem for irrigating fields. Near his center in Pune, he is instructing local farmers how to conserve water by growing cash crops near channels where water flows to irrigate their main crops. He has involved the area agronomists to further study the situation and increase productivity. Second, he is concerned about the rise of corruption in all aspects of Indian life. He attributes the problem to "the evils of politics." In order to find a solution to this demoralizing situation, he is attempting to bring some retired justices, teachers, and lawyers together in a dialogue to discuss the national scene. Third, he is working tirelessly toward the establishment of Gram Panchayats. In his view, "The only way to save democracy in India is to ensure the establishment of Gram Panchayats in every village in India." To this end, he travels to different states in India to talk to the villagers and convince them of their rights to solve their own problems and not depend on the state government.

Thought:

As a committed Sarvodaya worker, Govind Rao Deshpande regrets that "since independence we Indians have failed to create a new society." He believes that Gandhi's vision went beyond India's independence from the British. His insistence on Ram Raj was nothing more than the creation of a new society with a just social, political, and economic order. Rao feels that "the failure to do so has perpetuated a society filled with all forms of injustices causing inequality resulting in violence." The new society that Gandhi envisioned had the village at its center, but today, observes Rao, "The metropolis is perceived to be the center." The metropolitan culture is ruled by capitalism which "satisfies human greed, not his need."

Rao asks the question; "In India today, who is suffering the most?" He answers his own question by pointing to poor peasants, craftsmen, the harijans, women, and children. It disturbs him that India tolerates poverty, joblessness, caste based prejudices, mistreatment of women, and exploitation of children. He attributes class and cast disparity, social inequality, and the plight of the poor masses to India's imitation of the west. He firmly believes that had the leaders of the Congress Party listened to Gandhi at the time of independence, India would have avoided the mess that she is in now. Gandhi had over and over insisted that the real India was found in the villages. Instead of focusing on the grass roots development of agriculture and cottage industries, the government went for larger industries. For Rao, the policy was a "selling out to the western model of development." India is reaping the consequences of this mistake. Along with many other Gandhians, Govind Rao is critical of the so called "educated Indians." It pains him that these Indians, steeped in western ideologies, have now become the enemies of the poor. This class, which controls the power structure of the society, is "blissfully ignorant" of what it is doing to India. For Govind Rao, the so called "educated Indians" have failed to understand the real values of the Indian culture. Such ideals as affinity to the land, love for nature, self-control, discipline, and an ascetic lifestyle are beyond the grasp of "modern Indians." Gandhi understood this problem and his fight was a fight to save the Indian culture.

Govind Rao is critical of modern technology which relies on heavy machinery to produce more and more. He is guided by the insight that heavy industries are exploiting "material" resources. He insists that "matter" is limited and will eventually run out. He calls technology "a short lived balloon." Eventually it will be deflated and "then what?" Today, there is a real tension between the desire to consume more and more and the reality of depleting resources. The failure to satisfy our desires in the absence of resources will eventually produce violent behavior. Rao sees this violent struggle already taking place all over the world. In India, those who have been left out of this "modern dream" to have more and more are now demanding their rights. He points to the 'Dalit Movement,' the tribals and other groups which are becoming politically aware. A violent class struggle between the haves and have-nots is inevitable. Rao is not certain as to the magnitude of the revolution which is in the making, but he believes that there is a crisis in India today and incidents of violent conflicts between the rich and the poor are breaking out. Gandhi was quite aware of this conflict, and wanted to address it through the concept of Trusteeship. As we have seen, Govind Rao is taking a keen interest in experimenting with this concept.

For Govind Rao Deshpande, at the center of the notion of 'trusteeship' is the welfare of the 'individual.' It has a holistic view of the 'self' and its development. He contrasts this with the capitalistic understanding of the 'self'. Although, profit driven capitalism promises great prosperity for the individual, in fact it alienates the individual causing much pain and suffering. This is one's alienation from nature, society, and the inner self. The self loses a sense of belonging and there is no growth of personality. Under a capitalistic system, work has become monotonous, and the individual apathetic toward society. The work must provide pleasure and a sense of belonging. In trusteeship, there is no private ownership of the resources. The capital belongs to God, and humans are entrusted to be its caretakers. Consequently, the use of resources is for communal development, not private development. Within trusteeship, capital (resources), organization (corporate personalities), the human factor (workers), and the community at large are all equal. Thus, they participate in the decision making, production, and profit sharing. This creates a sense of belonging, personal growth, and community building.

Rao's thought and actions are informed by his philosophical and religious thinking. He believes that the purpose of human existence is to move toward a peaceful state, and something "noble" in human nature demands that humans reach this state in harmony with others. His understanding of human nature is that "it is basically good." Thus, all humans deserve happiness and want to live in peace. However, due to the lack of proper understanding and selfishness, they enter into conflicts with others. In the realm of economics, he feels, "Trusteeship will bring you to your true nature as God intended you to be." Thus, the practice of trusteeship is not only practical, but essential in the process of self-discovery. Rao feels that Gandhi had this basic insight into "the meaning and purpose of life," and therefore his notion of trusteeship was motivated by his spiritual insights. Rao realizes that the society at large is moving away from religious concerns. However, he firmly believes that, "Sooner or later our own actions will make us see the wisdom of the practice of Trusteeship." As for Gandhi, so for Rao, the economic, social, political, and religious dimensions of life are inter-related. It is the separation and the compartmentalization of various human activities that deter us from seeing the total picture.

In 1992 Govind Rao met with Manmohan Singh, at the time India's Finance Minister, and the architect of the 'New Economic Policy.' Manmohan Singh was concerned at that time about India's depleting foreign exchange. He talked about India's public sector investing with the multinational corporations to earn foreign exchange. Govind Rao talked to him about Trusteeship and prompted him to ask the entire nation to solve the problem. This will pull the entire nation together and the solution it finds will be permanent. Govind Rao regrets that Manmohan Singh favored inviting the multinationals to invest in India. This is what is happening now and India is being held hostage to the wishes of the World Bank and the International Monetary Fund (IMF). Rao does not see this trend as helping India in the long run. He is hopeful that the people of India will see the wisdom in the concept of Trusteeship. If the rich of India give up the ownership of the resources and hold them in a trust for the benefit of all, India would not have to look for outsiders to solve its problems.

Central to Rao's thinking is the concept of freedom. He maintains that in the coming century, humanity must experience three kinds of freedoms. First, the 'freedom from all national boundaries.' In his mind, the world is changing so rapidly that the concept of a nation-state is no longer useful. It creates barriers between people and confines them to a geographical locale. As a believer in Vinoba's Jai Jagat (hail to the world), Rao wants people to drop national identities in favor of a universal humanity. It is his belief that this change will bring unity and eliminate divisions. Second, he calls the 'freedom from ideology.' The defense of an ideology is perceived by him as narrow minded and shortsighted. It is based on the conviction that "my thinking is the best." Such a view is exclusive and encourages the conversion of others to one's point of view. This hinders an individual's freedom to think and choose on one's own, and exercise freedom of the will. Third, he calls for 'freedom from poverty, disease, and oppression.' For Rao, every human being has the right to the basic necessities of life. Today, he feels the cause of poverty and disease is due to the disparity that exists between the rich and the poor. Recalling Gandhi's statement that the world has enough for everyone's need and not everyone's greed, Rao feels that much of the poverty is artificially created. He blames the capitalistic economic system for this condition. Sarvodaya wants to change this system and make people free from the oppression it has perpetuated. Many of the programs that Govind Rao has been involved with are about freeing people from various forms of bondage. For him, working to make the people free is to work for Ram Raj.

Endnotes: Chapter IX

[1] Govind Rao Deshpande, pub., <u>Humanized Society Through Trusteeship</u> (Bombay: Trusteeship Foundation , 1973), p.32.

[2] <u>Ibid</u>., p.33.

[3] Based on an interview with Rao in 1993 at the Gandhi Peace Foundation in New Delhi.

X

Embracing The Tribals
Harivallabh Parikh

It is estimated that approximately 200 different tribal groups, collectively known as <u>adivasis</u> (original inhabitors), live all across the vast land of India. While the British remained oblivious to their existence, many efforts have been made since independence to bring the tribals into the mainstream of Indian life. Although Gandhi expressed concern about their lot, it fell upon his followers to begin serious social work among them. Today several Sarvodaya leaders have well established ashrams that cater to the adivasis needs.[1] Once dependent on the forest for livelihood, many tribals have been forced to take up agriculture for their survival. But, as farmers, they have been exploited by money lenders, forest contractors, landlords, and others. With the rise of technology and the development of city culture all over India, as it became necessary to cut the forests, the plight of the adivasis took a serious turn. Thousands were evicted from their homelands and displaced forever. More recently, the construction of the Sardar Sarovar Dam, commonly known as the Narmada Dam, has raised serious issues about the re-establishment of thousands of adivasis in the state of Gujarat, Madhya Pradesh, and Maharashtra.[2] Those environmentalists who oppose the project are worried that much of the land that would be submerged under the water due to the construction of the dam will not only cause ecological problems, but will drown many villages inhabited by the adivasis. The supporters of the project feel that the tribals can be adequately compensated and comfortably relocated. The matter of relocation is not a simple one. It involves uprooting and re-seeding an entire civilization that is thousands of years old.

During my research in India, I had been most interested in witnessing the process of relocating the tribals. While meeting Gandhians in Gujarat, I was

155

repeatedly asked not to leave the state without visiting the Anand Niketan (the abode of joy) Ashram in the village of Rangpur in the vicinity of the city of Vadodra. Established in 1949, this ashram is located in the heartland of the adivasis, and is actively involved in the relocation program of many tribals. I learned that the area was primarily occupied by the Rathwa and the Bhil tribes. Not knowing what to expect, I boarded a bus at Vadodra for a three hour journey to Rangpur. I was accompanied by an ashram aide, whose language I did not know, making conversation impossible. As the bus made its way to small villages and towns, I was filled with excitement. In a matter of a few hours I was to meet none other than Harivallabh Parikh, about whom I had read a chapter in Mark Shepard's book, Gandhi Today. It was late at night when the bus arrived at an unknown destination. As we got down, I was motioned to stay put by my guide while he disappeared in the darkness of the night. I understood that he was going to arrange for some means of transportation to reach the ashram. Standing on the roadside in complete darkness was not very comforting. I had visions of the Bhils coming out of the bushes with their bows and arrows to kidnap me -- images I had acquired in grade school in India - while reading about the adivasis. The darkness intensified the beauty of the stars and the chill in the air. The guide reappeared and gestured what I understood to mean that the ashram jeep was coming to fetch us. A few minutes later two head lights became visible at a distance piercing through the darkness. A jeep did arrive and we were on our way to the Anand Niketan Ashram.

As the jeep entered the ashram complex, signs of civilization were visible everywhere. The ashram was lit with electricity. About two hundred children were gathered under a shed, and were being entertained by a color television set. In the midst, gently swinging back and forth on a porch swing, was Harivallabh Parikh, affectionately called as 'bhai' (brother) by all who know him. Suddenly I was in the presence of a man who had been trained by Gandhi at the Wardha ashram and had settled in Rangpur in 1949 soon after the death of Gandhi. He welcomed me with a smile. After the ashram children left, we exchanged greetings, and bhai invited me to attend a prayer meeting in a nearby village. By the time we returned to the ashram it was close to midnight. His day had started at 7 a.m.. Suddenly I remembered reading in one of his news letters that sometimes he works sixteen hours a day. I was privy to his activities for the next several memorable days.

156

Life:

Harivallabh Parikh was born in 1924 in the princely state of Pratapgarh in Rajasthan. Since his father was the Diwan (minister) of the state, Hari was raised in a privileged family and was groomed to follow in his father's footsteps. The Maharaja of Pratapgarh was so impressed with his intelligence that he wanted to send him to England for higher education. As fate would have it, instead, Harivallabh found himself in Gandhi's ashram in Wardha. His fascination for Gandhi began at an early age when nationalists like Thakkar Bhappa and Madan Mohan Malaviya came to his father to raise money for Gandhi. His father was impressed with Gandhi's fight for freedom and wanted to help. However, little did he know that the help would include losing his son to Gandhi. It was Malaviya who passed some Gandhian literature to Harivallabh to read. The young man absorbed what he could, but, accompanied by two servants, landed at Gandhi's Wardha ashram in 1938. Having been raised among the nobility, Hari found the ashram life quite difficult. Recalling those days he states, "I did not even know how to wash my own plate, and getting up at 4 a.m. for prayers was most difficult. So I slept." He wrote a letter to Gandhi explaining his problems. He was advised to be patient and discipline himself. The determination paid off. He learned how to spin, along with many ashram chores, and gradually gained mastery on his senses. He became adept in Satyagraha philosophy and began to see himself as a Gandhian freedom fighter.

During his early years at the Seva Gram Ashram, Harivallabh was attracted to Dr. J. C. Kumarappa, the well known economist. As Kumarappa worked with Gandhi on Science for Village Industries, Harivallabh worked with the scientist-economist for the development of the villages. To this end he traveled in many villages to learn about their problems and to teach them about Swaraj. In 1942 when Gandhi launched the Quit-India Movement, Harivallabh took an active part in various Satyagrahas. As an individual Satyagrahi, he was targeted by the police for initiating subversive activities against the Raj. During this period he was sent to Tamil Nadu to teach Hindi as the national language. However, through the teaching of the language, he was sowing seeds of nationalism and mobilizing people for the fight for independence. In 1942 he spent some time at Gujarat Vidya Pitha in order to learn Gujarati, but also traveled to Sindh and in Karachi particularly he joined the underground movement to overthrow the British. Meanwhile he continued to teach spinning to the villagers. He recalls, "Gandhi was saying that he will win swaraj through the charkha. So we spun Khadi with passion." Eventually the police caught up with Parikh, and he was imprisoned. He spent nearly one year in jail as a freedom fighter.

During the Cripps Mission to India, many nationalists were released from jail. Harivallabh was freed in 1944, and returned to Wardha to participate in Gandhi's training program for comprehensive village development. In 1946, Gandhi sent him to assist in the work of the Kasturba Memorial Trust. He was to train women in education as well as various Gandhian constructive work programs. He remained with the Trust for two years. Once again Harivallabh was forced into the village life. Since his work was primarily with the village women, he organized many welfare programs for the uplift of the poor villagers. During the independence in 1947, Harivallabh rejoiced over the occasion, but his heart was with Gandhi who had gone to Noakhali in Bengal to pacify the Hindu-Muslim riots. Reflecting on this period, he states, "We knew that independence had come, but the real freedom was far away. We all felt that there was so much work to be done for social justice." When the Hindu-Muslim riots broke out after the partition and the creation of Pakistan, Harivallabh volunteered to help the relief-work of Lady Mountbatten. The work had many facets. It involved taking care of victims, providing food, shelter, medical care, and safety. It also involved holding meetings with many Hindu and Muslim leaders and convincing them to maintain communal harmony. Harivallabh recalls, "I saved many Muslim lives as they moved from place to place." It was during this time that Hari was seriously injured. While helping the victims of the communal riots on a railway station, he was struck on his neck from behind. The blow nearly paralyzed him, but he was saved. The effects of this injury are still visible as he must tie a handkerchief on his head to apply pressure on the back of his neck. This head dress has now become his trademark, and he is hardly seen in public without this head covering.

On January 22, Gandhi sent a circular letter to all Gandhian workers to meet him in Seva Gram ashram on Feb. 4th. Gandhi was to launch an experiment in what he called 'Moh Nivaran' (freedom from sensual desires), along with his close associates. The meeting never took place since Gandhi was assassinated on January 31st. At the loss of his guru as the nation mourned, Harivallabh contemplated his fate. He wanted to return to Rajasthan, but then the secretary of Congress, Balwant Ray Mehta asked him to go to Gujarat. Not knowing exactly what he would do in Gujarat, his fate brought him to a Gandhian Sarvodaya worker, Manubhai Patel. The veteran Gandhian had been concerned with the problems of educating the adivasis in Gujarat. He took Hari to the village of Konsindara, and a meeting was arranged between the adivasis and Harivallabh. He heard about their plight. He remembers, "I took a map of the area in my hand and traveled the radius of 200 kilometers studying the situation. I heard stories about their exploitation and wanted to help." After a close scrutiny he decided to work in the village of Rangpur, the present site of his Anand Niketan Ashram. Initially he was not welcomed. He was seen as an outsider who could not be trusted. For two days, Harivallabh with his wife camped under a tree. They started singing bhajans (devotional songs), offering prayers, and cleaning children. After two days, the suspicion that Hari and his wife Prabha were agents of their oppressors (money lenders and landlords) began to lift like a fog. They were invited into a house for temporary stay. As Harivallabh gained their confidence, a hut was constructed for him and his wife, which he named, Anand Niketan (abode of joy). What follows is a remarkable history of achievements of his life long work among the tribals.

As Harivallabh surveyed the area of his work, he realized that the aborigines settled in the neighboring villages were plagued with many problems. Commonly identifiable problems were: poverty, illiteracy, alcoholism, lawlessness, slavery to the landlords, deforestation, land erosion, drought, etc. Initially he decided to fight the problems on the following fronts:

1) To stop exploitation and addiction.

2) To eradicate corruption and harassment.

3) To increase food production.

4) To control population growth.

5) To eradicate illiteracy.[3]

Harivallabh started a door to door campaign to meet the tribals and gain their confidence. He went to their fields and worked along with them, bathed their children, educated the women and the children, told them stories, met the oppressive landlords, and started mediating between rival groups to find peaceful solutions to their conflicts. Within a short time Harivallabh began to be addressed as 'bhai' (brother) by the people. Impressed by his social work, the collector of Baroda (now Vadodra) donated 11 acres of land to 'bhai' for his ashram. The site chosen was located on the banks of the Heran river.

Early on in his work, Harivallabh Parikh recognized that the tribal society was beset by many feuds. He recalls, "I was astonished over the frequency with which murders took place. They fought over money, women, land, and often over trivial things. Alcoholism was a major contributing factor." The local police did not help much because adivasis lawlessness had become a source of income for them.

159

This led to further corruption. Furthermore, often the police sided with the rich and the resourceful. Harivallabh had an idea. He decided to become an arbitrator between the parties in conflict. This was the genesis of the concept of Lok Adalat (People's Court),[4] for which Harivallabh has received international fame. According to the scheme, both parties are required to appear in an open court before village leaders, relatives, friends and neighbors. A four-man jury is appointed, two by each side. There are no advocates, but both parties are allowed to speak for themselves. The jury hears both disputants and their witnesses, and delivers a verdict which is binding. Harivallabh acts as a judge, but relies on the jury for their wisdom. Speaking of the judgment, bhai states, "The principle of mutual consent is applied before the judgment is written down and signed by all concerned." Often the court ends with the ceremonial partaking of sweets as a sign of goodwill and reconciliation.

When 'bhai' moved to Rangpur village, the entire area was thickly forested. The adivasis were mostly dependent on the forest for their survival. However, after W.W II, the topography of the land started changing rapidly as the forests began to be cut. According to one estimation, "The deforestation was so drastic that the tribals, who traditionally depended upon the forest to survive, turned to agriculture. On the one hand, nature has played its role in deforestation by soil erosion and the land has become barren and open. On the other hand, the proponents of deforestation, usually business interests and corrupt government officials were a fierce lobby to resist to. The inevitable result was that once deforestation of a particular area had begun, it did not stop."[5] To his horror, Hari discovered that before the merger of the princely states (to which Rangpur area belonged) to the Indian Union, the king had already given permission to many contractors to cut the trees. Not only that, up until the 1960s the government continued to give new contracts to various co-operative bodies to fell trees despite serious opposition from Harivallabh and the adivasis. Discouraged by the government policy, 'bhai' began organizing Satyagraha against the contractors. Through his efforts an agreement was reached and one contractor, Ismalbhai agreed to delay the cutting until the government provided him other trees that were to be cut in preparation for the building of two dams. In this manner, Harivallabh was able to save 7,000 precious trees for the area. In the 1980s the Gujarat government attempted to force many tribals to leave their homeland without providing them with decent compensation. Bhai organized 1,200 tribals and fought their case in the High Court and won. Soon he launched 'Jangal Lagao, Jungal Bachao' (grow forest, save forest) movement and mobilized nearly 84 villages for this task. By 1980, he was able to persuade the government to join forces with the tribals to save the forest. This resulted in the growth of an aggressive afforestation program.

From the beginning, Harivallabh was committed to educating tribal children. Thus, he started a residential school at his ashram. The program was named, Life Education School. Here, 'bhai' implemented the Gandhian concept of Nai Talim (Basic Education). The goal was to educate children, but also teach them skills that could be used for self-sufficiency. Therefore, the education also included learning special trades that are used for the running of the ashram. Such programs as dairy maintenance, bio-gas plant maintenance and nursery maintenance are integrated into the curriculum. Advance students are given vocational training in farming, repairing machinery, and handling farming equipment. For the elderly, an adult education scheme was initiated under the National Adult Education Program. The villagers were asked to nominate their own teachers who underwent training at the ashram. Over the years many adult education centers have been opened throughout the area.

Soon after the ashram work began, the villagers were faced with water shortages of serious nature. Harivallabh immediately got busy in devising a plan to conserve water. The government had many plans to create dams on local rivers, but the work was proceeding on a very slow scale. Through the help of the tribals, he began constructing Bandharas (small dams) over streams and rivers. For the areas where such dams were not practical, he introduced small lift pumps with the help of the government, banks, and donor agencies. More than a few hundred pumps are currently running providing much needed water for the farmers. Agriculture in the villages has taken a new meaning since Anand Niketan Ashram started providing assistance to the tribals. The farmers are not only encouraged to grow food but also experiment with raising many nurseries, which helps in the afforestation program. The Ashram works as a hub for various agriculture related activities. As the word spread to neighboring villages, the work has been expanded beyond Gujarat state. Today, due to the efforts of 'bhai', food production has been raised to a satisfactory level. The self-sufficiency scheme has led to the construction of many bio-gas plants. Easy to maintain, these units are run on animal dung and water mixture. The waste is recycled in the form of natural fertilizer giving nourishment to the crops. The gas produced is used for the purpose of cooking and light. The bio-gas project has contributed immensely in saving the trees. In the villages where such plants are installed, the people are no longer a threat in destroying the forest for their fuel and fodder. Several villages have already been converted to the bio-gas concept where every family owns a bio-gas plant. Harivallabh calls these villages, 'Urja villages' (Energy self-sufficient villages).

It was not very long after 'bhai' settled in this area that he realized how much the tribals were harassed by money lenders, merchants and landlords. In some cases, the landlords who employed the tribals were also the money lenders. Like in many other parts of India where a Zamindar (land lord) controlled the lives of his tillers, so among the adivasis the problem was acute. For generations, many farmers were in debt and could never hope to repay the loans they had taken. Whatever they cultivated was collected by the landlords in repayment for the money they owed. Harivallabh divested a lot of his energy in touring many villages studying the problem and looking for solutions. The answer came in the form of establishing co-operatives. Naturally, the merchants threatened the tribals not to form co-operatives and harassed them to the point of committing violence against them. In 1951, the Ashram helped form a multipurpose co-operative society. Over the years many co-operatives have been formed to help the villagers.

Harivallabh's involvement with constructing Bandharas (small dams) and water lift projects have already been mentioned. He has also taken a keen interest in the construction of many dams by the government. For some he had to organize Satyagrahas with the tribals to stop the construction or to negotiate a proper settlement. For others he had to convince the tribals to let the project be finished since they were meant to irrigate their land. This involvement began in the 1960s and is continuing until the present time. For example, in the 1960s when the villagers took violent action against the construction of a dam on Rami river at Geleswar village, 'bhai' mediated a settlement, the dam was constructed, and the people are still benefiting from its use. In the 1970s, a Satyagraha was launched by the tribals against the construction of a dam near Karajwant village, and the work was stopped. In 1974 when Sukhi Dam was to be constructed, several villages were going to be submerged. Bhai mediated a settlement through which the tribals were properly evacuated and given land to resettle. In 1976, Karjan Dam project, which was primarily for the benefit of the people, was allowed to be completed after the government gave in to the tribals demand of cash and land compensation. Likewise in the case of Hiran Dam, the government had to look into alternative sites because, under the leadership of 'bhai', the tribals opposed the construction of the dam. Presently, Harivallabh is deeply involved in the controversy over the construction of Narmada Dam.[6]

Harivallabh's international involvement began in 1951 when he was asked to chair the Indian chapter of SERVAS by Bob Luitweiler of USA. Servas (an Esperanto word meaning 'serve') was started in Europe in the 1940s as was Resister's Movement. Its goal is to promote peace and understanding among people of different nations through traveling and serving. Impressed by the Gandhian activities of 'bhai', he was asked to start an India chapter, which he did with some reluctance. However, under his auspices many foreign travelers soon began traveling to India. His ashram has hosted many such visitors over the years. In connection with Servas conferences, 'bhai' has visited many countries of Europe, Asia, Australia, Switzerland, Canada, and U. S. A. Through his influence, the Gandhian philosophy of Sarvodaya has been introduced to many visitors abroad as well as in India.[7] Harivallabh's work for Servas was greatly appreciated both by Vinoba Bhave and Jai Prakash Narayan. In 1958 when Vinoba visited the ashram, he was asked to inaugurate an 'Open Door House' for Servas, which he agreed to do. At that occasion he praised the philosophy of Seva (welfare) and compared Servas' vision with his own. In his speech he used the phrase "Vasudev Kutumb Kam" (the whole world is my family). Certainly, his slogan of 'Jai Jagat' (hail to the world) carries the similar sentiments. In 1961 when J. P. visited Anand Niketan, he named Rangpur village as a "Global Village," where people from different parts of the world as well as India could come, work, and study.[8]

One of Harivallabh's most ambitious projects has been the care for thousands of tribals who have been affected by the Sardar Sarovar Project (or Narmada Dam Project). Since Prime Minister Jawaharlal Nehru laid the foundation stone for the construction of the Dam in 1961, a steady stream of Project Affected People (PAPs) began pouring into the Anand Niketan Ashram. Bhai, who supported the construction of the Dam and called it Anivarya Anist (necessary evil), was faced with the challenge of how to keep the tribals whose land was about to be submerged under water. Estimated to be 455 feet high with the canal stretch of 460 kilometers, the Dam will irrigate 1,800,000 hectares, and provide drinking water for thousands of villages in the states of Gujarat and Rajasthan. Furthermore, Madhya Pradesh and Maharashtra will receive the upstream water for irrigation and electricity. The PAPs whose land would be submerged are estimated to be 30,142 families from the tri-state area.[9] As Harivallabh listened to the woes of the people, he formed Lok Sangharsh and Lok Sahkar Samitis (People's Struggle and Cooperation Committees) to negotiate with proper authorities. He also studied the project and realized that the construction of the dam will benefit a large number of people. Hence, he has been involved in relocating thousands of families from the flood prone areas to new relocation sites. He has also persuaded the government to provide the PAPs adequate money, land, and other resources.

A brief summary of Harivallabh's constructive work programs at Anand Niketan Ashram gives us some insight into his life and work. The following statistics are useful to illustrate the current status of many of his activities:

The Peoples Court activity is as impressive as ever. To the date, 70,000 disputes have been settled. The idea of Lok Adalat has spread across the country and the government is trying to promote the model.[10] The afforestation program has achieved new heights. Bhai states, "To date, over 22.5 million trees have been planted, and are being raised and protected by our societies. Now we are planting more fruit trees, bamboo, teak, acacia, etc. We have established a network of nurseries to raise 2.5 million additional saplings for this year."[11] The Life Education School is flourishing as new buildings have been added to accommodate the students. Currently there are approximately 120 boys and 45 girls enrolled in the program. Since its inception, thousands of tribal children have gone through the ashram education. For Harivallabh, "the essence of education for peace, human rights, universal brotherhood and democracy lies in inculcating a respect for the views of others in the minds of our younger generation."[12] He is attempting to impart these values to his children. Water conservation remains a top priority. Up until now 37 Bandharas (small dams) and 125 lift irrigation projects have been completed, and more will be installed in the near future. The number of bio-gas plants continues to increase. At present approximately 798 households have their own bio-gas plants for energy needs. The Ashram continues to be the resource for bio-gas technology. In order to make the tribals self-sufficient economically, new co-operatives have been formed in different areas. At present 180 co-operatives are functioning in 350 villages. Local banks have been involved to make this program a success. As a consequence the harassment from the merchants has been practically wiped out. Servas work continues to gain momentum. Through the efforts of 'bhai' in 1992, the Indian Servas had 700 members. Today, the membership has increased to 826. The Ashram continues to host foreign visitors from many lands. It has been estimated that within the past five decades, approximately 5,000 foreigners have come to Anand Niketan. The ashram has hosted several international conferences, and 'bhai' has been consistently invited as a spokesman for Gandhian ideals in many countries. On the Narmada Dam front, Harivallabh has been an ardent supporter for its construction. However, he firmly believes that the dam should not be constructed at the cost of tribal culture, property, and other resources. Thus, he has been aggressively involved in the resettlement program. So far he has been instrumental in resettling 9,000 families in his area. He has consistently fought with the government for the proper compensation for the PAPs. Anand Niketan itself has constructed 500 permanent houses for them.

Besides major programs discussed above, 'bhai' has been responsible for a variety of projects dealing with family planning, eye clinics, women's upliftment, cattle camps, relief work, freedom from addiction to alcoholism, training unemployed youth, sanitation programs, etc. It is not an accident that in 1994, one of the national magazines in India, 'The Week', named him "Man of the Year."

During my recent visit to the Ashram in 1998, Harivallabh enthusiastically described his most recent activities in favor of the tribal uplift. While the forest conservation program had been progressing well, Harivallabh has now established 104 Forest Growers Cooperative Societies to protect more than 12,000 hectares of forest land. He has introduced a scheme under which a team of native villagers patrols the forest all night long to see that no damage is done to the trees by thieves. This program has been introduced into 73 villages. It is hoped that other villages will follow suit. His water conservation plan of building small dams (Bandharas) has now been adopted by the government of Gujarat in the hope of providing water for more villages. Impressed by his program of settling PAPs (Project Affected People), the government has asked him to help the state to build more low income housing. Currently, 5,000 more houses are under consideration for construction. He is in the process of forming Tomato Cooperatives and Sugar Cane Cooperatives to help the farmers who grow the crops. Most significantly, his staff has grown to 285, who work quite independently of him and only come to him for advice "as a last resort."

Thought:

Harivallabh Parikh believes that the world today is seeking Vikalpa (alternatives) to many problems produced by the worldview most nations hold. We live in a society where violence in all spheres dominates our lives, may it be social, economic, religious, or political. There is a general unrest and a search for change. He states, "When we look for alternatives, we are faced with Gandhi. We may deny him, but we cannot ignore him." For him, Gandhi gave us a blue print for the creation of a non-violent society, and this is what 'bhai' is trying to achieve through his Rangpur Ashram.

When I asked 'bhai' about the present state of Gandhian organizations and what they are trying to achieve in India, he offered the following ideas. He stated that there were about 32,000 Gandhian organizations, big and small, that have been working in India for a long time. What they have been able to achieve is difficult to measure. However, it is an indication that "Gandhi is alive and well." He believes, "Today we have taken the work of Gandhi beyond Gandhi. All kinds of constructive workers are now engaged in a variety of social work programs." However, he fears that the Gandhian family is "like a house divided against itself." He is particularly concerned that the 1974 split between Vinoba and J. P. hurt the movement tremendously. The division between the two great leaders got national attention. People lost faith in Gandhians, but not Gandhi. When I asked 'bhai', "Why do you think that the Gandhian movement was suffering from the lack of co-operation among the leaders?" He responded by stating, "Perhaps they became victims of their own egos. Or, perhaps, they heeded to Gandhi's advice to follow one's own conscience. Also, now there are various types of Gandhians. Some are intellectuals, some social workers, some politicians. Some are operating as NGOs (Non-governmental Organizations) and receive help from the Indian government or foreign donor agencies to run their projects."

Harivallabh thinks that today the younger generation is getting interested in Gandhian philosophy. Many educated youth, who are frustrated with the conditions in India, are coming to work as social workers, engineers, and teachers in the villages. Among these are some who are frustrated at the lack of opportunities to find jobs. So some are turning Marxist Naxalites, and others seeking opportunities to work in Gandhian ashrams. Bhai is hopeful about the youth involvement. He has organized several youth camps in his area to initiate young people into Sarvodaya ideology. He has also been an invited guest at other camps to speak about his work at Anand Niketan. While I was visiting Anand Niketan, he introduced me to several youth volunteers, who had come from bigger cities to work for his ashram. As far as attracting the youth is concerned, Harivallabh believes, "We should not try to sell Gandhi to them as if they have to become contractors for Gandhi. We have to change our approach to how to present Gandhi to them." He feels that there are many young talented social workers across India, who are doing the work of Gandhi without mentioning the name of Gandhi. I concur with 'bhai's' observation since I have interviewed several such young people in India. Many of them feel that the name of Gandhi has been misused by so many selfish people (some within the movement) that it has lost its respectability. In fact, in many instances, mentioning

166

Gandhi produces negative reactions. Therefore, says Harivallabh, "When talking to the youth I talk about humanity, truthfulness, love, and other ideals, not Gandhi." What is Gandhi, he rhetorically asks? "Gandhi is helping humanity," he answers the question.

Bhai has the view that after the death of Gandhi, there were generally two types of Gandhians whom he called 'Faith Gandhians' and 'Head Gandhians' respectively. He holds that 'Faith Gandhians' are the ones who came to villages and started their constructive work. For them, reading Gandhi's autobiography was enough for inspiration. 'Head Gandhians' entered into politics and took on other professions. However, Harivallabh feels that today the village needs both 'Faith Gandhians' and 'Head Gandhians'. "Faith alone is not enough," he proclaims, "We need intellectuals who can apply the new 'know-how' to their work." However, he insists that a distinction has to be made between 'Sarvodaya' and 'development.' "We don't want development, we need Sarvodaya," he explains. 'Development' is based on the capitalist worldview which calls for more production for larger consumption. It uses the latest technology, but dehumanizes production by minimizing human power. It promises a better life, but at the expense of many spiritual values. Sarvodaya is not against technology, but wants technology with a human face. Bhai learned many of these ideas from J. C. Kumarappa, who advised Gandhi on such issues.

When one visits Anand Niketan, it is quite evident that Harivallabh is an environmentally conscious Gandhian. He once told me, "I think the most significant issue for Gandhians should be the environment." When I pursued the issue, he indicated how ecological crises were affecting the political, economic and social developments all over the world. He was concerned that many Asian countries blame the West for polluting the environment, but are not willing to take responsibilities of cleaning up their respective countries. He pointed out the degrading condition of India's rivers, forests, and the trash-infested landscape. "... the industrial countries are responsible for the acid rains and ozone depletion", says bhai, "but there are other forms of pollutants for which we are all responsible." Therefore, Anand Niketan has implemented many programs where environmental concerns are the primary focus. On the issue of population control, while most Gandhians still promote abstinence as the Gandhian way, Harivallabh has organized many camps to educate people about birth control methods. He has also promoted surgical methods in clinics and camps. His efforts in the areas of afforestation and bio-gas use have already been mentioned. He is quick to point out that all of his new homes built to resettle the PAPs use environmentally safe materials. His support for many dams is motivated by the need to provide clean drinking water (as well as for irrigation) for thousands of families. He expresses concern for the fact that a great number of diseases in India are water related which can be controlled by taking care of water resources. In his ashram school, bhai uses a curriculum that in environmentally conscious. He feels that children must be instructed if we are going to change the future.

On the issue of Sarvodaya's involvement in politics, Harivallabh's views are clear. He explains, "Gandhians should not run for political offices, but have an impact on politicians." Due to his efforts, one of his tribal young men was appointed to Rajya Sabha (India's Upper House in the parliament). He does not hide the fact that he has helped Marxists as well as others to be elected in provincial elections. He supported these candidates because he believes that a moral leadership is important.

Harivallabh believes that when Gandhi was speaking of Ram Raj, he was speaking about making the village self-sufficient. This is what bhai is trying to achieve through Anand Niketan. The process involves "decentralization of power." He does not think that the "center" (Federal Power) will ever go away, but its effects can be minimized. "If there is a center of power within the Indian family system," says bhai, "then how can we eliminate the 'center' altogether." However, as a family must share power and responsibilities, so should other political, social, religion, and industrial institutions. Then, Harivallabh supports 'Panchayat Raj.' He has mentioned to many politicians that if they want the villages to become self-sufficient, they must hand over the power to the villages. He hopes that the Indian law makers will see the wisdom of a decentralized institutional structure.

Bhai is a great believer in the importance of moral values. He states, "Change comes from within. Gandhi taught us that without moral change there will be no effective social change. Vinoba Bhave's Bhoodan was an example of moral change. Both were spiritual beings." Because he is committed to spirituality, he holds regular Bhajan Mandalis (religious song gatherings) among the tribals. At these occasions, talks on moral issues are also given. He also believes that morality is not necessarily taught through religious services, rather through actions. He has instituted a program which promotes spiritual development of a person through conscious change. Those who meet the criteria of being "good" are given the title of Bhagat (a religiously dedicated person). This individual becomes a model for the community.

168

Over the years, Harivallabh Parikh has devised a most comprehensive approach of Sarvodaya for the benefit of the tribals in Gujarat. However, his impact is not limited to Gujarat. He has become a national as well as an international figure, whose advice is sought by many.

Endnotes: Chapter X

[1] This author visited three such ashrams in three different states; Vanvasi Seva ashram in U. P., Samanvaya Ashram in Bihar, and Anant Niketan Ashram in Gujarat. Many other ashrams all over India are working for the uplift of the tribals. According to Mr. Chinchalkar of Bharatiya Adim Jati Sevak Sangh in New Delhi, it was Thakkar Bappa of Gujarat who persuaded Gandhi to include adivasis in his constructive work program, which he did.

[2] Narmada Dam, when completed, will be the biggest Dam ever constructed in India. The project began in 1947, and proposed to have been finished by the year 2000.

[3] The information provided in the brochure 'Anand Niketan Ashram'', published by the secretary, Anand Niketan Ashram, 1992.

[4] For examples of the cases solved by the 'People's Court', see Mark Shepard's, Gandhi Today, Ch. 5

[5] Afforestation - A Mass Movement of the People, a booklet written by David C. Thomas, 1992 (No Publisher) pp. 3,4.

[6] For a detailed information on dams, see Our Involvement For Dams by Harivallabh Parikh, published by the secretary, Anand Niketan Ashram, 1994

[7] For a detailed information on Servas, see 41 years of Indian Servas 1951-1992 by David C. Thomas. The booklet available at Anand Niketan Ashram.

[8] Ibid., pp. 3-4.

[9] Harshkant Vora, Not Submergence But Emergence, Rangpur: Anand Niketan Publishers, 1991, p.4

[10] Information obtained from Anand Niketan Newsletter (Jan 1994-April 1995) and supplemented by the 1997 report obtained at the Ashram in 1998.

[11] Ibid.

[12] Ibid.

XI

Fighting for the Peasants
Jagannathan

After the monsoon soaks the dry land, parched with intense heat of the summer, a new lease on life is released all over India. The rainy cool breeze, that sweeps across the countryside, is a messenger of new hope for yet another season of an abundant harvest for the peasants. But the joy and enthusiasm of cultivating the land is limited for a few. A large segment of the Indian peasantry relies on the good will of the landlords who control the lives of the tillers. While traveling in the state of Tamil Nadu in 1993, I was painfully made aware of the agonies of the peasants by a Gandhian constructive worker, who was none other than Jagannathan. As we sat on the verandah of a modest house, which was built of the stones that he himself towed for days between 4 a.m. and 8 a.m. in 1947, he recalled Gandhi's last interview given to one of his biographers, Louis Fischer, toward the end of his life. When Louis Fischer asked Gandhi what was the next problem he was going to confront, evidently Gandhi replied," the land problem." When asked, how was he going to solve it, "the land owners will have to voluntarily give up the land, if they don't, the landless will occupy it," came the reply. "Wouldn't there be a civil war then?", persisted Louis Fischer. Gandhi paused and said, "yes, but the land must go to the poor." Having finished the story, Jagannathan looked deeply into my eyes. I could sense his concerns, disappointment, and hope when he said, "You know the land must go to the landless, this is an all-India problem." Jagannathan is a veteran Gandhian, who has committed his life to tackle the land problem for the sake of the landless peasants.

I first met with Jagannathan in 1980 on the campus of Gandhi museum in Madurai, South India. I was sent to him by Dick Keithahn, an American Lutheran Missionary to India, and a dedicated Gandhian worker in his own right.[1] I had

171

written to Jagannathan from New Jersey, and he agreed to meet me. His first comment on meeting me was, "you don't look American." I guess, with a last name like Harris, he had been anticipating meeting a white American. It was Jagannathan's smile and his sense of humor that captivated me. His friendly demeanor, unassuming manner, and frankness will impress anyone. This is the man who had been with Gandhi, worked with Vinoba, associated with J. P., and had been the president of the Sarva Seva Sangh. I thought I would be lucky if he gave me a few minutes of his time to ask him something about Sarvodaya. Instead, he offered me a place to live for a few days, personally accompanied me to visit Gandhi Gram,[2] and arranged for me to tour several of the villages where he had launched an impressive program to distribute the land to the landless peasants under the organization, ASSEFA.[3]

Over the years I have been drawn to Jagannathan and visited him several times to understand Sarvodaya. One of the most memorable meetings occurred in 1985. I had been staying at Vinoba's ashram in Paunar, when I learned that Jagannathan was coming there for a short visit. After his evening talk to the sisters at the Ashram, I asked him for time to discuss his work in Tamil Nadu. He said, "I am walking tomorrow morning at 4 a.m. to Duttapur to visit a Gandhian leper asylum, why not join me?" This was one invitation I did not want to refuse. So, the next morning we walked a few kilometers and talked about the problem of the landless, and the solutions that he was working on. I was to meet him again in 1986 at a conference in New Delhi, but it was in 1993 that we had a chance to spend some time together. I met him at a conference in Seva Gram, Wardha, and wanted to do an intensive interview. I approached him at his cottage where he was hanging some clothes to dry. He held my hand and said, "for a deep conversation about my life, we should be in the environment in which I live. Why don't you come to Madurai, and my temporary home near Gandhi Gram." I agreed. Subsequently, I met him with his family on January 16, 1993 and stayed for a few days. Other meetings followed in 1996 and 1997.

After the evening meal which we ate sitting on the floor in a traditional Indian fashion, Jagannathan and I retreated to the verandah. I suddenly realized why he wanted to be in his environment to talk about his life. Next to us was the empty room where his dear friend Dick Keithahn used to stay. It was Rev. Keithahn's love for God that had attracted Jagannathan immensely. Together they had worked for years on various projects along Gandhian lines. We were sitting adjacent to the campus of Gandhi Gram, a rural university based on Gandhian

172

ideals that Jagannathan helped found. Not too far from here was the Kodi road on which stood a sugar mill. Jagannathan had led a Satyagraha against this mill, which was oppressing the poor. There was a long history of personal transformation, leading to the call of Gandhi to join him in the Indian struggle for independence, participating in Quit-India campaign, going to jail, working with Vinoba for Bhoodan, working with J. P., being arrested during the emergency, and so on. This was indeed his environment. As he settled in his chair to begin talking, I glanced at his face. At the age of 83 he seemed strong, relaxed, and energetic. I was about to hear his story.

Life:

Jagannathan was born in the state of Tamil Nadu in 1912. His family came from the line of tillers (Kisans), who worked for a landlord (Raja). His father had very little education, but dreamed of going abroad to Burma, which he managed. He joined many Chittayars (a caste) who had migrated to Burma in the hope of making their fortune. Due to his father's success in Burma, Jagannathan lived a good life. By the time he entered high school, Jagannathan was attracted to drama, and became an accomplished actor. He entered the American College in Madurai with the liking for a western style education. He wore western clothes, a hat, and boots. He took to tennis and was hailed at the college as someone who was, "tip top and fashionable."

During the second year in college a major change occurred in Jagannathan's life. His soul was tormented as he read the writings of Vivekananda and Mahatma Gandhi. Both inspired him toward self-discipline, simplicity, and concern for the poor of India. He shaved his head and discarded his fashionable clothing. While his mother was shocked and wept over his uncanny behavior, Jagannathan felt that a change had come over him. In 1932 Gandhi gave a call to the youth of India to give their time for India's struggle for independence. "The air was filled with excitement," recalled Jagannathan. Many youth throughout India left their studies and pledged to follow Gandhi. As Satyagrahas were being organized all over India, Jagannathan joined in. The reality of oppression hit home when he was beaten and the head injuries left him delirious. During this time he corresponded with Gandhi and wanted to join him at his Ashram. Gandhi advised him to stay in Tamil Nadu and go to the Thiruchangodu Ashram of Raja Gopalachari, where Gandhi's own son, Devadas was to join. Since there was no reply from Raja, Jagannathan came to Christakula (Family of Christ) Ashram in Triputur, where he assumed the

173

educational and medical work among the peasants. Soon he befriended a Lutheran missionary, Richard Keithahn, who had a lasting influence on Jagannathan's life. They ended up working together for 40 years.

He was so impressed with Keithahn's religious life and faith in God that he hoped to nurture the same faith in his own life. Even though Rev. Keithahn was a Christian missionary, it did not matter to Jagannathan. His belief in the equality of all religions helped him appreciate the faith his new friend was expressing. Rev. Keithahn was not an ordinary preacher. He had been influenced by Gandhi and found no difference in the teachings of Jesus about helping the poor, and what Gandhi was attempting to do in India. When the Lutheran church questioned his involvement with the Gandhian movement, Dick left the church and joined Sarvodaya. Together, Jagannathan and Keithahn pledged to help the poor and they went around as mendicants, begging for their daily food. During this period, Jagannathan recalls meeting Khagawa, the legendary Christian leader from Japan, who visited Bangalore in 1934. Under Khagawa's inspiration, Jagannathan intensified his social activities by organizing camps, taking up the cause of the poor, and mobilizing students to help in this effort.

By the time Gandhi launched the 'Quit-India' movement in 1942, Jagannathan had returned to Madurai, Tamil Nadu a year earlier to start a Gandhian student home in Madurai. The early years of the Quit-India movement were full of violence. Dissatisfied countrymen had taken to agitation, disrupting communications, damaging properties, and burning and looting. Jagannathan, under the guidance of Gandhi struggled to turn the situation around to promote a non-violent Satyagraha. He was arrested three times during the Quit-India movement. By this time Jagannathan had become a confirmed Gandhian social worker. On one hand he was involved in India's struggle for freedom, and on the other he was becoming a constructive worker to lay the foundation for a new society. He became actively involved in Harijan Sevak Sangh (Servants of the Untouchables Organization). Under this organization he established several schools and hostels for the untouchables in Tamil Nadu. As he immersed himself in the cause of the underprivileged classes of the Indian society, it dawned on him that the untouchability was mainly due to economic reasons. It was an "economic slavery" from which the poor of India needed to be freed.

During his struggle to find a solution to the problems of the poor, he came in contact with Dr. Soundram Ramachandran, the Nai Talim (New Education) expert at Gandhi's Ashram in Seva Gram. She wrote to Jagannathan to join him in

174

starting a Gandhian school at Chunalpatti, where a piece of land had been donated. Together with Jagannathan and Dick Keithahn, Dr. Ramachandran started the well known Gandhi Gram in 1947. "It was meant to be like the Tolstoy farm that Gandhi started in South Africa", recalled Jagannathan. Gradually it became an educational center, and stands today as a rural institution based on Gandhian ideals. During the same year, he organized a major Satyagraha against the owners of the sugar mill located on Kodi road. The problem arose when Kisans (tillers) were being forced to sell their sugar cane to the mill instead of making their own jagiri (sugar cubes) as they had been doing for generations. They were being forced to give up this trade under the pretext that they had no license to make jagiri, only the sugar mill had the right to do that. As the police came to confiscate the equipment the people were using to make the jagiri, the women tied themselves along with their children to the wheels of the police trucks. Jagannathan himself laid down in front of the vehicles to block their entrance to the premises. Many Satyagrahis were arrested and taken to jails. The next day, the State Ministers arrived from Madras and a meeting was arranged among the state officials, village leaders, and the Sarvodaya workers. As a result, the government lifted the ban it had imposed on making the jagiri. The Satyagraha was a success. Recalling the spontaneous act of the village women to hug the wheels of the police vehicles in protest, Jagannathan states, "The action to hug the wheels took place long before the <u>Chipko</u> (Hug the Trees) movement was born in the Himalayas."

In 1948, all India Basic Education Conference was being held in Coimbatore, and Gandhi's protégé, Vinoba Bhave was to attend. During the conference, Jagannathan handed Vinoba a note which stated, "take up the land problem." "Vinoba did not respond" remembers Jagannathan, "but he was compelled to take up the problem as early as 1948." When the Bhoodan movement was born in 1951, Jagannathan went to Vinoba, leaving his wife Krishnammal behind, whom he had married from an untouchable caste in 1950. During those initial years of Bhoodan, Jagannathan walked with Vinoba in U.P. and collected land. "There was a great excitement in the movement that Vinoba had taken up the land problem which Gandhi wanted to tackle, but was assassinated," recalls Jagannathan. After a year Vinoba asked him to return to Tamil Nadu and organize the Bhoodan March. Jagannathan protested that he was a small person; there were bigger leaders working back home. On this Vinoba retorted," in <u>Ramayana</u>, even the small squirrels helped <u>Rama</u> to conquer <u>Ravana</u>." It is interesting to note that Jagannathan did not remain a small squirrel; he became the <u>Hanuman</u>, as he is called today by many Sarvodaya workers.[4] He returned to Tamil Nadu and got busy with his social work activities, organizing the Harijans and the peasants. He did the ground work in planning Bhoodan routes, organizing leadership, training workers, and setting up camps, which facilitated Vinoba's Padyatra for Bhoodan in Tamil Nadu in 1956. By now Jagannathan had become a confirmed Sarvodaya worker, and a trusted lieutenant of Vinoba.[5]

On the eve of Vinoba's departure from Tamil Nadu, the land problem had not been completely solved. In 1957 Jagannathan began a Satyagraha against the absentee landlords. Many such landlords were holding a large track of land, but were not cultivating it. They were exploiting the tillers by employing their services but not paying them enough in money or kind. Not only that, even those landlords who had donated their land to Bhoodan were still occupying it, and not letting it be distributed among the landless, who had been granted that land. Jagannathan approached Vinoba on this issue, who advised, "leave it, what can we do," recalled Jagannathan. Against Vinoba's advice, he began a calculated Satyagraha against these landlords. He succeeded in getting a large portion of the land distributed to the landless.

During the same period he organized a Satyagraha against the Meenakshi temple land in Madurai, which was occupied and cultivated by an influential landlord. In this struggle he was joined by Keithahn and Gora. Meenakshi temple owned several acres of land on which many peasants worked. However, the profits were enjoyed by the big landlord. Jagannathan succeeded in freeing the land from the landlord's control and handing it over to the poor.

In 1968 when several harijans were burned to death by the landlords in Venmani, Jagannathan organized peace marches in protest, mobilizing thousands of Harijans. A major Satyagraha was organized by him in 1969-70 against the Valivalum temple in Tanjore. Here the temple had illegally occupied a large amount of land to be cultivated by Harijans for the temple's profit. The Mahant (head priest) of the temple had created 18 trusts to keep control over the land. Again Jagannathan approached Vinoba, who responded by saying, "leave it, you are banging your head against the rock," remembers Jagannathan. He was not ready to give up. After he explained to Vinoba that he was not fighting the temple but a corrupt landlord, he was given a "green light" by Vinoba to go ahead. He began a 14 day fast against this atrocity, and J. P. came to visit him in his anguish. In 1972 Jagannathan launched yet another Satyagraha against the Mahant of the Bodh Gaya temple. "The Mahart of Bodh Gaya was most cruel, worst than the one in Tamil Nadu," states

Jagannathan. "He controlled 30,000 acres of land and 50 temples while the peasants were eating boiled leaves to satisfy their hunger." Jagannathan came to Bodh Gaya at the request of J. P., who supported his struggle against the temple.

During the Bihar Movement (1970s) while J. P. was active in Patna, Bihar, Jagannathan stayed in Bodh Gaya. His task was to train and supply Satyagrahis to J. P's movement in Patna. As Indira Gandhi declared the state of emergency, many Sarvodaya leaders were arrested and imprisoned. Jagannathan was severely beaten, arrested, and jailed for eighteen months. His wife, Krishnammal was also arrested, but escaped and found her way back to Tamil Nadu. Having spent sometime in Gaya and Baxar Jails, Jagannathan was transferred to Madras Jail at his family's request. He recalled how during this period of his life he joined J. P's 'Total Revolution', while Vinoba was against it. To his disappointment, Vinoba refused to bless the J. P. Movement, and many Sarvodaya leaders, including Jagannathan felt abandoned by Vinoba. Jagannathan sent his "notebook" to Vinoba which recorded the events of the Bihar Movement in detail. "Even though Vinoba kept the book for a long time, he did not act in favor of his recommendation." Since that time, Jagannathan's relationship with Vinoba became strained, but his respect for him did not diminish.

Upon his release from the prison, Jagannathan plunged into his social work activities to help the landless peasants. On one occasion he met Giovanni Ermiglia, a representative of <u>Movimento Sviluppo E Pace of Torino</u>, who had been touring India to find ways to help in solving the problem of poverty. In 1978, both Jagannathan and Ermiglia founded an organization called ASSEFA (Association for Sarva Seva Farms). Within the Sarvodaya community, ASSEFA received high praise and support. Many saw it as a continuation of the work of Bhoodan because Jagannathan began the work of settling many harijans on the land received during the Bhoodan movement. In its early stages, Sarva Seva Sangh blessed this movement and lent its support. However, gradually ASSEFA emerged as an independent organization as Sarva Seva Sangh dropped the issue of land from its platform. The work of ASSEFA spread to other states beyond Tamil Nadu and thousands of acres of land was distributed to the harijans. Not only that, ASSEFA developed a sophisticated plan to help the landless to settle, cultivate, and eventually own their own land. Their statistics are quite impressive and warrant serious attention. In 1980, Jagannathan along with his wife began another organization named LAFTI (Land for the Tiller Inc.), which is currently headed by his wife, Krishnammal. This movement not only persuades landlords to donate a portion of their land for the poor, but also purchases land from them on a low cost to be distributed. Once the landless are settled on these lands, they are encouraged to learn other skills in running various cottage industries besides cultivating the land.[6]

Jagannathan has always perceived himself as a custodian of Gandhi's legacy. This legacy has a long history of organized satyagrahas to fight the injustices done against the poor. When I visited him in 1996 at the Vinoba Ashram in Kuthur (Nagai Quaid-e-Milleth District) in Tamil Nadu, Jagannathan had removed himself from ASSEFA and launched a people's movement called Tamil Nadu Gram Swaraj Movement. In 1991, he resigned as the Chairman of ASSEFA because he felt that under the younger leadership, ASSEFA was no longer a revolutionary movement. It was taking the shape of a Development Organization. As such, they were seeking cooperation with the government and other money lending agencies. Under these circumstances, Jagannathan felt constraint to oppose the government policies if they went against the people. Thus, he decided to focus his energies to mobilize a people's movement at the grass root level. In 1991, he organized a mass Satyagraha against the making and selling of cheap alcohol in Tamil Nadu. Many women were organized under the Gram Swaraj Movement to launch this Satyagraha. In 1992, he brought together 10,000 people to march against the multinational companies. This was a major effort on his part to raise the consciousness of the people in the South about India's New Economic Policy, which he opposes.

In 1992, Jagannathan conceived of Gram Swarajya Padayatra (Foot March for Village Self Rule) in the region of Nagai Quaid-e-Milleth District of Tamil Nadu, where most of LAFTI's operations are spread out in the hundreds of villages. As he put it, "The aim was to spread the message of Gram Swaraj, true freedom for the villages, with one month to be spent touring each of the twelve taluks or blocks in the overall distribution". In December of 1993, the twelfth month of the journey, he arrived at Sirkali block. It was here that he heard the woes of the people regarding the Prawn industry owned by the multinational companies and the havoc it was causing to people's lives. Jagannathan was dismayed to learn how the prawn fisheries were purchasing fertile land, creating unemployment, draining the ground water for their prawn tanks, causing salination of the soil and the drinking water supplies, polluting the earth and the atmosphere with their affluent and waste. In the process this new industry was not only destroying the local ecosystem but also the way of life of the local agricultural and fishing communities. Jagannathan decided to halt his march and mobilize the people for a

178

Satyagraha against the Prawn Aqua-Culture. At the time, Jagannathan had no idea how long the struggle will be, and what it would take to achieve success against the powerful multinational companies.

The problem turned out to be much bigger than anticipated. Known as 'Blue Revolution', the prawn cultivation is one of the largest projects undertaken by the government of India to earn foreign exchange. The environmental damage caused by this industry has been reported in such countries as Bangladesh, Taiwan, Philippines, Indonesia and Thailand.[7]

According to Jagannathan, "India is its latest victim." The justification for the promotion of this industry has normally been "the removal of protein deficiency among rural communities by increasing productivity beyond those obtained in marine ecosystem. However, the ecological and economic impacts of the Blue Revolution indicate that such aqua-culture projects have actually aggravated the poverty of fishing and farming families."[8] The irony is that the products of this industry are exported to foreign countries and virtually nothing reaches the poor as protein supplement. Moreover, their fertile land (used for the cultivation of rice) is sold to be converted into the tanks, which are filled with sea water to grow the prawns. The destruction caused by this form of aqua-culture is manifold. The eastern coast of Andhra and Tamil Nadu are cyclone and flood prone. The destruction of coastal vegetation (trees and rice fields) to make room for the prawn tanks (which are dug up to 6' into the ground where rice paddy are grown), destroys the buffer zone against the damaging wind, increasing flooding. The salination of ground water occurs due to the seepage from the tanks which spoil the drinking water. The flushing of the effluents and wastes back into the sea kills the marine life, effecting the lives of the fishermen. Most importantly, the land becomes foul and unfit for rice cultivation. The list goes on.

In 1994, Jagannathan along with the fellow workers of LAFTI started a non-violent Satyagraha against the prawn companies.[9] The police, who had been paid off by the companies arrested the Satyagrahis and more than three thousand men and women were charged with criminal cases. About 120 village leaders were thrown into jails. Several LAFTI workers were beaten and had a narrow escape. The agents of prawn companies set fire to the houses of the people in the middle of the night at Thennampattiam Village and drove the people out.[10] However, with prayers, fasts, and marches, the Satyagraha continued. In 1995 the State government of Tamil Nadu passed an Act, known as 'Tamil Nadu Agriculture Act 6 of 1995'. Since the Act did not forcefully condemn the act of the Prawn

179

Companies, Jagannathan filed a case in the Supreme Court. The Supreme Court appointed a team of scientists drawn from NEERI (National Environmental and Engineering Research Institute) in Delhi. Upon their recommendation, the Supreme Court gave a remarkable judgment on Dec. 11, 1996 stating that all the prawn farms in India should be closed by the end of March 1997, except the scientific and improved traditional farms. The Central Govt. (according to Jagannathan), instead of protecting the victims, introduced the 'Agricultural Authority Bill' in an attempt to stall the Supreme Court decision.[11] In protest, Jagannathan began a fast in Delhi at Gandhi's grave site. On May 14, 1997, the Agriculture Minister came to visit Jagannathan to assure that the Parliament will take no decision on the issue in the summer session, and that he will personally tour the coastal areas to decide the matter.[12]

In the midst of court battles, several Prawn Companies are continuing to expand their operations. In protest, Jagannathan continues to plan new satyagrahas despite the threats of the police and the company's musclemen. While the struggle continues, Jagannathan has been recognized nationally for his remarkable work. In 1996 he and his wife were awarded the prestigious Bhagwan Mahaveer Foundation Award for their work among the poor, and also nominated for Right Livelihood Award. While continuing to lead a Satyagraha against the Prawn Aqua-Culture, Jagannathan's most recent venture is the establishment of the Gram Swaraj Kendra (The Center of Gram Swaraj) at Workers Home at Gandhigram University campus near Madurai. Here he wishes to train the youth in the ideology of Gram Swaraj.

Thought:

Jagannathan firmly believes that Gandhi's vision of establishing Ram Raj can only be achieved by working for Gram Swaraj (independence of the village). And, Gram Swaraj will not happen unless the land problem is resolved. He holds that the real India is found in the thousands of villages. Gandhi wanted to see them as republics, autonomous in running their own affairs. Today their fate is decided by the Central Government, which controls the power, and resources. Jagannathan laments that Vinoba Bhave left the land issue after the <u>Bihar Dan</u>. After Vinoba, even Sarva Seva Sangh did not make the land issue as their priority. Perhaps it felt that since the states were legalizing Bhoodan Boards as agencies to oversee the distribution of Bhoodan land, their was not much that SSS could do. For Jagannathan this was a mistake. The government can never bring about Gram Swaraj, because their policies favor urban development. It is for the reason that

180

independently of SSS, Jagannathan launched his own land distribution and development program first through ASSEFA and then LAFTI.

In his thinking, Jagannathan makes a sharp distinction between Development and Ram Raj. He claims that many Gandhian organizations in India today have fallen pray to the temptation of development in the name of progress. Under development, many government and non-government organizations are focusing on economic development, industrialization, urbanization etc. Ram Raj on the other hand is a spiritual concept which focuses on self-discipline, sacrifice, non-violence, reduction of desires etc. Furthermore, for Jagannathan, "The development mentality" does not have the spirit of Satyagraha. Many Gandhian constructive workers have lost this dimension of Gandhi." After Gandhi, Jagannathan found the spirit of Satyagraha in J. P.. One basic element in Satyagraha for J. P., according to Jagannathan, was "non-violent confrontation." From J. P., Jagannathan learned to become a revolutionary. Now, he holds that a revolution requires the movement through four stages; "organization, education, construction, and confrontation." As a constructive worker, he spent his entire life in organizing, educating, and constructing. Now, more than before, he is involved in confronting, whether it is the government, landlords, or the multinationals. This is the primary reason for him for stepping down from the chairmanship of ASSEFA, an organization he founded, and work for Satyagraha.

Jagannathan considers "decentralized economy" as a cure for many of the world's problems. Both communism and capitalism followed "centralized economy" of one form or another. "As communism collapsed, capitalism will collapse also." Gandhian economics can be an alternative if we see the wisdom in decentralizing power in the economic, political, and social spheres. In the case of India, Jagannathan wishes for the villages to draw their own Five Year's Plan than to follow a plan drawn by the central government. If, the villages are to control their own economic future, "I would push for Gram udyog (village industry)" maintains Jagannathan. In this regard he firmly holds that the technology should be in the hands of the villages, not some capitalist industrialist, who squeezes the village to make a profit. Therefore, today he is opposing the multinationals who will do nothing short of exploiting the masses and impose an economic slavery. Jagannathan grieves that today many villagers suffer form chronic poverty, bonded labor, malnutrition, and decease. These are land related problems. The economic independence will come when the land is handed over to those who cultivate it.

181

This is what Gandhi wanted to do, and this is what Jagannathan is struggling to achieve.

Endnotes: Chapter XI

[1] Keithahn's life story is told in his book, Pilgrimage in India (Madras: The Christian Literature Society), 1973.

[2] Gandhi Gram is a rural Gandhian institution, deemed to be a university near Madurai, Tamil Nadu.

[3] ASSEFA (Association for Sarva Seva Farms) initially launched in the state of Tamil Nadu in 1969 with the help of Movimento Sviluppo E Pace, Torino, Italy.

[4] Hanuman, half monkey and half human legendary figure found in the epic Ramayana, and is known for his devotion to Rama and his strength.

[5] Jagannathan's son, Dr. Bhoonikumar (with ASSEFA) told this author that in the presence of Vinoba, Jagannathan always sat straight and alert as a soldier.

[6] For details on the work of LAFTI, see the chapter on Krishnammal.

[7] Vandana Shiva, 'Social and Environmental Impact of Aquaculture' in Jagganathan, People's Appeal to Government for Total Ban On Prawn Farm (Kuthur : Vinoba Ashram, 1994), p.17.

[8] Ibid., p.17.

[9] Some of the companies active in the area are; BISMI, BASK, Magna, Spencer, Swarna Mathsya, Aqua Farm, and Ramakrishna Marine Foods.

[10] In 1996 this author personally toured the village and saw the burnt houses and talked with the victims.

[11] The information given to this author in a letter by Jagannathan dated Aug. 15, 1997.

[12] Ibid.

XII

Parenting the Landless
Krishnammal

While traveling in the state of Tamil Nadu, one cannot miss the lush green rice fields that adorn the countryside along the Eastern Coast. Known as the bread-basket of Tamil Nadu, it commands a serious attention from state officials, landlords and cultivators alike. Over the years this area has been the center of major conflicts and peasant uprisings. The most infamous incident occurred in 1968 when at the village of Khilvenmani, 44 Harijan women and children were burnt to death when supporters of an influential landlord set ablaze a house where these unfortunate souls had taken shelter. Today, a reconstructed building stands as a monument in memory of those who lost their lives at the very spot where the incident occurred. Decorated with the insignia of the sickle and a hammer, it is a constant reminder of the fact that the local communist party manages the monument and lets its presence be known among the people who live there. In January of 1993 when I visited the sight, I interviewed a young communist leader of the village. With a determined face and virtually no smile he stated, "we will never let this happen again." Later when I asked my Gandhian host, who had arranged this trip for me to the village, about the problems in this area, I was invited to tour many other villages and "see for myself". My host was Krishnammal, who in these parts is known as 'the mother of the landless' among the peasants.

Krishnammal, in her late 60s, is a symbol of love, patience, hope, and strength. Decorated as Padmasiri in 1989 by the government of India for her work among the untouchable peasants in Tamil Nadu, an honor reserved for a few civilians, she is an unassuming down-to-earth woman of small stature. When I asked her about her simplicity and easy going mannerisms, she said, "I guess I never forgot my roots. I was born in an untouchable family, and I work and live

185

among them now." The conversations I had with Krishnammal lasted for several days as we traveled by trains, buses, and a jeep. We visited the homes of some landlords, homes of untouchable cultivators, hamlets of many villages, and centers of a variety of Gandhian activities overseen by Krishnammal's staff. She heads the organization called LAFTI (Land for the Tillers) and supervises nearly 60 workers in the field. For years she traveled from village to village in her district riding on the back of a bicycle, until recently the Christian Aid, impressed by her perseverance, donated her a jeep. On one trip to view the problem of the landless, she brought me to a village named Mudikondan, where she has a base. This is the village where during my visit in 1993, the untouchables were still not permitted entry to the local temple controlled by the Brahmins. The village, I was told, consisted of primarily three groups; the Brahmins, lower Castes, and the untouchables. Most of the landlords were Brahmins. While touring the village we passed through a street which carried the ambiance of a Hollywood movie set.[1] The street was lined with rows of opulent houses which had the aura of mansions. Away from thatched roof mud houses of the peasants, these were the houses of the landlords who owned the rice fields. They had made their money at the cost of the hard labor done by the poor tillers. The problem was clear. Most of the land was owned by the rich, who exploited the lower castes by keeping them totally dependent on the wishes of the landlords. Many peasants were bonded laborers, who had virtually sold their families to the landlords, who provided money for their marriages, burials, and day to day living. The wages were low and the peasants could never repay their benefactors. Thus, they were trapped in the cycles of horrid exploitation. These were Krishnammal's constituents among whom she worked to free them from "a living hell" as one worker put it. This village was not unique. There were hundreds in the same predicament, affecting the lives of millions of low caste members.

Life:

Krishnammal was born in 1926 in a Harijan family in Tamil Nadu. She experienced the discrimination as her community was ostracized by the upper cast Brahmins. Growing up she witnessed the misery of her people, but pledged to help them as she struggled to break out of her suffocating environment. "All the time I used to think why was God allowing this suffering upon us," she recalled as we talked about the life and work. Her mood was reflective but jovial as she curled up in an easy chair and her mind wandered through the pages of the past history. "How did you survive those early years knowing that a whole segment of society

186

did not want you ?" I asked. "Oh, they wanted us, but they wanted us on their own terms. After all Harijans were needed to do their dirty work," she quipped. "Gandhiji tried to change our image, and a lot of changes have taken place, but we have a long way to go," she reflected. "There are thousands of children today who are in the same situation as I was during my childhood. My heart goes out to them," she continued adjusting her posture in the chair. Two days later, I met some of those children in small villages where Krishnammal was helping to educate them. They came in groups to hug her as she gave me a guided tour of the villages. These were the children of rice cultivators who had been freed from the oppression of the land lords, who once controlled their lives. Through LAFTI, Krishnammal had convinced many landlords to sell their land to LAFTI which was later redistributed among the Harijan families. Now these Harijans families own their own plots and have become self-sufficient. For her this was the first step toward Gram Swaraj.

Krishnammal had a very difficult childhood. Her father was very strict with the children and disciplined them with corporal punishment. Since he was not educated, he blamed his poverty and unfortunate lot on the lack of education. Consequently, he pushed his children to study hard, and often deprived them of the company of other friends. In retrospect, Krishnammal is thankful for the disciplined life she lived as a child. She speaks of her mother with fond memories. "My mother was a saint", remarks Krishnammal. After her father died of cancer, the mother had to struggle very hard to feed the family. During the day she was the landless laborer, and during the night she worked with the paddy to separate the rice from the husk. "Sometimes she worked till three or four in the morning, and let us sleep through the night," remembers Krishnammal. Watching her mother's suffering was hard for Krishnammal. "Her life touched me so much that I decided to work for the uplift of women as a youth," she remarked as she wiped her eyes. She realized that to be a peasant woman was hard enough, but to be a Harijan woman was most difficult. Krishnammal decided to become a sanyasin (renunciate) like the convent sisters she used to see. However, she was persuaded by her mother not to take that step.

Reflecting on her youth, she told me how she was adopted by Dr. Soundram Ramachandran, one of the founders of Gandhi Gram, the Rural University outside of Madurai. It was here that she learned about Gandhi and his freedom struggles. Dr. Ramachandran had been a close associate of Gandhi at Seva Gram Ashram and was trained in his vision of Nai Talim (New Education). At Gandhi Gram students came to be educated along Gandhian philosophy of

187

Sarvodaya. Krishnammal recalled how her life was shaped here as she participated in various constructive work programs and attended lectures on Gandhian Thought. Her teachers were visionaries, who wanted to reshape the destiny of India by inculcating in their students certain spiritual values. She was taught to help the underprivileged by raising their self esteem in order that they may help themselves. "One of the problems with the Harijans is that they have no feeling of self-worth. Years of oppression has convinced them that they are nothing. I try to teach them that they are something," she remarked. Teaching self-esteem and self-worth has not been an easy task for Krishnammal. Her approach has been to teach them the sense of responsibility. When LAFTI gives them a piece of land, they have to work with many families and repay LAFTI the cost of the land plus any loan they have taken. Krishnammal tells many success stories where the low caste peasants have achieved total independence by working on the land that LAFTI helped them obtain.

"Why is it important for the Harijans to work the land in these parts, why don't they do something else ?" I naively asked Krishnammal. She smiled and gave me a brief lesson in Harijan culture in Tamil Nadu.[2] "You see the harijans here love to get their hands dirty in the mud. The mud to them is like pudding. They love to touch the soil, work in the muddy water, and grow rice," she remarked. What I discovered was that most cultivators had worked the land for generations. Their identity as a people came from their affinity with the land. Their festivals and celebrations centered around the harvest. They observed the seasonal changes and patterned their life styles around the cycles of nature. The urbanization posed a serious problem for them because it meant replacing their culture and values by which they lived. By no means all Harijans are cultivators, but those who are, want to sustain their life style against many odds. The most serious obstacle is that while they cultivate the land, the land is owned by someone else. While they shed their blood, sweat, and tears in hard labor, someone else reaps the rewards. While they get poorer and poorer someone else gets richer and richer.

A momentous event in the life of young Krishnammal took place when she met Mahatma Gandhi. On Feb. 26, 1946, Gandhi came to Madurai to collect funds for his work for the uplift of Harijans. To her amazement, Dr. Soundram Ramachandran, chose Krishnammal to sit next to Gandhi at an important function, disregarding the hopes of her own relatives. Krishnammal was touched by her principal's affection for her. She spent three memorable days with Gandhi as she, Gandhi, and others around them went about collecting money for the cause of the untouchables. At one occasion Gandhi took her hand as she walked him around a famous Hindu Temple. She participated in a day of fast with Gandhi, which left a lasting impression on her. Meeting Gandhi gave the young Harijan girl a moral boost in her conviction to work for the liberation of the untouchable women.

Krishnammal finished her college education at the American College at Madurai. She was fortunate, she recalls, "because for a Harijan girl to reach that stage was difficult." Many Harijan girls were not so lucky, and Krishnammal was determined to help them when the time came. On July 6, 1950, Krishnammal married Jagannathan, a young man who had come back from Bangalore to set up Harijan hostels in Tamil Nadu. They met in a Gandhian youth camp, and waited for eight years to get married. Jagannathan was a young idealist, who had corresponded with Gandhi, worked with Rev. Kiethahn, and inspired by Vinoba Bhave. Their common goal to improve the conditions of the untouchables brought them together. Krishnammal put two conditions to Jagannathan before they could get married. One, that she would be wed wearing a white sari (traditionally the bride wears the red). Two, she would not wear any ornaments but put a spinning thread (used to make Khadi) around her neck as a symbol of simplicity. Jagannathan not only agreed, but surprised her "by spinning the wedding sari himself while fasting". Their marriage was blessed by the Gandhian constructive workers. As Jagannathan put it to me, she was his "inspiration." Together they plunged into the work of Sarvodaya. Through Jagannathan, Krishnammal was painfully made aware of the plight of the landless not only in Tamil Nadu, but all over India. They decided to join Vinoba's Bhoodan Movement. First, it was Jagannathan who went to Vinoba in 1951 leaving his young bride behind. When Vinoba asked Jagannathan to return to Tamil Nadu, Jagannathan agreed only if he were to be replaced with his wife Krishnammal. As Jagannathan returned to Tamil Nadu, Krishnammal took to traveling with Vinoba in Bihar and Uttar Pradesh.

In 1952, Krishnammal returned to Tamil Nadu to lay the ground work for Vinoba's visit to that state to spread the message of Bhoodan. Krishnammal recalls that she worked hard along with Jagannathan to get land for Vinoba. However, after Vinoba completed his pad yatra, even though thousands of acres were collected in Bhoodan-Gramdan, the land problem was far from being solved. Vinoba's movement made no significant change in the lives of the Harijan cultivators in Tamil Nadu. The most significant contribution that the Bhoodan Movement made was to raise the consciousness of the people regarding the plight of the Harijan peasants. It also generated respect for the Gandhian non-violent approach to solve the problem particularly when the communists in Tamil Nadu (as elsewhere) were bent on following violent means. From Krishnammal's perspective, the Bhoodan Movement was not making much progress "because there was no organized follow-up and a plan to properly redistribute the land among the poor." She recalls how many landlords began reclaiming their land even though they had once donated it.[3] Hence, many rich landlords evicted the poor cultivators from the land they had received under Bhoodan. Of course, there was also the problem of receiving the foul land, which was not fit for cultivation at all. Last, but not least, the Bhoodan movement had lost its revolutionary character as Vinoba lowered his demands by introducing Sulabh dan (easy gift) and Toofan dan (speedy storm gift). Krishnammal loved Vinoba and supported his program throughout 1950s. However, gradually she came to the recognition that something else needed to be done for the landless peasants to improve their lot.

The reader will recall the Khilvenmani village incident of 1968 when 44 Harijan women and children were burnt alive when a major conflict had arisen between a landlord and the peasants who worked for him. Soon after this brutal incident, Krishnammal moved to this area to launch a program of social work. She started a school in the village to educate the young. The villagers were suspicious of the outsiders, but Krishnammal won their confidence through her love. Through the school she began dialoguing with the villagers about their problems. Knowing that Krishnammal herself came from an untouchable caste, they opened themselves to her. With patience, she began assessing the conditions of the Harijans all around this area. Her goal became to give these people some hope for the future. She met the temple priests, the landlords, the communists, and the government officials to discuss the conditions of the poor. "It was difficult to step into a situation," recalled Krishnammal, "where the people did not trust each other and tension filled the air." As she began surveying the area riding on the back of a bicycle, she discovered that the problems were multidimensional:

1. A good portion of the land was owned by large temples, which received an enormous income from rice cultivation.
2. Most of the land was owned by the land lords, who employed Harijan farmers as cheap labor.
3. There was a problem of "absentee landlords." Many landlords were not living in the area but had rented out their properties to others to manage.
4. The wages paid to the cultivators was extremely low.

5. A good number of peasants were "bonded laborers" and owed their lives and their children's lives to the land lords. Since they could never pay off their debts, they were trapped in working for their masters for ever.

6. There was a serious drinking problem among the male cultivators, who sought to drown their problems in liquor.

7. The women were subjected to hard labor, and physical abuse at home.

8. The children had no hope to break away from cycle of poverty, disease, and child labor.

9. The police were often paid off by the landlords and therefore sided with them in the time of conflict.

10. There was a persistent violent conflict between the landlords and the police on one side against the Naxalites and communists, who supposedly were fighting for the harijans on the other side.

In 1969, Gandhi Smarak Nidhi financed Krishnammal to start a school and dig a well in the village where she stayed.[4] Thus began a life time adventure that has brought her joy and sorrow as she struggles to free her people from the exploitation of the rich and powerful. "In those initial years," recalls Krishnammal, "my husband, Jagannathan provided the moral support for me. Often he was the brain behind much of my planning." Jagannathan had already launched a Satyagraha against the temples that owned a lot of land. Krishnammal launched a Satyagraha against the absentee landlords. Reflecting on her strategy, she remembers, "my goal was never to fight against the landlords. I wanted them to co-operate with me to come up with a solution that will prove useful for all of us." Consequently, she made friends with many landlords, government officials, and the communists alike. She worked on creating a mutual trust between the Harijan community and the land owners. For her "this was following the spirit of reconciliation in a Gandhian way." Together with Jagannathan she founded LAFTI (Land for the Tillers), an organization that she heads now with a support staff of about 60 people.

The success to LAFTI did not come easily. Initially the local government officials were not extending a helping hand, and there were no funds. Krishnammal approached the local bank, but failed. "For two months I sat in front of the bank in the hope of attracting the attention of the bank manager," she recalls, "but the manager was reluctant." She noticed that the rich were being granted loans without any problem, but the poor were turned down. Eventually, the bank manager agreed to help her draft a letter to the legal adviser of the bank. The scheme worked, and

Krishnammal got her first loan. With money in hand, she purchased eighty-two acres of the Trust Land which was being sold, and distributed it among the poor peasants. She devised a scheme by which the poor peasants became the owners of the land, but paid to LAFTI from their income. Sooner than expected the loan was paid off. Now other banks began approaching Krishnammal, and offered her loans to purchase other land. She decided to focus on the absentee landlords. She remembers putting a friendly ultimatum before the landlords. She simply said, "donate or sell." It was not easy to convince the land owners, but some began to see her point of view. "I had to touch their hearts," recalls Krishnammal, "they had to be persuaded that helping the poor was a noble thing, and the exploitation of the Harijans must stop." She had several meetings with the owners and the cultivators separately and together. Sometimes she invited the local communists, government officials and constructive workers to dialogue together on various problems. Gradually a climate of mutual understanding and trust was created and peace began to prevail in tension torn areas. The landlords were reluctant to sell because they feared enduring great losses. "The land in this area is so rich that a single acre goes for as much as Rs. 100,000. I was offering them Rs. 10,000 or slightly more," reported Krishnammal. Some began selling to LAFTI and moved out of the area. At the time of writing this story, Krishnammal reports that she has succeeded in sending 120 landlords away from this area, and soon hopes to send another 100 away. However, the fight had not been without problems. Some landlords filed law suites against Krishnammal that she was "cheating them out of money." In due time some cases were settled out of courts, others were withdrawn. As the distributing and resettling process began for the Harijans, they could not be more happier. Krishnammal was hailed as "The Mother of the Landless."

Krishnammal began appealing to the State and Central governments to financially support her work. In 1985, Rajiv Gandhi, then the prime minister of India initiated a massive program to help the Schedule Caste (the Harijans) all over India. Under his auspices an organization called National Schedule Caste Finance Development Corporation (NSFDC) was created and a budget of Rs. 150 crores (1 Crore=10 million) was allocated. Krishnammal began corresponding with the Central government in the hope that they would pay attention to the problems of the Harijans in Tamil Nadu. Eventually, she was called to participate in a conference in New Delhi where 150 officials, who were made in charge to oversee the untouchable problem, had gathered. When her turn came to speak, Krishnammal addressed them by saying, "Give them the land and within three months they can

192

grow their crops and eat." The meeting was cordial but produced no results. The Center referred the matter to the state and one year passed. A year later she received a letter from Madras asking her to meet with the State officials. "They listened to my story" recalled Krishnammal "and agreed to send a high level executive officer to tour her villages." The government wanted to provide all possible comforts for the state official, but Krishnammal protested. "I wanted this man to come and stay with our people so he could really see the conditions and associate with them," remembered Krishnammal. Her wishes were granted. The NSFDC sanctioned Rs. 2 Crores for LAFTI. One Crore was given as subsidy and another as loan. The conditions were that LAFTI will repay the loan within 10 years. The farmers who were lent money, with the help of LAFTI, were able,to make enough profit on rice paddy to save for themselves and pay back the loan. Consequently, LAFTI was showered with praises by both the state and the Central governments. To this date, this organization, under the leadership of Krishnammal, has distributed nearly 10,000 acres of land among the poor farmers. Roughly 2,000 acres of the land was purchased at a low cost from the land owners.

It is about 9 a.m. in the morning and several LAFTI workers have gathered for an organizational meeting. Krishnammal sits on a mat on the floor surrounded by several men and women. Annie Louisa, a middle aged woman from Italy, who had been traveling with us for the past three days and I sit along side the workers as Krishnammal directs the meeting. The meeting turns rough as heated words are exchanged back and forth. Krishnammal bursts into tears as some other women workers do also. Annie Louisa, who has become a close friend of Krishnammal becomes concerned. We don't follow the conversation due to the lack of knowledge of Tamil language. Krishnammal does not lose control of the meeting and at the end a peaceful resolution is reached and there are hugs and greetings. All is well, but Krishnammal is not at peace. Later she explains to Annie and I, "our organization is not free from problems. Right now there are conflicts between the upper caste and the Harijans within my workers." Evidently some upper caste workers feel superior to Harijans and want to dominate them in many ways. The more I talk to Krishnammal, I see her organization (which she calls family) as a microcosm of Caste related problems of what she is determined to solve on a macrocosmic level. Later that evening Annie, Krishnammal and I were driven to a railway station to catch a train for Madras. As her driver bid good-bye, he burst into tears. She hugged him and tried to pacify him as her own son. I wanted to find out what the problem was. Krishnammal, as she held on to the young driver, said to me, "he is crying because he feels sad that the upper caste workers treated us badly in the meeting today. He is a Harijan boy and so am I. He is wondering why must such a condition exist within a Gandhian organization." The train arrived, the driver left us, and I had many questions for "the mother of the landless."

Krishnammal explains that she has to face many problems on various fronts, and the caste discrimination is one of them. Within her organization she has employed both the high and low caste individuals. "They must learn to co-exist and work together if they are going to change the society," she states. She also employs women, many of whom are intimidated by the presence of men. However, for Krishnammal "if we are going to talk about the women's rights to the villagers, we must show them a working model." Then there are the educated trained social workers, who have a different vision for LAFTI. She needs them also, but wants them to learn to deal with uneducated, poor, landless farmers. "You know these degree holders have lofty ideas, but lack practical experience," she remarks. They have a vital role in society, but must be "willing to get their hands dirty." Some times the educated and trained people bring an attitude of superiority and discriminate against the low caste workers. "I want to say that we are all equal. We must work together to bring equality for all people. If we cannot do it within our own organization, how are we going to do it in society?"

In terms of what she has been able to achieve, Krishnammal does not quote statistics. When I pressed her, she offered the following information:
Currently her organization is working with 10,000 families scattered in many villages. She has started a carpentry shop and a masonry training center to train untouchable caste boys. LAFTI is also involved in a mat weaving center where several people work and sell their products. Krishnammal started Apna Bhandar (our own store) to sell various products at a very low cost for the poor villagers. She is now working on establishing a large scale co-operative system to buy and sell goods. She explains that a chronic problem in her villages is "the middle men." They buy from the poor farmers at a low cost and sell to the city vendors at a high cost, pocketing the profit. It is her hope that through the co-operatives, she will empower the peasants to take control of their economic resources. She has an intensive training program for the Harijan youth to start their own work in weaving, masonry, and carpentry. So far approximately 50 people have gone through the training program. She has launched an aggressive campaign to replace many mud houses inhabited by the poor peasants with PAKKA (concrete) dwellings. Several such units have been completed. She has also mobilized women to launch a

Satyagraha against the production of liquor. On one occasion while I was touring several villages with Krishnammal, she pointed to a man at a distance who was carrying a bundle of rice paddy on his head. "See that man," she burst into a loud voice, "he is carrying his day's wages given to him by his landlord in kind (the rice). He will now go and sell this to buy liquor and get drunk, while his family has nothing to eat." I learned that this was a common practice among many poor peasants who drowned their misery in liquor. Krishnammal has organized women to march against the liquor shops, the majority of which are controlled by the state license system. On the one hand the government preaches "leave liquor," and on the other turns around and grants licenses to "produce liquor." "This is a source of revenue for the government," explains Krishnammal, "but it is ruining the lives of my people."

My tour of Tanjore district (now called Nagai Quaid-E-Milleth District) was over and we all parted in Madras. Two days later Krishnammal knocked at my hotel room door. I was excited to see her so soon. "Why did you come to see me, we just said good-bye two days ago," I blurted out. "Oh, I wanted to come by and see if you were all right. You know there was a cholera epidemic in the villages where we had travelled. Several people had died. I just wanted to make sure that you were all right." I gasped for air, and gave her a hug.

Most recently, Krishnammal's LAFTI has joined hands with the Gram Swaraj Movement headed by her husband, Jagannathan. Together they have launched a Satyagraha against the Prawn Farms (Shrimp Industry) owned by several multinational companies in the Quaid-E-Milleth district of Tamil Nadu.[5] Their struggle began in 1993 and is still going on. Their goal is to force the multinationals to stop buying the rich paddy fields, filling them with salt water, and raising shrimps. As a consequence, thousands of peasants, who used to work in rice fields have lost their jobs. Furthermore, when people have opposed the Prawn Farms, their houses have been burnt and they have been forced to evacuate the area. Over the years, due to the Satyagraha against the multinationals, many of LAFTI workers have been beaten, and several thrown in jail. Krishnammal has spent her boundless energy caring for the families who are affected by this serious problem. Her organization is now involved with several law suits in an attempt to solve the problem through the courts.

Thought:

Krishnammal insists that she is not an intellectual, but a social worker. She does not quote Gandhi or Sarvodaya ideology to the people she wants to change. "My life should reflect my beliefs. I am a person of action", she explains. Needless to say that the Gandhian philosophy influenced her deeply in her early years, and continues to inspire her in her work. She married a well known Sarvodaya worker, Jagannathan, and moved about in an "extended Sarvodaya family" all her life. She read Vinoba Bhave and worked in close association with him during the Bhoodan-Gramdan Movement. She participated in J. P.'s Total Revolution Campaign in Bihar. She was arrested for her activities in Bihar as she trained Satyagrahis for J. P.'s movement along with her husband, Jagannathan. However, she escaped from the truck in which the prisoners were being transported, as her captors stopped at a restaurant to have some tea. Her husband, Jagannathan chuckles when he tells the story of her escape. "You know, she left me there in prison and ran away to Tamil Nadu," he recalls. So, how did the Bihar Movement influence her thinking? "I became convinced that freedom is a precious gift," she stated, and went on to explain how even today a large segment of the Harijan society that she works for is not free. "I must work to free them. That is my thinking. That is my hope," she stated. For Krishnammal, Gandhi was not simply fighting for India's freedom from the British, he was fighting for freedom from all forms of injustices and oppression. In her small way she is struggling to free her people from the economic, political, and religious bondage.

"How does the idea of Ram Raj play a role in your thinking about freedom?" I once asked Krishnammal. "Ram Raj and Gram Swaraj are lofty ideals. I believe in them but I don't discuss these ideas with the poor peasants," she responded. "They can understand Gram Swaraj more easily than Ram Raj, so sometimes I talk to them about the freedom of the village," she went on to say. "It is hard for people to grasp Gandhian philosophy," she interjected and proceeded to tell me about an incident. "You know, one day my husband, Jagannathan was discussing Gram Swaraj with our daughter, who is a medical doctor. She got so fed up with his idealism and shouted "go buy it in the market." Exasperated, Jagannathan replied, "you are a doctor, I am a Gandhian social worker. We have nothing in common." So we have discussions like that at home. How can I explain Gram Swaraj to the peasants?" So, she tells them about Ramalinga, a Tamil saint who lived in the Middle Ages. At the age of eleven, Krishnammal learned about Ramalinga's teachings and latched on to one single idea that has proven to be most powerful for her. The idea was that everyone has a "divine light" (Jyoti) inside. One must pray to it, awaken it, and worship it. "In all of my work there has been a divine light," explains Krishnammal. Convinced of its force, she has taught Ramalinga's devotional songs to hundreds and thousands of women in numerous villages. On one occasion, Krishnammal took me to a Harijan house, and we participated in a short worship service which entailed primarily lighting of the candles and singing devotional songs. "I get my energy from Ramalinga, I get my tolerance from Ramalinga, I get my hope from Ramalinga. And this is what I teach to my women in these villages, and they believe in it," went on Krishnammal as she concluded the brief ceremony of awakening the "inner light."

Krishnammal feels very strongly that the women need to be empowered. Thus, all land donated by her through LAFTI to the poor families is registered in the name of the woman in the family. Generally, it is the wife who works the land right along with her husband. This practice has proven to be economically and socially viable. Economically, if a woman owns the land, she is not likely to sell it to pay off loans or to support a drinking habit. Socially, if land belongs to the wife, men tend to stick around and the family stays together. This minimizes many social problems the villagers face. Furthermore, when women feel secure their self-esteem goes up and they become agents of many reforms. Presently, Krishnammal is contemplating organizing thousands of women to launch a Satyagraha against several multinational companies that are selling their products in the villages. The women are also organizing themselves to protest against the liquor shops, and the licensing of the liquor production. Krishnammal believes that through the help of the "inner light" women are empowered and can achieve higher goals.

I confronted Krishnammal with a criticism of her work that I had heard from other Gandhians in India. I told her that in the eyes of some Gandhians, her work was perceived to be non-Gandhian since she was receiving money from some foreign donor agencies as well as from the Indian government. The argument is centered around the notion that Gram Swaraj cannot happen unless the villages are self-supportive. Krishnammal dismisses the charge as superficial. As far as receiving money from the government is concerned, she feels that the funds are allocated to help the poor, and must be used by the poor. "It is their money and it should be spent on their welfare. There is nothing wrong with it," she claims. As to the funds coming from abroad, she feels no objection. "There are donor agencies who wish to support our projects because they are helping the poor," she claims, "and there is nothing wrong with it." She sees the outside help as "seed money" to get the peasants started, and eventually become independent, which they do. They return all government loans earlier than expected, which is a great accomplishment.

Unperturbed by the criticisms of her work, Krishnammal is a commanding voice in the state of Tamil Nadu for the rights of the poor untouchables. She moves among the government officials in Delhi and the peasants in Tamil Nadu with remarkable ease and poise. She is contented that after years of struggle her work is recognized by the officials on the state and national level. Still, she feels that her mission is far from over. "Until my last breath, I will work for the poor," she proclaims.

Endnotes: Chapter XII

[1] The village visited was Modikondan.

[2] Jagannathan's life and thought are treated in Ch. XI.

[3] Evidently reclaiming the land which many landlords had donated to Bhoodan was a common phenomenon. The problem was widespread and several Gandhians are still dealing with it.

[4] Gandhi Smarak Nidhi, based in Delhi, is the main Gandhian organization that coordinates the Sarvodaya Constructive Work programs.

[5] For details on 'Prawn Satyagraha' see the chapter on Jagannathan (Ch. XI).

XIII

Schooling the Revolutionaries for Peace
Narayan Desai

When Jai Prakash Narayan gave a call for Total Revolution during the Bihar Movement (1974), many Sarvodaya leaders responded to his invitation. Their goal was to launch a program of reform that would affect all aspects of life. There was a Satyagraha against corruption from the top to the bottom in the government and other agencies created to serve the people. Since it challenged the Prime Minister of India, and labeled her government as 'corrupt', Vinoba called it a 'negative Satyagraha' and advised his followers to stay away from the Total Revolution. The conflict between J. P. and Vinoba on this issue has been discussed elsewhere.[1] Here, my purpose is to focus on the life and thought of one man, who had been called 'the right hand of J. P.' during the years that J. P. led the movement to transform India along Gandhian lines. He is none other than Narayan Desai, the founder of the Institute for Total Revolution in Vidchi, Gujarat.

I first met Narayan Desai in April of 1985 when I attended the annual meetings of the Sarva Seva Sangh in Jai Prakash Nagar, a small village near the town of Balia. I had waded across a portion of the river to come to this village, where the Sarvodaya family had gathered. When I approached Narayan for a conversation, he invited me to join him in his regular after-dinner walk that he so much enjoys. We walked on a narrow path in the fields, back and forth, as he expounded on the Gandhian vision of Sarvodaya. I felt privileged to be invited to share his evening walk with him unaware that the ritual was going to be repeated nearly eight years later at his ashram in Vidchi. During my 1992-93 wandering all over India to interview the living Gandhians, I decided to revisit Narayan Desai. The visit nearly turned out to be a disaster as a hand grenade exploded on the railway platform at Surat, killing several people. It happened to a train that I was supposed to be boarding, but had changed my mind, and left a day earlier. In retrospect, the agony of trying to reach Vidchi via bus turned out to be a blessing compared to the travesty I would have had to face had I traveled a day later by the ill-fated train. I reached Narayan Desai's residence (his ashram) unannounced on March 11, 1993. The family (his daughter and son-in-law) were about to have their lunch, and I was graciously invited to join them. I discovered that he had an extremely busy schedule, and an interview might not be possible. Disappointed, I accepted the possibility of returning to Delhi without having talked with Narayan. After the noon rest, Narayan pleasantly surprised me when he extended me the offer to talk with him on his after dinner walk. My thoughts returned to 1985 when I had taken my first walk with him. The ritual was about to be repeated and I was elated.

Vidchi is a small village nestled among the fields, a few miles from the city of Surat. One has to leave the main highway and travel on a gravel road for quite a while to reach Narayan's ashram where the Institute for Total Revolution is situated. Narayan Desai started this institution after the death of J. P. to train young men and women in Gandhian though and action. Over the years young people have come here from different parts of India, and abroad. Recently, Narayan is encouraging only those foreigners to come who know the native language. His goal is to train the Indian youth to become 'the revolutionaries for peace'. Set among beautiful shaded trees, the schooling of the youth puts them in touch with nature. They study and work in the fields with Narayan on their side as a model of the ancient Indian gurus.

Life:

Narayan Desai does not remember when he was born, but claims, "I must have been conceived at Sabarmati Ashram where my parents lived with Gandhi." He spent the first 12 years of his life in Sabarmati Ashram and then 11 years in Seva Gram Ashram. He breathed the air where Gandhi walked, talked, and taught. For him, "there is no memory of a significant moment when I met Gandhi." He lived with him, played with him, and was raised under his influence. He remembers, as a young boy, he rode bike with Gandhi, went on walks, played games, and sought advice on the play that the kids were going to put on in the ashram. Narayan was aware that often foreign dignitaries and visitors descended upon the ashram, and addressed him as 'Mahatma'. His parents addressed him as 'Bapu' (father). For Narayan, "Gandhi was my friend, that's what I remember

202

about him." When I asked him about how Gandhi treated other people, Narayan recalled one particular incident. He thought that this incident gave some insight into Gandhi's notion of non-violence. He remembers seeing a sign near Gandhi's kuti (cottage) which read, "Be Quick, Be Brief, and Be Gone." Perturbed over its usefulness, Narayan decided to ask one visitor what he thought about the presence of the sign. The visitor's response gave Narayan some insight into the mind of Gandhi. What Narayan learned was that during a short visit with anyone, Gandhi gave 100% of his attention to that person. This made them feel that they were human beings who were important. When the visitors left, after a brief meeting, they had been in perfect communion with Gandhi, and the shortness of time did not matter. Narayan calls it, "a positive love, feeling that one is a part of another, than one is in an I and Thou like encounter." As Narayan related this story, I felt that he was imparting the same attention to me as he had experienced with Gandhi.

As a young person, Narayan did not receive any formal schooling, but was educated at the ashram. Since Gandhi believed in practical education, all ashram children learned how to spin, work in a garden, help in the kitchen, and study. Like others, Narayan Desai was subjected to Gandhi's experiments in Nai Talim (new education). He was partly educated by his father, Mahadev Desai, who was Gandhi's senior secretary. Until Mahadev died, Narayan had assisted him in his secretarial work. In that capacity, he was privy to enormous amounts of correspondence, editing Gandhi's talks, an recording activities around Gandhi. During the Salt Satyagraha in 1930, Narayan was a young lad to take any serious notice of the Satyagraha. However, by 1942 when Gandhi launched the Quit-India Movement, Narayan was beginning to grasp the fundamentals of the Gandhian approach to Satyagraha. After his father's death, Narayan began helping Pyarelal, Gandhi's Junior Secretary. After a while the work was not satisfying and Narayan wanted to leave the Ashram. As he put it, "the secretarial work was getting to be a routine, and I felt that I was not growing." So, Narayan decided to seek Gandhi's advice. While accompanying him on one of his walks, Narayan presented his problem to him and expressed the desire to leave the ashram and work for Nai Talim as a teacher. Narayan remembers how distraught he was over the situation. On one hand, he was pulled by the love for Gandhi to stay with him; and on the other, he wanted to be fulfilled as a teacher. With Gandhi's blessings he left and came to Vidchi in 1946.

During the 1940s, Narayan Desai faced the real challenge of implementing the Basic Education of Gandhi and developing it. He became interested in Tagore and was attracted to Tagore's ideas on freedom, art, literature, and music. He felt that Tagore's philosophy of education could be integrated into the Gandhian ideas on the Nai Talim. Thus began his work of schooling the tribal children in Vidchi. When he studied the situation of the tribal children, he realized that giving them a traditional education will be of no use. He remembers that when he took charge of the local school in Vidchi, he had 63 students. The students were dirty, unfed, and night blind. The conditions of the tribals were so bad that they could not properly feed and clothe their children. Narayan recalls how he set up a cleaning tent to wash the children. The next day they looked the same. It was learned that the children had no changing clothes, and lived only in one pair of clothing. Narayan Desai decided to begin Nai Talim by instituting a program of making clothes. This led him to perfecting the art of spinning, weaving, and stitching. After some effort the children were making their own clothes. Since many of the children were night blind, the problem of nutrition had to be addressed. They were put on a milk program for a month and the children became well. Through his experiences in running the school, Narayan came to realize that the basic problem of the tribals was economic. Educating them meant nothing unless their basic needs were met. He recalls how Gandhi used to say that "God comes to the poor in the form of bread". Thus, Desai concentrated on the economic problems through Sarvodaya.

His conviction that the source of violence could be traced back to economic disparity was strengthened when Vinoba launched the Bhoodan Movement in 1951. In 1952, Narayan decided to join Vinoba in his pad yatra for Bhoodan. He grew closer to Vinoba, who accepted him as Mahadev's son. "There was a personal relationship I had with Vinoba due to my father," remembers Narayan. Bhoodan made Narayan a spiritual person, but it was a long process. As he walked with Vinoba, he was amazed how people longed to see him. Once he stopped a man to ask him why he was rushing to see Vinoba. The man replied, "I am going to see Mahatma Gandhi." Narayan interrupted, "but don't you know that Mahatma Gandhi is dead." To his surprise the man responded, "Mahatmas never die, they come back in another form. Gandhi has come back in the form of Vinoba." Narayan went through a personal crisis, because he was failing to grasp Vinoba's spirituality. He contemplated on leaving the movement because he failed to see the connection between economics and spirituality which Vinoba insisted upon. He recalls how Vinoba will greet people and say, "I see god in you." Narayan thought that Vinoba was being a "sly fox", as he put it, as he appealed to people's religious sentiments. Not wanting to be a hypocrite, he decided to quit the movement.

However, before leaving he decided to confront Vinoba with his problem. Narayan recalls how Vinoba changed his mind by showing him "the goodness of human beings." He told Narayan not to worry about believing in God and being spiritual. He said, "believe in human goodness." Narayan stayed and ended up walking 8,000 miles and collecting hundreds of acres of land in Bhoodan. He now believes, "Bhoodan made me more spiritual. It gave me my faith."

In early 1960s when Bhoodan/Gramdan Movement was spreading all over India, Narayan Desai, with the permission of Vinoba, moved to Varanasi where the headquarters of Sarva Seva Sangh was located. He became the founder editor of Bhoomi Putra, one of Sarvodaya's main literary feat. The work of editing the magazine was crucial since it became one of the major vehicles to propagate Gandhian thought, and also keep the people informed about the progress of Bhoodan. Having worked with his father, Mahadev Desai, and Pyarelal, Narayan well prepared to publish the magazine. During this period, Narayan came in close contact with J. P., who had been pressed by the Sarva Seva Sangh to become the chairman of Shanti Sena. After much pressure, J. P. agreed on the condition that Narayan be appointed it's secretary. As a member of the executive committee of the Sarva Seva Sangh, Narayan was the youngest person of that group and did not want to accept that position. He wanted to remain a volunteer. However, J. P.'s acceptance of the chairmanship of Shanti Sena left no choice for him but to accept the position of the secretary. Thus, for the next sixteen years (1962-1978), Narayan worked closely with J. P..

Narayan Desai talks about J. P. with great admiration and respect. He states, "J. P. was a very soft-hearted person." Under J. P.'s guidance, Narayan pushed Shanti Sena to an international level. Gandhi had first used the term Shanti Sena in 1922 during a major riot between Hindus and Muslims. During the Quit-India Movement some Shanti Sena work was done as riot control. However, it was during the time of independence in 1947 that Gandhi had thought of organizing it on a national level. However, he was assassinated before a conference could be called for organization purposes. In 1957, while walking through South India for Bhoodan, Vinoba was disturbed over the fact that riots between the Hindus and the Muslims had broken out in Gramdan-villages. He attempted to revive Shanti Sena as a means to curb the violence. However, it was not until 1962 when J. P. became the chairman of Shanti Sena that a concerted effort of organization began. The credit to educate and train members of the peace brigade goes to Narayan Desai. Besides being mediators for peace, the peace soldiers have also engaged in relief work during various natural disasters. The idea of creating an international Shanti Sena was entertained in 1961 when activists from several countries met in Beirut, Lebanon. Narayan Desai represented India and took an active role in setting its agenda. In subsequent years the activities of the World Peace Brigade included an international freedom march into Northern Rhodesia, the Delhi-Peking Friendship March (1963), Nagaland Peace Mission (1964), Cyprus Resettlement Project (1972), involvement in peace keeping during the Bihar Movement, work in Central America etc.[2] Within India Narayan also organized a Tarun Shanti Sena (Youth Peace Brigade). Many of its members during the 1970s are now the emerging Gandhian workers in India.

For Narayan Desai, 1970s were the years of intense struggle for the Indian politics. Many factors had caused a general unrest in the nation, some of which included ; famine, poverty, unemployment, rise in prices, atrocities committed by the police, and the inability of the government to fight general corruption and lawlessness. The Sarvodaya Movement found itself in the midst of a crisis as it attempted to respond to the situation through Satyagraha, constructive work programs, and other efforts. Many Sarvodaya workers felt that Bhoodan/Gramdan movement had been a failure or marginally successful. Years of working in the villages had produced no significant result in generating people's power. The entire Gandhian agenda of building the nation was suffering. During this period, Narayan Desai sided with J. P. and agreed with his agenda for Sarvodaya. Among other things it included harnessing the youth power to fight the corruption (as seen in the Gujarat and Bihar student uprisings), and ultimately challenging the power of the Central Government (as evidenced by the Indira Hatao (remove Indira) movement during this period).[3] The readers will recall that Vinoba had opposed J. P.'s strategy of oppressing the Central Government whom he held responsible for much of India's problems. Since, Narayan agreed with J. P., he decided to part company with his spiritual guru, Vinoba Bhave. His face turned somber and reflective as he talked about his decision to part company with Vinoba. He recalls, "I put my head in Vinoba's lap and cried like a baby when I told him that I was leaving." He told Vinoba that he was leaving because it was Vinoba who had taught him to follow his conscience. Now his conscience was dictating that he must follow J. P.'s program of Total Revolution. At that point Vinoba had put his hand on his head in an affectionate manner and said, "that is your way, go ahead." Narayan Desai was now the 'right-hand' of J. P..

As Sarva Seva Sangh split between two factions (Vinoba vs. J. P.), Narayan became quite "vocal" in opposing Vinoba, for which he endured heavy criticisms from many of his friends who had sided with Vinoba. Narayan plunged into the work of mobilizing Tarun Shanti Sena and working with youth volunteers and training them as revolutionaries for peace. He also organized the Clean India Campaign and Youth Against Corruption Campaign. The aim of the first was to clean up India by working to rectify the unhygienic conditions, environmental hazards, industrial pollution, filthy slums etc. The latter addressed the general corruption and unethical practices in the courts, industries, and the government. As the tension rose and Indira Gandhi declared the state of Emergency, Narayan almost got arrested. On J. P.'s advice he went underground to continue to fuel the Total Revolution. Once while visiting Vinoba at Paunar during Emergency, the police searched for him as they accused him of plotting to kill Vinoba. Narayan views this incident as a political move on the part of the government to harass him. Due to the efforts of his friend, Gautam Bajaj, who as a member of Vinoba's ashram convinced the police that there was no conspiracy to assassinate Vinoba, Narayan was able to escape arrest. He recalls, "I opposed Vinoba's policies on favoring the oppressive government. I always had great respect and love for him."

After the demise of J. P. and Vinoba, Narayan continued to work of Shanti Sena, training young people in Gandhian non-violent resistance. However, his concerted effort came when he opened his Institute for Total Revolution in Vidchi. I had the opportunity of sitting in one of Narayan's typical classrooms in 1993. As a teacher, I was impressed by Narayan's teaching skills and his dynamism. The class began with a few minutes of sharing student's thoughts with the entire group. Some spoke of the problem they were facing in the field, some reflected more philosophically on the nature of non-violence, truth, love etc. Narayan himself shared his feelings about how grateful he was to God that he saved him from making a mistake. The mistake he was referring to was the possibility of turning me away from Vidchi without granting an interview since he was so busy. I shared my feeling about the privilege I was being granted to join the class. After the moments of sharing, Narayan opened the class with a dialogue on the Gandhian vision of Gram Swaraj. His pedagogical style was Socratic, engaging students to interact and enter into a dialogue. He was animate, reflective, and discursive. The students responded with thoughtful questions and discussion followed. After the class, the next day's schedule was discussed as to who was going where to work on the land, to teach young children, or to engage in some constructive work activity in the village. In the morning when I left his ashram, I kept reflecting on what the state of Gandhian Volunteerism would be in India if many such institutions were running around the country. Although, he has a few students, his is an extraordinary experiment in training the revolutionaries for peace.

In 1995, Narayan Desai was elected the president of Sarva Seva Sangh, a post he had denied in the past. The single most priority of the Sangh today is Gram-Swaraj. Under his leadership, Sarvodaya workers are called to invest their energies in the villages to build more Gram-Sabhas (village assemblies) to generate people's power. During our meeting in early 1998, Desai reported that during the past few years he had been focusing on strengthening the Gram Swaraj Movement. As the president of Sarva Seva Sangh he had established several goals for himself;

1. He had been working to create a community spirit among the people who inhabited various villages. He felt that the villages were torn between communal and caste related problems which needed to be addressed before they could reach self-sufficiency.

2. He was intensifying the Gram Swaraj Movement by setting the goal of making 11,000 villages in Gujarat alone as members of the movement. So far only 6000 villages are part of the movement on the all India level.

3. He set the goal of increasing the number of lok sevaks beyond the current number of 9000. He was organizing training camps to involve more people.

4. He was challenging the khadi workers to stop taking government subsidies and work towards asarkari (non-government) khadi.

5. He was proposing that Sarva Seva Sangh should change its constitution and let kisans (cultivators) become the lok sevaks rather than limiting the membership to those who ran the khadi stores. He felt that the current number of 9000 lok sevaks on all India level was too little to work for Gram Swaraj. By opening the membership to others this number could be increased.

6. He was appealing to students to work for Basic Education along the Gandhian lines in the villages. He had already launched Basic Education in many villages on the primary level, and wished to bring it to the high school level.

7. He was encouraging Sarva Seva Sangh to either sell or distribute their land holdings to the poor, in order that they may concentrate more on Gram Swaraj.

8. He was initiating a move to improve the quality of a well-known Sarvodaya magazine, Bhoomi Putra, widely circulated in India. His goal was to make the magazine available to more people in order that Gandhian thought may spread.

With his busy schedule, Narayan Desai had still found time to publish various books. The most notable is The Fire and the Rose, a biography of his father Mahadev Desai, a senior secretary to Mahatma Gandhi. He edited his own biography prepared by Paul Hare of the U. S. A., entitled Non-violent Revolutionary. He also completed The Spring of the Independence Movement, in Gujarati, and is working on his magnum opus, Gandhi As I Knew Him. In 1998, he was continuing to teach his students at the Institutes of Total Revolution, although he admitted that he was gradually relinquishing his responsibilities to his daughter and son-in-law in this regard.

Thought:

When you talk to Narayan Desai, it is evident that he is a person with global vision. He is aware of the economic, socio-political, and cultural revolution that is sweeping across the world. He is also aware that India cannot develop in isolation from the rest of the world. Thus, he thinks that Gandhian philosophy of life must speak to the world situation. He appreciates Vinoba's slogan of 'Jai Jagat' (hail to the world), but feels that it was merely a slogan without any substance. When he confronted Vinoba on this issue, Vinoba agreed that much work needed to be done to bring the world together. Narayan feels that many of India's problems are world problems, and therefore Gandhians must co-operate with other organizations outside of India to involve them in a co-operative effort. His work with the World Peace Brigade was based on this conviction. Although after the Delhi-Peking March, the World Peace Brigade faded away, an important step had been taken to bring resisters like Michael Scott (Britain), A. J. Muste (U. S. A), and J. P. (India) together to work on non-violence techniques. Today, admits Narayan, many foreign visitors are coming to India, and Indian social workers are going abroad. Through this process of exchange of ideas a great deal can be accomplished. It is important to note that Gandhian ideas found their way into the Civil Rights Movement in the United States through Martin Luther King Jr. Likewise, many communities in Europe and Latin America have found inspiration in Gandhi. Narayan feels that the world is increasingly becoming a global marketplace where exchange of ideas is becoming a way of life. However, what shape the globalization will give to Sarvodaya remains to be seen.

Narayan is a great believer in following one's conscience. For him, one's freedom to act according to one's conscience is the legacy of Gandhi and Vinoba. He had the experience of leaving both of them as conscience dictated him to follow his own program of action. For him freedom of conscience is the real freedom because it refuses to be subjugated to mental slavery. When Gandhi fought the freedom of India, believes Narayan, he first worked on freeing the people in their minds. After having understood the concept, people were ready to embrace Satyagraha. However, following one's conscience is not a matter of following one's "whim." It requires spiritual discipline. Narayan gives credit to Vinoba for teaching him spirituality through Bhoodan. During this movement, Narayan was forced to examine his own ideas on divinity and humanity. Vinoba brought him to divinity through his faith in humanity. Through such experiences, Narayan developed his personal faith. Subsequently, his conscience became the conscience of a spiritual man, producing self-determination and love for truth. Narayan passes his faith to his students and encourages them to come to terms with their own feelings regarding Gandhian philosophy rather than accepting what they have been taught.

Since most of Narayan Desai's life is spent in promoting Nai Talim (Basic Education), he is a great believer in properly training the volunteers as Satyagrahis. He is the author of several monographs on shanti sena and the basic techniques of Satyagraha. His well known book, Hand Book for Satyagrahis has been widely used by Sarvodaya workers. In his foreword to the book, George Willoughby has said the following:

> ... the Handbook focuses on the need to change social, political, and economic institutions, and the necessity of the social change agent, the Satyagrahi, to perfect oneself, to build a disciplined way of life that will enable the social change agent to continue in effective struggle. .... the Handbook, like training manuals in the United States, can be seen as the useful tool to stimulate transitional network building, the reaching out and linking up of non-violent revolutionary groups all over the world.[4]

Indeed, much of Narayan's thought is focused on spiritual development of the Satyagrahis. However, it also teaches them strategies of direct action that are universally applicable in the Gandhian tradition. George Willoughby is correct in assessing his book as a "training manual" because it deals with such issues as; how the Satyagraha should act, how one should prepare spiritually, changes needed at home, learning from the people, working with the people, building mass organization, constructive work, and direct action.[5] Only a skillful teacher like Narayan Desai could have written such a manual. His strategy of teaching also includes the use of the arts. As a gifted poet, and playwright, he has composed many songs and written short plays that are performed by his revolutionary students and Sarvodaya volunteers. He believes that for the Gandhian message to reach to the people, it must be presented in a manner which is skillfully designed to attract their attention. The use of dance, drama, and music helps to gain the attention of the people, and make favorable impressions on their hearts and minds.

Since Narayan Desai worked closely with Jai Prakash Narayan, he became one of the architects of J. P.'s Total Revolution. He was in total agreement with J. P. that the corruption must be tackled at all fronts, even if it meant challenging the power of the government. When I pressed Narayan on the issue why Vinoba's followers disagreed with the ideology of Total Revolution, he explained it in this way; in a nutshell, they misunderstood Gandhi's warning against participation in party politics. Gandhi and Vinoba, both, did not join a political party, but they were political people. They influenced, challenged, and criticized political power as they saw fit. For Narayan, J. P. was not any different. He also did not seek political power after he gained Sarvodaya. Thus, to say (as the Vinoba faction does) that through Total Revolution, J. P. was "entering into politics" (which they oppose) is wrong. For Narayan, then, Total Revolution is a moral revolution based on essential Gandhian principles. He explains the content through the diagram he created to educate the people, which is reproduced below.[6]

WHEEL OF TOTAL REVOLUTION

1. VALUES:	INNER CIRCLE
2. ATTITUDES:	SECOND CIRCLE
3. RELATIONSHIPS:	THIRD CIRCLE
4. STRUCTURES:	FOURTH CIRCLE
5. POWERS:	OUTER CIRCLE

As the diagram illustrates, Narayan's thought is methodical and based on the conviction that Total Revolution has the potential to change society and lay a firm foundation for Gram Swaraj as both Gandhi and Vinoba wanted.

Narayan Desai views the world as a place where the forces of life and forces of death are at war with each other. This is the struggle between the oppressor and the oppressed. The oppressor is rich and powerful, the oppressed poor and powerless. Those who oppress are few, but the oppressed in majority. The political, social, economic institutions are in the hands of the few, who control life. This is not only the case of India, but the world at large. The goal of Sarvodaya is to stop the exploitation of the poor and the have-nots. Narayan is not discouraged that Gandhi is losing the battle at present. His vision is that the forces of life will unite and eventually defeat the forces of death. Here, Narayan gets philosophical and begins to explore such issues as the meaning of life, purpose of creation, and humanity's final destination. He finds answers in the thoughts of Gandhi, Vinoba, and J. P. while Ram Raj is the final goal through Gram Swaraj. Narayan believes in fighting all forms of injustices along the way. This is the vision behind Total Revolution. He calls himself "a man of faith", who has "faith in himself, his colleagues, goodness of man, and God." His faith gives him hope, hope to win the struggle against the forces of death.

Endnotes: Chapter XIII

[1] See the chapter on J. P.

[2] A brief discussion of Shanti Sena's activities is found in Mark Shepard's <u>Gandhi Today</u>, Ch.3.

[3] The developments of this period are covered in some detail in the chapter on Jai Prakash Narayan.

[4] Narayan Desai, <u>HandBook for Satyagraha</u>, p. ix, x (Foreword).

[5] <u>Ibid.</u>, see table of contents.

[6] The diagram is reproduced from the book, <u>Handbook for Satyagrahis</u> by Narayan Desai (New Delhi: Gandhi Peace Foundation, 1980).

XIV

Caring for the Harijans
Nirmala Deshpande

In recent years the term harijan (Children of God), a designation given to the untouchables of India by Mahatma Gandhi, has come under intense scrutiny. The criticism has mainly come from a group of socially deprived classes, who prefer to call themselves dalits (deprived). In their eyes harijan is a demeaning term, and Gandhi is indited for having applied the term to a particular socially deprived class of people. While they attempt to replace the term harijan with the term dalit, the plight of the untouchables continues.[1] Although the constitution of India outlawed untouchability many years ago, the social reality of the Indian life is that untouchability still exists, and there are millions of people who are treated as outcasts. Gandhi called them 'Children of God' (harijans) because he earnestly wanted to raise their social status. Thus, he made the eradication of untouchability a primary focus of his constructive work program. While he was intensely criticized by the upper caste Hindus for associating himself with the untouchables, he remained firm in his commitment to befriend the harijans and to fully integrate them into the Indian society. To this end he lived with them, ate with them, and worked with them through his social work organizations. It was he who founded the Harijan Sevak Sangha (Organization of the servants of harijan) for the uplift of the untouchables, an organization which boasts the existence of many social work programs in every state of India today.

Over the years while studying the Sarvodaya Movement in India, I was repeatedly asked the question by many Gandhians; Have you met Didi (older sister)? It was clear to me that if I wanted to investigate Sarvodaya's involvement with harijans, I had better meet this lady they addressed as an elder sister. I met didi several times, but it was not until the February of 1998 that I was able to conduct a thorough interview with her. Nirmala Deshpande, affectionately called didi within the Sarvodaya family, is one of the most controversial figures among the contemporary Gandhians. A disciple of Vinoba Bhave, critic of J. P. for his politicizing of Sarvodaya, a confidante and personal friend of Indira Gandhi, a literary figure well known in Marathi literature, and presently nominated to Rajya Sabha (the upper house of the Indian Parliament) by the President of India, has been president of Harijan Sevak Sangh since 1983. She also heads the Akhil Bharat Rachnatmak Samaj (All India Society of Constructive Work Programs) which she set up in 1982 as a new organization to Sarva Seva Sangha. Totally committed to the Sarvodaya vision of Gandhi and Vinoba, she believes that Sarva Seva Sangh has been hijacked by the supporters of J. P., while Vinoba had demanded its abolition in the early 1970s during the split between J. P. and Vinoba which rocked the Sarvodaya world.[2] Since against the wishes of Vinoba, the followers of J. P. continued to work under the organization of Sarva Seva Sangha, Nirmala Deshpande saw it fit to set up a new organization to carry on the work of Gandhi and Vinoba. Although severely criticized by the supporters of J. P. for her role within the Sarvodaya Movement in the 1970s, and supporting Indira Gandhi's emergency measures in Indian politics, she commands respect of thousands of Sarvodaya workers, who run nearly 300 Sarvodaya organizations which are presently associated with her All India Society of Constructive Work Programs. Despite her involvement in a variety of constructive work programs, she remains committed to her service to the harijan in India. Proud to be heading the organization, Harijan Sevak Sangh, which was started by Gandhi, she is determined to fulfill the dreams of Gandhi and Vinoba to fully integrate harijans into the main stream of the Indian society.

Life:

Nirmala Deshpande was born on Oct. 17, 1929 in a family of committed Gandhians in Nagpur, presently in the state of Maharashtra. Her father was a prominent lawyer, who took part in Gandhi's freedom movement in 1920, eventually giving up his law practice in 1930 to fully join him. Her mother was a scholar who studied philosophy at Fergusen College in Pune, and became a successful writer and a poetess. Recalling her childhood, didi remarks, "My parents were quite active in the Freedom Movement. Gandhi's name was familiar to all or family. As for me, I became a devotee of Gandhi from my early childhood. As we say in India, it may have something to do with my previous life." She took to

216

spinning Khadi at an early age and would not take any food until she had finished her daily quota of spinning. She remembers, "My father used to taunt me that when it came to spinning I was like a staunch brahmin. I was fully determined." Even though she was living in an affluent family with servants and many helpers, she took to a disciplined life of cleaning, sweeping and washing. She attributed her disciplined life to the inspiration of Gandhi. Impressed by her dedication to Gandhi, her grandfather used to encourage her to become like the medieval saint, Meera Bai, who was a legendary figure in the Indian history for her dedication to Lord Krishna. She comments, "Everybody in my family knew that one day I would join Gandhi."

Though as a young child, Nirmala longed to meet Gandhi, but the opportunity only came in 1945 when she was studying at Fergusen College in Pune. Gandhi happened to stay at the Nature Cure Center at the Din Shah Mehta Clinic in Pune. There he held regular prayer meetings which Nirmala began attending. She recalls, "At my first darshan (seeing) of Gandhiji, I was overwhelmed by his presence. I felt an inner joy and peace. I knew that he stood for the right cause. I considered it to be a rare fortune to have had his darshan." Evening after evening, Nirmala stood in line with others, as Gandhi came to lead the prayer meetings. She recalls, "Many leaders of the Congress Working Committee like Nehru, Patel, Azad, Rajendra Babu etc. used to be there. We volunteered ourselves as young students to work with them." She sees this period of her life as formative years when she internalized Gandhi's philosophy of Satyagraha and Sarvodaya. He challenged the youth to get involved in the process of nation building. Nirmala accepted the challenge, but due to her mother's advice, concentrated on her studies of political science. She stood second in her M. A. exams and taught political science at Morris College in Nagpur for one year.

In 1947 when independence came to India, Nirmala joined in the celebrations. She recalls, "On the night of August 14th everyone took to the streets. People lit oil lamps in their homes, distributed sweets to each other on street, sang and danced in a festive mood. India was free." On the morning of the 15th of August, the radio had announced that Gandhi had undertaken a fast in Calcutta against the communal riots on account of the partition of India. As Gandhi observed the day of silence and prayer in Calcutta, Nirmala took to her fast in Nagpur. While other family members and friends continued to celebrate by partaking of sweets, Nirmala refused to indulge in merry making while allowing her friends to do so. She remembers, "Through his fast Gandhiji was teaching us self-purification that

217

was responsible for 'the miracle of Calcutta' when the rioting finally ceased and the harmony was maintained." The news of Gandhi's assassination came as a shock to didi. She had plans to join him in Noakhali (in Bengal) during his peace march, but the plans did not materialize due to her studies. Now Gandhi was no more. She felt robbed of the opportunity to work with him closely. With a sad voice she states, "When I heard that Gandhi had been killed, as a devotee I wanted to live no more."

Her dream to work along Gandhian lines was materialized when she met none other than Vinoba Bhave, who was to become her mentor till he died. From 1945 when she briefly met Vinoba till 1952 when she actually joined his movement, Nirmala Deshpande read Vinoba's books that shaped her life. She wanted to join him in Telangana where Bhoodan was born.[3] Since she received no reply from Vinoba regarding her wishes to join him, she remained at Morris College. In 1952 Vinoba wrote to her and she joined him in his Bhoodan Pad Yatra. Her job was to take notes as Vinoba spoke, prepare press releases, and mainly propagate his ideas through writing. She remembers how Vinoba used to jokingly call her friend, Mahadevi Tai, as the Home Minister and Nirmala as his Foreign Minister. For most of Vinoba's active life in the Bhoodan-Gramdan movement, Nirmala accompanied him on his foot marches all across India. She willingly accepted whatever assignments he gave her which included such activities as organizing Sarva Seva Sangh in Banares, working for the Kashturba Trust [4] in Indore, and managing the post-Gramdan work in Bihar.

After Vinoba retired at Paunar Ashram in 1969, Nirmala was among those sisters who stayed with him at Paunar Ashram. When I asked her about the conflict between Vinoba and J. P. and the role she played in the events that led to the split within the Sarvodaya movement, her mood turned pensive, but she did not avoid the question. She emphatically refuted the charges that she was anti-J. P. and that she totally opposed his Total Revolution and favored the Emergency imposed by Indira Gandhi. As far as J. P. is concerned, she remarks, "J. P. was a friend of my father. I disagreed with him because he was making the Sarvodaya movement an instrument of politics. He could have left the Sarvodaya, as Vinoba had suggested, but he did not. As you know, for Vinoba Sarvodaya was meant to be apolitical." She regrets that some people accuse her of making inflammatory remarks against J. P. in her speeches. She claims, "My speeches are recorded and I have always spoken of J. P. with respect." As for siding with Indira Gandhi when she took harsh measures to stop J. P. and his activities to bring Total Revolution to entire India, Nirmala Deshpande remarks, "My relationship with Indiraji was a personal

218

one. I was her friend, not a political adviser. I remained her friend even in those years when she lost power and was lonesome. However, the very day she became Prime Minister for the second time on January 14, 1980, I said good-bye to her. I told her "My work is over". Indira knew me very well. She knew that I was not interested in politics." Didi reflects that she was instrumental in saving Indira's life two or three times. She also feels that if she had been with her the day she was killed, she would have saved her life by facing some bullets .[5]

During the split within Sarva Seva Sangh, Nirmala took Vinoba's side and ideologically has remained a follower of Vinoba ever since. She claims, "I took Vinoba's line of keeping Sarvodaya out of politics. I have not voted till today." When I reminded her that she was now a member of Rajya Sabha (Upper house of Parliament), she politely retorted, "Yes, but I am a nominated member and not an elected member. Since 1980 I have been approached to accept this nomination but I said no! But, this time because of my regard for the president, I accepted the nomination. I don't see that as joining politics." She contends that under J. P.'s influence, Sarva Seva Sangh was highly politicized. Therefore, it became necessary for the close associates of Vinoba to resign from it. After leaving the Sarvodaya organization, Nirmala, along with other supporters of Vinoba, continued to work for the Bhoodan-Gramdan movement.

In 1983, Nirmala Deshpande was offered the presidency of Harijan Sevak Sangh, an independent Gandhian organization set up by Gandhi himself for the uplift of the harijans. Located on the outskirts of Delhi in the area known as the King's Way Camp, Harijan Sevak Sangh had a humble beginning with Gandhi, but today thrives as a busy campus. Nirmala admits, "Even though the responsibility to head this organization was awesome, I accepted the position because it connected me with something Gandhiji had started. Many legendary figures of the Freedom Movement had been associated with it, and it had the noble goal of changing the lot of the untouchables." Under didi's leadership, the organization has grown tremendously. It has undertaken numerous constructive programs ranging from schooling the children, training craftsmen, empowering women, to designing new toilets that will free the harijans from manually collecting the night soil from door to door as they had been doing for generations. Nirmala Deshpande believes that the real stigma of untouchability on the harijan is due to their work of cleaning toilets. There was a time when bhangis (a caste of toilet cleaners) literally carried the baskets of human waste on their heads to dispose it off outside the city. They were considered unclean and undesirable. No one wanted to touch them. The upper caste people had to ritually purify themselves if they felt defiled by them. Gandhi sought to change all this by himself scavenging and cleaning the toilets. He also encouraged devising of new types of latrines and septic tanks. Today the work has reached a high level of achievement. Nirmala states, "We want to liberate the scavenger community and give them alternate jobs. Today our work is in every state of India."

Currently Harijan Sevak Sangh runs nearly 20 schools all over the country for the harijan children. They are not only taught the state curriculum, but are also instructed in Basic Education (Nai Talim) along Gandhian lines. Lately, Nirmala Deshpande has worked in South India (in particular the state of Tamil Nadu) where the problem of untouchability is more acute. She has taken a major Pad Yatra along with her associates, held camps, toured the villages, organized clinics and workshops in order to educate the masses about the evils of untouchability. The state branches of the Harijan Sevak Sangha carry out their own programs effecting the lives of thousands of people. She boasts, "Today you will find the finest products of our institutions; teachers, writers, politicians, doctors, lawyers, administrators and university vice-chancellors in every walk of life. I am proud to say that the current president of India Sri R. K. Narayana is a product of one such institution in Trivendrum, Kerala."

In 1982, Nirmala Deshpande founded Akhil Bharat Rachnatmak Samaj (All India Society of Constructive Work Programs). Her main aim was to bring together was many Sarvodaya organizations together as possible that worked along the visions of Gandhi and Vinoba. She claims, "I perceived it as a federation of Sarvodaya organizations, particularly when Vinoba had dissolved Sarva Seva Sangh. Of course the followers of J. P. sought it fit to continue to work under Sarva Seva Sangh, which they are doing today. My goal is to give expression to Gandhi and Vinoba's ideas." Nearly 300 Sarvodaya organizations have associated with her organization and the number is increasing. Although this organization encourages the work of many constructive work programs, its primary focus seems to be on the problems connected with Bhoodan. Nirmala and her associates continue to work for the distribution of land which was not completed under Vinoba. They have organized several farming communities to reclaim the land which was distributed to them under Bhoodan, but had to be repossessed by rich donors. They have organized satyagrahas against the landlords who are evicting the rightful owners of the land. Some work still needs to be done in the area of developing the foul land which was donated for the wrong reasons. In some cases

220

litigations involving several parties connected with the land have to be resolved. Thus, the work involves dealing with the land problems on various levels. A major success has been achieved in the area of making waste land fertile again.[6]

Much of the work of All India Society of Constructive Work Programs is accomplished by people's support. In some cases the local and state governments have provided financial support. In recent years, the World Bank and some foreign donor agencies have also lent a helping hand. The work has become quite wide spread as a wide variety of projects dealing with land, khadi, reforestation, environment, health, education, hygiene, and the uplift of women have been taken up. Nirmala Deshpande views these projects as the work of Sarvodaya which seeks to empower the weaker section of society.

Nirmala Deshpande's personal involvement in the area of peace making, human rights issues, communal harmony, and promoting a mutual respect for all religions is also praise worthy.

In mid 1980s, didi was instrumental in organizing a peace march in the state of Punjab. She recalls, "In 1983 and 1984, terrorist activity in the Punjab was at its height. There was a movement to create Khalistan (Land of the Pure) as a separate nation and free Punjab from India. The Sikhs and the Hindus were fighting and the communal tensions were on the rise. Innocent people were being killed and there was a serious problem of maintaining the law and order in the state. It was risky to travel in Punjab." Nirmala trained 2000 volunteers in Delhi in non-violent resistance and prepared them to travel into the interior of the state. She remembers, "Many people told us that the mission was too dangerous and that we should not risk people's lives. I told my volunteers that there was a good chance that some of us may not come back. They had the choice of leaving the march. None of them quit. So we divided ourselves in different groups and marched on." The mission of the marchers was to reach the remote villages and teach the people the way of peace. Many volunteers from Punjab also joined the march, covering the entire state. Their worst nightmare came when Indira Gandhi launched the Operation Blue Star[7] and the Sikh's holiest shrine of the Golden Temple in Amritsar was bombarded by the Indian army to chase the terrorists who had occupied the temple. Nirmala's team remained in Punjab during the crisis but none of them were harmed. They kept on bringing Gandhi's message of non-violence and communal harmony to the people. Didi remembers, "People were afraid for us, but we small Gandhians took a giant step in the name of peace. It was because of Gandhi and Vinoba that we achieved something in Punjab."

221

In 1994, Nirmala didi extended her peace making work to the region of Jammu and Kashmir. She believed that for centuries Hindus and Muslims have lived in peace in the region. However, now some outside forces (infiltrators from Pakistan) were determined to ruin their peaceful co-existence. She recalls, "When we went into Kashmir the situation was extremely tense. In every town there was a military presence and often long curfews were imposed. At night we could hear the gunfire." Under adverse circumstances, the team undertook the project of rebuilding the burnt houses. She asked both the Hindu and the Muslim communities to rebuild their houses together. She remembers, "When we asked for donation for our work, the very first donation came from a mosque. Sometimes even the militants put their guns aside to help us."

Didi's organization has been actively involved in the Freedom for Tibet movement. She supports the Dalai Lama in his attempts to solve the Sino-Tibet conflict through peaceful means. She believes that the Dalai Lama is a follower of Gandhi and encourages his people not to hate the Chinese for their aggression against the Tibetan people. Nirmala organized a peace march for Tibet but the Indian government stopped them from entering into Tibet. When stopped at the border, her group held a prayer meeting to reaffirm their commitment to peace. Impressed by her work, the Lithuanian parliament passed a resolution to support the movement. To bring her movement to the people of the world, in 1996 Didi and her associates sent a peace memorandum in support of Tibet to various embassies in New Delhi. She recalls, "To my surprise many embassies opened their doors to us on Oct. 2, the day of Gandhi's birthday. Some politely refused to receive us, others gave a different date to visit their embassy. The Chinese embassy did not reply to the letter." Many organizations from Europe and America have lent their support to Nirmala's movement in favor of freeing Tibet. "Our goal is," states Nirmala, "to convince China to start a dialogue with Dalai Lama and save the environment and culture of Tibet." To this end, in 1997 she organized a Satyagraha in Kalimpong (West Bengal) where many support groups for Tibet from India gathered to take a joint pledge to work for the freedom of Tibet. The European and American friends prayed and fasted for three days for self-purification.

In 1994, under Nirmala Deshpande's leadership, an organization, Association of Peoples of Asia, was founded. "I took inspiration from the Asian Relations Conference which Nehru had organized in 1947," she states. Like Nehru, didi's goal is to create a feeling of friendship and brother/sisterhood among the peoples of Asia. The first meeting was held in 1996 in New Delhi , India. In 1997,

Pakistan recipocrated by inviting an Indian delegation to Pakistan. She remembers, "We were received so warmly by our Pakistani brothers and sisters. We discussed issues of peace, non-violence, and disarmament in a friendly atmosphere." Since its inception, her newly founded organization has established contacts with Kazakhstan, Uzbekistan, Turkmenistan, Indonesia, Taiwan, and Burma. Her plans are to continue to spread the message of peace and harmony to the rest of Asia, forming an alliance among various people's.

Nirmala Deshpande's most recent activity involves organizing what she calls "Inter-faith Meets." Inspired by the Gandhian notion of Sarva Dharma Sambhava (respect for all religions), didi believes that inter-faith meets can be a source of maintaining peace and harmony among various religious communities in India. Her mentor, Vinoba Bhave, also had a firm commitment in promoting the inter-faith activities. She claims, "Communal conflicts are often caused by the lack of understanding and respect for other religions than one's own. Particularly in India, where we have so many diverse religious communities, an open dialogue among religions is necessary." To this end she has organized several inter-faith meets in such towns as Mathura, Varanasi and Ayodhya, which are prominent Hindu centers. On Feb. 1, 1998, her meeting was inaugurated by the Dalai Lama at the famous Muslim university, the University of Aligarh. She claims, "This was a first meeting of its kind ever held at a Muslim university. Many of our Muslim friends urged us to return to Aligarh at a later date."

Thought:

A woman of small stature, but a dynamic personality, Nirmala Deshpande tirelessly goes about heading various organizations and working for Sarvodaya. She says, "I am taking a small step toward bringing what Gandhiji used to call Ram Raj and Vinoba interpreted it as Gram Swaraj." Although in her thinking, she is a follower of Vinoba's thought, she has taken independent initiatives to implement her ideas.

Nirmala believes that there is no dearth of Gandhian Vichar (thought) in the world, but what is lacking is the Achar (practice). Therefore, her goal is to put into practice what she has learned from Gandhi and Vinoba. When I asked her about the source of her motivation, Didi began to expound her personal theology which has guided her over the years. She states, "I have always been a spiritual seeker. My social work is worship to me." When I probed further, she repeatedly talked about Sadhana (spiritual quest) as the heart of the Indian spiritual traditions. According to

223

this notion, individuals must turn within themselves to find the source of their strength. She explains, "According to my religious tradition, God is to be found within, and when you experience God, your experience his grace. I am a strong believer in the grace of God. It is this grace that gives me strength, courage, and motivation to do what I do." As I listened to her I was reminded of Krishnamal (Part Two, Ch. 6) who speaks of Jyoti (inner light) that has been a source of her inspiration and power. Both of these women are intensely religious and see their social work as an extension of their spirituality. For Nirmala, like for Gandhi and Vinoba, spiritual preparation is absolutely necessary while undertaking any action against social injustice. Thus, whether it is a peace march, a protest, or a form of Satyagraha, she encourages her associates to engage in prayer meetings, vigils, and fasts for self-purification.

In her thinking, the self-sufficiency of a village is the beginning of Ram Raj. She remembers that Gandhi wanted 7 lacs (700,000) village workers to work in the villages to help the people achieve economic, social and political self-sufficiency. To this end she, as a Sarvodaya worker, has personally adopted Itoria, a village in the state of U. P., where she is determined to create a self-sufficient village. She has encouraged many other workers to do the same throughout India. In many villages this kind of initiative has been taken. She reports, "Although this work is done in small pockets, it is my hope that it will gain momentum and more workers will adopt villages and prepare them to achieve self-sufficiency." She realizes that she has to face enormous challenges to make her plans work, specially when the villages are increasingly affected by modernization and the western models of development. She believes that through proper education and creative planning the villages can be shown the way toward their freedom from outside forces. However, dedicated workers are needed who can live and work in the villages. She believes, "Sarvodaya workers must accept the challenge, sacrifice their own comfort, and plunge into the service of the common folk. This is the way for Gram Swaraj."

Like Vinoba, Nirmala Deshpande advocates the marriage of science and spirituality. She believes that the days of traditional religions are over, and it is science that is paving the way for true spirituality to surface. She makes a distinction between science and technology on the one hand and spirituality and religion on the other. By science she means a systematic progressive quest for knowledge which is concerned with the nature of Truth. Technology, on the other hand, is utilizing scientific knowledge to produce instruments for human comfort.

However, it obstructs the investigation of Truth. Science encourages the quest for spiritual truths, while religion confines truths to various doctrines and dogmas. Nirmala's efforts in the area of creating Sarva Dharma Sambhava (respect for all religions) are inspired by her commitment to scientific knowledge and the quest for spirituality beyond religiosity. She attributes communal conflicts to the failures, on the part of many people, to focus on the spirit of science and spirituality. In the context of India, she is saddened by the fact that so many riots and violent actions are perpetuated in the name of religion. Through her inter-faith meets, prayer meetings, and activities, she hopes to encourage the spirit of 'secularism' which in India refers to as "respect for all religions". She admits, "I realize that in India today there are many forces which are working against the spirit of secularism, and there is a movement toward religious fundamentalism. However, Sarvodaya must challenge it and I am committed to do so."

Didi advocates Vinoba's slogan of Jai Jagat (hail to the world). Vinoba believed that no country of the world would remain isolated from other countries. He condemned close minded nationalism based on ethnic, religious or political superiority. Like Vinoba, Nirmala believes in the spirit of true internationalism which is based on love for all human kind. Today, more so than ever before, the world is coming together through constant telecommunication, rapid transportation, and migration of people. No longer are our problems and achievements isolated events. They affect all of us for better or worse. By proclaiming 'hail to the world', Vinoba attempted to bring the world together in order that all people may share their joys and sorrows together. Nirmala's efforts in the area of peace making, rallying the world for the cause of the freedom of Tibet, and forming alliances between Asian countries are inspired by her firm belief in the slogan of 'Jai Jagat'. She claims, "When we proclaim 'Jai Jagat', we take the attention off of us and focus on others. The problems of others become our problems. We share in each other's sufferings." It is quite obvious that in her work she gets support from her friends in Europe, America, and Asia.

Nirmala Deshpande is critical of those Sarvodaya workers who, she claims, have become actively involved in politics. She believes, "Sarvodaya can remain a moral force only if it stays away from politics and does not succumb to political pressures. It is for this reason that I have never voted for a particular political party." It is her understanding that both Gandhi and Vinoba discouraged Sarvodaya's involvement in party politics. However, with Jai Prakash Narayan the emphasis changed. He and his followers, against the advice of Vinoba, courted

225

politicians and formed the Janta Party against Indira's Congress. For Nirmala such an activity lessened the credibility of Sarvodaya in the eyes of the people as a non-partisan movement. She believes, "Sarvodaya has not yet recuperated from the damage that was done to its image during the 1970s." And, it is for this reason that she launched the Bharat Rachnatmak Samaj to bring Sarvodaya back to its original intent. When I asked her whether it was possible to bridge the gap within Sarvodaya caused by the split between the followers of Vinoba and J. P., she responded, "Our ideological differences are too profound. However, I have no hard feelings against those who view Sarvodaya from the eyes of J. P. Many workers of that camp attend our meetings and I welcome them."

Didi gets most excited when she talks about her work for the Harijan Sevak Sangh. She believes that one of the most valuable contribution that Gandhi made for the improvement of the Indian society was that he made freedom of the untouchables as an integral part of the Indian Freedom Movement. For her, inherent in the freedom movement was Gandhi's utmost wish that "the exploiters of yesterday should become the servants of today." Thus he wanted the upper caste Hindus to give up untouchability and embrace the harijans. For Gandhi, the problem was not with the harijans, but with the upper caste people who needed to reform themselves. India's freedom from the British meant little for Gandhi if the Indians continued to oppress their own people. Nirmala believes that Gandhi wanted the privileged castes to "atone for their sins by doing penance as they served the harijans." As such giant personalities of Congress as Mata Rameshvari (Nehru's sister-in-law), J. D. Birla, Rajagopalachari , Rajendra Prasad, and Govind Vallabh Pant willingly associated themselves with the Harijan Sevak Sangh, "they were engaged in their penance," says Nirmala. She emphatically declares, "I am doing my penance for the atonement of the sins of my fore-fathers, who mistreated their fellow human beings in the manner in which they did."

Nirmala Deshpande is critical of those members of the Dalit Movement who condemn Gandhi for lowering the standard of the untouchables by calling them harijans. For them the term harijan has become derogatory because, according to Nirmala, "They don't understand what Gandhi has done for them." She explains, "It was the Harijan Sevak Sangh that was responsible for fighting for the 'Reservation Status' for the harijans and the tribals.[8] Gandhi had sent his close associate Thakkar Bappa to the Constituent Assembly to convince them to include the harijans in the political decision making process." Not only that, she reminds us that it was Gandhi who appealed to Nehru to include Dr. Ambedkar (now claimed leader of the Dalit Movement) in his council of ministers. She states, "Gandhiji told Nehru that unless he accepts Ambedkar as one of his ministers, he will not bless his ministry." Later on, the work of drafting the constitution of India was given to Dr. Ambedkar by Gandhi. According to Didi, Dr. Ambedkar once told her father, "I became a minister (in the government) because of Gandhi." Nirmala regrets that today a rift has developed between Ambedkarites and the Gandhians. After independence, Dr. Ambedkar saw very little change in the lot of harijans and he converted a large segment of that society to Buddhism. Whether this conversion has really changed their status in the Indian society remains a debatable question. Nirmala Deshpande believes that the real change in the status of the harijan will come when the upper classes change themselves. "Under Gandhi's influence," she claims, "thousands of upper class changed their attitude toward the harijan and they suffered at the hands of other upper class people." She cites the example of her own family which was ostracized by the Brahmin priests who did not want to come to her ancestral home to perform religious rituals because "we associated with the harijans."

In the person of Nirmala Deshpande, lovingly known as Didi, we have a dedicated individual who is willing to sacrifice her own comforts for the uplift of the have-nots. Her enthusiasm and energy to work for the poor stem from her faith in God and the following of Gandhi and Vinoba.

Endnotes: Chapter XIV

[1] The term Dalit is primarily being used by the followers of Dr. Ambedkar, a contemporary of Gandhi, who disagreed with him over the issue whether the harijans should be given a separate electoral status. While Gandhi believed in integrating the untouchables into the main stream of the Indian society, Ambedkar believed that this was not possible. He managed to convert many harijans to Buddhism since it stressed on a casteless society. Today, these so called neo-Buddhists are engaged in an anti-Gandhi rhetoric in order to hail Dr. Ambedkar as the true leader of the untouchables. It is primarily they who favor the term dalit over harijan.

[2] See part one (Ch.3) on J. P. for details.

[3] For Telangana story see part one (Ch.2) on J.P. for details.

[4] Kasturba Trust was an organization Gandhi founded after the name of his wife, Kasturba. Its primary function is the upliftment of women.

[5] Nirmala did not elaborate on how she saved Indira's life two or three times. However, she narrates that once a holy man from the Himalayas had told Indira that as long as Nirmala was with her, no harm will come to her. Nirmala regrets that on the day Indira was killed, she was not with her although she had planned to do so.

[6] The author visited Vinoba Seva Ashram in the village of Bartara in Shahjahanpur district in the state of U.P., where experiments are being carried out to make the Ooser(barren) land Upjaoo(fertile). The state government in co-operation with the ashram is carrying out the experiments on a larger scale too help the farmers affected by this problem.

[7] Launched in the summer of 1984, Operation Blue Star was a military code name for the army operation to purge the Golden Temple in Amritsar of the terrorists who had taken shelter there. In this operation many Sikhs as well as the army soldiers were killed, but the temple was freed from the hands of the militants.

[8] Through the Reservation Status, the harijans and the tribals were assured certain seats in the state assemblies and the Parliament. Today the system is used to ensure the uplift of the lower castes to assure them government jobs and admissions to schools and institutions of higher learning. Though the government continues to adhere to this policy, the upper caste people are highly against it. They advocate 'merit' as the basis of social advancement.

228

XV

Spinning for Gram Swaraj
*Ramachandran**

In the feature film, <u>Gandhi</u>, when the character of Gandhi asks the American reporter Margaret Bourke-White why she wanted to interview him, the reporter humorously responds, "Well you are the only man I know who makes his own clothes." Perhaps what Margaret did not know was that hundreds and thousands of people had been spinning cotton to make their clothes before the British occupied India, and many continue to do so still today. Spinning and weaving were two cottage industries that the Colonial Empire tried to destroy, as the factory clothes made with the Indian raw materials were sold back to the Indian people. As the Industrial Revolution was fed by the materials acquired in the colonies, the natives bore the cost through poverty. When Gandhi came on the scene, he realized how <u>Charkha</u> (the spinning wheel) was losing its momentum in Indian homes. The factory made clothes were being preferred in the name of fashion and cost efficiency. He attempted to revive spinning in Indian homes to challenge the British economy. Thus the Swadeshi Movement (one's own) was born which sought to promote local goods for local consumption. <u>Khadi</u> (homespun) was given a particular attention by Gandhi because Indian cotton was being shipped outside of India to be resold to Indians in the form of cloth at a higher price. This was a case of double jeopardy. The indigenous people not only lost their raw material, but also lost the local market for the home spun.

Among the Gandhians in India today, there is an intense debate on the status of Khadi. It revolves around the argument whether or not Khadi should be supported with government funds. Those who oppose the government support claim that Gram Swaraj is a people's movement. Therefore, unless the people

229

themselves take interest in spinning, they will not be completely freed from the industrial control which comes from the government support. Those in favor, see no harm in receiving government funds to increase the production of Khadi so that it may be exported abroad, sold in big cities, and become an industry. Both ideologies are involved with the spinning schemes in India. In 1953 when the government of India formed the Khadi Commission to oversee the Khadi work on the all India level, many Gandhian Khadi organizations joined this body in the hope to attract more people for the cause of spinning. Many remained opposed and are working independently to promote self-sufficiency in the villages and providing the poor means to earn their livelihood. When traveling in India, I was advised by several Gandhians to meet and talk with one Gandhian who had spent his entire life in the Khadi movement. This man was V. Ramachandran. Working from the city of Coimbatore in the state of Tamil Nadu, Ramachandran heads the Bharatiya Gramodyog Sangh (Indian Village Industries Organization). The primary task of the organization is to promote the production of Khadi throughout South India. His work has been so successful that over the years 70 some other organizations such as this have splintered from the mother organization under Ramachandran's leadership. I met up with this veteran Gandhian in Madurai where he had traveled from Coimbatore specially to meet me. I was in the presence of a man who believes that one of the keys to Gram Swaraj is the survival of Khadi in India.

Life:
 V. Ramachandran was born in 1921 in the state of Kerala. His family was attracted to the Nationalist Movement, but had no contact with Gandhi. His orientation to Nationalism came when he heard stories about his great grandfather, who had been involved in helping the Muslims on the Malabar Coast during their rebellion against the British. He recalls, "during 1857-1920, the Muslims were more nationalists than the Hindus in South India. They took up arms against the Raj on the land issue. This was the second mutiny."[1] Even though the grandfather was a brahmin, he sided with the Muslims and provided them food during the rebellion. Ramachandran's father was not interested in party politics, but he wore khadi in support of the nationalist movement.
 Ramachandran's first encounter with Gandhi took place in 1936, when Gandhi visited his school. As a young boy of fifteen, Ramachandran was overtaken by emotions when he heard Gandhi speak about the British oppression in India. He recalls how he put his entire monthly school fee in the collection plate for Gandhi-

230

the money which had been sent to him by his grandmother. This was the beginning of a new Ramachandran. He became a radical leftist leader among the students. He entered college as a confirmed nationalist. He began leaning toward Marxism having heard the speeches of Namboodripad, who was a great Congress leader of the South. "In those days", recalls Ramachandran, "people of all different ideological persuasion were in the Congress". Thus, Namboodripad, though influenced by Marxism, remained within the Congress and attracted many youth. Ramachandran was particularly attracted to the Marxists because of their uncompromising attitude toward the caste system, and their zeal to bring about social change. In the meantime, Gandhi had also started a campaign against untouchability, and was speaking up against the prejudices perpetuated by the caste system. The issue of caste based discrimination came to the forefront when Ramachandran was a student at Annamalai University. He organized the student body against the administration which was favoring the students of higher caste. In the student union election, Ramachandran and his friends defeated the brahmin candidate in favor of a student from a lower caste. The issue became so politicized that the university had to be closed down for a period due to the student agitation. This was Ramachandran's early venture into revolutionary activity.

V. Ramachandran's involvement with Khadi as a Gandhian constructive work program began in the 1930's when he met C. Rajagopalachari. He was a nationalist leader who had been greatly influenced by Gandhi, and had been in touch with him. Within the Nationalist Movement, Rajagopalachari was a well recognized figure in South India. In 1936 he had been elected the Chief Minister (then called Prime Minister) of Kerala,[2] when Ramachandran came in contact with him. Since, Ramachandran was a student leader, many of Rajagopalachari's cabinet ministers became friendly with him. Gandhi also had interest in youth, and was giving a national call to the youth to join the nationalist movement and postpone their studies. Consequently many students were leaving colleges and universities to join the cause of India's independence. Ramachandran was also presented with this choice. As the second world war broke out, the British dismissed the state government, and many ministers were sent out to run the Khadi institution. Rajagopalachari asked Ramachandran to join them in this work. As Ramachandran remembers, "there was no turning back for me now, I ended up spending all my life in Khadi work." Since, he was college educated, soon he rose to the level of high management within the Khadi organization. In that capacity he met various political leaders, as he pushed the cause of Khadi in the South.

Through his involvement with Gandhi and his managing of the Khadi organizations, Ramachandran began to understand the importance of spinning, weaving and marketing for the nationalist cause. He came to realize how the British were destroying the local economy by introducing the 'mill cloth'. Before the British ever came to India, there were thousands of pockets of traditional spinning in the villages. Men, women, and children were spinning and weaving during the months they were not cultivating the land. Since they were poor, Charka provided them some extra income for sustenance. This practice was prevalent all over India. Ramachandran believes that it was partly due to spinning and weaving that India managed to get gold from abroad as they exported their materials. Ancient India was called the 'golden bird of the East', because India was rich. However, with the coming of the Europeans, the situation began to change. Ramachandran agreed with Gandhi that it was high time that Khadi was saved. "It was the genius of Gandhi that he launched a movement to save Khadi. Khadi was already there, he revived it," says Ramachandran. Gandhi inherited a 'built-in system', but he refined it. "He was the first person to introduce the concept of a minimum wage for the spinners" recalls Ramachandran. This was the way to stop the exploitation of the poor. Even the British in India did not have a system of minimum wages, which upset Gandhi and his co-workers.

By the time India became independent in 1947, V. Ramachandran had spent many years in promoting Khadi. He recalls, "I had to convince the villagers that Khadi was a means of their social security in the absence of any other means of income". He walked through numerous villages preaching 'Swadeshi' and pushing the Gandhian program of spinning. He also became an expert on various aspects of production as he managed various divisions of the Khadi work within the Khadi organization. When Gandhi was assassinated in 1948, Ramachandran and his associates decided to improve upon the existing system of spinning. Soon, the Ambar Charkha was to be invented, which ran on electricity and could spin several spindles simultaneously. In spite of the controversy among many Gandhians whether the Ambar Charkha promoted Gandhian values or not, Ramachandran favored its use not only for greater productivity, but also for increased earnings by the artisans. According to Ramachandran, between 1952-58 different workable models of Charkhas were invented. By the time 10,000 new spinning wheels were produced, Ramachandran and associates decided to submit a plan to the government for financial support. The plan was accepted and Khadi received a boost. For Ramachandran, governmental support not only brought the financial backing, but "gave the movement a moral support". The people came to recognize that their government was behind them in changing their economic conditions. Ramachandran remembers how he realized that from Coimbatore to Kanya Kumari, there was a 'cotton growing belt' where thousands of spinners lived. Through the use of newly developed technology he decided to take the production of Khadi to a new height. His efforts were so successful that he was asked to become the director of the Khadi work for the state of Tamil Nadu by a leading Gandhian, Dr. Arunachalam, who was a member of All India Khadi and Village Industries Commission. To his disappointment, Ramachandran refused the offer, but continued to work independently.

In the 1950s V. Ramachandran's attention turned to Vinoba Bhave. At Paunar, Vinoba had been experimenting with Kanchan Mukti (freedom from money) and Rishi Kheti (cultivation without the use of animal power). Ramachandran was impressed by Vinoba's spiritual ideas, but his interest remained with the work of Khadi. However, his liking for Vinoba grew when he learned how he had pushed the cause of the Indian villagers in front of the First Planning Commission session called by India's first Prime Minister, Jawaharlal Nehru. Vinoba had walked to Delhi to attend this meeting at Nehru's invitation, but left in disappointment when he realized that the government was more interested in industrialization than saving the village industries. Ramachandran's ideas about the village industries, including Khadi, coincided with the ideas of Vinoba. When Vinoba launched the Bhoodan Movement, to Ramachandran's liking, he sought to link Khadi with the movement. Ramachandran decided to work for the cause of Bhoodan. When Vinoba took his walking tour through Tamil Nadu, Ramachandran and his Khadi workers organized Vinoba's program throughout the state. Since Ramachandran already had a net-work of several hundred workers who worked for Khadi, he mobilized them for the Bhoodan work as well. Through their efforts, Ramachandran collected fifty to sixty acres of land every day for Vinoba, while he walked through Ramachandran's region. Vinoba was pleased and Ramachandran became his confidant.

Over the years as Khadi work intensified in South India, Ramachandran broke away from the All India Spinners Association which worked under the guidance of Sarva Seva Sangh. Thus, the Tamil Nadu Sarvodaya Sangh was formed. The reason for this break was not ideological but a matter of convenience. Ramachandran felt that Wardha, where Vinoba was living, was geographically too far removed from the South. Furthermore, the problems that Ramachandran was encountering were different from the North. The break however did not result in isolation. Ramachandran remained a frequent visitor of Vinoba. As he likes to put it, "Khadi and Bhoodan had a good marriage." Vinoba continued to express his support for Ramachandran's work in the South. In the North, Meerut (near Delhi) became a great center for Khadi as well. Both North and South followed the Gandhian ideology of Gram Swaraj through Khadi. Both had the blessings of Vinoba. "The major difference between the North and South" recalls Ramachandran, "was on the issue of the use of technology in the production of Khadi. While the North insisted upon the 'traditional means' of spinning, the South was committed to the new technology." According to Ramachandran that difference can still be observed as the Khadi work continues. Breaking away from the All India Spinners Association gave Ramachandran more freedom to develop his Khadi work. He began to be recognized as a leading Sarvodaya worker from Tamil Nadu. Many state and central government officials sought his advice for the development of village industry. For himself, Ramachandran sought no political power. In spite of recognition and good reputation in the South, he never became a candidate for elections.

In 1953, shortly after the independence, the Central government decided to create a commission to better oversee the work of Khadi all over India. It was government's way to support Gandhi's constructive work program in the area of spinning. Its main function was to set a uniform policy to promote Khadi, and to help various Khadi organizations throughout India. Ramachandran supported the work of the Commission, and in 1977 even became one of its board members. However, he became aware that the creation of the commission started a debate among Gandhians; whether Gandhi would have approved of a corporate-like set up for Khadi. The Commission's goal became high productivity through technology. Soon, Khadi became an industry, promoting export overseas. It also set up a budget to financially support many Khadi organizations. It bothered many Gandhians that it had become a business. Several problems arose when the government sliced its budget and the commission could not fulfill its financial obligation to the member organizations. In the eyes of concerned Gandhians, Khadi had been hijacked and become a hostage of the government. Soon, Sarvodaya workers began distinguishing between what they termed as Sarkari Khadi (government supported) and asarkari (non-governmental) Khadi. Few experiments in Asarkari Khadi are now being conducted in different pockets of India. Much of large scale Khadi work is connected with the Khadi Commission. Ramachandran supports the Khadi Commission, but his own organization is quite autonomous. It does not depend on the Commission's financial backing as many small organizations need to. Since Ramachandran is a believer in the use of technology, his goal is to continue to increase production. To this end, he does not frown on the government's support of Khadi.

During the 1970s, Ramachandran was one of the influential board members of the Sarva Seva Sangh. For thirteen years he served the organization as one of its managing trustees; giving particular attention to legal matters. He had that position until the time of the Emergency, when he turned it over to the Sangh. During his tenure as a managing trustee, Ramachandran was greatly distressed over the split between Vinoba and J. P., and the tension it created for the Sarvodaya workers. Not wanting to take a side in the dispute, he became a mediator for peace between the two camps. He recalls, "I was among the few who became the bridge-builders between the supporters of Vinoba and J. P." It was partly due to his efforts and the efforts of others like him, that a compromise was reached when Vinoba proposed that those who wanted to support J. P.'s 'Total Revolution' might take a two year leave of absence from the Sarva Seva Sangh. In fact this policy was adopted. He regrets that many of Vinoba's supporters chose to leave the Sangh all together. As a consequence, majority of the Sarvodaya leaders, who belong to the Sangh today, are the supporters of J. P.'s Total Revolution.

Today, Ramachandran heads the <u>Bharatiya Gramodyog Sangh</u> (Indian Village Industries Organization), which he started nearly thirty years ago. Located in Coimbatore, South India, his work is spread out in hundreds of villages where his organization supports the local spinning and other cottage industries. His work takes him to the people who are deprived of basic necessities of life. Over the years he has provided for their economic, educational, and medical needs. He has performed over 1500 marriages among the villagers, and many of their sons and daughters have taken high profile jobs in the government as well as the private sector. Some have become engineers, doctors, teachers, and at least one is a leading scientist in India's Atomic Commission. Ramachandran attributes the success to Gandhi's Khadi initiatives. "And now", he humorously says, "Khadi has skyrocketed".

Thought:

Like many Gandhians, V. Ramachandran's thought is intrinsically related to his work. Although the primary motivating factor in his life is the philosophy of

Sarvodaya, he interprets Gandhi in his own way to make him relevant to the contemporary situation. During our conversation, Ramachandran reflected a great deal on the current social situation in India as a whole and in the areas of his work in particular. He believes that over the years, India has gone through tremendous social changes. These changes are brought about due to economic growth, industrialization, and technological advancement. Compared to the time of Gandhi, India now has a growing middle class, whose appetite for consumption is increasing day by day. However, as custodians of progress, this class has also become the oppressor of the poor. For Ramachandran, something has gone wrong in the process of nation building, when the poor who are the majority, are denied of their fair share of the economic growth. On the contrary, they have become the victims of the middle class' exploitation. Under the capitalistic economic framework, it is believed that the lives of the poor will change when the capital gains will trickle from top to the bottom. V. Ramachandran believes that the process should be reversed. The emphasis should be put on the bottom (the poor) and bring them up. This is what Gandhi had proposed, Vinoba had requested, and Ramachandran is after. He sees his Khadi work as an attempt to give the poor an opportunity to change their economic and social status.

Even though Ramachandran supported the work of the Khadi Commission, he has come to believe that the Commission helps only those who already have technological resources. Thus, those Khadi organizations that have a high volume of productivity receive financial backing of the Commission. Ramachandran believes that this process leaves the poor spinners out of the system. He asks the question; "How can we generate people's power if the majority of the poor villagers are not shown how to be a part of the economic process ?" Therefore, he believes in establishing various co-operatives which involve spinners, weavers, buyers, sellers etc. He has already started various associations of these groups to take control of their own economic resources. This scheme keeps the profit on the local level, and also eliminates the exploitation by the middle man. He states, "When people become in charge of their own lives, then the people's power is generated." Through his work in the region of Coimbatore, Ramachandran has altered the lives of thousands of poor families. His work has been so successful that thousands of villagers have now become full time spinners because through spinning they have achieved economic independence. Many such villagers are freed from years of dependence on landlords, who kept them economically dependent by lending them money for their survival. Many such loans have been repaid, and the villagers are no longer victims of the exploitation. This is an example of creating people's power in which Ramachandran believes.

Ramachandran believes in the value of decentralization of power. Needless to say that he agrees with Gandhi that the best government is the one which governs the least. "But the real question is", asks Ramachandran, "why should we decentralize power?" In his mind, the issue is directly related to the welfare of the poor. In the centralized structure, the power is seldom shared with the poor and the socially deprived. So, he has always been in favor of the Panchayati Raj for the villages (village council of five). He is disheartened that India is so slow in bringing this transformation. "If we had taken Gandhiji seriously", he states, "we would have implemented a Panchayati raj a long time ago." In his own work, he has used the decentralization of power as a basic tool to empower the people. That was the main reason why he broke away from the All India Spinners Association which was under Sarva Seva Sangh to form Tamil Nadu Sarvodaya Sangh. He further branched out to create the India Village Industries Association, which is further divided into small organizations. This process has given the spinners a sense of belonging as the decision making has increasingly come in their own hands. Ramachandran speaks with great delight about the changes he has observed in the lives of the people he works with. He believes, "they are more confident, happy, and satisfied."

One of the major differences between Marxists and Gandhians, according to Ramachandran, is that Marxists want first to get power and then work for change, whereas the Gandhians wish to work to bring change without the desire for power. This is one of the reasons that Ramachandran left the Marxists and became a Gandhian social worker. Of course the real division between the two groups remains on their attitude toward the issue of 'the means and ends'. Like Gandhi, Ramachandran believes that the end does not justify the means. During his involvement with the Marxist Communists, he was disturbed over the fact that the communists were willing to use any means (often violent) to achieve their goal. As a young man, he knew many youth who were attracted to Marxism because of its appeal to overthrow oppression. However, Ramachandran realized that such an approach will court disaster. Through his Khadi work, he has been able to show his people how important it is to solve their problems through non-violent means. Today, he is in a constant dialogue with the young people in the villages where his work is spread out. "Youth have not changed," he states, "they are energetic and want a quick fix to long standing problems. Many young people are still attracted to Marxist ideology. My goal is to bring them to Gandhi."

When I asked Ramachandran how he has gone beyond Gandhi, he reflectively replied, "Gandhi has not been fully tried as yet, how can I go beyond him." I was not surprised by his response because it echoed the sentiments of many Gandhians I have interviewed. Some go as far as to say, "Gandhi has not only been not tried, he has been betrayed." Nonetheless, Ramachandran believes that Gandhi is being further removed from our time. A lot of changes have occurred in Indian life since Gandhi lived. Therefore, we have the difficult task of recovering Gandhi. He realizes that it is hard to know how Gandhi would have reacted to every situation if he were alive today. Therefore, for Ramachandran, it is important to change with the times, but remain as honest as possible to the values that Gandhi gave us. That means we should not be afraid to experiment with his ideas, and if they proved to be true, we should try to implement them. One Gandhian ideal that has haunted Ramachandran till his youth, is the notion of Ram Raj. Like Vinoba he understood it to mean Gram Swaraj. He is convinced that his Khadi work is a means to bring Gram Swaraj. He recalls, "when we were fighting for independence from the British, we said to them that we have the right to self-determination. Today the villagers are crying out that they have the right to their self-determination." Ramachandran feels that through his Khadi work he is helping them to attain this freedom.

Endnotes: Chapter XV

[*] After the chapter was completed, the author regretfully learned the demise of Ramachandran.

[1] The First Mutiny was the rebellion of 1857 in the North after which Queen Victoria had taken the direct control of India.

[2] In the 1930's the British had a program of self-determination for various states. They could form their own government

XVI

Generating Women's Power
Shobhana Ranade

While assessing Gandhi's contribution for the uplift of women in India, it would be fair to say that he brought women out of their homes into the streets to fight for the cause of justice. Today, his legacy to generate women's power survives in numerous constructive work programs undertaken by various Gandhians throughout India. Named after Gandhi's wife, Kasturba Trust became an independent Gandhian organization to oversee the social work among women and children after the death of Gandhi. It has inspired thousands of women to train along Gandhian lines and invest their energies in the villages and cities of India to work for the uplift of women and children. Walking through the beautiful gardens of the Aga Khan Palace in Pune, India, one finds a steady stream of women (and men) paying respects to Kasturba at her memorial. The palace which has been turned over to the Gandhi National Memorial Society, and which houses a Gandhian exhibit, is also a great center of learning for women. This is a unique center, because it trains women to become Gandhian social workers and commit themselves to five years of active service in a village to work with women. It accepts only twenty-five women per year, but teaches them Gandhian values, and equips them with skills that can empower women. The woman who trains them is Shobhana Ranade.

I had first heard about Shobhana Bahen(sister), as she is called, at Brahma Vidya Mandir, one of the six ashrams founded by Vinoba Bhave for women. For a long time Shobhana had been associated with the ashram as she came closer to Vinoba. Although at Vinoba's advice she spent more time at Maitri Ashram (one of Vinoba's ashrams) in Assam, the sisters of Paunar regarded her as "one of their own." I was asked to meet her at the earliest opportunity and to learn from her

241

about the Gandhian work among the women. The opportunity came in 1993 when I met with her at her office at the Aga Khan Palace in Pune. At a first glance, Shobhana Bahin gives you the impression of being a "modern woman". A master of several Indian languages, she converses in impeccable English. Clad in her beautiful sari, she gives you a "determined" look, a look of a person who is confident and in control. She is a habitual Khadi user and often spins at home as many Gandhians do. But, when you talk to her, you know that she is seasoned in Gandhian ideology and social work. For her Gandhi, "is not a man, but an idea". And, it is the "idea" that she takes to thousands of women in the villages through her students she trains. When the government of the state of Maharashtra advised her to turn her training center into a university, she refused. Her idea is to generate women's power through committed trainees who can go to the villages, and not demand a comfortable life as many university graduates are expected to do.

Life:

Born in 1924 in Ratnagiri in Maharashtra, Shobhana Bahen was made aware of India's independence struggle at an early age through her family. Her uncle was a Congress leader and through him she caught the revolutionary spirit. Earlier in her life, she was attracted to the ideas of Subhash Chandra Bose whom she had the privilege of meeting as a student. Once she had the honor of garlanding Bose when he came to attend the Haripura Congress near her home. She felt the charisma of Netaji (Leader Bose), and was inspired by his struggle to free India. While meeting Bose was a transforming experience, listening to the fiery speeches of Veer Savarkar was even more overwhelming. Both Savarkar and Bose shared their views on fighting the British imperialism. They conceded to the use of violence if necessary to achieve their goal. Shobhana recalls that she was so impressed with Savarkar's ideas that "she used to sell tickets to promote the attendance in his lectures". She used to be spellbound by the fervor of his patriotic speeches. She even sold his literature on the streets which was banned by the British. The youth were particularly affected by both Bose and Savarkar because they wanted to change things and preserve Indian values. When Savarkar was captured and sent to the prison, Shobhana was disheartened. Yet, she never lost hope. She was convinced that the freedom will come through revolutionary means. Then came Gandhi.

Shobhana Ranade met Gandhi for the first time in 1942. He organized a prayer meeting at Dr. Dinsha Mehta's nature cure clinic in Pune. Shobhana was in the audience. Little did she know that the man was about to change the direction of her life. Unlike Bose and Sarvakar, Gandhi spoke of non-violent resistance. Shobhana, who was attracted toward building bombs and fighting with guns, became a changed person. She became a volunteer for Gandhi. "This was the time of Quit-India Movement, and there was tension everywhere. As Gandhi was gaining ground for his philosophy of Satyagraha, I was attracted to it," explains Shobhana. One day she brought her young baby daughter to be blessed by Gandhi. She was afraid that Gandhi might not have time for such insignificant things. When she told Gandhi of her fear, he responded by saying, "live fearlessly". Shobhana recalls, "that was the message for me". Gandhi not only blessed the baby, but took personal interest in both the mother and the child. Shobhana could not believe that such a busy person like Gandhi would have time for them. She explains, "you see, that was the greatness of Gandhi. He took special interest in the personal lives of the people. He had a genuine interest in their well being". To live "fearlessly" became Gandhi's mantra for Shobhana. She decided to take heart in his advice and to teach fearlessness to other women became important for her. The man who helped her achieve her goal was none other than Vinoba Bhave.

Shobhana got involved with the All India Women's Conference as she worked for Congress as a young woman. However, in 1951 as the Bhoodan Movement got notoriety, Shobhana Ranade found herself in Pochampalli near Hyderabad, where Vinoba was working for Bhoodan. She had traveled there with one of Assam's greatest Sarvodaya workers, Amal Prabha Das and her associates. Meeting with Vinoba was another life transforming experience for Shobhana. She was persuaded that the Gandhian ideal of Swaraj was possible through Gram Swaraj (freedom of the village). Vinoba had discovered the Bhoodan/Gramdan was one way to bring Gram Swaraj. Shobhana immersed herself into the Sarvodaya literature, but what she found to be most useful were conversations with Vinoba. She calls Vinoba, "a walking university". His discourses centered around spirituality, philosophy, politics, economics, sociology and other subjects as well. Shobhana was awestricken by the amount of knowledge Vinoba imparted to his associates. What was most touching was that Vinoba showered his affection on Shobhana. Recalling her association with Vinoba, she states, "I know many people saw Vinoba as a stern sanyasin, but my memories of him are nothing but of an affectionate person." Once she committed herself for the Bhoodan/Gramdan work, Vinoba took interest in her intellectual development. He sent her to Anna Sahib, one of Maharashtra's well known Sarvodaya leaders, for further studies. According to

Shobhana, "Anna Sahib was another gentle soul". A trained economist, he had a wide variety of interests. He made Shobhana read Russell, Bernard Shaw, Kumarappa, and Gandhi. As she matured intellectually, she saw the wisdom of Gram Swaraj even more clearly and dedicated herself for the Bhoodan work.

While Vinoba was on his pad-yatra (walking tour) of Assam, Shobhana Ranade became one of the key workers in Assam to facilitate his Bhoodan/Gramdan work in that state. At Vinoba's suggestion she learned the Assamese language as she went door to door selling the Sarvodaya literature and explaining it to the people. Vinoba put a challenge to her. She was to excel in selling most copies of the Sarvodaya literature on a daily basis and then report to him. "Selling about four hundred copies was enough," recalls Shobhana. Her dedicated efforts soon posted the sale of 1,000 copies a day. When that happened, "I became a favorite of Vinoba", she remembers. Impressed by her enthusiastic efforts, Vinoba began taking more interest in her as a Sarvodaya leader. He had a humorous way of showing this interest. He made sure that she had her morning tea. As a consequence her co-workers began asking her daily, "Shobhana, have you had your tea today?" Vinoba also enjoyed the humor of the situation. In the midst of the light side of life, hard work continued. Shobhana intensified her study of the Assamese language and fell in love with it. She traveled all over Assam distributing Sarvodaya literature and collecting land for Bhoodan.

Shobhana had a long standing commitment to the Congress Committee. Because of her work in Assam, the Assam Congress Committee decided to pull her into the political arena. In late 1960's, the committee decided to nominate her to the state assembly. Her popularity was widespread, and she was told that she would not even have to contest the elections. She decided to consult Vinoba on the issue. His initial reaction was of great joy. He was impressed because as an outsider (she was from the state of Maharashtra) she had won the affection of the people of Assam. Vinoba told her to go ahead and join the state assembly, but continue to work for Sarvodaya from inside. The day she was about to leave the camp and enter politics, Vinoba called her. She remembers, "I had reached the compound gate when a man approached me and said that Vinoba wanted to see me." Vinoba looked at Shobhana and said, "Shobhana, don't do it." Recalling that incident, she states, "I was saved." Vinoba's idea was that as an outsider one should serve the people and not become part of the power structure. Since then Shobhana has not been inclined to hold any political office. She continued to work for Sarvodaya until 1972 when the workers of Assam honored her by bestowing upon her the title, "the daughter of Assam." Perhaps this honor might not have come if Vinoba had not "saved her" as it were, from her involvement in the politics.

In 1972, Shobhana Bahen returned to Paunar Ashram in Maharashtra. Soon Vinoba selected her to take charge of the Kasturba Trust, and work for the uplift of women. Like Gandhi, Vinoba had been most concerned about the plight of the Indian women. In 1958 he had published Stri Shakti (Women's Power), and always wanted to implement his ideas to change the status of women in Indian society. The basic thesis of the book was that women were equal to men. He criticized the Hindu tradition by idealizing women on the one hand and downgrading them on the other. He wanted women to take charge of their own lives and refuse to accept the second class citizenship. He wanted men to realize that in the liberation of women is their own liberation. He advised men to share in household work and not make it as a women's domain. He also predicted that unless there is a woman leader born of supreme character like that of Shankara charya (8th century South Indian philosopher) the liberation of women will not be completed. Vinoba knew that the Kasturba Trust had been created for the uplift of women, but needed an able leader to run it. Shobhana was deemed to be the right person to head the organization. Thus began her long association with the Kasturba Trust. For about seven years, she gave her heart and soul to the women's work. Her ambition was to reach the women in remote villages. The work involved hygiene, child care, nutrition, cottage industry etc. Shobhana saw that the trained volunteers reached the right places to carry out their work. This was hailed by Vinoba as the work of Stri Jagaran (the awakening of the women). Shobhana went into the field herself only to return to Paunar once a month to report to Vinoba. She agreed with him that women's liberation was not merely an Indian issue, but an international issue. Also, the Indian approach to cause of women's power was not divisive. It represented a holistic approach which called for men's support and co-operation as well. Thus, Shobhana organized three international seminars at Paunar on women's issues under Vinoba's guidance.

In 1979, while visiting Paunar, Shobhana was approached by Vinoba, who suddenly asked her to give up the Kasturba Trust and work for the Gandhi National Memorial Society. "In the presence of such veteran Gandhians as Arunachalam and Diwakar," recalls Shobhana Bahin, "he asked me to go and work for Aga Khan Palace." Morarji Desai, the prime minister of India had asked Aga Khan to donate his palace in Pune to a voluntary agency rather than turning it over to the Indian Government. Morarji wanted the building to be used for some constructive work rather than to be turned into a mere museum. It was, therefore, donated to Gandhi Smarak Nidhi, which in turn assigned it to the Gandhi National Memorial Society. Shobhana decided to turn it into a center to train women who can work for women throughout India. Thus, although she changed positions, her work remained preoccupied with women's uplift. The building which houses the Gandhi National Museum, also houses her office and a school for training women. She offers a one year diploma in Gandhian studies, but selects only twenty-five students, who come and stay together, and train as social workers. Their curriculum changes year to year, but focus remains, 'women's power'. After graduation the candidates are required to spend a minimum of five years in a village. After three years they are called back for a reunion and a reevaluation of their particular project. The goal of the program is to teach self-reliance and self-sufficiency to the trainees. Upon graduation they are encouraged to develop their own projects related to the women's issues. Shobhana never gets tired of telling the success stories about her students in the field.

Shobhana Bahen sees herself as a Gandhian social worker, who has many fronts. Not too long ago she was elected the president of All India Women's Conference (AIWC). This was an old organization started by an English woman, Margaret Cousins. Gandhi had supported Cousins' efforts to fight for the rights of women. However, it had remained an urban organization. Shobhana has taken it to the villages. Supported by volunteers, this organization has similar goals as the Kasturba Trust. As if this was not enough, Shobhana is also involved with the work of the S. O. S. Children's Villages. At the same time she remains a managing trustee of the Kasturba Trust. Currently, her time is spent coordinating the work of these four organizations. Through this work she wants to make Vinoba's dream of women's uplift a living reality.

Thought:
After I finished my interview with Shobhana Bahen, her words, "Gandhi is an idea", kept resonating in my mind. She is of the opinion that when people call Gandhi a 'Mahatma'(great soul), there is a tendency to put him on a pedestal and remove themselves from him. In this case Gandhi becomes a distant saint whose actions can never be matched by the ordinary people. Shobhana feels that idealizing Gandhi to this extent is wrong because it takes us "off the hook", so to speak, from applying his thought. Therefore she proclaims that Gandhi is an "idea" that needs to be applied. I was intrigued by her explanation because, a year earlier, Arun Gandhi,

246

one of Gandhi's grandsons had given a similar explanation to me when we were discussing the notion of Gandhi being a Mahatma. Shobhana Bahen is in good company when she calls our attention away from the man, Gandhi, to his actions. In all of her social work with various organizations that she is involved with, she uses Gandhi's thought to achieve success. When I pushed her on this issue, she readily mentioned four principles; hard work, discipline, cleanliness, and Swadeshi. In her training of women social workers, these values are instilled in them, who in turn teach these values to the people they work with. For Shobhana these are the fundamentals of building a society, leading to Gram Swaraj that both Gandhi and Vinoba were preaching.

Today, Shobhana is not directly associated with the Sarva Seva Sangh, but she feels that she belongs to the extended Sarvodaya family. She admits that Sarvodaya movement is going through a period of crisis, and that its leaders are faced with many challenges. She realizes that the level of commitment is dwindling and that there is a need to bring more youth in the movement. Therefore, she remains committed to the work of children's education along with the uplift for women. She remains in contact with other Gandhians, many of whom are well recognized within the Sarvodaya movement. In fact before she started the work of women's training program for the Gandhi National Memorial Society, she called a day long meeting of many Gandhian leaders at the Aga Khan Palace in Pune. The day began with a prayer meeting followed by a day long discussion on how Gandhian ideas be implemented in the work she was about to undertake. The women's training center, which is now a major Gandhian constructive work program that she runs, was a product of this community effort. As a result of her success, she is often invited to various Sarvodaya functions, and her advice is sought by many co-workers.

Since much of Shobhana's work is with women, her primary concern is with generating women's power. She believes that the key to women's power is to teach them 'fearlessness'. She will never forget that Gandhi had once advised her, "live fearlessly". This advice changed her life and made her a leader among women. Later, Vinoba, through his ideas on women's liberation, gave her further insights into how to convey this message to the women in villages. As Shobhana Bahen ponders the plight of Indian women, she realizes that the years of oppression has made them afraid and incapacitated to change their situation. Vinoba taught women to get rid of their fear through courage, hard-work and self-sufficiency. He invited men as well, to the discussion of women's liberation. Shobhana believes that men and women should fight together to liberate themselves from that many fears that plague their lives. However, the fundamental fear of women in the villages is related to the issue of 'self-worth'. It is the question of self-identity, pride, and positive self-image. As Vinoba saw this as a spiritual problem, so does Shobhana recognize the religious dimension of the problem along with its economic, social and cultural connections. She trains her women social workers in such a way that they may recognize these problems and find ways to empower women in the field. She restrains herself from giving them solutions, rather encourages them to find individual solutions based on the unique situation they face as they deal with women and their families.

Shobhana Ranade believes that the central theme of the Gandhian thought is the creation of a non-violent society. For her, the creation of such a society begins with the family. It is for this reason that the focus of her work is on women and children. She remembers that when Vinoba founded his Maitri Ashram (Friendship Ashram) in Assam for women, he wanted to extend friendship and love beyond the ashram to the family. He advised Shobhana that she should work to make every family that she came in contact with as an extension of the Maitri Ashram. That meant creating an environment within the family where peace and love might abound. This was the real essence of non-violence. As Vinoba wished to extend peace and harmony to the neighbor, Shobhana carries this message through her trainees to the villages. Furthermore as Vinoba proclaimed the message of Jai Jagat (hail to the world), Shobhana believes in extending this message to the world as well. That is why she has approached the United Nations to support her 'Children's Village' program. It has already been mentioned that she has organized three international seminars dealing with women's issues at Paunar. She has been able to convince some international donor agencies to come to her aid. This author was invited to attend one function organized by the Children's Village in Pune where several foreign guests were present. Here, Shobhana spoke of extending peace to the rest of the world, and help in creating a non-violent society.

Like many supporters of Vinoba Bhave, Shobhana Bahin believes in staying clear from party politics. She contends that Gandhian social workers must devote their energies to constructive work programs and not get involved in politics. Consequently, she does not support any political party or candidates. Ever since Vinoba advised her not to accept the nomination to join the state assembly of Assam, she has never fought an election. The only vote she ever received was the vote of the governing members of AIWC when they elected her as the president of the All India Women's Conference. She cites the examples of Gandhi and Vinoba, who never joined a political party, and yet their influence was felt in making political decisions.

Shobhana Ranade's life and thought are extensions of a legacy left behind by Gandhi, Vinoba and other Sarvodaya thinkers. She has tirelessly given her energies for the welfare of all in whatever capacity she has served. By giving her life to the cause of the uplift of women, she is creating a legacy for many to follow.

XVII

Working for National Integration Through Youth
Subba Rao

As the train reaches its destination, it is greeted by hundreds of people, some of whom hold the ever popular marigold garlands in their hands. These are the well-wishers and friends of the occupants of the train that has finally arrived at the platform. This is not an ordinary train. It is 'Sadbhavana' (Goodwill on Wheels) that will carry some 250 young people all across India over the period of eight months covering thousands of miles. It carries the message of 'national integration' and 'goodwill' to the masses all over the vast land. From Oct. 2, 1993 to May 31, 1994, 1,867 young men and women from 26 states would have volunteered to be on this train, about a hundred changing every ten to twelve days. Some will travel the entire distance and spend all eight months on this train. On the way they will be greeted by state governors, chief ministers, members of the parliament, mayors, chiefs of police, various dignitaries, social workers, and ordinary people. Among the greeters would be Mother Teresa of Calcutta, who would hand each of the participants a written prayer.

After the customary fanfare, two hundred and twenty or so youth will unload their bicycles on the platform and will descend upon the city in groups. Their goal: to visit schools, colleges, universities, religious and cultural centers, business organizations, and slums. They will carry with them Gandhian literature, sing songs of peace and harmony, give talks on national integration, perform street plays, and preach non-violence. In the aftermath of the 1992 communal riots,[1] and the subsequent bombings in Bombay in 1993 which caused further riots and deaths of thousands of people all across India, one man had a dream to mobilize the youth and take them on a train of 'Good Will' on a mission of peace and national unity. This man was S. N. Subba Rao, who is affectionately called 'Bhaiji' (brother) by

251

hundreds and thousands of youth across India. A veteran Gandhian who spent most of his life for the cause of various Gandhian constructive work programs, he now spends most of his time organizing Gandhian youth camps.

I first met Subba Rao on the roof of Gandhi Peace Foundation in New Delhi where he was hanging his laundry to dry. I was standing next to a man who had worked closely with Vinoba and J. P. and had courted hundreds of decoits and persuaded them to surrender their arms in the name of Gandhi. I had read accounts of Subba Rao's work with the decoits of the infamous Chambal Valley, and had awaited the opportunity to talk to him about his experiences. Our initial meeting was cordial and friendly. He invited me to attend a youth rally for national integration where Arjun Singh, then the minister for Human Resources Development, was to be the guest of honor. The rally was packed with youth from all over India. Arjun Singh spoke, but what was most impressive was to hear Subba Rao sing songs of patriotism, love and harmony in various Indian languages. It was obvious that he commanded the respect of the young people who had gathered under his leadership to pledge for a non-violent and peaceful society. In subsequent meetings, I was to learn more about Subba Rao's life and his thought.

Life:

Although there is a friendly debate within his family about the date of his birth, it is agreed that the year was 1929 and the place was Bangalore. Having no serious knowledge of Gandhi at an early age, he grew up in an environment where the atmosphere was charged with the devotional songs of Ramakrishna and the teachings of Vivekananda. In the beginning, Subba Rao admits that, at a young age, he was attracted to the Vivekanand mission because the children were given candies at the end of devotional meetings. However, gradually he was pulled towards the mission for singing devotional songs and listening to religious teachings. He does not recall if Gandhi was much mentioned, but he remembers visiting many homes where people were spinning Charkha (spinning wheel) and producing their own clothes. Just for fun, he started spinning also. He vividly recalls that after a month when he was given a sheet of cloth for which he had spun, he was amazed. This event brought him to Khadi, and he started wearing it.

In 1942 when Gandhi launched his well known "Quit India" campaign, Subba Rao was in sixth grade in school. He was the only young boy wearing Khadi at school, which brought attention to him. He recalls how Gandhi was becoming popular and mass rallies were being organized all over India to oppose

British rule and demand complete freedom. At one occasion some protesters entered his school and demanded that classes be suspended and that students should join the mass protest. Subba Rao found himself in the crowd yelling, "Quit India" and writing it on the street. Soon the police arrested him, and he found himself being interrogated at the local police station. Although he was detained for only five to six hours and never put in jail, the experience was instrumental in shaping his life for the future. This was a "turning point," recalls Subba Rao, because he "became a school hero at the age of thirteen." Moreover, now the boy started to learn about Gandhi and began taking interest in volunteer work. First he joined The Student Federation and later The Student Congress, and eventually The Rashtra Seva Dal (National Volunteer Corp.). This organization had Gandhi's blessing as Nehru became its first president. Soon the British charged it to be subversive and arrested Nehru and Dr. Hardekar, leaders of the movement. In 1943, Subba Rao remained quite active in the Rashtra Seva Dal, and gradually took charge of its leadership, conducted its youth camps, organizing new centers and training campers for the hard life in prisons. While studying for his law degree, he was asked by Dr. Hardekar to come to Delhi and give one year of his life for the work of Seva Dal. Subba Rao hesitated, but compelled by the need for nation building, he arrived in Delhi on May 17, 1951, never to leave again.

Although he never met Gandhi (he first saw him in Bangalore at the age of six), Rao felt deeply connected to him during the years of India's independence struggle. "It was Gandhi's genius," he recalls "that he made everyone feel that they had contributed to the freedom struggle." Charged by Gandhi's call for volunteerism, Rao threw himself wholeheartedly in the work of Seva Dal. He organized youth camps, met young people in remote villages, mobilized women for spinning Khadi, and led marches in Bangalore and Delhi for the cause of freedom. "There was a national euphoria," recalls Rao, "when India achieved its independence in 1947." He felt that he had personally contributed to the success of the Gandhian movement. "The reality of the partition hit us all, but we never lost sight of communal harmony that Gandhi so passionately believed in," says Rao. So he continued to work with the youth, and the seeds of national integration were being sown everywhere. After Gandhi's assassination, Subba Rao never lost hope, but tenaciously trained the youth in Gandhian thought and action for the creation of a non-violent and peaceful society. He traveled the breadth of India organizing many youth camps. It was during this period that he focused on "youth discipline." Today he feels the young people lack wholesome living because there is an absence of discipline in their lives. So, he teaches them drills, exercises and mental constrain to become fit.

Subba Rao had a unique experience in 1952 which not only brought him closer to Vinoba and J. P., but transformed his life. A fellow worker in Seva Dal invited him to Central India to visit the Chambal Ghati (Chambal Valley) which was infested with decoits. The legendary decoits like Man Singh, Madho Singh, and Tahsildar Singh had their hideouts in this valley from where they carried out their activities. Subba Rao agreed to the visit fearlessly. During his stay, once his host became restless and informed Rao that Man Singh was aware of Rao's presence in the village as an outsider. Paying no attention to the advice that it might be dangerous for him to stay there longer, Subba Rao decided to hold a public meeting of the Seva Dal in the usual manner. As the villagers gathered under a tree to listen to Rao, he was made aware that the most infamous decoit of India, Man Singh, was in the crowd with his gang. They were dressed as policemen (their usual disguise) in order to mingle freely with the crowd. Subba Rao opened the meeting with devotional songs and then spoke of Vinoba Bhave and the Sarvodaya movement. He explained the Bhoodan (land gift) movement and explained how Vinoba was tackling the problems of poverty, violence, and other social ills through the movement. He explained how this was all connected with Gandhi's dream of bringing Ram Raj (Kingdom of God) to India. As a consequence, Man Singh's gang became quite friendly toward the members of the Seva Dal. Man Singh's son, Tahsildar Singh, became Rao's personal friend. Thus began the initial negotiations for a settlement of disputes between the decoits and the state police. Consequently, for the first time, twenty hard criminals surrendered to the police in 1960.

Under the inspiration of Vinoba Bhave, Subba Rao contemplated leaving Seva Dal and joining Shanti Sena. Due to the Bhoodan movement there was a great need for community organization as well as settling disputes as they arose. At the suggestion of Vinoba, Rao joined forces with Vallabh Swami and Narayan Desai, two veteran Gandhians, to head the Shanti Sena (Peace Brigade) activities.[2] Since Subba Rao had been working with the youth, he used his experience to organize Shanti Sena youth camps. While he still walked with Vinoba occasionally for the cause of Bhoodan, he concentrated on training the youth for non-violent resistance and peace keeping. He particularly recalls the Shanti Sena camps he helped organize between 1966-67. By this time, Jai Prakash Narayan (J. P.) had assumed the presidentship of Shanti Sena, while Narayan Desai became its secretary. These camps were successful not only because they trained future Gandhian leaders, but

254

because they brought broader ideas of Gandhian philosophy of life to the youth. For Subba Rao, Gandhi's vision of nation building was a part and parcel of his understanding of real <u>Swaraj</u> (independence). It was on this basis that Vinoba had formulated Sarva Seva Sangh to carry out the program of Sarvodaya. Through Shanti Sena camps Rao was drawn closer to J. P.'s ideology.

The year 1969 was the year of the Gandhi centenary. As the nation made plans to celebrate the occasion, Subba Rao had an idea. He was haunted by the notion that the Gandhi centenary should not be celebrated only by publishing more books and installing Gandhi's statues here and there. He wished to bring Gandhi's message of peace and harmony to the masses. He wanted a train full of Gandhian exhibition that could travel all over India. With the help of the president of India, Dr. Radhakrishnan, J. P., Indira Gandhi, then the prime minister, and other associates, the dream was realized. The exhibition, "<u>Mohan to Mahatma</u>" was displayed in ten coaches that made up the train. As expected, many youth volunteered to work on the train as they brought Gandhi to the masses. To his delight, Subba Rao was given two trains. One for the Broad Gauge and the other one on the Meter Gauge. The trains moved for ten months, carried 60 to 70 youth from 25 different states who explained the exhibits to the people. A year later, impressed by the work, the centenary celebration committee insisted on giving Rs. 6,000/- to Subba Rao for his efforts. He decided to take that money to the Chambal Valley and work among the decoits. When he put the proposal to his friends, the money grew to Rs. 16,000/- through generous gifts. Rao called it "Gandhi money," and with it he purchased some land in a place called Joura. Thus, in 1970, under his patronage, Mahatma Gandhi Seva Ashram was started in Joura which still thrives with vitality.

For a decade, since the opening of the Mahatma Gandhi Seva Ashram, Subba Rao plunged into various Sarvodaya based constructive work programs. However, improving the conditions in Chambal Valley became his main focus. He viewed this as an extension of his work of Shanti Sena. At this juncture, an important event marks the history of Sarvodaya. In 1972, certain decoits approached Vinoba Bhave only to be told that they should contact J. P. Even though Vinoba was instrumental in bringing some decoits to surrender in 1950s, he was now weak and retired. He felt that J. P. could be of more help to them. One decoit disguised as a contractor approached J. P. at his Patna residence in Bihar. He introduced himself as Ram Singh. For three days he tried to persuade J. P. to come to Chambal Valley and mediate between the police and the decoits. J. P. refused to travel to Chambal due to his ill health and more pressing involvements in the crisis of Bangladesh. Tired of hearing J. P.'s excuses, Ram Singh finally told J. P. that his name was not Ram Singh but Madho Singh, and if J. P. called the police right then, J. P. could collect a reward of Rs. 150,000/- for turning Madho Singh over to them dead or alive. This got J. P.'s attention and he learned that Ram Singh was in fact Madho Singh, one of the most feared decoits in India of this time. J. P. was awe-stricken. He agreed to come to Chambal where Subba Rao hosted him at his Mahatma Gandhi Seva Ashram. Recalling the incident, Subba Rao narrates how the surrender of decoits under J. P. took place. At one meeting between J. P. and the decoits, Rao began the meeting with a song, "Lord, I have come to surrender at your gate", in the native language. "The atmosphere was so charged with emotion," recalls Subba Rao, "that many decoits with weapons on their shoulders were crying and wiping away their tears. One by one they laid down their arms at the feet of J. P." Altogether, 654 criminals surrendered to the police in various installments. Now they are out of jails after serving their sentences.

During the 1980s, Subba Rao turned his attention to the problem of national integration seriously. Once again he sought to train the youth for this work. He felt that after the breakup of the former Soviet Union, Yugoslavia, and the Referendum (through defeated) to divide Canada between the French speaking and the English speaking, there was a threat that India might suffer a similar fate. The problems in Kashmir, eastern India, southern India, and the Hindu-Muslim conflict in northern India warranted that the forces of division must be checked. The rise of Hindutva and its impact on the Bharatiya Janta Party and Shiva Sena, and Muslim reaction to Hindu militancy concerned Gandhians all over India. It was quite obvious that religion was being politicized to gain power and control by groups which had vested self-interests. The political events which led to the assassination of Indira Gandhi in 1984 had already divided the Hindu and the Sikh communities. But, the events that led to the destruction of the Babri mosque on December 6, 1992, and the subsequent riots that took the lives of several thousand Hindus and Muslims, was a clear indication that communal harmony in India was at stake. To anyone who traveled throughout India during this period, as I did, it was obvious that the Indian government, social and religious organizations, many volunteer organizations, and colleges and universities alike were organizing various programs to promote national unity. Subba Rao was not far behind.

Subba Rao's program for national integration was the "Good Will Train." He realized that in 1993, India would be celebrating Vivekananda's centenary of his

256

visit to the World Parliament of Religions in Chicago. Vivekananda's message had been for religious harmony through the belief in <u>Sanatana Dharma</u>, the Eternal Religion. Committed to religious universalism, Subba Rao realized that one cause of disunity within the religious communities was their narrow minded views of religion. Gandhi, like Vivekananda, had preached respect for all religions and denounced religious exclusivism. Subba Rao decided to take this message on his <u>Sadbhavana</u> (goodwill) train. The government of India gave him the train, which traveled 18,075 kilometers, visiting 120 major stations, over the period of eight months. The train was not only greeted by people belonging to various religious groups, but by members of various political parties as well. Subba Rao undertook this venture under his new organization called, The National Youth Project. The response to this train has been overwhelmingly positive, and Subba Rao has a follow-up program to launch a Sadbhavana Express. Until the next train, Rao continues to hold national integration youth camps all over India. The largest camp he has ever organized was attended by 23,500 youth. For some years now he is also holding Gandhi youth camps during summer months in the United States. The focus of these camps is to impart Indian cultural values to the children of Indian immigrants who attend these camps. The camps also emphasize community building through Gandhian teachings.

In 1997, when India was celebrating its 50th anniversary of independence, Subba Rao had an idea of bringing various voluntary organizations in India together for a convention to discuss the future of India.[3] He approached Prime Minister Gujral, who enthusiastically supported the idea. Unfortunately, due to lack of funds, the government was unable to act on its promise. Disappointed, Subba Rao approached a Hindu swami, who was also his friend, and the convention was organized in Bangalore at his ashram. To Rao's credit, 127 volunteer agencies sent their representatives for the convention and 850 men and women gathered under his leadership. After three days of deliberations, the group decided that they needed to focus on two main issues for the future of India: the <u>building of character</u> and <u>national integration</u>. The group vowed to take these ideas to their respective states, where they are continuing to work on these issues within their own organizations. As a result of the convention, Subba Rao is currently being invited all over India to hold youth camps and discuss the state of the nation with the young people of India. Impressed by his activities in this area, the government of India invited him to address 3,000 youth in Madras at a government sponsored camp in 1998. Subba Rao spoke on 'national integration.'

257

For the past two years (1997 and 1998), Bhaiji Subba Rao has taken a keen interest in curbing violence in Champaran, Bihar.[4] In the absence of a strong government in Bihar, many villages in this state are witnessing gang-related activities. The people are terrorized, their properties looted, and many are killed. The problem is acute in Champaran, particularly with reference to the crimes against women. When the government failed to respond to Subba Rao's request to deal with the violent situation in Champaran, he decide to hold his camps there and work among the people. So far he had held four camps in that area bringing the message of non-violence through music, songs, work-shops and work projects. He states, "The people's response has been overwhelmingly favorable. They have welcomed us and are willing to solve their problems through Gandhian ways." The basic problem in Champaran is access to guns. At one point, guns were needed for self-defense against the decoits and gangsters.[5] However, Subba Rao is convinced that guns are not the answer to lasting peace. He is working on a plan to ask the villagers to surrender their guns and work peacefully. "I am hopeful," says Rao, "that I will achieve my goal in Champaran in due time."

In 1998, Subba Rao wanted to organize the fourth <u>Sadbhavana train</u>, and began negotiating with the government on the procedures. He felt that 1998, being the 50th anniversary of Gandhi's death, Gandhi's life could be best commemorated by having a mobile exhibit in a train that could travel throughout India. His idea was well received by government officials, but nothing was done to encourage him to take up the project. When he approached the government for the last time, he was shocked to learn that two trains had already been prepared to roam the country. He stated, "The government has taken my idea, but changed the focus of the exhibit. Although they fully depicted the life of Gandhi, more emphasis was put on showing the achievements of India since independence." Subba Rao is saddened by the fact that he lost the opportunity of reaching the people of India through a network of volunteer youth who could have managed the train and performed religious music, drama, songs, and held prayer meetings with different communities wherever the train went. After all, he had managed three train exhibitions before with his youth groups. Their way of bringing the Gandhian message to the people had a spiritual basis.[6] However, with this opportunity lost, Subba has not lost hope. He continues to look for other avenues to bring Gandhi to the people.

Most recently, Subba Rao met with the Planning Commission to discuss the state of poverty in India.[7] His goal was to impress upon them that, despite India's industrial development, poverty had been on an increase. He wanted the Planning Commission to think seriously about the majority of the people of India and devise programs for their uplift. While discussing this issue with me, he states, "Today about 48 million people are registered in our Employment Exchanges throughout the country. This is the urban situation. The villages have even more unemployment." He wants the Planning Commission to stop promoting the cause of the multi-national companies that make the rich richer.

When I asked Subba Rao about his achievements over the years, he referred to his work with the youth. He takes satisfaction in the fact that he has been able to reach the youth of India through hundreds of camps that he has organized. He has been able to inspire them to adopt certain ethical values in the face of corruption rampant in the Indian society. Not only that, he has trained so many youth who have entered into every field of occupation in India. It is his earnest hope that the young people will bring a desirable change in the nation. He is also encouraged by the kind of work his youth groups have done for national integration in India. His efforts in this area continue.

Thought:

By his own admission, Subba Rao's thought is highly influenced by the thinking of Vivekananda, Gandhi, Vinoba and J. P. Collectively, the primary concern of these men was the creation of a just social order locally as well as globally. This is what Subba Rao is engaged in doing.

In terms of his thought, Subba Rao is convinced that no just society can be established without a spiritual renewal. He learnt this early through his association with the Ramakrishna Mission in Bangalore. He saw the expression of this ideal particularly in Vivekananda, Gandhi and Vinoba. The basis of this spiritual renewal is the belief in Sanatana Dharma (Eternal religion). For Subba Rao, two aspects of Vedanta, which support the notion of the Eternal Religion, are crucial. First, it calls for an individual's commitment to a devotional life and the belief that spiritual practice is as important for self-transformation. Second, it insists that religious tolerance is necessary for peace. He has been attempting to utilize these ideals in his life's work. He is a great believer of holding prayer meetings in his youth training camps. Here young people learn to sing devotional songs and pray universal prayers. In his camps religious tolerance is practiced by incorporating devotional readings from all religions. Subba Rao believes that it was Vivekananda who taught us the ideal of 'Sarvadharma Sambhava' (equality of all religions). However, it was

Gandhi who extended the emphasis to 'Sarvadharma Mamabhava' (all religions are mine). Subba Rao believes that the youth must be instilled with the Gandhian notion if they are to carry the message of religious harmony to the society at large. He explained, "India is home to the world's great religions. Many others are given shelter here because of religious tolerance." It saddens Subba Rao that currently in India its ideal of religious tolerance is being challenged by many political, social, as well as religious forces. This is a challenge that must be faced with "discipline, training, and a message of love."

Subba Rao is a firm believer of training the youth in mental and physical discipline. He brings his own training that he received in Vivekananda Mission, Seva Dal and Shanti Sena to the National Youth Project that he now leads. In all seasons, Rao can be seen wearing Khadi shorts (half pants) as a symbol of his discipline. He explains, "In the military, soldiers are put to rigorous exercises to toughen up. I train my youth with drills and exercises. Our drill consists of community manual work for the benefit of the needy. I want them to be mentally and physically fit." He laments that modern lifestyles of luxuries and comfort have made the youth weak. In his camps, he trains them to become fit to face the hard work of nation building.

Subba Rao is a great supporter of Sarvodaya ideology and the constructive work programs undertaken by its followers. He agrees with Gandhi that Swaraj (independence) did not simply mean India's independence from the British. Rather, Swaraj meant a continuous struggle to build the Indian nation. It was for this reason that Gandhi had established several constructive work programs. He often started a program on the basis of need. This is exactly what Rao continues to do. Many of his youth camps are organized to build roads, dams, wells, etc. He believes in working with local communities in identifying needs and then mobilizing youth to get the job done. The real integration between the community and the youth takes place when they work together. Often the community provides the food and lodging. Through their cooperative efforts a climate of trust, love, and harmony is created. "This is doing the Gandhian work. Sometimes, Gandhi is not even mentioned, but he is acted upon," says Rao. He is concerned that every youth that participates in his camp "must feel that he/she is actually doing something for the nation. This can be done only by getting their hands dirty with the soil," explains Rao. So they pick up the spade, dig the earth, collect the rubble, and move the earth. In Bhaveian tradition, this is Shramdan (donation of labor), but Subba Rao has given it a new meaning by calling it "Shramsamskara" (a tradition of labor).

Thus, for his youth, nation building is not a matter of donating a few hours for hard labor, it is developing an "attitude of working hard for the nation."

Central to the notion of "Continued-Swaraj" is the spirit of "Volunteerism" according to Rao. He explains that since independence most Indians have become "government reliant." They expect the government to solve all their problems. Gandhi had warned people against this tendency. In fact the notion of Jan Shakti (People's Power) was partly directed towards self-sufficiency. Under this idea, Gandhi wanted people to tend to their own affairs. This did not mean that a political structure was not needed; but, as we have already seen, he felt that the best government was that which governed the least. Thus, he advocated decentralization of power through a Panchayati Raj. As for Gandhi, so for Subba Rao, decentralization of power meant transferring power to the people. And the exercise of such power was made possible through the spirit of 'volunteerism'. Rao believes that it is through participatory volunteerism that people can really feel that they are contributing to nation building. This is "Continued Swaraj." As Gandhi attracted many youth to his movement, Rao is attracting the youth also through his organization and teaching them the spirit of volunteerism.

According to Subba Rao, Gandhi had four major constructive work programs initially which Rao calls "the pillars" of Gandhi's movement. Later these were elaborated into 27 programs. Subba Rao has taken the initial four programs and made them the focus of his work. The four programs were: Hindu-Muslim unity, removal of untouchability, eradication of poverty, and stopping alcoholism. He realizes that many Sarvodaya leaders as well as other volunteer work agencies are also working in these areas. Likewise, his work is not limited to these four areas either. Nonetheless, he feels that for the present the issue of Hindu-Muslim unity is an important one. Therefore, he is directing most of his energies towards national integration work camps. After his participation in the Sadbhavana train ride, Rao realized that there are numerous obstacles to the mission of national integration. Briefly, he observed that politically all political parties have resorted to political extremism by patronizing organizations formed purely on the basis of caste, creed, and religion. Some parties, in order to create a vote bank in their favor, do not hesitate to create communal tensions. Some state governments motivated by political reasons have undertaken the task of rewriting textbooks along communal lines. Socially, there is a general lack of knowledge among the masses about the elementary teachings of world religions. This ignorance leads to bigotry and religious tensions. Caste alliances, gender differences and exploitation of the

261

have-nots creates serious impediments for the work of integration. Economically, the disparities that exist all over India make it difficult to bridge the gap between the rich and the poor. The new economic policy which favors multi-national companies in India has further contributed to economic disparities. In the midst of all these impediments to Sadbhavana (good will) the youth are in a sorry state. Subba Rao observes that many youth organizations are being formed along caste and religion lines. They are often under the control of a political party that uses them as pawns for their own selfish goals. In the face of these adversities, Rao believes that Gandhian thought can provide that glue which is needed to keep India together. Subba Rao firmly believes that his efforts to bring national integration through the work of the youth will succeed.

Endnotes: Chapter XVII

[1] The riots that occurred after the destruction of the Babri mosque at the hand of certain Hindu extremists in December of 1992.

[2] Shanti Sena refers to the peace brigade that Gandhi initiated and Vinoba fully realized.

[3] India has the largest network of volunteer organizations in Asia. Some of these are termed NGOs (Non Governmental Organizations) which are involved in various forms of social work throughout India.

[4] Champaran is a historical village where Gandhi had led the famous Indigo Satyagraha against the British.

[5] Evidently, one retired army man, Badri Narayan Pandey, mobilized the villagers and taught them how to shoot to defend themselves. His efforts were praised by many people as he was able to keep the decoits and gangsters out of the villages where they once terrorized the people. Badri Narayan was hailed as a hero.

[6] Subba Rao's earlier trains (1969, 1993) were managed by the Gandhian youth fully committed to Gandhian values and the desire to bring his message to the people.

[7] The Planning Commission is the government body that oversees India's Five Year Plan for national development.

XVIII

Saving the Environment

Sunderlal Bahuguna

Anyone who has traveled from Hardwar to Badrinath in Northern India is struck by the beauty of the Himalayas. The towering peaks, the green valleys, the lush country sides, and the deep gorges that cradle the river Ganges leave a lasting impression on one's mind. The entire Uttara Khand (the northern region) that stretches from Kashmir to Arunachal Pradesh leaves the visitor awestricken by its natural beauty, rich culture, and simple life of its inhabitants. It was here, in the deep forests, that the ancient sages of India reflected upon the philosophical and religious meaning of life, producing immense literature that contributed to the creation of the Indian civilization. Sometimes referred to as Tapo-bhumi (land of austerities), it has attracted many rishis and munis in search of their Sadhana (spiritual quest), who made the Himalayas their abode. To make a pilgrimage to many holy sites scattered all over Uttara Khand is a lifetime dream for many pious Hindus who come to the Himalayas every year from all over India. To those who inhabit the mountains, its forests and rivers are the very source of their livelihood. And for many who have never seen the Himalayas, they are the source of their life-giving water through hundreds of rivers that flow into the plains. To the natives of the region it is unthinkable that the Himalayas are threatened by the environmental degradation, The sad reality is that it is true.

Protection of the natural environment is of major concern to many Gandhians all over India. However, among those active in the northern region, the name of Sunderlal Bahuguna stands out. The founder of Himalaya Bachao (Save Himalayas) and Chipko (Hug the Trees) movements, he was the recipient of the Right Livelihood Award in Sweden in 1987. Known throughout India as a Sarvodaya Gandhi, he has been involved in many Satyagrahas to save the

265

environment. For his commitment to clean air and water, he has trekked throughout Uttara Khand, opposed the government policies of development, fasted, been beaten, and arrested. Most recently he is involved in a major Satyagraha to stop the building of a mega-dam in Tehri, Garhwal. As an environmentalist, he has been an outspoken leader in many international and national conferences. Inspired by Gandhi, Vinoba, and J. P., Sunderlal Bahuguna is one of those Gandhians who has surrendered his life to the Gandhian ideals. Committed to a life of self-discipline, simplicity, and hard work, along with his wife Vimla, he lives at Navjivan Ashram in a remote village of Silyara, near Tehri, in the district of Garhwal. Currently, one is likely to find him in a small hut on the banks of the Bhagirathi river, near the site of the building of the Tehri Dam. He is in a state of a protest.

Life:

A native of Uttara Khand, Sunderlal was born in 1927 in the village of Marora in Garhwal. Life was tough in the remote village, but his father, through hard and dedicated work, succeeded in becoming a forest officer. Sunderlal grew up marveling at the beauty of nature surrounded by lush trees, clear air, and pure water. He admired his father's love for the holy river, Ganga, which was closely visible from where Ambadatt Bahuguna had built the house for his family. As a young child, Sunderlal heard stories of the river, which was addressed as Mother Ganga. The tranquillity of life was interrupted when his father died while Sunderlal was quite young, and his mother had to assume hard work to provide for the family. Sunderlal witnessed the ordeal of the mountain women, as his own mother tried to make ends meet. The forest, the land, and the river were sources of livelihood, and the people respected them. From his mother, Purna Devi, he learned the value of hard work, discipline, and self-sacrifice. Unaware of Gandhi's existence, Sunderlal spent his early childhood attending a village school, trekking the hillsides, and playing on the banks of the river.

The year 1940 was a crucial year in young Sunderlal's life. At the age of 13 his life was about to change. One day, he saw a man carrying a small wooden box, walking in the village street. Thinking that a magician had come to town, many children followed him around. To their surprise, when the man opened his box, he displayed a portable spinning wheel. He said he was a follower of Gandhi and was going to achieve Indian freedom through the means of a spinning wheel. Attracted by his strange talk, Sunderlal began listening to him more attentively. He recalls, "I

266

used to get 6 annas (few pennies) per week as pocket money. I decided to buy the books this man was selling with this money." These books were: <u>Swaraj Kaise?</u> (How freedom?), <u>Nava Yukon Se Do Baten</u> (A Few Conversations with Youth), and <u>Rashtriya Geet</u> (National Songs). These books had great impact on Sunderlal. He began keeping the old man's company. One day the man asked the boy a question, "What will you do when you grow up?" "I will serve the king," responded Sunderlal. "Who will serve the poor?" retorted the man. "We will do that also," responded Sunderlal. "You cannot serve two gods," remarked the young man. "Then tell us what to do," demanded Sunderlal. "If you don't want to sell yourself for a few pieces of silver, then follow me," proposed the man. With a gleam in his eyes, Sunderlal states, "So we followed the man." The man was none other than <u>Sri Dev Suman</u>, a well-known Gandhian and freedom fighter who worked in the hills.

While Gandhi was busy organizing the Quit-India movement, young Sunderlal got busy reading Gandhi and learning about Sarvodaya and Satyagraha from Dev Suman, his guru. During this time, Garhwal was governed by a king who was oppressive toward his people. Dev Suman organized the people to oppose the king as well as the British occupation of India. In 1944 Suman was jailed and tortured for his activities. Soon Sunderlal organized a youth group for the independence of India, which annoyed the king as well as the British. His activities brought him into the public eye, and the police began to keep a watch on him. While Dev Suman was in jail, Sunderlal smuggled news of his tortures in jail to the press. As a consequence, he was also arrested. Imprisoned for nearly five months, he was subjected to many maltreatments by the police who wished to silence him. While himself incarcerated, he heard the news that his guru and benefactor, Dev Suman had died in jail. He had fasted for 84 days, and according to one account, "All the while he was tortured, heavy weights were tied to his body and he was even flogged.[1] After his release, Sunderlal continued to work for his guru, for which he had to hide from the police. For one year he disguised himself as a Sikh with a beard and a turban, moving from one place to another. At the age of 18 he decided to go to Lahore (now in Pakistan) to complete his studies. Without any money, he shared a room with his brother, but ate meagerly. He began losing weight and became ill. Due to his scholastic achievements, he caught the attention of Prof. Roshan Lal Verma, who arranged for him a better place in which to live and concentrate on his studies. Due to his activities in Garhwal, the police followed him to Lahore. He managed to escape from the school with the help of his friends

267

until the police slacked off. After the life of a runaway, he managed to return to Lahore and finish his B. A. degree.[2]

Sunderlal's return to Tehri, Garhwal, marked a new era in his life. Along with some friends, he joined a protest movement against the oppressive king of the area. As the movement grew, he came in contact with various congress leaders in Delhi, and presented them a plan for the liberation of Garhwal. Gradually, he found himself being pulled into the Indian politics, but he resisted the temptation of fighting the elections and being elected to the Indian parliament. He was more drawn toward Sarvodaya and the Gandhian thought. He was aware that one of Gandhi's English disciples, Mira Behn, had an ashram in Rishikesh at the foothills of Garhwal. Sunderlal recalls, "Meera Behn used to tour the hills on horseback because she was concerned about the flood problems in the region which started in the mountains. I used to walk nearly 40 kilometers to work with her." The association with Meera brought Sunderlal into the Gandhian constructive work. It was she who insisted that if he wanted to change the conditions in Garhwal, he must work for the uplift of the poor. Sunderlal took her advice and opened a small ashram in 1956 in Silyara. Another prominent Gandhian, Sarla Behn, was engaged in the women's work in the hills of Kumaon. Sunderlal met her also and their association proved to be fruitful. Sunderlal's wife-to-be, Vimla was being trained as a Gandhian social worker in Sarla Behn's ashram. After their marriage, both he and Vimla began their work among the poor hill people.

By the time the Bahuguna's began their work in the remote village of Silyara, the Gandhi Smarak Nidhi, an institution that coordinated the Sarvodaya constructive works had been formed in Delhi. Sunderlal could have received the financial support from this organization for his work. However, he deliberately decided against it. He remembers, "Gandhi's last will and testimony was before me. That's all I needed. I did not want to be dependent on the Smarak Nidhi for financial support." Nonetheless, the money was needed for their work. Therefore, Sunderlal took on various labor jobs while Vimla taught school. Armed with Gandhian ideals, both of them worked hard to free the people from their miseries. Soon, Sunderlal came face-to-face with the problem of untouchability. Since both Sunderlal and Vimla belonged to a high caste but freely mixed with the harijans, many families began opposing them. One manifestation of this opposition was that they were refused entry into many homes. The stage was set for organizing a movement against untouchability, which they did. A movement was organized to oppose the authorities who did not allow the harijans to enter the Buda Kedar temple. Sunderlal and Vimla were beaten and insulted but continued their struggle. At this point, Sunderlal took to a long pad yatra, (foot march) bringing the message of love and acceptance of all to many villages. Simultaneously, he launched a Satyagraha against the selling of liquor in the hills. The consumption of liquor was responsible for many social and economic problems. Sunderlal mobilized the people and went on a 16-day fast "to express solidarity with the people's desire for the removal of the liquor vend."[3]

In 1960, while the Bhoodan movement was gaining momentum, Vinoba Bhave asked Sunderlal to join him in his pad yatras to obtain land. Leaving his wife behind to look after the work of Navjivan Ashram, he joined Vinoba's movement. Recalling his decision to take that step, Sunderlal ponders, "And that is how I joined the Sarvodaya family." He looks upon the years spent with Vinoba with fond memories. "Vinoba was a living example of how the Gandhian ideals should be put into practice, it states Sunderlal, "and I was so touched by Vinoba's spirituality." Although his Bhoodan Yatras were satisfying, his heart was in Garhwal, to which he longed to return to continue his constructive work.

In the 1970's, Sunderlal plunged wholeheartedly into the work of saving the forests of Garhwal. It is well known that during the British occupation of India, the British developed the lumber industry which allowed various contractors to cut down the precious trees. They also planted pines which could be used for extracting resin and making a variety of turpentine-based products. They also invented the method of transporting the logs by floating them on mountain rivers to be collected in the plains. Sunderlal began protesting against the big industries that were exploiting the natural resources. He favored forest-based, small-scale industries that were beneficial for the local people. However, when he saw the environmental degradation that the felling of the forest was causing, he became determined to save the forest. Between the years 1973-75, he traveled 4,200 kilometers on foot in the hills to observe the problem of deforestation and related environmental issues. He also encouraged the youth to spread the news about the depletion of forest resources. In many villages, the efforts were underway to block the contractors from cutting the trees, and the famous Chipko Movement (Hug the Trees) was in the making. Soon, Sunderlal was working with other environmentalists in the Himalayan regions. Among these was Chandi Prasad Bhatt, who was another Gandhian Sarvodaya worker and well known for his work with the Chipko movement.[4]

With the rise of the Chipko movement, people were hugging the trees in many villages and frustrating the government as well as the contractors. In some cases violence broke out when police tried to remove the protesters. Sunderlal organized the non-violent satyagrahas to keep the Gandhian ideals alive throughout the struggle. While Chipko was being associated primarily with the felling of trees, Sunderlal realized that the problem was much larger. The trees were connected with the problem of water shortages, land erosions, floods, depletion of herbs, etc. In fact, due to the process of symbiosis, attention needed to be paid to the entire region of the Himalayas. Thus, Sunderlal founded the Himalaya Bachao (Save Himalayas) movement to address many problems. It was his effort to force the government of India to formulate a "Himalayan Policy" rather than to ignore the problems that existed there or to act without any knowledge of the conditions of the hill people. Due to his efforts, the movement has gone beyond the region of Garhwal. Other Himalayan provinces have also become conscious of the problems. As a result of his efforts, which included mobilization of the people, pad yatras, satyagrahas, and many fasts, the government has taken some actions. Today, the felling of trees at heights over 1,000 meters has been banned.

Sunderlal's ecological concerns led him to organize a major pad yatra, which is well known as Kashmir to Kohima March, lasting over 2 years and covering the distance of 4,870 kilometers. The purpose of the March was to bring China, Nepal, and India to a common platform to discuss the conditions of their dwindling forest resources. More than that, it was a gigantic effort to raise the consciousness of the hill people about the environmental degradation in their backyard. The march went through four stages, starting in Kashmir and ending in Nagaland. Several concerned citizens and the environmentalists walked with Sunderlal to a great distance. However, he was the only marcher who walked the entire distance. Over the period of 300 days, Sunderlal studied the conditions of the forests, the problems of soil erosion, the malpractice of the contractors, indiscriminate road building, and other forms of environmental damages. According to Sunderlal's biographer, Bhart Dogra:

> Six reports on different areas and aspects of ecological ruin in the Himalayas were prepared and submitted to different governments -- report on Kashmir, report on Himachal Pradesh, report on W. Bengal hills (Darjeeling), report on U.P. Hills, on resin tapping and report on Nepal. The message of the march was presented at several conferences at home and abroad, including the U. N. Energy Conference in Nairobi.[5]

What is most significant about Kashmir to the Kohima march is that it uncovered the years of neglect of the Himalayan regions. The problem included indiscriminate cutting of the forest by the lumber companies, excessive extraction, building of saw mills in the remote forest areas, destroying trees to build roads, corruption of the officers to accept bribes from contractors, etc. The ecological crisis has resulted in landslides, floods, droughts, depletion ^of forest-based resources, and related problems. However, due to Sunderlal's efforts, the government has become more watchful, and the people are more informed of their rights. He admits, "It is people's power that will bring changes," and he is committed to building that power.

Sunderlal Bahuguna's recent activities center around his Satyagraha against the building of the mega Tehri Dam. Based on geological findings, Sunderlal claims that this dam is being built in a region that is most prone to earthquakes. It will not only dislocate thousands of people upstream, but it will also present a real danger to hundreds of villages and towns down stream. Not only that, it proposes to supply the water and electricity to the larger cities of North India, while the local people are not benefited by its presence. In order to stop its construction, Sunderlal has courted arrests, imprisonment, and loss of life through rigorous fasting.

The Tehri Dam project was conceived under Primer Minister Nehru's government in 1949. When the project report was completed by 1969, it was revealed that a fault 20 meters wide existed along the bed in the dam site.[6] The potential dangers from the fault as well as the weak rocks that will support the dam were kept a secret from the general public. However, when a document regarding the dam leaked during the Janta Party regime in 1980, the people of Tehri organized themselves to oppose the construction of the dam. In 1983, having read a report on the ecological disaster, caused by the Aswan Dam in Egypt, various groups, including Sunderlal's Chipko group, filed a petition with the Supreme Court to stop the construction of the dam in Tehri. Ever since then, Sunderlal has become the protagonist in the Tehri Bandh Virodhi Sangharsh Samiti (the Committee in opposition to the dam).

At the height of 850 feet, with the estimated cost of millions of dollars, the dam has been declared a seismic risk by many experts. Despite oppositions from various NGOs, the government is determined to complete the project with help of a substantial financial aid from Russia. Sunderlal believes that this construction will bring havoc to the hills as well as to the plains. The problems are many. According to S. P. Nautiyal, President, Wadia Institute of Himalayan Geology, Dehra Dun,

271

"the rocks of the dam site are highly fissile, phyllites, quartzschist with variously thick gouge zones in between the foliation and along numerous other shear zones."[7] His recommendation: the area is not safe for a dam of this size. Due to the problem of silting, the life of the dam will be 30-40 years instead of 100.[8] There is also the estimate that the reservoir created to hold the millions of gallons of water will submerge the entire town of Tehri. It will change the ecological balance, creating mud slides along the reservoir, and weakening the structure. The main concern is the earthquakes as evidenced by a major disaster that occurred in 1991, and took the lives of thousands of people. The government's claim that the Tehri Dam will withstand the shocks of a major earthquake is not acceptable to the Satyagrahis who oppose its construction. What bothers the environmentalist, Dr. Vandana Shiva, is that the government keeps the development of the project a secret. It encourages powerful contractors who build dams to "...buy up engineers, experts, and politicians while local people's prosperity is destroyed and independent and free scientific knowledge is stifled and marginated. It is inherent to projects like Tehri Dam that they must kill both nature and democracy for 30 short years of electricity generation."[9]

Since the Uttara Khand earthquake of 1991, which destroyed many lives and property in and around Tehri, Sunderlal has taken many fasts in an attempt to call the government's attention to the problem. In 1992 after the police raided his Satyagraha site near the dam, he went on a 45-day fast. While several of his social activists were jailed, as a consequence of their protest, many political leaders began visiting the site. In 1996, he again went on a longer fast until the Prime Minister, H. D. Deve Gowda, persuaded him to end the fast. Due to his efforts, the heavy blasting at the site of the dam has been stopped. While the government studies the problem, the construction has been delayed.

Thought:

Even though Sunderlal Bahuguna met Gandhi only once, just before the Mahatma's assassination in 1948, the Gandhian legacy has been the cornerstone of his thought. Inspired by Gandhi, Vinoba, and J. P., he considers himself a member of the Sarvodaya Family. Although he has never held an office within the Sarva Seva Sangh, he is readily recognized by many Sarvodaya workers as one of India's leading Gandhian activists. Like many Gandhians, his goal is to lay the foundation of a new society where the welfare of all will be the basis of all human endeavors. In pursuit of this goal he is critical of those forces that are taking the world in the direction of materialistic progress at the cost of spiritual bankruptcy. Within the philosophies of Sarvodaya and Satyagraha, he sees Gandhi's spiritual concerns as central to the creation of a new social order.

Bahuguna is an ardent critic of what he calls "the tradition of Development." As an environmentalist, he sees modern development as one of the major causes of ecological crises. He believes that the tradition of "development" began with President Harry Truman, who on January 10, 1949, declared that the world's greatest problem was the lack of development of the poor countries, for which America was willing to give financial and technical assistance.[10] Sunderlal asks the question; what kind of development was America going to promote? He answers his own question by stating that this development was based on two faulty premises:

1. That nature has no identity of its own, and it can be bought and sold.
2. That society is made up of human beings only.

For Sunderlal, these assumptions disregard a holistic approach to life, where all life is interconnected. Taking the example of America, he believes that the effect of this thinking was that the Europeans who came there began cutting the forests for settlements. In the name of development, the natural resources were exploited and slowly people were alienated from nature. Gradually science and technology became servants of development. He concludes that today all over the world human life is totally dependent on oil, gas, chemicals, and other natural resources that have limited supplies. In the race to produce more and more, consumption of goods has become the basis of human happiness. The result is that the world suffers from environmental degradation, and happiness is nowhere to be found.

Sunderlal is fond of quoting the Buddha, who, he believes, had a better understanding of development and the source of happiness. In his Four Noble Truths, the heart of Buddhist spirituality, the Buddha stated: 1. There was universal suffering. 2. The cause of suffering was ignorant craving. 3. The craving needed to be abolished. 4. It could be done by following an 8-fold path, leading to true happiness (Nirvana). For Sunderlal, craving is the basis of development. He feels that modern capitalist economic theories promote the proliferation of desires. We are all told to consume more and more to be happy. "Just look at the advertisement industry," he says. "you don't have to be much educated to understand the message they are giving us." He argues that not everyone can buy more and more. Even if they could, the Buddhist insight is that it will not bring happiness. Sunderlal links

Buddha to Gandhi through Sarvodaya. He believes that Gandhi was supportive of Buddha's insights as introduced by his formulation of Sarvodaya philosophy. In fact, Ruskin, the Buddha, and Gandhi have common insights when it comes to controlling desires and seeking the welfare of all. He is also indebted to Ivon Illich, the Mexican thinker, who, under the influence of Gandhi, sold his assets and lived in a hut to experiment with "simple living and high thinking." Sunderlal paid a visit to Illich during his travel to Mexico and found in him a kindred soul.

As an alternative to development, Sunderlal wishes to promote the notion of "sustainable economy." Since the natural resources are limited and the over consumption is causing environmental havoc, the only alternative is to use "renewable" resources. The best means for providing such resources are the trees. Thus, Sunderlal promotes the planting of fruit and nut trees in place of focusing on agriculture. He quotes Gandhi, who, in 1926, wrote to Kaka Kalelkar that for India the next step should not be toward unified agriculture but toward planting the gardens with fruit trees. For Sunderlal this is the new scientific thinking from which the world can benefit. He agrees with Gandhi that planting fruit trees will save labor (more labor is needed in agriculture), provide nourishment, stabilize rainfall, save the soil, and provide general well-being. Furthermore, they both believe that fruit-culture has economic, political, and spiritual benefits.[11] Since the dawn of the Chipko movement, Sunderlal has been advocating the planting of fruit trees along with saving the forests of India. He feels that the government will not move in this direction, and that the people must organize themselves to work for sustainable economy.

Although Sunderlal is concerned with the world-wide ecological crises, he is particularly concerned about the region of Garhwal in Uttara Khand. He believes that until the 19th century the historical evidence shows that Garhwal was a very prosperous Himalayan region. It produced sufficient grains, fruits, spices, herbs, oils, leather, etc.[12] However, by the end of the 19th century its prosperity began to decline. The main reason for the decline was the British exploitation of the region for their own good. The East India Company expanded its trading practices in the hill regions. The forests were cut down for the lumber industry and more profitable pine trees were planted to extract turpentine. When the people objected, they were pacified by promises of developing agriculture in the hills. After independence, the policy of exploiting the hills continued. The forests were cut down to promote the cultivation of potatoes and apples. It affected the animal husbandry since the means of fodder became scarce. During the previous several five-year plans the government did not pay any attention to the proper development of the region. It was not until the 7th plan that some attention was given to the Himalayas, but that was to develop more trade. The attention was given to the planting of pine trees. The people opposed the pine plantation because it increases the acidity of the soil, depletes the water resources, and provides no fodder for the livestock. Sunderlal sees the benefit of the pine trees only for the contractors who are in the business of promoting the turpentine related industry. For the hill people it is a means of destroying the valuable resources of water and soil.[13] Thus, Sunderlal through the Save The Himalayan Movement is trying his best to empower the people in order that they may chart their own destiny. Today, there is an intensified movement to claim for Uttara Khand a separate statehood. The present government favors the move, but the actual creation of a separate state remain to be seen.

In his writings and speeches, Bahuguna often makes a distinction between knowledge and wisdom. He maintains that in today's world there is so much emphasis on gaining knowledge and less on using our wisdom. He is particularly concerned that we attempt to solve most of our problems by so-called "experts." There are technical experts who want to solve the village problems. The fact is that the villagers have the wisdom, but no power to change their fate. Thus, in the name of development, urban values of the intellectuals are often imposed upon the rural people. Sunderlal believes in nurturing Jan-Shakti (people's power) among the rural people so that they may instruct the "experts" with their wisdom. He links the utilization of wisdom with Sarvodaya. The welfare of all, according to Sarvodaya must begin with the bottom upward. This means that for Sarvodaya the wisdom of those who are at the bottom of the social scale must be given utmost importance. Sunderlal believes that Ivan Illich was thinking along the same lines when he wrote his book, De-Schooling Society. Like Illich, Sunderlal maintains that the ordinary people are the victims of the "tyranny of knowledge." However, "to run the affairs of the world only on wisdom will be foolhardy," says Bahuguna. Nonetheless, he feels, "the knowledge must be supplemented with wisdom." What concerns him is that in the name of knowledge, the wisdom of the people is ridiculed by those who claim to be guided by "reason."

Along with many other leading Gandhians, Sunderlal has been an arch critic of India's current liberalization of economic policies which allows the multinational companies to do business in India. He feels that such a step will deepen India's ecological crises. He states, "by aggressively propagating the concept of liberalization, the West is trying to make third world countries, including India, a dumping ground for their polluting industries and are avidly eyeing the resources of these countries as fodder for their future economic growth."[14] He also says, "there is an urgent need to orchestrate a nationwide movement against the impending danger to Indian ecology in the wake of the ongoing liberalization process."[15] Sunderlal is also critical of various political parties in India who have no serious concern for protecting the environment. In his words, "the environment does not figure anywhere on the agenda of any political party in India. Political parties in the country have started believing in a new found religion of economy. For them market is the temple, the technocrats the high priests, and dollars are the new God.[16] On the issue of the environmental crises in India, Bahuguna has the support of many scientists. Among them is Anil Aggarwal, director of the Center for Science and Environment in New Delhi. Dr. Aggarwal believes that India is in the middle of an environmental disaster, and its cities are among the world's most polluted areas. Like Sunderlal he warns, "the only hope lies when environmental issues become part of electoral politics. People must have control over the environment, but for that to happen, we need political change. Nothing will happen unless there is electoral pressure."[17]

Through such movements as Chipko, Save The Himalayas, and the Tehri Dam Virodh Samiti, Sunderlal has been tirelessly engaged in raising the consciousness of the people regarding many environmental issues. For him, his work is primarily about creating Jan Shakti (people's power) as Gandhi would have it. It bothers him that "while 5% of Indians are running the country with the bureaucratic support of another 20%, the other 75% are the silent majority." His goal is to wake the majority up in the hope of bringing a Sarvodaya society into reality. In his acceptance speech on the occasion of being honored with "The Right Livelihood Award" on December 9, 1987, in Sweden, Sunderlal exhorted the life and message of Gandhi for the entire world. His own life has shown that he is committed to bringing Gandhi's vision of Ram Raj into fruition. However, no Ram Raj is possible unless the environment is saved.

Endnotes: Chapter XVIII

1 Bharat Dogra, Living for Others: Vimla and Sunderlal Bahuguna, (New Delhi: Multiplexus, 1993), p. 24.

2 Ibid., p. 26

3 Ibid., p. 28

4 For Chandi Prasad's involvement with Chipko, see Mark Shepard, Gandhi Today (Washington, D. C.: Seven Locks Press) 1987, Ch. 4 ("Hug the Trees").

5 Bharat Dogra, Ibid., p. 37

6 Sandhya Jain, "A Dam of Sorrow for the Tehri People," in Tehri Dam (The Intach Environmental Series, New Delhi: Intraprastha Press, 1987), p. 38.

7 S. P. Nautiyal, "Notes on the Tehri Dam Project," Ibid., p. 13-14.

8 Ibid., p. 15.

9 Vandana Shiva, "Veil of Secrecy and Silence," Friends of Chipko, Ignoring Reason, Inviting, Disaster, New Delhi: Vision Wordtronic Pvt. Ltd. (no date), p. 28.

10 Sunderlal Bahuguna, Chipko Ka Sandesh (The Message of Chipko) published by Chipko Information Center, Navajivan Ashram, Tehri Garhwal (no date), p. 2

11 Ibid., p. 10

12 Ibid., p. 16

13 Ibid., p. 18-20

14 Dhanaijjay Kumar, "Liberalization called Ecological Disaster" in India Abroad, Vol. XXVII No. 10, Dec. 6, 1996, p. 24

15 Ibid., p. 24

16 Ibid., p. 24

17 Tanni Pande, "Political Pressure Urged to Avert a Disaster," Ibid., p. 24.

XIX

Challenging the Multinationals and Centralized Polity
Thakurdas Bang

In January of 1993 I had the privilege of attending a conference at <u>Seva Gram</u>, the well known Gandhian ashram at Wardha, Maharashtra. Several of my Gandhian friends had insisted that I should plan to attend the conference if I was to understand the nature of the current crisis that India was facing. It was the theme 'Azadi Bachao' (Save Democracy) that was most intriguing. Initiated by <u>Sarva Seva Sangh</u>, the conference brought some of India's leading Gandhians to a common platform. The conference was a follow-up on an earlier meeting of the like-minded Gandhians, who had met a year earlier to discuss the pressing national problems. With mutual consent 'Save Democracy' was chosen to be the famous Seva Gram Declaration. Many of the participants were fresh from traveling around the country for national integration after the destruction of the Babri Mosque in Ayodhya on Dec. 6, 1992. I thought that most of the speakers would focus on Hindu-Muslim unity since that issue was still fresh on everyone's mind and directly related to the issue of democracy. However, the issue turned out to be different. The focus of the conference was India's 'New Economic Policy' and its implications for the survival of village India. It was concluded that since India had opened its door to the multinational companies, its economic independence was threatened, and India was being held hostage by foreign investors. Thus, the democracy was being threatened.

Among Sarvodaya Gandhians who are challenging the presence of the multinational companies in India, the name of <u>Thakurdas Bang</u> is quite prominent. In an unpublished survey which I conducted among the Sarvodaya workers in 1992-93, the name of Thakurdas Bang was repeatedly mentioned as "a leading contemporary Gandhian in India today" by a majority of the people. I had first met Professor Bang (he was a professor of Economics before joining the Gandhian movement) in 1981. He had facilitated my visit to Vinoba's ashram in Paunar, which began my journey to study the Sarvodaya Movement. At that time he was the president of Sarva Seva Sangh, and an ardent supporter of J. P.'s Total Revolution. Today he has authored several books, an is widely recognized as a leading theoretician of Gandhian Sarvodaya philosophy.

Life:

Professor Bang was born in 1917 in the state of Maharashtra. Though his early years were uneventful, his family knew about Gandhi who had just returned from South Africa. Thakurdas grew in an environment that was charged with the freedom struggle. By the time he entered college, he was recognized as a high achiever by his teachers. He had a brilliant academic career, and obtained his Bachelor's degree with distinction. He was attracted to economics as a subject and aspired to be a professor of economics some day. Due to his excellent academic record he was admitted to a postgraduate program and passed his M. A. exams in First Division. His friends and family intended for him to proceed to London for further studies after he had successfully completed a degree in law. Thakurdas recalls, "in those days young men aspired to go to England in order to pass the Indian Civil Service (I. C. S) examinations, and enter the government service." As fate would have it, he accepted a position as a lecturer in a degree college in Wardha. By the time Gandhi sent a call to young people of India to join him in the freedom struggle, Thakurdas became restless at heart. He had a brilliant career in front of him, but his conscience was dictating that he must fight for his country's freedom. Consequently he plunged into the Quit-India Movement of 1942. He was arrested and spent two years of his life in a British jail.

The imprisonment was the time for reading, reflection, and learning more about Satyagraha. Gandhi had made an impression on him, and he was convinced that the uplift of the villagers was extremely important. He contemplated on joining Gandhi's constructive work program after his release. Upon being freed from the jail, he rejoined the college as a professor, and formed a 'Village Service League'. This was a forum of students who organized themselves under his leadership to work in several villages near Wardha. Their goal was to help in rural reconstruction along Gandhian lines. Thakurdas set up Gram Seva Kendras (centers for village service) in several of these villages. Through these centers he sought to organize the villagers. They identified their problems and began exploring ways to end their exploitation. Like elsewhere in India, their biggest problem was the apathy of the people and exploitation of local vested interests, besides the demand for higher taxes. To his credit, Thakurdas mobilized the people of Chimur-Ashti villages, who had been particularly harassed by the British.

In Chimur - Ashti villages which are situated in adjoining districts of Maharashtra, the local people had taken massive part in hoisting the national flag, instead of the Union Jack of the British, on police stations -- vestiges of British authority. The police officers resisted this attempt and fired, resulting half a dozen casualties. This infuriated the people, and they beat several constables and officers to death and burnt government buildings. For a few days People's Raj remained in these villages. Afterwards, the army was sent to these villages by the British authorities to capture these citadels of freedom, arresting and imprisoning over 200 people, sentencing most of them to very long terms of imprisonment, including capital punishments to a dozen patriots. The people were under the spell of fear for several months, and many women were raped by the army. One of Gandhiji's foremost disciples, Professor Bhansali, resorted to an indefinite fast against these atrocities and ended it after 60 days only when an impartial inquiry by the British government was undertaken. Up on his release from jail, Thakurdas undertook a tour of these villages along with over 30 students from the college and helped them to shed fear. Also a fund to assist the needy was raised and distributed amongst them. Contact was established through the village service league with several villages near Wardha and economic and social surveys of these villages were undertaken through the students. This resulted into deeper knowledge of the problems of the villages. So sanitation, adoption of simple measures of naturopathy (simple medicines for common ailments), were taught to villagers through the village service league. All of this resulted into a dialogue on the present situation and helped to generate the spirit of struggle against the British Raj.

Professor Bang met Gandhi for the purpose of conveying to him the message from Kumarappa -- the foremost Gandhian economist -- since he was also in jail with Thakurdas. Since he was also a firm believer in Gandhian thought, Thakurdas did not feel the need to meet Gandhi frequently. He focused on working with his students and imparting them the Gandhian outlook on life. Recalling those years, Prof. Bang states, "I had no desire for personal publicity. I believed in working quietly through the constructive work program. So I changed my abode from the city of Wardha to an adjoining village along with a dozen students. Along with our college studies we helped the villagers in adult education, sanitation, preparation of organic manure, etc." Through this work, Prof. Bang was able to raise "a land army" from amongst the villagers to do the community work. For him this was an exercise in "discipline, sacrificial living, and self-reliance."

The excitement of independence in 1947 soon turned into depression at the assassination of Gandhi. Greatly distressed, Thakurdas gave some serious thought as to how he must propagate Gandhian ideas. He kept coming back to the notion that true independence will not be achieved until the villages of India become self-sufficient. He was haunted by Gandhi's dream of Ram Raj, and Vinoba's notion of Gram Swaraj. During this period, he grew close to Vinoba Bhave and was impressed by his interpretation of Gandhi. On Vinoba's advice, Prof. Bang with several of his associates took up the constructive program in the village of Mahakal, near Paunar ashram. He resigned from his college post to freely dedicate himself for the work of Sarvodaya.

When Vinoba launched his Bhoodan Movement, Thakurdas was right along with him. He recalls, "We were so impressed and hopeful that a new revolution was in the making. Hopeful, because Vinoba was tackling the most chronic land problem." Vinoba sent him to Bihar to work for Bhoodan, an assignment he willingly accepted. In Bihar, along with other associates, he worked on the strategy of the 'pad-yatra' that Vinoba was to undertake. He mobilized several groups that could organize the Bhoodan work, reducing the burden of collecting and distributing land by top Sarvodaya leaders. Thakurdas then moved to the state of Madhya Pradesh and other states of India for the purpose of organizing the Bhoodan work in 1954. Pleased with his work, Vinoba paid him the highest compliment at Kanchipuram Sarvodaya gathering in 1955. He recalls that Vinoba said, "...like what Khruschev did in Russia to establish collective leadership, Prof. Bang and his associates did in the field of organizing padyatras in groups of ordinary workers. This he called 'the search for people's servant'." For the next two years, Thakurdas was entrusted with the task of organizing many groups for the Bhoodan work all over India. he intensively engaged himself in the service which brought him highest of praises from Vinoba and the fellow Sarvodaya workers.

While the Bhoodan Revolution was on, Thakurdas was directed by Vinoba to go to Dhule district of Maharashtra, and work among the tribals. Thus began his adventure in the jungles of Dhule from 1958 till 1960. During this period he lived among the adivasis with three of his close associates. He remembers, "in the beginning the tribals were suspicious and perceived us as outsiders. We were also concerned about gaining their confidence." However, it was not too long before the tribals saw them as their friends. Thakurdas and company began by educating the adivasis' children, caring for their health, and improving their farming methods. They discovered that the tribals suffered from addiction to alcoholism, gambling, and many other social vices. They were also victimized by the rich contractors who used them as cheap labor. Thakurdas held regular gram sabhas (village meetings) to discuss their problems with them. As a result of these meetings they were educated about their rights and were empowered to deal with the exploitations they suffered. Reflecting on those years, Prof. Bang states, "My work with the tribals was most satisfying, since it gave me a chance to meet and know a group of people who were completely ignored under the British rule. I hope I made a difference in their lives by teaching them."

In 1960, Thakurdas returned to Seva Gram ashram, and for the next few years he concentrated on working for Nai Talim (Basic Education). His entry into the program of Nai Talim was due to personal reasons. He was faced with the issue of educating his own sons who were in their teens. Disillusioned by the traditional college education which he deemed as "bookish and impractical in India", he was searching for an alternate method of education. When he came to the Gandhian ashram of Seva Gram, he learned that the Nai Talim that Gandhi had envisioned had been stopped. He realized that many of his colleagues were faced with a similar situation, and were in search of an alternate model. Therefore, Prof. Bang, along with his wife, gathered some school age children and began an education program for them. However, they soon ran into a practical problem. To their astonishment they learnt that their Nai Talim was not recognized by the universities and colleges. Not only that, even the government did not look upon his method with a favorable eye. He recalls, "The problem of further education after the termination of Seva Gram school stared us in the face. So we came to the conclusion that unless the whole system -- political, social, economic and cultural institutions -- is changed, the single school experience of ours will not work. Furthermore, it will frustrate the students." Therefore, Thakurdas abandoned the Nai Talim experiment and plunged into the Sarvodaya social work to change the Indian society. He is still involved with this process.

Since 1964, Prof. Bang has been primarily working as one of the chief organizers in the Sarvodaya Movement. He became the President of The Maharashtra Sarvodaya Mandal and then appointed General Secretary of the All

283

India Sarva Seva Sangh. From 1979 to 1985 he was elected the president of the same body. One of his goals during this tenure was to organize the Sarvodaya workers all over the country. His primary concern became to educate them and mobilize them for the village work along Gandhian lines.

Prior to his election as President of the Sarva Seva Sangh, Thakurdas came in close contact with Jai Prakash Narayan(J. P.). During the J. P. and Vinoba split, he sided with J. P. and became a protagonist for J. P.'s Total Revolution. Reflecting on those years(mid 1970's), he states, "I had always respected Vinoba and still do. I was affected by his spirituality and wholeheartedly supported him in his Bhoodan Movement. But, many of us thought that after his retirement at Paunar, Vinoba was gradually losing touch with reality. J. P. on the other hand had his finger on the pulse of the country." Prof. Bang feels that he never really completely left Vinoba, but, rather, took a leave from Sarva Seva Sangh as Vinoba had advised his associates to do, as they sought to mobilize against the dictatorial tendencies in Indira Gandhi's government. In defense of J. P., he states, "J. P. was not entering politics as some followers of Vinoba charged him. He was challenging the corruption of the government. When Janta government was formed, he took no political office, which he could have easily done." For Thakurdas, J. P. was a loknayak (guide of the people) and the founder of Loktantra (people's freedom) movement. J. P.'s Mushahri experiment, which he narrates in his book, Face to Face, convinced him that the political corruption flowed from the top (central govt.) to the bottom (local govt.). Thus he challenged Indira's government but never gave up building from the bottom. "J. P. was always for Gram Swaraj," says Thakurdas, "he encouraged us to build people's power by working with the villagers." Today, he is continuing the work for Total Revolution through a variety of programs he has launched with his Sarvodaya colleagues. Some of these include organizing the youth for Swadeshi (self-sufficiency), full employment for the poor, formation of new Gram Sabhas, communal harmony, Shanti-Sena, youth for Gandhi, and challenging the New Economic Policy and the presence of the multinational companies in India.

For communal harmony, Thakurdas provided the major leadership in organizing a group of Sarvodaya workers to fast in protest against the religious fundamentalism and militancy of the Hindutva movement. They chose the site of Ayodhya, where the controversial Babri Mosque was located and was about to be destroyed by the hands of the Hindu extremists. Thus, in 1992, about a hundred Sarvodaya workers pitched their tents on the banks of the Sarju River and commenced their fast to stop the communal violence against the Muslim community at the hands of the supporters of Hindutva. The Hindu extremists destroyed their tents, threw away their spinning wheels, and beat them up. The police intervened and the protest was broken up. After the Dec. 6, 1992 event of the destruction of the Babri Mosque, Thakurdas Bang and associates decided to tour the country to preach communal harmony. About fifty thousand people participated in this activity. Their goal was to reach the villages and control violence. Reflecting on his tour of the nation, Prof. Bang stated, "our goal was not only to preach the Gandhian thought, but to tell them about Gram Swaraj as well."

Since 1993 Thakurdas has taken it upon himself the task of visiting many colleges and universities. When I interviewed him in 1993, he stated, "India has 175 universities and about 7,000 colleges. We must approach them and tap the hearts and minds of the youth. It is our experience that the youth have a positive attitude and desire to change." He has been contemplating to start a youth movement under the name of 'youth for Gram Swaraj' or 'youth for Gandhi'. He further stated that Sarva Seva Sangh had initiated a 'Peace College Project' in order to reach the students. These projects were inspired by J. P., who had started Tarun Vahini (Youth Brigade), but suspended it during the Emergency Period. Thakurdas wants to revive such a youth force for nation building. He is deeply concerned that today most of the colleges and universities have become centers of political activities. Consequently, the students are pawns in the hands of various political parties who use them for their selfish gains. However, their use of youth force is for destructive purposes. Even the student union elections are supported by the political parties and funded by controllers of power. Thus, we witness violence on college campuses and more often the colleges and universities are closed down due to unrest. Prof. Bang feels that the youth force can be harnessed for the benefit of society. Currently, Thakurdas Bang is working through Rashtriya Yuva Sangathan (National Youth Organization) in assisting youth to organize themselves. The objectives of this organization include the promotion of non-violence, economic and social equality, self-reliance, and equality of all religions.

Thakurdas Bang's most recent efforts have been in the area of challenging India's New Economic Policy. Under this policy, India has opened its door to foreign investors through multinational companies. Now many foreign companies are permitted to hold more than 51% of the shares. This policy enforces the idea that India must produce more consumer goods and consume more and more. Its implications for import and export are to purchase high tech machinery at any cost, borrow more money through International Monetary Fund (IMF) and the World Bank, establish credit by selling Indian goods to foreign countries to earn foreign exchange to pay off the debts, send the best products overseas, and in general exhaust nation's raw materials for the benefit of the rich and powerful. Prof. Bang's 'Save Democracy' campaign is a movement to educate the people of India about the manner in which they are being exploited by the government, industrialists, and the foreign companies. To this end he continuously organizes conferences, seminars, and satyagrahas. He feels that if under the New Economic Policy the rich succeed in imposing their economic agenda on the masses, then democracy in India will be endangered. The only way to combat this situation is to empower the villagers so that they may raise their voices. He has participated in many Satyagrahas against the multi-national companies. He states, "Small successes have been achieved here and there. For example, a powerful multi-national, Cargill, which started to construct a jetty on the western coast to start overseas trading, had to withdraw before people's power generated by Satyagraha." Thakurdas Bang calls this a "lonely instance" and feels that a lot of work needs to be done to defeat the interest of the rich companies in India.

In 1993, Prof. Bang established <u>Lok Swaraj Sangh</u> (People's Freedom Organization) for the purpose of educating the voters in order that they may properly utilize their voting power. For this effort he traveled the length and breadth of the country to seek people's support. Again, his goal was to reach the villages, where many political parties have their centers. The goal of <u>Swaraj Sangh</u> is not to support any political party or candidate, rather to mobilize voters on the local and national level on issues of importance. None of the members is encouraged to hold political offices. In a recent interview Thakurdas stated that even though the work of 'voter's councils' for the purpose of freedom was good, he did not achieve much success in this area. He and his associates came to the realization that unless an all-round changes take place, progress on this solitary front is impossible. Meanwhile, new problems like mounting unemployment due to the destruction of almost all village industries, spread of consumerism due to television, mounting corruption in all walks of life, environmental degradation (of water, air and soil), mounting casteism and communalism needed the immediate attention of the Sarvodaya movement. Therefore, in 1997 (the Golden Jubilee year of India's independence) Prof. Bang under the patronage of Sarva Seva Sangh launched a renewed movement for building from below. This is the new phase of the Gram Swaraj movement.

In the Golden Jubilee of Gandhi's assassination (1998), Prof. Bang, along with the leadership of Sarva Seva Sangh, had made Gram Swaraj the main platform of the Sarvodaya movement. It is their goal to declare a minimum of 5000 villages in the states of Gujarat, Maharashtra and Rajasthan as Gram Swaraj villages. What that means is that these villages, based on Article 40 of the Constitution of India, will declare autonomous Gram Panchayats and settle their problems themselves. To this end Thakurdas is busy establishing Gram Sabhas (village assemblies) in many villages, which will in turn elect the Gram Panchayats. When I asked him how this emphasis on Gram Sabhas was different from that of Gandhi, Vinoba, and J. P., and what made him think that Sarvodaya will succeed now, he responded by stating, "This is a good question. For fifty years people listened to us (on the issue of Gram Sabha), but did not take us seriously because they felt that the government will bring the Panchayati Raj as the Constitution mandated. However, the government was not effective in fulfilling its promise. Now the people have lost faith in the government, and they are ready to act on their own. They are realizing that Gram Swaraj is the only way to their freedom. Many crises have brought them to this awareness." He reports that many villages, where he works, have declared "village autonomy" and started many constructive works like enriching the soil by producing and using organic manure, self-reliance in primary necessities of life like food, clothing and shelter, starting village funds for social welfare and development, settling the disputes in the village thereby boycotting courts and police, prohibition against liquor, etc. For Thakurdas, these are the steps towards Gram Swaraj.

Thought:

As a prodigious thinker and writer, Prof. Bang has written extensively on various aspects of the Gandhian thought.[1] Most of his writings are responses to the crisis that India has faced since independence. His well known book, Whither India (1988) summarizes his thought in a nut shell. During our conversation in 1993, he directed me to this book, which I found to be quite useful in understanding his ideas on a variety of issues. His main thesis is that in spite of some gains in establishing the Indian democracy since 1947, India has suffered many losses. The losses are primarily due to the fact that the makers of independent India did not heed to the advice of Mahatma Gandhi. This is particularly true in the area of political governance and economic development. Thakurdas feels that the main cause of the general unrest in the Indian society (poverty, lawlessness, corruption, instability etc.) is the centralization of economic and political power in the hands of the Federal Government. As a consequence, the villages of India are neglected. The economic resources are vested in making the Central Government strong. The path of decentralization which Gandhi had outlined is not applied. In the area of economics, most resourceful industries were nationalized and controlled by the center. The people were told that India will be better of with Russian type of socialism. In reality, India mixed the capitalist system of England and America with socialism of Russia. The goal became to industrialize India according to the western model of development. Even in the agricultural sector, the power was entrusted in the hands of the landlords and the industrialists.[2]

Thakurdas Bang believes that the dream of making India an industrialized nation has been a failure. He recognizes that according to some estimates, India is included among the seven industrialized nations in the world. However, he regrets that along with development poverty in India has increased. As India became industrialized, the cottage industries began to suffer, and unemployment arose. For an ordinary Indian in the village, life became miserable.[3] India increasingly became slave to modern western technology, something the people were not equipped to handle. Thakurdas correlates this development with the increase in crime and corruption. The government made promises to make India a land of 'milk and honey', but, in reality, it could not provide a decent meal per day for all. As a result, the public became disillusioned, and the 'pie in the sky' dream crumbled. Today bribery, dowry, illegal money laundering, smuggling, drug trafficking for easy money etc., have reached a high level. Thakurdas states, "Just look at the scandals around us. There is a general feeling among the people that if you are a politician, you are corrupt. The people have lost faith in the government." All of these vices can be traced back to the mistake India made when it adopted a western model of development. For Thakurdas, Prime Minister Nehru, the architect of modern Indian Economic Policy, realized his mistake when on Dec. 11, 1963, in his speech to the Indian Parliament, he admitted that India had failed to solve the problems of unemployment through big industries, and that perhaps India should have paid attention to Gandhi's advice.[4]

Professor Bang emphasizes that the Indian culture was based on the cultivation of the land. What that meant was that the entire value system on which the Indian religious, social, political, and economic life was based, had its origin in agriculture as a way of life. In this way of life, the village was the primary unit. One can say that the village was a co-operative system under which the good of the

288

individual depended on the good of all. The entire nation was a republic of these villages. The government was 'decentralized' and the power rested in the hands of the panchayat (group of five). The village produced for its necessities and shared resources. When the British occupied India, this 'cultural system' was disrupted. In the interest of high productivity and to feed the European Industrial Revolution with Indian resources, the people were forced to give up their cultural values. When Gandhi returned to India from South Africa, he had the foresight to recognize the destruction of an ancient civilization. As we know, Satyagraha was his way to fight the British, and Sarvodaya to reconstruct the country. What Thakurdas Bang wants is Gram Swaraj in the same manner that Gandhi had advocated.

Thakurdas admits that his thought parallels the thinking of J. P.. When I pressed him on why he was so impressed with J. P., he remarked, "with J. P. I found the completion of Gandhi." He elaborated by illustrating that Gandhi was a man of action, but his actions were directed in two main areas. First, he confronted the oppressive power structure of the government. Second, he accepted the village as a basic unit where the development should take place. J. P. followed a similar line of thinking. He opposed the dictatorial government of Indira Gandhi, and strongly believed in the 'bottom-up' theory of development. Like Gandhi, J. P. was working on all fronts because he believed in the holistic approach towards Gram Swaraj. His slogan of 'Total Revolution' embodied Gandhi's comprehensive plan of action. Like J. P., Prof. Bang is also working on different fronts in order to make the Gandhian dream a reality.

Like many of the fellow Gandhians, Thakurdas is deeply concerned about the environmental problems in India as well as in the world. This is one of the reasons that he opposes the 'new technologies' for India's industrialization. He once stated to me, "you know some of the technologies for big production that we are receiving from abroad are no longer acceptable in the countries they come from. The environmentally unsafe techniques as well as materials are dumped on us."[5] Furthermore, the safety measures that are required in the developed countries are no where near the requirements put on them by the Indian government. It bothers Thakurdas that the Indian civilization which had such a close affinity with nature, where sages deified natural phenomena, and people worshipped the mountains and rivers, is now threatened to the point of facing destruction. He states, "our war is a war between the urban culture and the village culture. If we want to be environmentally safe, we will have to move toward preserving the village culture." That means preserving the agricultural lifestyle with emphasis on small scale industries and traditional technologies. He is excited over the fact that many youth are beginning to understand India's environmental problems and are willing to do something about it. However, he also realizes that the majority of the youth are being lured into the urban centers for modern living. Thakurdas is engaged in a mission of 'consciousness raising' among the youth, and is hopeful that many will turn themselves around.

Professor Bang's work in the area of Hindu-Muslim unity has already been mentioned earlier. It is of concern to him that some Sarvodaya workers have become supporters of Hindu extremism propagated under the banner of Hindutva. They are misled by the propaganda that the Hindus in India are disadvantaged because the government policy is to favor the Muslims, even though they are in a minority. Thakurdas believes that the Hindu-Muslim problem in India is caused by ignorance on both sides about their respective religious beliefs and practices. In 1993 he wrote a small, but valuable book entitled, Hindu-Muslim Manas (The Hindu-Muslim Mind-Set). In this work, he tries to show that for the past 1300 years Hindus and Muslims have lived together side by side in India. Most Muslims who converted to Islam (for whatever reasons) were Hindu Indians.

Over the years they grew suspicious of each other, resulting in many communal riots. He tries to show that what we call 'Indian Civilization' is a mixture of both Hindu and Muslim cultures. If they fought each other, the fight was among the kings not the people. Furthermore, the invasion of India by many 'so called Muslim kings' should not be perceived as the invasion by Islam. He attributes much of the Hindu-Muslim conflict to the British policy of 'divide and rule' which they adopted in India. Today the differences (misunderstandings) between the two communities are being exploited by certain politicians for their selfish goals.[6] Thakurdas' purpose of writing this book was twofold: to bring the Hindus and Muslims together and to see through the politics of keeping them apart. He asserts the secular nature of the Indian Constitution which guarantees the freedom of all religions. On religious grounds he proposes the notion of Dharma Samanvya (The essential unity of all religions) to emphasize religious tolerance.

Thakurdas Bang's Satyagraha against the multinational companies is a part of a nationwide movement supported by many Gandhians. In his thinking, the issues of the new economic theory, environmental crisis, growth of the multinationals, industrialization, centralization etc. are all related to the movement for Gram Swaraj. They are impediments to the freedom of the village. He views the control of the economy by the multinational companies as a new form of colonialism. He thinks, "We must not forget that the East India Company which opened the door for the occupation of India was a trading company. Where economic interest prevails, military action follows." He hopes that India will not make the same mistake again by opening its doors to foreign companies. Unfortunately the process has begun, and Prof. Bang wonders where it will end.

Endnotes: Chapter XIX

[1] Some of the well known titles are; Satyagraha: Kya, Kyun, Aur Kaise (Satyagraha: What, Why, and How?), Gaon Ki Satta Gaon Ke Hath (The Village Rule in Village Hands), Hindu-Muslim Manas (The Hindu-Muslim Mindset), and Bharat Kidhar (Whither India)

[2] Thakurdas Bang, Whither India, p.6

[3] Ibid.; p.6-7

[4] Ibid.; p.8

[5] 1993 interview in Gopuri, Wardha

[6] Thakurdas Bang, Hindu-Muslim Manas, pp. 3-4

Part Three

Assessment

Assessment

The story of Sarvodaya movement is a story of decades of struggle by a group of dedicated Gandhian social workers, whom Geoffrey Ostergaard has called, the Gentle Anarchists.[1] They are gentle because they are pursuing a non-violent path in their revolutionary activities. They are anarchists because they are challenging the power of the state in the hope of generating 'people's power'. It is questionable whether they have succeeded in establishing a non-violent society with equitable distribution of power among the people, a society that Gandhi had termed Ram Raj. In fact, the evidence points to the contrary. What shall we say then? Has the Sarvodaya movement been a giant failure -- an exercise in futility -- a vision turned nightmare? The cynics may reach that conclusion. As for the contemporary Gandhians, the fight is far from being over. They remain committed to the ideals of Sarvodaya. In fact, for them, it is either Sarvodaya or Sarvanash, meaning 'welfare for all' or 'destruction for all.'

Having looked at a brief history of the Sarvodaya Revolution through the eyes of Gandhi, Vinoba, J. P., and a selected group of contemporary visionaries, it is quite evident that Gandhism in India is alive, though ailing. In this final part of the book I wish to critically assess the Sarvodaya vision in order to fully comprehend its claim. I am convinced that many critics of the Sarvodaya movement and its leadership have valuable views that need to be heard and evaluated. I have made an attempt to integrate their criticisms in my assessment to look at a wider picture. Furthermore, I have stated some suggestions of my own, which I feel warrant serious attention.

After half a century since India's independence from the British Raj, the question that plagues the Indian mind still remains the same; whither India? Despite advancements in the areas of industrial development, space technology, computer

295

science, nuclear research, and self-sufficiency in food, India is beset with many crises of immense magnitude. On top of the list is widespread poverty. It is estimated that approximately 50% of the Indian population today remains below the poverty line. While India claims to have reached self-sufficiency in growing food (due to the Green Revolution), hunger, malnutrition, and curable diseases claim many lives. Dr. L. C. Thanu reports

> ... it is distressing to note that India continues to be the fifteenth poorest nation in the world with per capita income of Rs. 4010 (1988).... About 23.76 Crore Indians representing 29.9 percent of the population are living below the poverty line. The numbers of unemployed and under-employed are on the increase... We are becoming bankrupt as the government with a total debt (external and internal) of over Rs. 445,000 crores...[2]

In recent years, state terrorism, governmental lawlessness, police violence, political violence, criminalisation, communal conflict, terrorist movements, etc. have increased in high proportions.[3] "India has become "the land of bootleggers, smugglers and black-marketeers" (Acharya Kriplani). The thirst for power, self and position of the political bigwigs remains unquenched (Kamrajji), and sound democratic practices are thrown to the winds."[4] Pollution in Indian industrial cities has been increasing steadily.[5] Environmental degradation is rampant. According to a resent survey conducted by a popular Indian magazine, India Today, corruption in India has reached to an unprecedented height. Almost 41% of Indians believe that the nation is 'innately corrupt'.[6] The same poll states that 50% of the people hold that the police in India are dishonest, while only 6% hold them honest.[7] Many have lost faith in their politicians and the political system as a whole. "India is engulfed by self-doubt over its political system. Politicians are perceived as deceitful and ineffective, and there is lack of confidence in the police and administration."[8] Many elected MLAs (Members of the Legislative Assembly) have "criminal cases registered against them."[9] To the eyes of one observer, "if you see the political scene today it is a political lunatic asylum."[10] Disheartened over 50 years of progress and a life of freedom, Bal Thackeray, the leader of Shiv Sena has this observation to make, "You spit on the road. You shit on the road. And you take that as your freedom. Is that the freedom that you want after 50 years? The balance sheet of India of the past 50 years is ... bullshit."[11] That Mahatma Gandhi is not on people's priority list is confirmed when the India Today poll reveals that presently people rate Indira Gandhi over the Mahatma, "as someone who inspired people".[12] The same survey reveals the state of the nation when it reports, "The despair over the present has even led to a growing nostalgia for the efficacy of the British Raj."[13] If this is not a crushing blow to the spirit of the Gandhians, what is?

The present India has become a battle ground for many competing political, social, economic, and religious forces. It is a stage where the drama of power struggle is being played out with great intensity. As social workers, the Gandhians are caught in the midst of a larger revolution with a revolution of their own. As the stories of their lives depicted in Part Two of the book shows, the majority of them are inspired by the thought of Jai Prakash Narayan (J. P.). They uphold the ideals of his 'Total Revolution,' which some have called 'The Radical Sarvodaya'.[14] The reason for this allegiance, it appears, is that J. P. dared to ask the question; Whither India? We need not repeat J. P.'s vision here (See Chapter Three). What is crucial in his Total Revolution is that he understood the nature of the crises in India in the manner in which Mahatma Gandhi did. Like Gandhi, he perceived the 'Indian Dilemma' in terms of a 'civilizational crisis'. He recognized that during the regime of Prime Minister Indira Gandhi, the socio-economic and political situation, following a model of development which was contrary to the Indian value system, had reached a stage which was detrimental to the survival of India as a nation. J. P. wished to reform all social, political, economic, and educational institutions in search for a new society, hence he called for a Total Revolution. This was an attempt, as his followers view it, to save the Indian civilization and restore it to its pristine heights. This is what contemporary Gandhians are still engaged in -- the development of the Indian civilization -- a form of Ram Raj. They are forced to face the question; Whither India?

In the process of retrieving the Indian civilization, the contemporary Gandhians have taken up many common causes. The first, and perhaps the foremost, is their concern with the process of economic development. The underlying assumption in their critique of the current developmental process is that it has caused havoc to the Indian economy, created poverty, neglected the agricultural sector, and exploited the poor. For some, the culprit who took India toward the path of a western model of development was Jawaharlal Nehru, the first Prime Minister of India, followed by his daughter Indira Gandhi, and his grandson, Rajiv Gandhi. Rajiv, in particular, "believed that modern, front-line technology was the sure fire remedy for all the ills of the Indian economy. The vision of a socialistic India that inspired his grandfather and mother had little appeal in his flying jet-set life style and technocratic outlook. He resolutely placed the socialist agenda on the back-burner in the firm belief that India should first modernize herself from the technological manna falling from the Western skies."[15] As a consequence India began to experience serious foreign exchange problems and its debts increased. When Manmohan Singh, Rajiv's finance minister, took office in 1991, "foreign currency assets stood at $124 million, barely sufficient to meet the country's import bill for three weeks."[16]

Critics believe that the Congress leadership collectively is held responsible for taking India along a path of destruction. The economic development they pursued sought western technological know-how, industrial development, urban civilization, and the rise of an elite class. It is important to note that in this analysis of the Indian malaise, the Gandhians have the support of many credible thinkers in India. Consider the words of J. P. himself who wrote, "But the model itself was largely un-Indian (meaning western) and elitist and thus ultimately was bound to fail. It is no coincidence that the Nehruvian model produced the greatest disparities of income and wealth. It pushed more people below the poverty line than ever before. It created the most cynical elite class. And above all it caused the deepest permeation of corruption and immorality in our public life."[17] J. P. wrote these words in his foreword to a book by J. D. Sethi, an Indian economist. Sethi concurs with J. P. and writes, "...the frustrating experience of the development policies and programs of poor countries over the last three decades...shows that the economies of these countries have ceased to grow and that they are not able to solve any of the major problems of their societies, particularly problems of poverty and unemployment."[18]

The failure of the Western model of development is recognized by many social scientists. Professor Shankar Pathak of the Delhi School of Social Work has this to say on the matter. He writes, " The early euphoria and expectations of western model of development (and also the Soviet and Chinese models of socialist development) gradually led to a deep sense of disappointment as the efforts and achievements of the newly independent nations failed miserably in eradicating acute mass poverty, illiteracy, ill-health, and unemployment."[19] Another social scientist adds, "...a craze for 'development' which is the other name for the acquisition of wealth by a few at the cost of the others is expanding the areas of absolute poverty everywhere both in the rich as also in poor nations."[20] A political scientist in India joins the refrain when he speaks out, " Increasingly, we are displacing masses and masses of the poor in the name of development, forcing them to go into the cities, where the urban elite despises them and they are taken away to the so called resettlement colonies which are full of filth and disease, and are, in fact, becoming breeding grounds for crime."[21] In the same vein, R.R. Diwakar adds, " Even after a lapse of forty years of swaraj (now fifty) and the adoption of the Western type of development through seven five-year plans (now ten), India has not been able to make much headway regarding the problems which Gandhi had chosen as priorities for solution by the people of India."[22]

What is this monster called 'Development'? It is basically an 'Anglo-Saxon' concept[23] which has been applied towards the economic progress of the poor countries in an attempt to "save them" from destruction and make them civilized like the 'developed' countries. Hence, "fundamentally, development implies the replacement of general competence and abundant subsistence activities by the use and consumption of commodities. Development implies the monopoly of wage laborer over all other work."[24] Furthermore, "...(it) is a process of societal transformation from a traditional society to a modern society, and such a transformation is also known as modernization."[25] The idea of 'development' carries with it a sense of reaching an economic utopia, where all human wants will be fulfilled, and humans will live happily ever after. Central to this thinking are the notions of the maximization of wants, large production, consumerism, and the accumulation of wealth. However as many experts tell us, "...development activities have tended to create avenues for excessive consumerism of some against the continued deprivation of many others."[26]

It need not be emphasized that 'development' as described above was not the sort of development that Gandhi was after. "Affluence as a goal of development was not in Gandhi's mind. He believed that there is sufficient to meet the needs of the people, but not their greed... His was a holistic view of life. Accordingly, his development philosophy revolved around man, his society and environment (nature) and their respective and simultaneous development.[27] The contemporary Gandhians must find comfort in the fact that in their critique of the Western notion of development they have support from many members of the scholarly community. Whether or not they are able to check and control the developmental paradigm that India currently seems to have adopted for itself is a different, but critical matter.

Another major concern for the contemporary Gandhians, which is intrinsically connected to the problem of development, is the issue of technology. There has been an intense debate over the use of modern technology all over the world. India is no exception to it. For Gandhians it is clear that a blind faith in technology has caused many problems in India and around the world. Particularly for India, a heavily populated country, technology is replacing man with machine. It has disrupted the agro-culture by favoring an industrial culture. Furthermore, it has far-reaching implications for consumerism, urbanization, exploitation of the poor by the rich, environmental degradation, etc. Again, in their analysis of the effects of technology, Gandhians have the support of many intellectuals.

Ever since the appearance of Alvin Toffler's well known book, Future Shock, an intellectual conversation about the effects of technology has taken place around the world. Of course, Gandhi along with Ruskin and Tolstoy, had already initiated a dialogue on the topic in the wake of the industrial revolution quite early on. Toffler wrote, "Our technological powers increase but the side effects and potential hazards also escalate. We risk thermo-pollution of the oceans themselves, overheating them, destroying immeasurable quantities of marine life, perhaps even melting the ice caps. On land, we concentrate such large masses of population in such small urban technological islands - that we threaten to use up air's oxygen faster than it can be replaced."[28] Since Toffler's observations, many others have agreed with him. Today, worldwide conferences to discuss the depletion of the ozone layer, global warming, chemical waste, the effects of the nuclear fall out, etc. have become common occurrences. Soon after the appearance of Toffler's work, a prominent Indian engineer, author, and administrator wrote, "there is already a 'backlash' against the excessive materialism which modern technology is trying to foster."[29] The writer speaks of the counter-cultures that are emerging as a consequence of building a technological society. He quotes Rene Dubos, who says, "present day counter cultures probably are the expression of a deep seated, almost sub-conscious social wisdom capable of generating protective responses against this trend."[30]

That uncontrolled technological development is causing serious problems for us is increasingly being recognized. On the perils of technology an Indian political scientist writes, "In recent decades, a flood of light has been thrown on how modern technology has reached a stage wherein the very existence of mankind is exposed to danger....Urbanization, crime, social disorganization, smoke and dirt, desolation of nature, exploitation of labor and a host of harmful effects were pointed out in the nineteenth and in the beginning of the twentieth century."[31] An Indian Canadian economist says, "...I am against technology which is centralist and alienates humans from humans and humans from nature. Our modern technology alienates us both from humans and nature."[32] There is no doubt that science and technology define the value system for most modern people. But, as Ignatius

Jesudasan points out, "the end result of science, and industry and technology is war."[33] There is a feeling amongst some scientists and technocrats that technology can solve the problems created by technology. This view advocates that the solution of technology is in more technology. However, there are those who challenge this fanatic faith-like stance among the followers of the religion of technology. As Rajni Kothari, an Indian political scientist points out, when science became an instrument for technology it ceased to be a liberating force. Today, "technology has become Frankenstein".[34] On the consequences of our contemporary technological advancement, a Gandhian scholar has this to say, "As technological innovations take place leading to capital-intensive, large-scale mechanized production, wealth and income get concentrated in the hands of a few leading to sharp inequalities of income and poverty. Society gets sharply polarized giving rise to a dualistic nature of economy."[35]

That the contemporary Gandhians are challenging India's faith in modern technology should not come as a surprise. Gandhi in Hind Swaraj (1909) had warned against the perils of technology. However, many Gandhians are aware that Gandhi was not against all technology. As J. D. Sethi[36] and others have pointed out, Gandhi reworked his ideas presented in Hind Swaraj throughout his life. He preferred technology that was useful to mankind without exploiting humans and nature. The contemporary debate on the use of technology has shown that Gandhi had great insights into the future of the technological culture. The contemporary Gandhians firmly believe that his prognosis was true.

The issue of technology is directly related to the question of industrialization, which is another major concern of the contemporary Gandhians. Modern technology which celebrates technology inevitably glorifies industrialization. Throughout this book several references have been made to India's first Planning Commission, which was headed by Prime Minister Nehru, and met for the first time in 1951. It laid the foundation of India's first Five Year Plan, which continues to progress to this day. The readers will recall that Vinoba Bhave had walked away from the Planning Commission meetings because he felt that it favored a heavy industrial development of India and neglected agricultural concerns. Ever since 1951, Gandhians have been in protest against government policies to make India an industrial nation. Their reasons for protest are quite obvious. It is estimated that industrialization is responsible for the disappearance of many village hand-crafts, generally known as the 'cottage industry'. It affects agriculture as the capital gained from the agricultural products is diverted to sustain the large industries. It causes mobilization of the population from the villages to the urban centers. Since the industrial sector cannot provide jobs for all available hands, it leads to joblessness, poverty, and a life of crime.

The analysts from different walks of life have been critical of heavy industrialization around the world as well as India. Dr. M. V. Naidu, a political scientist and development researcher, suggests that the economics of mass industrialization needs large production, sophisticated technology, colonies to sell the goods, corruption mentality, indoctrination of the masses through media control, and various forms of monopolies. The end result is that it produces a culture of militarism, and a culture of imperialism.[37] An economist and one of the leading intellectuals of India, Dr. Amlan Dutta states, "Industrialization on a mass scale leads to the exploitation of the country by the city. Industry, commerce and major financial institutions tend to be concentrated in the bigger urban centers. With that goes the centralization of power, both economic and political. The cities impoverish the villages."[38] An economic model which supports heavy industrialization is criticized by yet another scholar who sees that "...the result is waste, destruction and structures of manipulation all over the place, in which man has lost both self-control and a sense of unity with the rest of creation."[39] In a nutshell, the culture of heavy industrialization is a culture of violence. As one professor of economics puts it, "The industrial revolution in the west was achieved at the cost of the exploitation of the colonies. If India wants to opt for heavy industrialization, it will have to colonize the neighboring countries."[40] It is interesting to note that countries like Nepal have already protested against India's heavy handedness in various trade agreements.

The issue of industrialization is linked with India's current New Economic Policy which contemporary Gandhians are against.

> A major thrust of the new policy (New Economic Policy) has been short term stabilization of the balance of payments. This has to be achieved by reducing the imbalance between the aggregate supply and demand by cutting down the deficit in the Central Budget. Encouraging exports, import liberalization by lowering import duties and seeking a stand by loan from the International Monetary Fund (IMF) were the measures adopted. At the same time, structural adjustment was sought to be achieved by reformulating the industrial licensing system, encouraging foreign investment....[41]

It is heavy industrialization that has led India into a borrowing pattern from the World Bank which has caused enormous problems. A few years ago, India's inability to pay back interests on loans caused it to transfer its gold reserves to England. As a consequence India became hostage to the wishes of lending agencies like the International Monetary Fund. It had to also succumb to the agreements with GATT (General Agreement on Trade and Tariff) set by industrialized nations of the world. As a part of the deal, India had to open its market to foreign investors, make changes in its import-export policies, devalue its currency, and thereby try to earn more foreign exchange to pay off its debts. Under the circumstances, India had no other choice. But, the real question is; how did it get in this mess? The critics hasten to point out that the New Economic Policy, though seemingly beneficial for the rich, is not benefiting the poor. In fact, the rich are getting richer and the poor poorer. The question needs to be asked; Why were the institutions like the World Bank, IMF (International Monetary Fund), and GATT created? Were they created to really help developing countries? Hardly, say the critics. They were created in the wake of the ailing economies of the highly industrialized nations.[42] Of course, the borrowers (under developed countries) support their existence in order to fix the economic bind in which they find themselves. If you don't play the game by the rules (set by the rich countries), you are threatened to be ostracized. Thus, in the name of progress and development, the Indian government has to justify its economic policies.

The way the World Bank and IMF extended help to India was through what is known as the "structural adjustment loan." These loans were provided to many third world countries around the world as long as they agreed to the western model of free economy and laissez-fair. As a return to this favor, the World Bank demanded the following changes.

1. Elimination of barriers to imports.
2. Removal of restrictions on foreign investments.
3. Elimination of subsidies for local industries.
4. Devaluation of the national currency.
5. Reduction of spending for social welfare.
6. The gearing of production for exports rather than for domestic consumption.
7. Drastic reduction of government regulation of the economy.
8. Privatization of state enterprises. [43]

Related to the issue of industrialization is the issue of the proliferation of the multinational companies, which is also opposed by the Gandhians. In that, they have support from many other groups as well. In the view of one scholar, "Foreign collaborations, multinationals in the name of transfer of technology are leaving

India dry. And this is true about all other Third World countries who have allowed foreign collaborations on their soil."[44] Comparing the effects of the multinationals between India and Japan, the same scholar wonders why the per capita income in India has not risen much. He states, "...there have been 13,000 foreign collaborations in India (at the time of his writing in 1990) since independence. There must be something drastically wrong with our country (India) because Japan with 25,000 collaborations has pushed its per capita income to $14,000 per year as compared to $200 in our country."[45] At the heart of the multinational issue is the problem of technology transfer from rich countries to poor countries. A prominent Indian economist, J. D. Sethi worries what the transfer of technology has done to developing countries, including India. He concludes that the technology transfer is designed, "to (i) exploit the resources of the poor countries for the benefit of the developed countries...(ii) create a dualism by isolating the sectors depending on Western technology...(iii) widen the already wide technological gap...(iv) stunt the very process of growth by creating a new consumer-oriented industry...(and) (v) create a kind of technological imperialism which demoralizes developing countries and makes them accept the superiority of Western civilization."[46] It is estimated that since the government of India opened its doors to the multinationals in 1991, a phenomenal 1243% increase in foreign investment has been registered. The number of foreign projects approved by the government have risen to 240%. Companies from such countries as U. S. A, Netherlands, Japan, Germany, Switzerland and the United Kingdom are among top investors. Their combined investments are assessed in billions of dollars.[47]

India's decision to open its doors to the multinational companies under its policy of 'liberalization' is undoubtedly being challenged. The invitation to foreign investors is seen as a threat to the whole concept of 'swaraj' (independence). In recent years, even the economic concessions made to the NRIs (Non-Residential Indians) by the government of India has been severely criticized. For one critic, "these people are not angels to soothen our poverty-stricken villages but are propelled only by selfish ends."[48] The critics are also concerned about the multinational's involvement in India's medical industry. One criticism of the foreign medical companies is that they invest very little in India, but take an exorbitant amount of profit outside of India. According to one research scholar, in 1981 alone, Hecht Co. invested Rs. 2,000,000 but took out of India, Rs. 50,000,000. The Ciba Co. invested Rs. 200,000, but took out of India, Rs. 47,000,000. Likewise,

Sandos invested Rs. 100,000, but profited Rs. 77,800,000. And finally, Glaxo invested Rs. 100,000, but took out Rs. 34,800,000.[49]

Another scholar points out how multinational drug companies are dumping fatal drugs into India which are banned by the World Health Organization.[50] Some companies are making drugs without license. He concludes by stating that there has been 345% increase in medicine prices. The adulteration in drugs with an alarming rate, which has caused many deaths in India over the years, is also pointed out by Dr. Meera Shiva.[51] That the multinational companies are taking away herbs from the Himalayan forests in large quantities is disturbing to Dr. Malhotra.[52] Dr. Rohtagi warns that India is increasingly becoming dependent on Western medicine that has serious side effects. He asks that people in the medical profession in India oppose the presence of the multinational companies.[53] Manoj Tyagi makes the claim that profits made in medicines has surpassed the weapons sale, and that the European prosperity is based on medicine industry. He goes as far as to say that on some medicines, the multinational companies in India make 1800% profit.[54]

The previous discussion shows that the present economic policies which promote mass industrialization, high technology, growth in multinational corporations was not the way Gandhi perceived of laying the foundations of Ram Raj. Since India did not heed to the advice of Gandhi, the consequences have been drastic. According to contemporary Gandhians, India's developmental policies are responsible for unemployment, pollution, loss of cottage industries, environmental degradation, corruption, energy crisis, increased foreign debts, etc. And, in their criticisms of the present industrial development of India, the followers of Gandhi have the support of many scholars.

Another major concern for the contemporary Gandhians is the place of the village in national development. It is their view, as we have seen, that the village has been a victim of economic exploitation since the British rule in India. It is claimed that villagers have been neglected, while the resources have been poured for urbanization. It is not an accident that the majority of the Gandhian constructive workers are, therefore, working among the villagers throughout India. And, their primary goal is to achieve Gram Swaraj -- village independence.

The concern for Indian villages is voiced by many researchers. It has been suggested that Gandhi was impressed by four factors of village life; 1. corporate community life, 2. smallness of size, 3. autonomous character, and 4. self-sufficiency.[55] With the exception of number 2, one wonders if the other factors are found to be true today. The corporate community life is shattered by caste and class conflicts. The autonomous character of the village is affected by centralization of power in the hands of the government. And, self-sufficiency is challenged by the desire to consume industrial goods produced at urban centers. The ideal village of Gandhi does not exist. However, the question is being asked; What has caused the villages of India to suffer where the majority of India's population lives? It should be noted that the answer to this question is connected with the issue of agriculture. The village in India was tied to the agricultural economy. With the rise of industrial economy, agriculture was affected, and so were the villages. It is suggested, and it is true, that "The British rule tied India to international capitalism. It led to the introduction of modern science and technology...The influence of capitalism has penetrated in a much larger way into the interior (villages) of the country."[56] It was hoped that the new advancement will increase agricultural production and liberate the villages from their antiquated ways of living. During the Nehru years (1947-64) this thinking continued. His administration focused on land reforms and cooperatives, but no significant progress was made on either front.[57] In fact, "...American -- not Indian -- farmers were feeding a large part of urban India."[58]

It cannot be denied that drastic changes have occurred in recent years in the agricultural sector. The Green Revolution of the 1970s (which is being called the Greed Revolution) has brought self-sufficiency (so it is claimed) in food production. Agriculture has become highly mechanized and technical. The achievements in this area are impressive. However, what worries many analysts is the question; what are the consequences of this progress in growth for the poor farmers? In this context, one social scientist writes:

> But the social cost of growth is also tremendous. Modern agricultural equipments, machineries for irrigation, and chemical fertilizers are supplied by large industries owned either by the state or by the private capitalists. It is beyond the capacity of the ordinary peasants to secure in the open competitive market tractors, power tillers, pump-sets, shallow tube-wells or threshing machines or to arrange for the servicing and repair of these machines, or to get the supply of electricity and diesel for running them.[59]

The same author reports that since agriculture has become a high-tech industry, other consequences have occurred. There is a rise in rich landlords, brokers who demand high prices (as middlemen) from the farmers to sell their produce, failure of the government subsidies to reach the poor farmers, and problems of small peasants forced to become landless agricultural laborers.[60]

The economic consequences of the agricultural industry are beneficial for the rich, but hardly for the poor. Besides, village life has been affected in a negative way. Most affected are small farms and cottage industries. This change has impacted the social organization of the village. It has destroyed the ancient system of "reciprocating relations in production and distribution between different social groups organized in a network of direct interdependence."[61] The ancient system that had made the villages self-supportive units is no longer there. That interdependence gone, there is a flight to the urban centers where life is even more difficult and jobs hard to find. No wonder one sees sprawling shanty towns and slums around all urban centers. As J. D. Sethi observes, "This situation is precarious. Villages cannot absorb the increase in population and, as people move from the villages to the cities, the reduced level of growth rate only results in the creation of massive and ugly slums. There is no technology which by itself can solve this problem."[62] This leads into a discussion of rampant poverty in India. And that the poor are being oppressed everywhere is a well known fact.

If Gandhians are concerned with the problems of the village, agriculture, and poverty, it should not come as a surprise to us. When Gandhi hailed the notion of Gram Swaraj (village freedom), he foresaw the problems that have been discussed above. He held that exploiting the village was a form of violence that he was fighting against. He was aware that urbanization and industrialization of India was being done at the cost of the village. That is why he stated, "The blood of the villages is the cement with which the edifice of the cities is built. I want this blood that is today inflating the arteries of the cities to run once again in the blood vessels of the villages."[63] Like a prophet he cried out "if the village perishes India will perish too."[64]

The final common concern that most Gandhians discussed in this book are preoccupied with, which I wish to analyze here, is the concern with the centralization of various forms of power. As we have observed through a discussion of their lives and thoughts, they seek decentralization of power in politics, social structures, economics, education, etc. Needless to say, in their view, the modern Western model of development, which has led India into various forms of problems, is responsible for the stagnation in the Indian society resulting in poverty, environmental problems, crime, terrorist activities, etc. Here also they have some support from the social and political scientists.

In the realm of the political order, it is quite obvious that the Indian democracy functions on the basis of centralization of power. It is a system in which the state demands power in order to safeguard the interests of the people. However, in reality centralization of power works against the people. As one political scientist points out, "The dominant tendency and the mode of thought today is to place the State above the people, the security of Nation-State above people's security. The removal of real or imaginary threats to the State has become more pertinent than preventing threats to the people and their interests."[65] In terms of control of power, India had always had the problem of power distribution to provincial governments. Indian politics is preoccupied with the state governments wanting to have more control over their own affairs, only to be told by the central government to relinquish power in favor of a strong center. The movement toward a Panchayat Raj, which works for the decentralization of power has long been recognized. However, to implement it properly in the villages has been a problem. One scholar suggests:

> The Panchayat should be vested with far greater administrative powers and responsibilities than it enjoys today. All taxes on behalf of government - whether state or central - should be collected by it out of which an agreed portion may be retained by it and the rest remitted to the local treasury. The Panchayat should also be given additional grants by state and central authorities for undertaking additional tasks required to be done by it.[66]

The failure of the Panchayat system is indicative of the fact how difficult it is to decentralize political power. As one author points out, many Panchayati Raj institutions have been, "sabotaged by the bureaucracy and vested local interests in many places. They had acted in connivance with legislators and M. P.s (members of parliament) from the respective areas under the hope that Panchayati raj would eventually die a quiet death."[67] Under these circumstances decentralization of power has been quite difficult. Nonetheless, the need to do so is widely recognized.

The problem of centralization of power is also recognized in the area of science and technology. It has been observed that the scientific and technological know-how is usually under the control of the government or powerful institutions. The decisions to control research, allocate funds, choosing of personnel, are usually in the hands of a select few. Therefore, "...It is impossible to ignore the fact that science and technology have come to be inalienably associated with centralization of authority. The combination of centralized power, science and technology constitute the dominant trend in modern organizations."[68] Dr. Sanyal is concerned that this situation creates many social tensions which lead to violence. He concludes that "under the conditions, it is necessary to change the environment fundamentally in its structure, values, and motivations. Essentially this is a question of moral regeneration."[69]

The issue of science and technology is directly related to the issue of economics. Whoever controls technology, controls the means of production. The more centralized this activity is, the more people are left out of the decision-making process that impacts their lives. However, "If the means of production are controlled by the community consisting of individuals enjoying equal rights and opportunities, and if knowledge is accessible to all, as it should be in a non-violent society, the centers of authority will automatically wither away. In the absence of centralized power, science and technology will acquire new dimensions in the usefulness to mankind."[70] The question of centralized economy is at the heart of capitalism. The critics of the capitalist theory of production are quick to point out that it is a major source of consolidating power in the hands of a few. In the case of India, it has produced a strong and powerful industrial class that controls economic as well as political power. As a consequence, the masses suffer under the oppressive economic order. The plight of the poor has made one scholar to cry out:

> Under the framework of Gandhian alternative, we want a decentralized economic order. We want participation of people in formulation and implementation of programs. The decentralized system in production, in planning, in decision making and in administration is required at all levels. Village and cottage industries in our rural economy can solve the problem of production, distribution, consumption and exchange. The concept of "truth", "non-violence" and "Swadeshi" will fit in our decentralized economic order.[71]

The centralization of authority and power is visible in numerous Indian social, religious, and cultural institutions. Gandhi was painfully aware that a major social reform was necessary to lay the foundation of a just society. Sarvodaya was his response to various forms of authoritarianism. Gandhians today are aware that many social scientists have come to recognize that decentralization of power is necessary if we are going to have a truly democratic and humane society.

In the preceding section an attempt was made to give a glimpse of some of the major concerns that the contemporary Gandhians have in order to answer the question; Whither India? The list is by no means exhaustive. The issue of communal conflicts, lack of a moral vision, and religious fundamentalism are also very much on their minds. Time and time again, the Gandhians I have interviewed have mentioned, "The crisis of India is a moral crisis." Most recently, the regeneration of the Hindutva (a form of Hindu fundamentalist movement) has caused many concerns. Since many references have already been made to this movement throughout this book, I refrain from treating it as a separate Gandhian concern. In sum, the Gandhian concerns are centered around social, economic, and political justice. Ultimately it is a concern to eliminate all forms of violence in the hope of creating Ram Raj.

*   *   *

In its quest to answer the question; Whither India? the Sarvodaya Movement has to face up to many challenges and criticisms. It is important to listen to the critics in order that a meaningful dialogue may follow.

The first and foremost criticism relates to the whole issue of 'Development.' Inherent in this larger issue are questions regarding capitalism, economics, technology, industrialization, urbanization, multinationals etc. The question that has been raised is; Has the western model of development failed in India? Since India's first prime minister Nehru is credited for applying this model to India, the question can be asked; Was Nehru wrong? The critics are quick to point out that 'Nehru bashing,' which has somewhat become fashionable in certain scholarly circles in India, is wrong. While it is true that he promoted industrial development, it is untrue to say that he neglected agricultural development. His rationale of development was based on his vision for an independent democratic India which had to establish itself as a growing nation in the eyes of the world. His vision, therefore, had an international dimension and was not narrowly focused on India. Knowing the mind of Nehru, Gandhi still chose him his successor in guiding the destiny of India. And, it was Nehru's international appeal that brought him support from all over the world which was necessary for the survival of the young country. He truly believed that the short comings of industrialization could be checked by governmental control. It should not be overlooked that Nehru's industrial India was an 'experiment' just like Gandhi's Gram Swaraj was an experiment. Both were subjected to the test. In tests like these there are no perfect scores. Some results are positive and some are negative. To conclude that Nehru primarily favored industrial development and neglected agriculture is short-sightedness. As Bimal Prasad points out, Nehru did not underestimate the importance of agricultural development.[72]

The supporters of development along the lines of industrialization are quick to point out that neither capitalism nor industrialization are inherently bad. Today, an enormous rise in economic productivity, tremendous increase in trade and

310

commerce, increase in income and high standards of living, scientific and technological progress, and dissemination of information, are all made possible due to an economic system which is based on capitalistic theories of development.[73] The collapse of the Soviet Union, and the western influence in Eastern Europe are being cited as examples of the success of capitalism. Even China, which continues to follow a socialistic communistic vision, is opening its doors to multinational companies. Outside of the United States, Germany, and Japan are hailed as examples of great economic success. The tremendous economic growth in South East Asia is attributed to its capitalist economic orientation. The economic growth of India since independence has largely been possible due to a western model of development. Despite chronic poverty, India has developed a middle class which is approximately 250 million strong. If the economists are right that for the economic growth of a country it is essential to have a middle class, a case is made that the Indian economic growth has been impressive. The fact that India can now send economic aid in the form of food, medical supplies, and scientific and technological expertise to other third world countries is made possible due to its own technological development. That a number of foreign students from Africa and Asia are studying in Indian universities is a credit to India's own advancement in higher education. The fact that the multinational companies are attracted to the Indian market is seen as a sign of economic growth and advancement.

In opposition to large scale industrialization, the Gandhian approach has been of promoting village based cottage industries for self-sufficiency. However, the critics feel that in this system, "the scope of economic activities will be drastically reduced. People will cease to create surplus over their daily needs and hence, there will be no generation of capital. Under such a situation, people will become inefficient and society will stagnate because the means of production at its disposal will not grow."[74] Since Gandhi was not completely against technology, there is also the view that "Gandhi also wanted large-scale industry to develop. In fact, cottage and large-scale industries were not competing alternatives, but complementary and helpful to each other... Besides, each sector will help the other by supplying certain requirements and by taking in some of its output."[75] The approach of combining the small scale rural production with the large scale industries seems to have been the vision of Nehru, which is still being followed in India. For the critics, this is the only viable way to go given the economic diversity that exists in India today.

311

The critics are apt to point out that, although Gandhi may have opposed capitalism in principle, he received much support for his movement from his capitalist friends. It is a well known fact that the industrialists like Birla and Bajaj provided money as well as land for Gandhian institutions. Even though Gandhi proposed 'Trusteeship' as a method to combat capitalism, in fact, he failed to convince his industrialist friends to adopt trusteeship. They never looked beyond 'charity' as a means of dealing with the poverty India was facing. A question, therefore, needs to be asked of present day Gandhians: To what extent have they given up a capitalist approach to development in their own respective constructive work programs? In theory they may deny their adherence to large-scale production, consumption, capital investment, etc., but in practice they are part of a capitalistic economic system. This is particularly true of those engaged in the production of khadi, agriculture, and production of goods that require buying and selling in the market place. Not only that, they are consumers of goods, banking facilities, industrial equipments, means of speedy transportation, medical technology, etc. that are products of an industrial based capitalistic economy. The differences do exist in terms of the degree of their involvement. Nonetheless, a complete freedom from such an engagement has become an impossibility.

There are those who claim that Gandhi has become irrelevant today (a debatable issue) because he did not leave an economic blueprint behind for India's development. One critic suggests:

> Gandhi was most ineffective when it came to a question of what sort of economic structures should be built up. He had his theory of small-scale industry, he had his theory of Trusteeship, but they were never developed to become a counter to the existing notion of bourgeois economic development. The only challenge to the notion of a modern, capitalist, industrialized society came from the socialists...[76]

The argument is that if Gandhi could not successfully challenge the economic model of development at the time of India's independence, how do the contemporary Gandhians hope to challenge it today? This is indeed a difficult question to answer. It requires a demonstration on part of the Gandhians that an alternate Gandhian economic model can succeed.

The idealization of the village and the preservation of agriculture have also come under the scrutiny of the critics. As far as Gandhi's ideal village is concerned, a case can be made that such a village does not exist and in fact never existed. In reality, villages in India suffer from unsanitary conditions, illiteracy, poverty, and various caste conflicts. Also, to argue that the condition of the villages deteriorated after the British occupation may have some truth, but not the whole truth. Before Zamindars (landlords created by the British to collect revenue), the rich Seths (money lenders) exercised their influence on the lives of the people. The exploitation of the poor was not the creation of the British. There is also evidence that all kinds of disease plagued the villages. In fact the innoculation against small pox, cholera, and the treatment of leprosy, tuberculosis, and malaria were discovered in the western world and then imported to Asia. Many such illnesses plagued the Indian society before the Industrial Revolution. Thus, to claim that the villages in India were the ideal habitats before the development of the urban culture will be shortsightedness. There were not 'Gardens of Eden.'[77]

Of course, the critics must know that Gandhi never idealized the illiterate, unsanitary, and disease stricken villages described above. It was his dream that in the future villages will be very different. In a letter to Jawaharlal Nehru in 1945 he wrote, "My ideal village still exists only in my imagination... In this village of my dreams, the villager will not be dull... He (man) will not live like an animal in filth and darkness. Men and women will live in freedom, prepared to face the whole world. There will be no plague, no cholera and no small pox....[78] Elsewhere he had broadened his vision to a worldwide network of "... innumerable self-sufficient villages, gardens of Eden where would dwell intelligent folk whom none could deceive or exploit. The villages will develop into ever widening, never ascending circles. Life will not be a pyramid with the apex sustained by the bottom, but an oceanic circle."[79]

Now that the responsibility of realizing Gandhi's dream has fallen on the shoulders of contemporary Gandhians, it is fair to ask what progress they have made in this regard. In my interviews with Gandhians I often received the following response, "We are trying to create gram sabhas (village councils) or we are trying to generate lok samitis (people's committees)." In other words, the achievements in generating people's powers for self-determination have been slow. There is no model village where Gandhi's dream has turned into a reality.

The charges that India, in the wake of the industrial development, has not paid attention to agriculture is not entirely true. As Ashutosh Varshney points out, in post Nehru years, India has made a steady growth in agriculture. He writes, "Between 1967-8 and 1970-1, however, India's food output continued to rise. In 1965-6 and 1966-7, its output had been 72.3 and 74.2 million tons, respectively. In 1967-8, food production reached 95 million tons; and by 1970-1, it was 108.4

million tons, one and a half times higher than the output achieved in 1965-6....
Largely as a result of these stocks, the drought of 1987-8, one of the worst in the
century, did not lead to a famine."[80] Under the Janta Party (1977-80), the agrarian
reforms continued under the leadership of Chowdhury Charan Singh, India's home
minister. It was his mobilization of the farmers (the farmers rally of 1978) that
facilitated his appointment as the Deputy Prime Minister of India. Since then India
has seen the rise of various peasant unions that look after the rights of the farmer.
Not only that, in the last decade, "A large number of its (India's) politicians (have)
come from rural backgrounds."[81]

The Gandhians do not deny the success of the Green Revolution and the
progress made in the agricultural sector. However, they argue that the progress has
created many other problems. Agriculture has been turned into an industry for the
rich farmers. It has squeezed the poor farmers out and created a serious problem of
landless laborers.

The fact that the Gandhians are for decentralization of power has also met
the eyes of the critics. The argument is made, as we have seen earlier, that in a
nation-state, power is centralized. Consequently, economics, technology, and
industrialization also form centralized structures. From the Gandhian side it is
argued that centralization of power causes oppression, and that it began with the
British colonialism in India. The critics can counter the argument by pointing out
that the system of centralized political structure predates the British in India. After
all, were not the rajas and maharajas ruling India for a long time? Were there not
feudal lords in ancient Indian culture who controlled the political, economic, and
cultural institutions? And what about the caste-system? Did not the twice-born
castes of Brahmins and the Kshatriyas dominate the social and religious scene? In
fact, a case can be made that the Indian society has always followed a hierarchical
structure. This hierarchy can be detected as early as in the Vedic literature, and
surely in the codification of the laws in Manu. In family relations, in social
relations, and in various institutions in India today, power is distributed
hierarchically. If this is the case, then the question can be asked; How did Gandhi
perceive of the process of decentralization of power? He must have realized that he
was fighting against the powerful forces operative in the Indian civilization. No
wonder his efforts in this area failed, and the efforts of his followers remain on the
experimental level.

Since the issue of decentralization of power relates to the power of the
government, the question can be raised; Why did Gandhi accept parliamentary

democracy? Was he making a concession to the wishes of the people of India? If he was, then he must have realized that by accepting the parliamentary system, he was accepting the evils of the system as well. One evil of the parliamentary system is the concentration of power in the hands of the few. In his Hind Swaraj (1909) he had bitterly criticized the British parliament (comparing it to a prostitute -- retracting the analogy later at the objection of a British lady for its sexist overtones). Yet, at the time of India's independence he was willing to accept this form of democracy. Perhaps, Gandhi had no other choice. However, he must have realized that his actions were allowing the flood gates to open for all forms of consequences that he opposed. How his followers can turn the situation around poses a serious dilemma.

No discussion on Gandhi or the Gandhians is complete without a critical reflection on the issue of non-violence. Whether it is the question of India's independence, Ram Raj, or running of the social, economic, and political institutions, the Gandhian thought inevitably deals with the power of violence versus non-violence. The basic assumption among the contemporary Gandhians is that our present structures of powers are breeding grounds for violence. Therefore, their constructive work programs are directed towards the establishment of a non-violent society. On this issue, the Gandhians cannot escape the challenge of the critics. The first question that a critic might raise is centered around the argument whether or not Gandhi's notion of non-violence is as absolute as it is made out to be in the Gandhian circles. The answer is an emphatic "No". As one critic observes, "He (Gandhi) never advocated absolute non-violence without a consideration of the circumstances, and he also realized that what India practiced under his leadership was the non-violence of the weak, as he called it."[82] Furthermore, ... "He wrote that we need not eschew violence in dealing with robbers, thieves, or nations who invade India.[83] It is also pointed out that in the First World War Gandhi recruited soldiers for the British, approved the operation in Kashmir in 1947, advocated fighting over cowardice and might have even accepted the overthrow of the Portuguese in Goa."[84] His views on the treatment of monkeys and snakes over the nuisance they caused at his Ashram are well known. So are his actions in dealing with the ailing calf. The point is that Gandhi accepted the principle of non-violence as an absolute good, he believed in it, for himself, but recognized its limitations.

Another criticism of Gandhi as it pertains to the issue of non-violence is raised in connection with his understanding of human nature. Central to his belief in the efficacy of non-violence is that human nature is basically good and even godly.

315

This belief may have been strengthened by his knowledge of Hinduism, which claims the centrality of Atman (which is the same as Brahman) at the core of all human beings. This allows for the belief that humans are naturally inclined towards an internal goodness which is common to all. Consequently, even in an inhumane person, one can appeal to his/her divine nature. Critics object to such an analysis. "Many simply disagree with the positive Gandhian assessment of human nature. While Gandhian literature regularly refers to the need to bring about nothing less than a "transformation of human consciousness", ... such a transformation simply is not possible and will not happen."[85] It will not happen because it is questionable whether human nature is basically good. "Very great moralists like Manu and Krishna, Aristotle and St. Thomas, Confucius, and the Buddha did not think so. To think that all men are alike is to ignore psychology and common experience... In the late nineteenth and twentieth centuries, Dostoevski, Freud and others have rediscovered the reality and power of evil."[86] Of course, the dilemma for the critics is that, on the one hand, Gandhi believes in the absolute goodness of human nature, which should allow for the practice of non-violence; but on the other hand he makes exceptions to its practice.

The final question on the above stated issue is, did Gandhi succeed in promoting non-violence or in establishing institutions (economic, social, political, etc.) that were non-violent? The answer is 'NO'. He had limited success with non-violence in his fight against the British, but no success in making Indians a non-violent people. It is revealing to read that "more people died in police firing in eighteen years of the Nehru regime than in the entire period of two hundred years of British rule, and more people were felled by police bullets in the years of Indira Gandhi's regime.... More than thirty thousand people died or were crippled in police firings during the thirty years of father-daughter rule."[87] At least one scholar-thinker believes that Gandhian non-violence will not succeed because the ethos of India today is much different from the time when Gandhi tried to mobilize people around his morals and values. India today ".... has been overwhelmed by problems of transitional history -- cataclysmic social, political and economic transformation."[88]

This line of thinking concludes that if Gandhi had a relative notion of non-violence, and if he did not create non-violent institutions, how do the Gandhians hope to succeed whose moral preparation may not be on par with that of Gandhi. Perhaps, the Gandhians will respond by suggesting that modern civilization, which has produced the institutions of non-violence, needs to be changed. And the success of the Gandhian principle of non-violence does not depend on producing a non-violent model, but in "trying" to construct such a model.

The burden of implementing Gandhian ideals fall on the shoulders of the contemporary Gandhian constructive workers. Much of this book has been dedicated to the telling of their stories. Needless to say that the constructive workers, and their projects, have been subjected to many criticisms. Consequently a discussion in this regard becomes imperative. It is interesting to note that Prime Minister Nehru viewed the work of Khadi and other village industries as "temporary expedients of a transition state rather than a solution to our vital problems."[89] Unfortunately, this line of thinking is widespread in India even today. The critics view the constructive works as "patch work" with no serious consequences towards solving national problems. Perhaps the most serious criticism has come from a Gandhian worker, Nirmal Chand (of the Gandhi Peace Foundation) who observed that, after his fifty years of experience in working with the Gandhians, he has come to the conclusion that he can no longer tolerate the problem of embezzlement, exploitation of the workers and the selfishness of many Gandhian leaders. He reports that many Gandhian organizations are caught up in law suits, have become rich institutions, and their leaders are not fit to give moral guidance.[90]

A common complaint that one hears about the Sarvodaya constructive workers (like the ones profiled in this study) is that while they preach decentralization of power, they themselves are not willing to relinquish their own power within the organization they oversee. They suffer from "the guru complex," i.e. they perceive themselves as gurus whose disciples should submissively follow them. Furthermore, they are reluctant to pass on their mandates to the younger generation.[91] My own observation in this regard is that not all Gandhians are rajas of their ashrams. Some have relinquished their power to different committees within the organization. However, in the eyes of the tribals or poor villagers, who are highly benefited by the existence of various constructive work programs, the Gandhian constructive workers are their heroes. Nevertheless, the social hierarchy, which is a basic feature of the Indian society, survives in Gandhian ashrams as well.

The lack of coordination among various Gandhian workers is also pointed out as a sign of their weakness. Sarva Seva Sangh is a loosely organized body. Many constructive workers do not even attend its organizational meetings. Often the leaders are engaged in their own social work programs without the knowledge or even the concern for what the others are doing. In the interest of national and international recognition, often the Gandhian leaders are self-occupied. Under this situation, they cannot be a viable force in society. As one observer puts it, "Gandhian organizations are like rivulets in search of the mainstream."[92] The problem of co-ordination and co-operation is also extended to the worker's relationship with the local panchayat in the village. One critic writes, "In their anxiety to stay out of local factions and personal and other conflicts, constructive workers have often failed to develop close working relations with local Panchayats and cooperatives and have tended to establish separate links with interested local workers and leaders."[93] Their attempts to create separate gram sabhas and lok samitis could also be seen in the same light. Of course, the constructive worker's response often is that the local Panchayats are so politicized and controlled by vested interest groups that it is difficult to work with them. Hence the creation of new working committees like the village councils and people's committees becomes necessary.

The most fundamental issue in the eyes of the critics is what did Gandhi intend the constructive work to be, and what has it become? What Gandhi proposed was that this kind of work should include a moral action, supported by voluntary co-operation, promote self-reliance, help building from below, practice non-violence, and implement decentralization.[94] If Rajni Kothari is correct, the constructive work program today has taken a 'developmental' approach and needs to move out of this paradigm. Although many Gandhian constructive workers make a theoretical distinction between development and welfare (Sarvodaya), in practice many of their projects follow the governmental policy of development. As such, the projects are funded by government aid and foreign donor agencies. Among certain young constructive workers, it has become a practice to prepare projects that could be funded by the governmental and non-governmental agencies. With these funds they are able to raise their own standards of living.[95] The critics fear that these tendencies are against the Gandhian principles.

An ardent critic of Sarvodaya, Devdutt, has called it, "the church of Gandhism" which is, to his mind, irrelevant today.[96] He argues that Sarvodaya is failing because it suffers from cult-thinking. "There is the cult of localism. It romanticizes and over-emphasizes the guilelessness of local bodies, particularly of the variety of Panchayats--as if, these communities are Gardens of Eden untouched by power and its corruptive influence."[97] There is also "the cult of consensus" which, in his view, "underestimates the value of conflict of ideas and it is not conceded that there is a creative force in competition of ideas."[98] On the whole, he finds the Sarvodaya leaders limited in their thinking who have an utopian vision to change society, who expect too much from an ordinary individual, criticize the developed societies, and have too much faith in spirituality. Although somewhat cynical in his assessment of Sarvodaya leadership and its vision, the writer raises some important questions about its dream to create a peaceful society. He challenges Gandhians to be more open minded and study the current trends which are now taking place in the Indian society. He is apt to point out that even though "the church of Gandhism" may be irrelevant, "it does not follow that the gospel of Gandhi is also irrelevant."[99]

The criticisms against various Sarvodaya ideologies and programs finally come down to questioning the viability of Ram Raj. As we have seen, Ram Raj (Kingdom of God) is about creating a social order along Gandhian lines. It is about a particular worldview which competes against many existing worldviews around the globe. Some such plans to create a renewed social order are religious while the others are secular in nature. After the recent reunification of Germany, the break up of the Soviet Union, and political changes in Eastern Europe, there has been talk of 'the new world order' in the West, spearheaded by the United States. This new world order envisions different military alliances, re-shifting of political powers, industrial development, and economic prosperity. The key to this new world order is economic development along the lines of the western model of development. The belief that the adherence to this world order will bring prosperity and happiness is sweeping across the continents. In this context, the question can be asked; What can the vision of Ram Raj offer? The critics are not certain that it can offer much.

The supporters of the Gandhian model of a social order claim that the Dwadash Vratas (the twelve vows) that Gandhi offered can be the basis of Ram Raj. These are; Ahimsa (non-violence), Satya (truth), Asteya (non-stealing), Brahmacharya (chastity), Asangraha (non-accumulation), Parishrama (bread labor), Aswad (control of the palate), Bhayavarjanam (fearlessness), Sarvadharma Sambhava (equality of all religions), Swadeshi (love for one's country), Sparshabhavana (abjuring untouchability), and Aninda (non-criticism). It is claimed that, "The observance of these twelve Vratas can lay the foundation of a non-violent social order because they can eliminate the inner or psychic sources of agitation, excitement, emotion, provocation, irritation, and violence, or they can effectively control the urge or craving for money, wealth, power, fame, and carnal desires."[100] The critics will argue that this is a purely religious vision and can never

319

be fully implemented. In fact, it comes in direct conflict with the new world order propounded along economic lines. At best, a few individuals can practice these vows, but it can never be a model for the entire society.

It has been suggested that there are four main pillars to the edifice of a Gandhian society -- decentralization of power, non-mechanization, non-industrialization, and ruralization.[101] However, none of these is accepted by the Indian society today. The critic observes, "For most Indians in the saddle today there is not enough philosophy in, nor sufficiently long application behind, these items (4 pillars) proposed in our most dynamic twentieth century for free Indian society since 1947, when all kinds of races have to be run and competitions to be faced on all scales, in all fields and at all levels."[102] It should be pointed out that many Gandhians will disagree that Gandhi was against mechanization, industrialization, and for ruralization. Nonetheless, it is true that people in power in India today are not interested in understanding Gandhi. They are not interested because Gandhism is dead as so pronounced by some. As one critic states:

> If we still hear of Khadi Boards, Bhudana (Bhoodan), Harijan Leagues, Sevak Samajs..., side by side with electrification, and science and technology pools, it is because our leaders and sub-leaders do not want to admit that Gandhism is dead; ...The organizations mentioned above are only fanning the ashes; there are no embers.[103]

One basic problem with the concept of Ram Raj is that Gandhi never fully defined what he meant by it. Sometimes he hinted that such a Raj may have existed in the past when perfect Dharma (morality) was practiced in Ayodhya. And yet he admitted that his Rama (ruler of Ayodhya) was not the Rama of the epic Ramayana. Sometimes he mentioned that Ram Raj was like the time of the Four Caliphs (the leaders of Islam) in ancient Arabia. However, at other occasions he put Ram Raj in the future, which was yet to be established. Whether this ambiguity was intended or it points to Gandhi's own unsettled development of thought is debatable. What is certain is that it has caused the critics to raise some serious questions on the matter. Since they are no certain paradigms of its existence, it is a futuristic dream. As one scholar has written, "The religious aspects of Gandhiji's Ram Raj -- the establishment of the kingdom of righteousness on the earth -- will still remain a distant dream for the world to work for. The idea of reducing economic inequalities through a Trusteeship system is far from realistic. Decentralization of political power in a country where there is a political instability may prove to be dangerous

320

and disastrous."[104] Another criticism is made that since the notion of Ram Raj is so elusive, it is a romantic ideal.[105] And many such ideals have existed in the past.

*   *   *

So far in this assessment of the contemporary Gandhians, the discussion has been centered around their ideologies and challenges to those ideologies. The voices of various scholars were presented to sharpen the issues and to evaluate the concern for a new social order -- the building of a non-violent society -- Ram Raj. There is no doubt that the cause that the Sarvodaya Gandhians have undertaken is a noble one, and demands a serious attention. However, there are areas of activities where their work needs to be more focused if they are to leave a meaningful legacy for the next generation. Following are some personal reflections on ongoing problems and future prospects concerning the Sarvodaya movement.

The most fundamental problem that the contemporary Gandhians face is the problem of "self-image." It is the problem of establishing their credibility in the eyes of the common people in order that they may be taken seriously. Unfortunately, for many Indians, Gandhians (identified with Khadi clothes and the Gandhian cap) are perceived as romantic idealists untouched by modernity, critics of the science and technology, and bent on taking India backwards to a rural society. A popular Hindi saying states: "Majboori Ka Naam Mahatma Gandhi." When translated it approximates the idea, "The name of helplessness is Gandhi." It is suggestive of the negative belief that when people are helpless due to the lack of power, they think of Gandhi. In this manner Gandhi and his thought are subjected to ridicule. Both are seen as irrelevant. Of course, the Gandhians would like to turn the image of Gandhi around. If so, they need to popularize the phrase, "Majboori hi Gandhi", which means, "The very helplessness is Gandhi". This suggests that the feeling of helplessness is an indication that Gandhi is needed. Therefore, he is relevant.

Central to the question of credibility is the question of education. Unless the Gandhian ideals are disseminated in the hearts and minds of children through a curriculum that includes Gandhism, no proper change in the self-image of Gandhians is possible. However, public education is in the hands of the government today. Unless Sarvodaya finds a way to educate the boards of education that set the curricula, it will be difficult to teach Gandhian values. One solution to this problem might be for the Sarva Seva Sangh to commission talented

321

Gandhians to write a model curriculum that could be presented to the state education boards for review and adoption. Such an activity could be undertaken in different states of the union where State Sarvodaya Mandals (organizations) are operative. This would mean organizing educated Sarvodaya workers who can dedicate their talents for this work. It is a well known fact that Gandhi had included Nai Talim (New Education) in his constructive work program (see the chapter on Gandhi). However, neither Vinoba nor J. P. could give it a national prominence. In fact, after independence, the government merely paid lip service to its importance, and no serious effort was made to implement it. Today, a modest office of Nai Talim survives as a museum piece among the buildings at the Seva Gram Ashram in Wardha.[106] If Sarvodaya is not able to influence the government to include Gandhian thought in its curricula, then the other option for it is to make education a community based enterprise. This would mean that every community will have its own schools taught by individuals committed to Gandhism. Today, many constructive workers are involved in the work of establishing balwadis (primary schools), yet there is a need to launch an organized national movement if Gandhism is to be promoted along side of other disciplines.

Sarvodaya desperately needs an organized youth movement. The plight of the youth can easily be observed in India today. With the exception of a few institutions of higher learning, many colleges and universities have become centers of political activities.[107] The lack of hope in a bright future has disillusioned millions of young people. The problem of discipline, cheating on exams, bribing examiners, rioting, and related problems plague many institutions. The youth are in search of a meaningful and useful life. My purpose here is not to evaluate the Indian educational system and the reasons for its success or failure. An analysis of those issues can be found elsewhere.[108] The point is that the Gandhians need to mobilize the youth who need a vision for the future. Many Gandhian leaders, who are profiled in this study, have been working with the youth all over India. However, there seems to be no co-ordination among them. The dynamic Gandhian youth leaders are scattered all over India. Increasingly, young engineers, social workers, and post graduate students are finding their way into the villages to set up their own institutions to help the villagers. Many are doing Gandhi's work but hesitate to invoke his name due to the problem of negative "self image" referred to earlier. There is a tremendous amount of energy and vitality that could be harnessed if the efforts of the youth could be channeled in a proper direction. Sarvodaya needs to create a 'youth cell' on a national level of high visibility. The function of the cell could be to disseminate information, co-ordinate activities, and promote training of youth leaders.[109] The main reason for its existence will not be centralization of power, but to co-ordinate the decentralized activities.

Ever since the well publicized split between Vinoba and J. P., there has been a crisis of leadership within the Sarvodaya movement. Time has not yet healed the wounds created due to the division between the so called 'followers of Vinoba', and the so-called 'followers of J. P.' The verbal attacks on the ideological differences between the two groups can still be heard among Sarvodaya leaders. There has been no effort to bring both groups to a common platform. As a consequence, the Sarvodaya leaders are more focused on doing their independent projects rather than joining their forces to create a national front. It is certainly the case of a house divided against itself which cannot withstand the forces which run counter to the Gandhian vision. Nationally, the leadership has no united voice, no effective platform to bring about social change, and no moral force to influence the masses. There is a serious problem of attracting dedicated Lok Sevaks (servants of the people) to the movement. The lack of a charismatic leader or a collective leadership has left the movement dry and ineffective. As Mark Thomson notes, "In some of the ashrams there still are dynamic persons, but for some reason they have not been able to perform a cadre of devoted and enlightened workers."[110]

The schisms among various religious, social, and political movements are a historical problem. However, in any case, the question of whether to view the split as a problem or an opportunity to do something creative rests in the hands of the leadership of the movement. Take the case of Christianity, which has been divided into so many groups and denominations. Here, the Ecumenical Movement through many dialogues among the parties, has achieved considerable success in bringing several denominations together within its Protestant branch. Dialogue also continues between Catholics and Protestants in the hope of bridging the gap between the two in the future. The Sarvodaya today needs an "ecumenical spirit" to work out the differences that exist between the followers of Vinoba and those of J. P. The possibility of a reconciliation exists if the leadership views the split dialectically rather than dualistically (see Devdutt footnote #98). What is needed within the movement is a unity-in-difference, rather than a difference-in-disunity. It is interesting to note that J. P., close to the end of his life, had sought a reconciliation with Vinoba by visiting him. It is the view of one observer that such a meeting was possibly sabotaged by some of J. P.'s followers.[111] It is not too late for the different "wings" of Sarvodaya, in order to live up to their name, to open a sincere dialogue among themselves in the interest of the welfare of the people. Immediate attention needs to be paid for organizing a national forum where different Sarvodaya leaders may come together to work out their differences.

For Gandhi, Sarvodaya was grounded in spiritual principles. He perceived it to be a moral force generated by the power of those individuals who practiced religious disciplines. His own religious beliefs and practices helped him sustain the value of Sarvodaya. After Gandhi, Vinoba Bhave became the spiritual guru whose dynamism was felt by millions of people. His personal <u>Sadhana</u> (spiritual quest), as well as the Sadhana of his ashram disciples prepared them for their moral actions. They were encouraged to build their character through a prayerful and meditative lifestyle. The source of their power was their faith in the spiritual efficacy of the religious disciplines. Thus, Satyagraha and Sarvodaya were imbued with spirituality. Today, Sarvodaya seems to have lost its spiritual base. No doubt, many Gandhians engage in personal piety, but there are very few visible manifestations of that piety in their work. There is no emphasis put on the religious training of their workers. In some ashrams, prayer meetings are held routinely without any meaningful discourse on the application of prayer in daily work. Many religious services are poorly attended, and often the places of worship are empty. Based on the model provided by Gandhi and Vinoba, there is an urgent need to revive the spiritual basis of Sarvodaya. The responsibility of bringing a spiritual revival in the movement is in the hands of its leaders. It must begin with a personal transformation and extended toward communal transformation. India adores spiritual gurus. It will not abandon the spiritually motivated Gandhians. Perhaps the key to this transformation rests on the issue whether or not they see their work as 'development' or as Sarvodaya.

Contemporary Gandhians need to ask themselves: Is there a positive force behind Sarvodaya? For Gandhi this force was pursuit of Truth, which he called God. At times he also expressed his belief in a personal God, who was not a metaphysical principle but a living force. For Vinoba, it was his spiritual experience of a divine reality. For others, it was jyoti -- the divine light within -- (see the chapter on Krishnammal), the grace of God (Nirmala Deshpande), and the power of prayer (Harivallabh Parikh). Others have their own testimonies of faith (Narayan Desai, Chunibhai Vaidya, Subba Rao, and Sunderlal Bahuguna). However, it appears that due to the split within the movement, its spiritual base was considerably weakened. Vinoba was labeled as "too mystical" and his spirituality was perceived to be "beyond comprehension." Consequently, many chose to follow J. P. who was viewed as "practical." J. P.'s own confession that he was not a very spiritual man may have attracted like-minded followers. It is not my intention to suggest that Sarvodaya is meant only for the theists and has no place for the humanists. The question is; from where do the members of the movement derive their power to continue to pursue their visions? I concur with Gandhi that ultimately power comes from a disciplined spiritual life. Sarvodaya then needs a creative program to renew its spiritual development.

The Sarvodaya movement has fared well in terms of producing and disseminating its literature. It needs to develop in the area of performing arts. Today, many talented young people (who have Gandhian association) have produced inspiring songs, poetry, and plays which are performed by various groups. However, there is no co-ordination among these groups, and there is no national organization that supports them. What if Sarva Seva Sangh takes the initiative to form a Sarvodaya Kala Kendra (Center for Sarvodaya Arts)? It will most assuredly attract talented youth, who would want to perfect their art for the cause of Gandhi. Such an institution could offer classes in music, drama, literature, dance, etc., and train 'Sarvodaya performers' to take the message to the cities and the villages all across India. One can hardly imagine what transformative effect such an activity would have on the lives of the people! India has a great example of the Bhakti Movement (Devotional Movement) that spread all across India during the middle ages. Its success was made possible by bands of devotional saints who marched together the breadth of India singing hymns of praise, and bringing the message of devotional piety to the masses. Today, Bhakti has become a central feature of India's devotional life. If Sarvodaya wishes to become a mass movement, it must bring its lok sevaks together, train them in the Sarvodaya arts, and send them out with the message of Ram Raj. The Sarvodaya Kala Kendra can help achieve this goal. There is no limit to how many forms of arts can be brought together to do the work of Gandhi. What is needed is a commitment and a vision to achieve this goal.

Today, more than ever before, we are witnessing a globalization of political, social, religious, economic ideas. Nations are linked through all forms of electronic media and thus the dissemination and the availability of information have become easier. It is predicted that the twenty-first century will be the "century of information." In this context, the Gandhians must contemplate the formation of Sarvodaya International. The function of such an organization could be to invite like-minded people to join Sarvodaya and promote Sarvodaya volunteerism in their respective countries. Years ago the International Peace Brigade (Shanti Sena) was formed to promote the means of non-violent conflict resolutions. It was instrumental in raising people's consciousness in the area of peacemaking, and inspired the work of many peace seeking organizations around the world. Sarvodaya International can take further steps in the process of the globalization of Gandhism. It can also encourage Gandhians to learn from other cultures their methods of improving conditions of their society. For example, a dialogue between Liberation Theology and its impact on the formation of Base Communities in Latin American can prove to be useful for the establishment of Sarvodaya communities in India. The plight of the poor and the have-nots is not unique to India. Many countries of Asia, Africa, Latin America, and the West suffer from similar problems. A Sarvodaya International can be helpful in bringing people from these countries together to work for finding solutions to common problems.

The various constructive work programs undertaken by contemporary Gandhians are highly praiseworthy. However, it is unfortunate that no one has launched a program to tackle the population explosion in India. Experts tell us that in countries where population growth is not controlled, economic progress is off-set by the rise in population. Most Gandhians oppose the artificial methods of birth control and fall back on the traditional notion of Brahmacharya (continence) advocated by Gandhi and Vinoba. It is reported that J. P. supported the idea of birth control, but no organized efforts were made by him to launch a national program in this area.[112] To my knowledge, Harivallabh Parikh is one veteran Gandhian who has organized birth-control camps among the tribals in his area. Generally one encounters several assumptions which some Gandhians hold that might prevent them from working in this area. Besides the advocacy of continence, the often quoted Gandhian axiom is that 'the world has enough to provide for everyone's need, but not their greed'. Sometimes it is also stated that if God provides a person two hands, he will provide the means to feed one mouth. At least one lok sevak emphatically stated that India has no population problem, it is a western conspiracy to defame India.[113] And finally, there is the view that the rising population has no adverse effect on India since life expectancy has risen, and the standard of living has also gone up. By reporting these assumptions I do not mean to suggest that all Gandhians hold these views. Similar views are found among the general population in India. The fact remains that population control has never been a part of Sarvodaya's platform. A movement which is concerned with the welfare of all must find ways to deal with this serious problem. Since the Sarvodaya workers work with the villagers, they are in a good position to instruct them on the necessity of birth-control by holding workshops and clinics and providing them with the necessary methods of birth-control.

Among the contemporary Gandhians there is an ambivalent attitude toward their participation in the political process. It is not as if they don't want any power to change the society, but they are not sure if they should gain power via political involvement. Ideologically they have attempted to create a parallel government by working for Gram Panchayats. However, efforts in this area have not produced any favorable results. Many Sarvodaya Gandhians feel that Gandhi never worked to control political power. He never joined any political party, and even refused to be a member of the Congress Party. It is believed that somehow his non-participation in a party was a moral act, and they should follow in his footsteps. However, it is a fallacy to believe that Gandhi did not enter into politics. He came into politics to spiritualize it.[114] As far as his gaining political power is concerned, he had plenty of it by remaining outside the party. He did not need to join the Congress, he was the Congress. Much of his success was in the political field through negotiations, Satyagrahas, and influencing important decisions. He did not need to hold a political office, because no office could be higher than the office of the Mahatma. Gandhi had no ambivalence about his role in politics, and he dictated his own brand of politics by infusing his religious ideals into it.

The ambivalence on whether or not to participate in the political process has cost Gandhians the opportunity to influence change. Like Gandhi, J. P. came to the realization that his participation in politics was necessary if he were to save the Indian democracy in the 1970s. Thus, he plunged into politics wholeheartedly and changed the political landscape of the time by supporting the creation of the Janta Party. But, when Acharya Rammurti (see the chapter on him) supported V. P. Singh in his bid for the prime ministership of India, many Gandhians turned against him. Many of his critics, however, supported the idea of setting up Lok Umeedvars (people's candidates) to fight parliamentary elections. Though the experiment has been a failure, some have even supported the formation of a Sarvodaya Party. Among the Gandhians, there is no general consensus as to what role they should play in the political process. This ambivalence is also extended to their relationship with the government. Some support the government to gain favors from the power structure to enhance their constructive work programs, while others stand in opposition to it in principle. Some are recipients of handsome government grants to

327

support their projects, while others refuse to take any money from the government at all.

If for Gandhians not voting for a candidate is being true to the spirit of Gandhi, so be it. However, involvement or non-involvement into politics does not rest on the issue of "voting." One can be seriously engaged in politics without ever joining a party or voting for a candidate. Both Gandhi and Vinoba are exemplars of this model. In this context, to accuse J. P. for entering in politics is not justified (see the chapter on Nirmala Deshpande). He entered into politics as much as Gandhi entered into it to effect change. For both it was not a question of being involved or not involved. They were aware that non-entry into politics did not mean the absence of a political consciousness. Recalling the chapter on her, Nirmala Deshpande's recent acceptance to the nomination to Rajya Sabha (the upper house of the parliament) could also be viewed in this light. The Sarvodayaites need not become politicians (and avoid the evils of politics), but they must not shy away from every form of political participation.

It is my contention that the Sarvodaya movement needs to unite in order to become a political force. As long as they have accepted parliamentary democracy (which Gandhi accepted and J. P. helped to save it), they must recognize that some changes can be facilitated by working through the parliamentary process. A case in point is the issue of Panchayat Raj. If the Gandhians support the government in finding ways to improve and implement the Panchayat Raj, they might find this to be more useful than attempting to set up parallel governments by establishing gram sabhas. On other issues it may be necessary to launch a Satyagraha against the government as Jagannathan is doing in the south (see the chapter on him) on the issue of Aqua-culture. In both cases, an involvement in the political process is necessary. This is the legacy of Gandhi. He was able to combine the moral force with political power to influence change.

Can gram swaraj be achieved by receiving money from foreign donor agencies? This is a serious dilemma. Today many Gandhian constructive works are supported by money that has come from abroad. Readers will recall that during Indira Gandhi's return to power (1980), she had set up the Kudal Commission to investigate various Gandhian organizations which were accused of receiving money from abroad and using it for political purposes. Today, the money continues to flow. It should be noted that many successful projects that are run by the Gandhians, are run with the help of donations from abroad. Although it is true that Sarva Seva Sangh had never officially supported this practice, some Sarvodaya workers connected with independent projects are open to receiving financial aid from abroad. For Gandhi and Vinoba, the notion of gram swaraj was intrinsically related to the notion of Swadeshi. It meant self-sufficiency based on local resources. The whole process of the freedom of the village was training people not to depend on outside help. Swadeshi (one's own) was hailed better than Videshi (someone else's). The critics of Videshi money are right in suggesting that no gram swaraj can be obtained by dependence on foreign donations. We can call it development, but not gram swaraj. Thus, the real question is; Are the Gandhians in the business of development or Sarvodaya?

The issue becomes even more complicated when the West is criticized for its model of development, and yet no remorse is expressed on receiving that money which is the product of that model of development. Furthermore, why criticize the multinational companies, if some of the money they produce supports the existence of donor agencies abroad. One answer to this dilemma is that an effort needs to be made to raise money within India. There is no dearth of wealth in India as every Indian knows. However, the spirit of giving is lacking.[115] Gandhi was able to raise funds for his projects because he had credibility. Perhaps, the Gandhians need to prove their credibility through their actions. Then the money will come. There are those who will not agree with this analysis. Several arguments are presented in favor of receiving foreign donations. One is that if we are seeking the globalization of Gandhism through Sarvodaya International, then the involvement of other people should be encouraged and welcomed. Also, the foreign money is viewed as "seed money" which is not enough to support the projects, but stimulates the activity in order that it may take the life of its own. It should be noted that it is precisely in the name of globalization that the multinational companies are permitted to come to India. If we are willing to accept one form of globalization (receiving money from the foreign donor agencies), then we should be expected to accept the other as well (the multinationals). The Gandhians who favor the foreign donations must ponder this dilemma with stark realism.

One of the most difficult challenges for the Gandhians is how to make non-violence palatable to the masses. Gandhi presented a holistic vision of non-violence in all aspects of life, may it be social, economic, religious, political, etc. He conducted non-violent experiments in these areas. Today, the Gandhians are not able to pursue this holistic approach. They have become experts of their chosen fields, whether it is Khadi, agriculture, trusteeship, etc.[116] The holistic approach will require establishing institutions of learning where students could be trained in various aspects of the Gandhian thought. One such experiment is conducted by Manubhai Pancholi in Gujarat through his well known institution of <u>Lok Bharati</u>. According to Manubhai there are approximately twenty five other institutions like Lok Bharati that are trying to achieve a similar goal. However, not all of them are succeeding. His advice for the Gandhians is to establish institutions of Gandhian learning where students could be trained in Gandhian economics, politics, education, etc. from an early age. Only then can a holistic vision of implementing a non-violent society be realized. One cannot preach non-violence to the masses and expect them to become non-violent. It requires behavior modification. This is only possible through a holistic education. Since Gandhi was against Gandhism, the purpose of such an education should not be to brainwash students in the name of Gandhi. His ideas and experiments need to be integrated with the study of other disciplines. Gandhism is about life. It is about discovering ways and means to authenticate what humans are meant to be. Gandhi believed that non-violence was inherent into the nature of things. However, he also realized that violence too was a part of nature. The resolution of this paradox poses a real challenge for everyone. For those who believe, as Gandhi did, that non-violence can be victorious over violence, there is the difficult task of creating models of non-violent institutions from which the society may benefit.

There is a general tendency among certain Gandhians to be relentlessly critical of the West, its culture, achievements, and economic prosperity. Some of these criticisms are well founded, but many are based on the lack of first hand knowledge of Western culture. To generalize that the West is materialistic while India is spiritual is foolhardy. To claim that Christianity is exclusive while Hinduism is all inclusive is short-sight. To believe that all Christian missionaries are interested in converting Hindus is a fallacy. Most importantly, to blame the West for its capitalism and materialistic progress is to wallow in the pride of self-righteousness. The drive toward materialism, success, and achievements are part of human nature. If India emulates the West, then the blame should fall on those who are so eager to copy. The blame of destroying the Indian values should really fall on those who are so willing to accept the foreign values. This was Gandhi's main concern when he wrote his famous <u>Hind Swaraj</u> (1909). He was criticizing educated Indians who were sold on the western model of development. It was they, he thought, who were bent on taking India on a wrong path. The analysis holds as true today as then. It is the Indian industrialists, technocrats and elite who should be the recipients of Gandhians' wrath, not the West. Their goal should be to put their own house in order first before pointing a finger elsewhere. Furthermore, it should not be forgotten that Gandhi, to a large extent, was the product of western culture. His love for punctuality, cleanliness, hard work, humanism, and the respect for an individual may have had western origins. The Gandhian non-violent approach would be to take the best of the West, learn from it, and try to change the rest. Today, as many westerners are traveling to India, and are coming in contact with the constructive works; Gandhi is best served when they are accepted as equals and appreciated for their values. Instead of preaching Gandhian moralism to them, it might be better to enter into dialogue with them in the quest for truth.

One of the most difficult and yet urgent tasks for the Gandhians is to save Gandhi from Gandhism. Within the Sarvodaya movement there is a tendency to elevate Gandhi to the level of a deity. As such he is put on a pedestal beyond human reach. As Arun Gandhi argues, one of the problems with the contemporary Gandhians is to focus on the Mahatma rather than the man. In doing so, we distance Gandhi from our humanity. Our responsibilities are lessened because who can match up with the Mahatma? What is required is the recognition that Gandhi was also a human being like we are. If he could reach certain heights in his experiments with the establishment of a non-violent society, so can we.[117] I concur with Arun Gandhi's observation based on my own interviews with many Gandhian workers. Another tendency which matches the deification of Gandhi is orthodoxy. It is the inability to study objectively the Gandhian principles and to test them. The legacy of Gandhi is the legacy of experimentation. To accept his ideologies as gospel truth without putting them to test has no authentic meaning. With orthodoxy come dogmas and doctrines. And adherence to dogmas leads to exclusivism. At this point Gandhism takes on a negative religious attire. As a faith it is subjected to an emotional defense rather than scrutinized by reason. Anyone who reads Gandhi will recognize that this is the last thing that Gandhi ever wanted. He was an evolving thinker, who sometimes annoyed his associates by rapidly changing his mind. The Gandhians must resist the tendency to turn Gandhism into a religion, and instead advocate a rational philosophy that can stand the test of time. Vinoba Bhave and J. P. both took Gandhism to a higher level of rational thinking. Vinoba did it by stressing the merger of science and spirituality. J. P. founded an institution for Gandhian studies and other institutions where scholarly activities could be carried out. It was his goal to bring the Sarvodaya social workers and thinkers together. Such a legacy must continue.

331

If Sarvodaya is truly based on universal religious principles, then it must make a conscious effort to use universal symbols to articulate Gandhi. Often, Sarvodaya operates within a Hindu framework. Its literature is permeated with stories derived primarily from the Hindu religious texts. Often the prayer meetings organized in Gandhian ashrams have the ambiance of a Hindu puja (worship). The songs sung are taken from Hindu poets, and prayers uttered are from the Hindu religious sources. Perhaps, the question needs to be raised whether Gandhi had completely rid himself of his Hindu background as he propagated communal harmony, peace, love, and non-violence as universal religious symbols. One cannot accuse Gandhi for practicing his Hindu faith because he claimed to be a Hindu. The problem arises when he advocates acceptance of all faiths, and yet favors the symbols of one faith. It is for this reason that many Muslims suspected his rhetoric of Ram Raj as a universal utopian community. In spite of his explanations that Ram Raj was not a Hindu Raj, the minorities were not convinced. Perhaps, Gandhi had to play his Hindu card since majority of the Indians are Hindus and can easily grasp Hindu symbols. However, it is unfortunate that Sarvodaya has not been able to attract many Muslims, Christians, Sikhs, etc. into the movement. Their participation has been quite minimal. Perhaps, today, the contemporary Gandhians need to address this issue. They must construct a truly universal Sarvodayan language to attract people of all faiths into the movement. This is important because communal tensions in India have been the primary source of violence. It is true that the Gandhians are always there endangering their own lives to make peace. However, often they are there after the violence has erupted and the damage is already done. If they could involve people from all faiths into their movement, their presence in the community might help prevent the violence from exploding.

Given the situation that the Gandhians are faced with, the problems of self-image, orthodoxy, emotional dependency, deification of Gandhi, etc., which make them suspect in the eyes of the general public, there is a need for a new generation of Gandhians, who can move beyond Gandhi without betraying his ideals. We could call them Neo-Gandhians, a group of well-informed individuals who do not see Gandhism as a panacea for all problems, but are dedicated to seek solutions to the perennial question; Whither India? These will include scientists, engineers, educators, economists, political scientists, etc. who are enthused by the spirit of volunteerism and sacrifice for the welfare of all. They will not follow the Gandhian dogmas but will be committed to experiments in the quest for truth and building an equitable society. A trend in this direction is already visible. Some educated youth are returning to the villages with projects to change the lives of the people. They are disillusioned by the promises of success made to them by technocrats in the Indian government. They have come to believe that the present economic prosperity will be enjoyed by a few while the masses will be left out of the process. They shy away from being associated with the name of Gandhi but are doing the work of Gandhi. To them Gandhi is more than a person, he is an idea. For them the power of the idea is not in symbolically spinning khadi and wearing khadi, it is in helping the deprived members of the society to regain their confidence and become self sufficient.

In the context of India's religious and social pluralism, the Gandhians need to evaluate the meaning of the term Ram Raj as the goal of Sarvodaya. The term is entirely too inclusive and subject to misunderstanding. It represents an idealistic state which is hard to achieve and difficult to follow. Ram Raj suffers from the same predicament as the term Mahatma. Both are beyond the reach of the common people. More than that, it invokes an imagery which might be suitable for one segment of the Indian society, but leaves the others unresponsive. Due to its religious connotations, it can easily be exploited and misused as evidenced by the propagation of Ram Raj by Hindu fundamentalists. In this case, Gandhi is used to support their cause. The term Gram Swaraj comes closer to what Gandhi had in mind when he spoke of Ram Raj. However, Gram Swaraj, while supporting the cause of India's villages, might alienate India's cities. It seems only appropriate that Gandhism should speak to all levels of the Indian society. Gandhi's own term Hind Swaraj suggests the uplift of all Indians. But, Hind Swaraj carries with it a certain negative imagery about technology, industrialization, and urbanization as the debate over Gandhi's book by the same title has revealed.[118] Perhaps, Gandhi will be better served if Gandhians emphasized the establishment of Sarvodaya Samaj (Sarvodaya society) as the goal of Sarvodaya. Such a society can exist in the cities as well as the villages, in India as well as globally. It embraces peoples of all faiths and different cultures. It invokes a universal appeal compared to Ram Raj.

There is no reason why the Sarvodaya Samaj may not appeal to the philosophy of Ram Raj as advocated by Gandhi without invoking Hindu theistic imagery. Central to this philosophy is the vision of hope, which is central to all religions. Implied in this futuristic vision is a view of history. On the level of vichar (thought), the contemporary Gandhians need to clarify their eschatology, and their perception of history. If they believe that history is guided by a Divine purpose, then they need to discern as to what that purpose might be in relation to the

333

Sarvodaya Samaj. On the other hand, if they follow a purely humanistic approach, i.e., "the future is what you make of it," then they need to act accordingly. While the first response calls for the establishment of a religious community, the latter calls for the improvement of a secular society. Observing the many constructive work programs as I did, it is not clear as to whether Sarvodaya is working for the establishment of a religious community or non-religious society. Based on Gandhi's belief in a personal God, who intervenes in human affairs, it is evident that he had a religious view of history. Vinoba followed a similar line of thinking. However, with the advent of J. P., such a view, if not totally abandoned, was neglected. His followers (the majority of Sarva Seva Sangh) have the necessary task of combining J. P.'s pragmatism with Gandhian idealism. The two can come together on a pilgrimage to find Truth, which Gandhi equated with God. The quest for truth can bring hope for a bright future and the ability to overcome the many crises Sarvodaya Samaj must face.

*   *   *

The people of all generations are faced with many crises. However, today the world is beset by many problems of immense magnitude. The reports of human rights abuses, genocide, ecological disasters, famine, chemical warfare, and the threat of nuclear annihilation are transmitted over the electronic media for instant access. While the developing world is still struggling to find ways of satisfying human hunger, the developed world is faced with handling crime, drug addiction, mental illnesses, and above all, loneliness and meaninglessness. Under these conditions, the whole world is searching for a new world order. It is quite clear that no political order can solve all human problems. In the eyes of the people, the governments have failed to fulfill their promises to provide a secure and meaningful life. In this context there is a worldwide call for 'Volunteerism.' In the case of India, so many voluntary agencies have stepped in to do what the government will never be able to do. The Sarvodaya movement in India embodies the spirit of volunteerism.

As custodians of a powerful legacy, the contemporary Gandhians are exemplary in many ways. They lead a disciplined life, sacrificing many comforts and luxuries desired by an average person. As the lives of many covered in the book shows, many Gandhian social workers left their comfortable lives to join the movement. Many emulated Gandhi through his examples set by a religious lifestyle. The ideals of the control of desires, selflessness, non-possession, self-denial, control of the palate as part of the twelve famous vows of Gandhi, also became their vows. Following an austere life style, these Gandhians are not ordinary social workers. They are <u>religious</u> social workers. Their commitment to the ideals of Sarvodaya, as exemplified in their activities, shows that they are thoroughly dedicated individuals. Their dedication stems from their firm belief that Gandhism is relevant today and can solve many of India's problems. Among Gandhians, many are quite educated and knowledgeable of Indian history and culture. They understand current problems that the world is facing. Some have traveled abroad and are internationally known for their social work activities. Many have written books and monographs that are used to train many lok sevaks. They are well-versed in Gandhian literature and can articulate it quite well. They are deeply concerned about the welfare of India. As many have participated in India's independence movement, they are infused by the spirit of nationalism. A large number of the present day Gandhians have suffered imprisonment for their cause.

The hallmark of Gandhism is training in non-violent Satyagraha. Gandhians today are quite exemplary in advocating and leading non-violent satyagrahas. Even today, they are insulted, beaten, and put in jails for their non-violent activities. They embrace these sufferings because they believe in the spirituality of non-violence. This is what separates them from many other groups which advocate mere volunteerism to achieve their goals. Despite their Hindu background, Gandhians have a genuine respect for all religions. They advocate religious universalism in order to promote religious tolerance. At times of communal violence, perpetuated by religious intolerance, they are not afraid to mediate peace. Gandhi taught 'fearlessness' as a virtue; the contemporary Gandhians exemplify this virtue through their actions. They have fearlessly gone to work among the tribals, the decoits, and the religious zealots, some of whom are fanatics. They are not afraid to put their lives on the line for the cause of Sarvodaya. In a country which is divided along caste lines, Gandhians have exemplified social equality. Despite their failure to eradicate untouchability, they have freely associated with the untouchables over the years to raise their status in society.

If it had not been for the Gandhians, there would have been fewer constructive work programs in India today. The fact is that today there is a larger variety of constructive work programs than during the time of Gandhi. Gandhism has gone beyond Gandhi, which is a mark of its success. There is more awareness of human rights violations, the plight of women, child abuse, bonded labor, exploitation of the landless, and the conditions of the poor. The Gandhians are instrumental in exposing these vices that plague the Indian society. They are fighting for social justice in an altruistic manner which is praiseworthy. What is remarkable is that despite many odds that are against them, they are keeping the Gandhian vision alive. In doing so, they are messengers of hope.

In spite of the dedicated work and an exemplary life style advocated by its followers, unfortunately today, Sarvodaya has no better status than a "Reform Movement" in India. Like the modern movements of Brahmo Samaj (society of Brahma), Arya Samaj (society of Aryans), the Sarvodaya Samaj will continue to be perceived as a reform movement that has graced Indian history. In light of the challenges faced by it in contemporary India, it cannot gain any better recognition unless it commands political power. Since it has opted to become only a moral force, it will have to be satisfied with its quasi-political position. My reasons for this conclusion are the following:

1) The Sarvodaya movement has no power to change the political power structure. It has chosen not to get involved in politics.

2) The people are not ready for any radical change. They have not responded favorably to Sarvodaya's difficult demands.

3) The Sarvodaya vision is too idealistic for the common person to follow.

4) The Sarvodaya philosophy is based on religious principles. Consequently it can never have a popular appeal. As Jesus witnessed, "the gate is narrow and only a few shall pass through it."

5) Sarvodaya has compromised with the existing power structure.

6) Sarvodaya has no unified leadership and consequently no unified platform.

7) Sarvodaya has not become a mass movement. It has difficulty in recruiting many lok sevaks.

8) Sarvodaya has many constructive work programs which have adopted the developmental model, and are therefore no different from other projects.

9) Sarvodaya is subjected to many other competing socio-religious movements in India.

10) Sarvodaya has failed to become the conscience of the people. It is not a moral force of the masses.

The often asked question is; "What have Gandhians achieved?" Those who pose the question sometimes have their own answer; "they have not achieved much". Needless to say that the real answer to the question depends on one's perspective. If we are expecting an answer to the problem of civilizational crisis that

Gandhi was so concerned with, the Gandhians have not been successful in bringing about a paradigmatic shift in this area. On the contrary the "agro-culture" is in the process of being transformed into the "urban-culture." Thus Westernization is winning and Gandhians are losing. But, then again, we must ask the question: Who has really been successful in dealing with the issue of Whither India? The answer is; no one has. The political, social, and religious movements have all been experiments of one kind or another to make a difference in India's future. As such, Sarvodaya has also been an experiment. And, as it is with experiments, some are successful and others are not. If, on the other hand, we are interested in analyzing various experiments that the Gandhians have been conducting, we will find that they have a pretty good record. From their humble beginnings in South Africa, Satyagraha and Sarvodaya have affected the political, social, and economic life of millions of people. Leaving aside India's independence struggle, the efforts of Vinoba Bhave and Jai Prakash Narayan are no small feats in Gandhians' struggle to chart the destiny of India. Today if one wants to know what the Gandhians are achieving, one would have to trek the dusty roads of India's remote villages, venture into the habitat of the decoits of the Chambal Valley, visit the tribals in various provinces, observe the Satyagrahas against the Aqua-Culture in the South, observe the felling of trees and the building of dams in the Himalayas, face the terrorism of the Naxalites and the violence in Bihar, to name a few; and then ask the question; What have Gandhians achieved? The answer will be quite revealing.

Sarvodaya embraces the soul of India. It is based on the conviction that there is such a thing as an Indian spiritual ethos. That ethos consists in the fact that despite recurrent crises, there is something in the Indian psyche that remains inseparable from the sense of the sacred and the practice of the sacred values. India has survived many incursions -- and so will Sarvodaya.

This study has shown that Sarvodaya is a viable force in the Indian society today. The Gandhians are curators of a noble legacy which they are trying to sustain with their blood, sweat, and tears. Despite their lofty ideals, they are subject to all human weaknesses. Often in the absence of material resources, human power, and moral support, they are struggling to keep the legacy alive. In a culture which promotes materialistic values, self-gratification, and individualism, it is to their credit that they promote volunteerism. In a culture which tolerates and nurtures violence, it is to their credit that they dare to establish non-violent institutions. In a culture which is victimized by wars, it is to their credit that they are the messengers

337

of peace. For Gandhians, there is no dearth of thought. The real test of their success is their actions, as they are for us all.

Endnotes: Assessment

[1] See, The Gentle Anarchists (A study of the leaders of the Sarvodaya movement for Non-Violent Revolution in India) Oxford: Claredon Press, 1971.

[2] L. C. Thanu, 'The Relevance of Swadeshi in the Present Economic Crisis,' in Gandhian Approach to Contemporary Problems by Anil Dutta Misra (New Delhi: Mittal Publication, 1996), p. 92

[3] Devdutt, 'Gandhi's Nonviolence and India Today', in Gandhi Marg (Special issue on Nonviolence), vol. 14, #1 April-June, 1992, pp. 201-214.

[4] Op. cit., p.92

[5] Ram K. Vepa, New technology A Gandhian Concept (New Delhi: Gandhi Book House, 1975), pp. 52-53.

[6] "India: State of the Nation", India Today, Aug. 18,1997,p.29.

[7] Ibid., p.29.

[8] Ibid., p.24.

[9] Devdutt, op.cit. p.206.

[10] Vimla Thakkar, quoted in Murphy, Stephen, Why Gandhi is Relevant in Modern India (New Delhi: The Gandhi Peace Foundation), 1990, p.51.

[11] An interview with Bal Thackeray reported in India Today, Aug. 18, 1997.

[12] Ibid., p.26.

[13] Ibid., p.24.

[14] Acharya Rammurti is an exponent of this idea.

[15] K. J. Charles, "The New Economic Policy or the Recolonisation of India", in Anil D. Mishra, Gandhian Approach to Contemporary Problems., 1996, p. 83.

[16] Ibid., p. 84

[17] Jai Prakash Narayan in Sethi, J. D., Gandhi Today, Second Edition (Delhi: Vikas Publishing House, 1979, p.viii.

[18] Sethi, J. D., op.cit., p.91.

[19] Shankar Pathak in Gangrade, K. D., Gandhian Ideal Development and Social Change (Delhi: Northern Book Center), 1991.

[20] K. D. Gangrade, Gandhian Ideal Development and Social Change (Delhi: Northern Book Center), 1991, p.1.

[21] R. Kothari, Politics and the People: In Search of a Humane India, vol. II (New Delhi: Ajanta Publications, 1989), p.418.

[22] Dr. R.R. Diwakar in foreword to Murphy, Stephen, Why Gandhi is Relevant in Modern India (New Delhi: The Gandhi Peace Foundation, 1990), p.X.

[23] K. D. Gangrade., op.c.t., p.4.

[24] Ibid., p.5.

[25] Ibid., p.5.

[26] Ibid., p.3.

[27] R. P. Misra, ed., Gandhian Model of Development and World Peace(New Delhi: Concept Publishing Company), 1990, p.61.

[28] Alvin Toffler, Future Shock (New York: A National General Company, 1971), p.430.

[29] Ram K. Vepa, New Technology A Gandhian Concept, (New Delhi: Gandhi Book House), 1975, p.16.

[30] Ibid., p.17.

57 Ashutosh Varshney, Democracy, development, and the Countryside: Urban-rural struggle in India (New Delhi: Cambridge University Press, 1995), p.7.

58 Ibid., p.27.

59 Hitesranjan Sanyal, op.cit., p.173.

60 Ibid., p.173.

61 Ibid., p.163.

62 J. D. Sethi, Gandhi Today, op.c.t., p.107.

63 M. K. Gandhi, Harijan, 23 April, 1946, p.198 as quoted by K. D. Gangrade in R. P. Misra, Gandhian Model of Development and World Peace, op.c.t., p.63.

64 Suresh Misra, "Gandhian Concept of India Village" in R. P. Misra, op.cit., p.202.

65 Rajni Kothari, op.cit., p.212.

66 Ram K. Vepa, op.cit., pp. 330-331.

67 K. D. Gangrade, op.cit., p.30.

68 Hitesranjan Sanyal, op.cit., p.182.

69 Ibid., p.182.

70 Ibid., p.182.

71 B. P. Pandey , "Toward A Gandhian Approach To Planning," in R. P. Misra, op.c.t., p.198.

72 Bimal Prasad, Gandhi, Nehru & J. P.: Studies in Leadership (Delhi: Chanakya Publications, 1985), p.137.

73 M. V. Naidu, op.cit., p.253.

74 D. Bandopadhyaya as quoted by Hitesranjan Sanyal, op.c.t., p.176.

75 Ibid., p.176.

76 Bipan Chandra as quoted in Stephen Murphy, Why Gandhi is Relevant in Modern India (New Delhi: The Gandhi Peace Foundation, 1990), p.65.

77 Ram K. Vepa, New Technology A Gandhian Concept, op.cit., p.58.

78 Gandhi's letter to Nehru as quoted in Nageshwar Prasad, ed., Hind Swaraj A Fresh Look, op.c.t., p.7.

79 Gandhi as quoted by Kathalene Jannaway, "Gandhi and Technology" in Science for Villages, # 160-163, ed., Devendra Kumar (Wardha: Center of Science for Villages), 1993.

80 Ashutosh Varshney, op.cit., pp. 48-49.

81 Ibid., p.6.

82 K. Satchidananda Murty, "A critique of Satyagraha" in S. C. Misra ed., Gandhi: Theory and Practice, Social Impact and Contemporary Relevance, op.c.t., p.355.

83 Ibid., p.355.

84 Ibid., pp. 355-356.

85 Stephen Murphy, op.cit., p.67.

86 K. Satchidananda Murty, op.cit., p.351.

87 Devdutt, "Gandhi's Nonviolence and India Today," op.c.t., p.205.

88 Ibid., p.210.

89 Mark Thomson, Gandhi and His Ashrams (Bombay: Popular Prakashan, 1993), p.227.

90 Nirmal Chand, "Not Self-Service but the necessity of Village-Service" (an unpublished article written in Hindi), 1993.

91 This information was received during a conversation with a lok sevak (servant of the people) during my fieldwork in the state of Gujarat. It should be noted that during my conversation with many Gandhians, while some agreed to this observation of the lok sevak, the others denied it.

92 Mark Thomson, op.cit., p.277.

93 Tarlok Singh, "Constructive Work in India: Directions for the Future" in Nageshwar Prasad, Gandhi and the Contemporary World (New Delhi: Radiant Publishers, 1993), p.166.

94 K. S. Bharathi, The Social Philosophy of Mahatma Gandhi (New Delhi: Concept Publishing Co., 1991), p.12.

95 Nirmal Chand, op.cit.

96 Devdutt, "Sarvodaya, Our Times and Gandhi" in S. C. Biswas, ed., Gandhi Theory and Practice, Social Impact and Contemporary Relevance, op.cit., p.108.

97 Ibid., p.107.

98 Ibid., p.107.

99 Ibid., p.108.

100 L. M. Bhole, "The Gandhian Model of Nonviolent Social Order," in Gandhi Marg (Special Issue on Non-Violence) April-June 1992, p.276.

101 Mohan Singh Uberoi Dewana, "Gandhism is dead: Long Live Gandhi-ji" in S. C. Biswas, op.cit., p.471.

102 Ibid., p.472.

103 Ibid., p.472.

104 K. J. Mahale, "Society and State (Ramraj and Swaraj) in S. C. Biswas, ed., op.c.t., p.316.

105 K. Satchidananda Murty, op.cit., p.354.

106 The work of Nai Talim was given to Mr. Zakir Hussein, who became the vice president of India. Among the Gandhians there is a feeling that he did not take much interest in promoting its ideals.

107 J. D. Sethi, Gandhi Today, op.cit., p.149.

108 Ibid. (See Chapter 6 for details)

109 During my interviews with many Gandhian youth across India, I found that many welcomed the idea of creating such a cell. Some suggested that the Gandhi Peace Foundation in New Delhi needs to initiate such an activity.

110 Mark Thomson, op.c.t., p.253.

111 It was reported to me by Mr. Balvijay, the secretary of Vinoba, that J. P. at the end of his life wanted to meet Vinoba. Vinoba agreed to meet him at the airport in Nagpur since J. P. was on dialysis and quite ill. It so happened that J. P.'s plane never touched Nagpur and went directly to Patna, his final destination. While the plane was landing in Patna, J. P. supposedly inquired if he had reached Nagpur. Evidently, he was never informed that he would not stop at Nagpur. The question remains whether this was a ploy on the part of some of his associates who did not want him to meet Vinoba, or simply a misunderstanding.

112 Based on a conversation this author had with the veteran Gandhian, Subba Rao, a close associate of J. P.

113 Based on a conversation with a Gandhian volunteer in Bihar.

114 More than once Gandhi spoke about Gokhale -- his mentor -- who he claimed had given the Indians the message according to which Gandhi wanted to live. The message was "to spiritualize the political life and the political institutions of the country." (See M. K. Gandhi, The Collected Works, Vol. XIII, p. 66, and Vol. XXXV, p. 295).

115 A Sarvodaya worker, Dick Keithan reported to this author how difficult it was for him to extract money from the Indian Corporations in donation.

116 A veteran Gandhian in Gujarat, Manubhai Pancholi holds the same view and wants Gandhians to adopt a holistic approach toward the establishment of a society based on Gandhian ideals.

117 Based on a private conversation with Arun Gandhi, one of the grandsons of Gandhi, and the founder of M. K. Gandhi Institute For Non-Violence, Memphis, TN, U.S.A.

118 See Nageshwar Prasad, ed., Hind Swaraj: A Fresh Look, op.c.t.

Bibliography

Sources in English

Basu, S. K., *Foundations of the Political Philosophy of Sarvodaya*, Delhi: Bliss & Light Publishers, 1984.

Bharadwaj, A. B., *Living Non-Violence*, Delhi: Gandhi in Action, 1986.

Bharati, K. S., *The Philosophy of Sarvodaya*, New Delhi: Indus Publishing Co., 1990.

Bharati, K. S., *The Social Philosophy of Mahatma Gandhi*, New Delhi: Concept Publishing Co., 1991.

Bhave, Vinoba, *Shanti Sena*, Varanasi: Sarva Seva Sangh Prakashan, 1963.

Bhave, Vinoba, *Thoughts on Education*, Varanasi: Sarva Seva Sangh Prakashan, 1964.

Bhave, Vinoba, *The Steadfast Wisdom*, Varanasi: Sarva Seva Sangh Prakashan, 1966.

Bhave, Vinoba, *The Essence of the Christian Teachings*, Varanasi: Sarva Seva Sangh Prakashan, 1969.

Bhave, Vinoba, *Random Reflections*, Varanasi: Sarva Seva Sangh Prakashan, 1971.

Bhave, Vinoba, *Third Power (A New Dimension)*, Varanasi: Sarva Seva Sangh Prakashan, 1972.

Bhave, Vinoba, *Women's Power*, Varanasi: Sarva Seva Sangh Prakashan, 1975.

Bhave, Vinoba, *Democratic Values*, Varanasi: Sarva Seva Sangh Prakashan, 1977.

Bhave, Vinoba, *Talks on the Gita*, Varanasi: Sarva Seva Sangh Prakashan, 1978.

Bhave, Vinoba, *The Principle and Philosophy of the Bhoodan Yagna*, Tanjore: Sarvodaya Prachuralaya, 1995.

Bilpodiwala, Noshir, *The Social Order and Sarvodaya*, Varanasi: Sarva Seva Sangh Prakashan, 1963.

Biswas, S. C. ed., *Gandhi: Theory and Practice Social Impact and Contemporary Relevance*, Shimla: Indian Institute of Advanced Study, 1969.

Bondurant, Joan V., *Conquest of Violence*, Princeton: Princeton University Press, 1985.

Bose, N. K., *Selection from Gandhi*, Ahmedabad: Navajivan Publishing House, 1957.

Brown, Judith, *Gandhi: Prisoner of Hope*, New Delhi: Oxford University Press, 1989.

Chakravartty, Gargi, *Gandhi: A Challenge to Communalism*, New Delhi: Eastern Book Center, 1987.
Chatterjee, Margaret, *Gandhi's Religious Thought*, Indiana: University of Notre Dame Press, 1983.
Chaudharay, Ramnarayan, *Bapu As I Saw Him*, Ahmedabad: Navajivan Publishing House, 1959.
Chaudhuri, Sandhya, *Gandhi and the Partition of India*, New Delhi: Sterling Publishers Private Ltd., 1984.
Choudhuri, Manmohan, *Exploring Gandhi*, New Delhi: The Gandhi Peace Foundation, 1989.
Dalton, Dennis, *Gandhi: Nonviolent Power in Action*, New York: Columbia University Press, 1993.
Dasgupta, S., *A Great Society of Small Communities*, Varanasi: Sarva Seva Sangh Prakashan, 1968.
Daster, Aloo J., *Gandhi's Contribution to the Emancipation of Women*, Bombay: Popular Prakashan, 1991.
Datta, Amlan, *The Gandhian Way*, Shillong: North-Eastern University Publications, 1986.
Datta, Dhirendra Mohan, *The Philosophy of Mahatma Gandhi*, Madison: University of Wisconsin Press, 1953.
Dayal, Parmeshwari, *Gandhian Approach to Social Work*, Ahmedabad: Gujarat Vidyapith, 1986.
Desai, Narayan, ed., *Guidelines for People's Committees*, Varanasi: Sarva Seva Sangh Prakashan, 1978.
Desai, Narayan, *Handbook for Satyagrahis*, New Delhi: The Gandhi Peace Foundation, 1980.
Deshpande, Govind Rao, *Humanized Society Through Trusteeship*, Bombay: Trusteeship Foundation, 1973.
Devadoss, T. S., *Sarvodaya and the Problem of Political Sovereignty*, Madras: University of Madras, 1974.
Diwan, Romesh & Lutz, Mark, *Essays in Gandhian Economics*, New Delhi: Gandhi Peace Foundation, 1985.
Dutt, Dev, *Report to Gandhi*, New Delhi: Gandhi Smarak Nidhi, 1982.
Erikson, Erik H., *Gandhi's Truth*, New York: W. W. Norton & Co. Inc., 1969.
Fischer, Louis, *Gandhi: His Life and Message for the World*, New York: A Mentor Book, 1954.
Fischer, Louis, ed., *The Essential Gandhi*, New York: Vintage Books, 1962.
Galtung, Johan, *The Way is the Goal: Gandhi Today*, Ahmedabad: Gujarat Vidyapith Peace Research Center, 1992.
Gandhi, Arun, ed., *World Without Violence*, New Delhi: New Age International (P) Ltd., 1994.
Gandhi, M. K., *Satyagraha in South Africa*, Ahmedabad: Navajivan Publishing House, 1928.
Gandhi, M. K., *From Yervada Mandir*, Ahmedabad: Navajivan Publishing House, 1932.
Gandhi, M. K., *Hind Swaraj or Indian Home Rule*, Ahmedabad: Navajivan Publishing House, 1938.
Gandhi, M. K., *India of My Dreams*, Ahmedabad: Navajivan Publishing House, 1947.
Gandhi, M. K., *Sarvodaya*, Ahmedabad: Navajivan Publishing House, 1954.
Gandhi, M. K., *My Religion*, Ahmedabad: Navajivan Publishing House, 1955.
Gandhi, M. K., *Truth is God*, Ahmedabad: Navajivan Publishing House, 1955.
Gandhi, M. K., *Ruskin's Unto This Last, A Paraphrase*, Ahmedabad: Navajivan Publishing House, 1956.

Gandhi, M. K., *Gandhi, An Autobiography,* Boston: Beacon Press, 1957.
Gandhi, M. K., *Discourses on the Gita,* Ahmedabad: Navajivan Publishing House, 1960.
Gandhi, M. K., *Village Swaraj,* Ahmedabad: Navajivan Publishing House, 1962.
Gandhi, M. K., *The Message of Jesus Christ,* Bombay: Bharatiya Vidya Bhavan, 1964.
Gandhi, M. K., *The Collected Works of Gandhi,* 90 vols. Publications Division, Ministry of Information and Broadcasting, Government of India, 1958-1984.
Gangrade, K. D., *Gandhian Ideal Development and Social Change,* New Delhi: Northern Book Center, 1991.
Grover, Verinder, ed., *Gandhi and Politics in India,* New Delhi: Deep & Deep Publications, 1987.
Handa, M. L., *Manifesto for a Peaceful World Order: A Gandhian Perspective,* Delhi: Paramount Publishing House, 1983.
Hingoram, Anand, T., *The Encyclopedia of Gandhian Thought,* New Delhi: All India Congress Committee, 1985.
Hoffman, Daniel P., *India's Social Miracle,* California: Nature Graph Co., 1961.
Ingram, Catherine, *In the Footsteps of Gandhi,* Berkeley: Parallax Press, 1990.
Iyer, Raghavan, *The Moral and Political Writings of Mahatma Gandhi* (Vols. I, II, III), Oxford: Claredon Press, 1986, 1987.
Jack, Homer, ed., *The Gandhi Reader,* 1, New York: Grover Press, Inc., 1956.
Jagannathan, *People's Appeal to Government For Total Ban on Prawn Farm,* Kuthur: Vinoba Ashram, 1994.
Jain, J. C., *Gandhi: The Forgotten Mahatma,* Delhi: Mittal Publications, 1987.
Jesudasan, Ignatius, S. J., *A Gandhian Theology of Liberation,* Anand, India: Gujarat Sahitya Prakashan, 1987.
Joshi, Nandini, *Development Without Destruction,* Ahmedabad: Navajivan Publishing House, 1992.
Joshi, P. C., *Mahatma Gandhi: The New Economic Agenda,* New Delhi: Har Anand Publications, 1996.
Juergensmeyer, Mark, *Fighting With Gandhi,* New York: Harper and Row, 1984.
Kapoor, Archna, *Gandhi's Trusteeship,* New Delhi: Deep & Deep Publications, 1993.
Kappen, Mercy, *Gandhi and Social Action Today,* New Delhi: Sterling Publishers Private Ltd., 1990.
Kripalani, Krishna, ed., *All Men Are Brothers: Life and Thought of Mahatma Gandhi,* Ahmedabad: Navajivan Publishing House, 1960.
Kothari, Rajni, *Transformation and Survival,* New Delhi: Ajanta Publications, 1988.
Kothari, Rajni, *State Against Democracy,* New Delhi: Ajanta Publications, 1988.
Kothari, Rajni, *Politics and the People* (Vol. I, II), New Delhi: Ajanta Publications, 1989.
Kumarappa, J. C., *Economy of Permanence,* Varanasi, Sarva Seva Sangh Prakashan, 1984.
Larson, Gerald James, *India's Agony Over Religion,* New York: State University of New York Press, 1995.
Lewis, Martin, D., ed., *Gandhi: Maker of Modern India,* Lexington, Mass., D. C. Heath and Co., 1965.
Macy, Joanna, *Dharma and Development: Religion as Resource in the Sarvodaya Self-Help Movement,* Connecticut: Kumarian Press, 1983.
Maharajan, M., *Gandhian Thought: A Study of Tradition and Modernity,* New Delhi: Sterling Publishers Private Ltd., 1996.
Mani, Mahajan, P., *Foundations of Gandhian Thought,* Nagpur, India: Publishers and Publisher's Distributors, 1987.

Mashruwala, K. G., *Gandhi and Marx*, Ahmedabad: Navajivan Publishing House, 1951.

Mashruwala, K. G., *Towards Sarvodaya Order*, Ahmedabad: Navajivan Publishing House, 1971.

Mathur, J. S., ed., *Non-Violence and Social Change*, Ahmedabad: Navajivan Publishing House, 1977.

Mehta, J. K., *Gandhian Thought: An Analytical Study,* New Delhi: Ashish Publishing House, 1985.

Mehta, Ved, *Mahatma Gandhi & His Apostles*, New Haven: Yale University Press, 1976.

Merton, Thomas, *Gandhi on Non-Violence,* Canada: Penguin Books, 1969.

Miller-Renefulop, *Dehumanization in Modern Society*, Ahmedabad: Navajivan Publishing House, 1953.

Mishra, Anil Dutta, ed., *Gandhian Approach to Contemporary Problems*, New Delhi: Mittal Publications, 1996.

Misra, K. P. & Gangal, S. C., *Gandhi and the Contemporary World*, Delhi: Chanakya Publications, 1981.

Misra, R. P., ed., *Gandhian Model of Development and World Peace*, New Delhi: Concept Publishing Co., 1989.

Murphy, Stephen, *Why Gandhi is Relevant in Modern India,* New Delhi: The Gandhi Peace Foundation, 1990.

Nanda, B. R., *Mahatma Gandhi*, Delhi: Oxford University Press, 1958.

Nanda, B. R., *Gandhi and His Critics*, Delhi: Oxford University Press, 1958.

Narain, Jai, *Gandhi's View of Political Power*, New Delhi: Deep & Deep Publications, 1987.

Narayan, Jaiprakash, *Face to Face*, Varanasi: Navachetna Prakashan, 1970.

Narayan, Jaiprakash, *Sampoorn Kranti*, Varanasi: Sarva Seva Sangh Prakashan, 1984.

Ostergaard, Geoffrey and Melville Currell, *The Gentle Anarchists*, Oxford: Claredon Press, 1971.

Ostergaard, Geoffrey, *Nonviolent Revolution in India*, New Delhi: Gandhi Peace Foundation, 1985.

Parikh, Harivallabh, *Our Involvement for Dams*, Rangpur: Anand Niketan Ashram, 1994.

Patil, V. T., ed., *Studies on Gandhi,* New Delhi: Sterling Publishers Private Ltd., 1983.

Patwardhan, Appa, *Chalanshuddi Or Nature Forging Towards Sarvodaya*, Ahmedabad: Navajivan Publishing House, 1967.

Pillai, N. P., *The Educational Aims of Mahatma Gandhi*, Trivandrum: Kalyanmandir Pub., 1959.

Prabhu, R. K., ed., *The Mind of Mahatma Gandhi*, Ahmedabad: Navajivan Publishing House, 1967.

Prasad, Bimal, *Gandhi, Nehru & J. P.*, Delhi: Chanakya Publications, 1985.

Prasad, K. M., *Sarvodaya of Gandhi*, New Delhi: Raj Hans Publications, 1984.

Prasad, Nageshwar, ed., *Hind Swaraj: A Fresh Look,* New Delhi: The Gandhi Peace Foundation, 1985.

Prasad, Nageshwar, ed., *Gandhi and the Contemporary World*, New Delhi: Radiant Publishers, 1993.

Pyarelal, *Mahatma Gandhi: The Early Phase* (Vol. I), Ahmedabad: Navajivan Publishing House, 1965.

Pyarelal, *Mahatma Gandhi,* (Vol. II), Bombay: Sevak Prakashan, 1980.

Pyarelal, *Mahatma Gandhi* (Vol. III), Ahmedabad: Navajivan Publishing House, 1986.

Pyarelal, *Mahatma Gandhi: The Last Phase* (Vol. I, II), Ahmedabad: Navajivan Publishing House, 1956.

Radhakrishnan, N., ed., *Gandhian Perspective of Nation Building for World Peace,* New Delhi: Konark Publishers Private Ltd., 1992.

Radhakrishnan, N., *Gandhi Youth & Nonviolence,* Delhi: Center for Development & Peace, 1992.

Radhakrishnan, N., *Gandhi: The Quest for Tolerance and Survival,* New Delhi: Gandhi Smriti and Darshan Samiti, 1995.

Ram, Suresh, *Vinoba and His Mission,* Rajghat: Akhil Bharat Sarva Seva Sangh, 1954.

Ramachandran, *Quest for Gandhi,* New Delhi: Gandhi Peace Foundation, 1970.

Rammurti, Acharya, *Total Revolution For All,* Varanasi: Sarva Seva Sangh Prakashan, 1978.

Rammurti, Acharya, *Marx and Gandhi,* Ahmedabad: Vimal Prakashan Trust, 1992.

Rao, Seshagiri, K. L., *Mahatma Gandhi and Comparative Religion,* Delhi: Motilal Banarsidas Pub., 1978.

Richards, Glyn, *The Philosophy of Gandhi,* London: Curzon Press, 1982.

Rottermund, Dietmar, *Mahatma Gandhi: An Essay in Political Biography,* Columbia, Mo.: South Asia Pub., 1992.

Rudolph, Lloyd & Susanne, *Gandhi: The Traditional Roots of Charisma,* Chicago: The University of Chicago Press, 1967.

Sachidananda, ed., *Sarvodaya and Development,* Patna: A. N. Sinha Institute of Social Studies, (no date).

The Servants of the People Society, *Lok Sevak Sangh,* New Delhi: Lajpat Bhawan, (no date).

Shepard, Mark, *Gandhi Today,* Washington D. C.: Seven Locks Press, 1987.

Sethi, J. D., *Gandhi Today,* Ghaziabad, India: Vikas Publishing House Pvt. Ltd., 1979.

Sethi, J. D., ed., *Trusteeship: The Gandhian Alternative,* New Delhi: Gandhi Peace Foundation, 1986.

Shah, Kanti, *Vinoba: Life and Mission,* Varanasi: Sarva Seva Sangh Prakashan, (no date).

Shah, Kantilal, ed., *Vinoba on Gandhi,* Varanasi: Sarva Seva Sangh Prakashan, 1973.

Sharma, A. K., *Gandhian Perspective on Population and Development,* New Delhi: Concept Publishing Co., 1996.

Sharma, K. D., *Impact of Gandhi on Rural Development and Social Change,* New Delhi: Mohit Publications, 1997.

Singh, Nirmala, *Non-Violence and Satyagraha in Gandhian Philosophy,* New Delhi: Janki Prakashan, 1997.

Singh, Ramjee, *Gandhi and the Twenty-First Century,* New Delhi: Peace Publishers, 1993.

Sinha, Archana, *The Social and Political Philosophy of Sarvodaya,* Patna: Janaki Prakashan, 1978.

Sonnleitner, Michael, *Vinoba Bhave on Self Rule & Representative Democracy,* New Delhi: Promilla & Co. Publishers, 1988.

Tandon, Vishwanath, *Sarvodaya After Gandhi,* Varanasi: Sarva Seva Sangh Prakashan, 1965.

Tandon, Vishwanath, *Selections from Vinoba,* Varanasi: Sarva Seva Sangh Prakashan, 1981.

Tikekar, Indu, *Integral Revolution: An Analytical Study of Gandhian Thought,* Varanasi: Sarva Seva Sangh Prakashan, 1970.

Thomas, David C., *Afforestation - A Mass Movement of the People,* Rangpur: Anand Niketan Ashram, 1992.

Thomson, Mark, *Gandhi and his Ashrams*, Bombay: Popular Prakashan, 1993.
Varma, Ravindra, *Gandhi's Theory of Trusteeship*, Wardha: Institute of Gandhian Studies, (no date).
Varma, Ravindra, *Five Fallacies and the Future*, Wardha: Gandhi Vichar Parishad, 1990.
Varma, Ravindra, *Is There An Alternative to a Non Violent Revolution?*, Wardha: Institute of Gandhian Studies, 1992.
Varma, Ravindra, *Gandhi and Fundamentalism*, Wardha: Institute of Gandhian Studies, 1996.
Varma, Ravindra, *Gandhian Philosophy of Swadeshi*, New Delhi: Gandhi Smriti and Darshan Samiti, 1997.
Varshney, Ashutosh, *Democracy, Development and its Countryside*, New Delhi: Foundation Books, 1995.
Vepa, Ram K., *New Technology: A Gandhian Concept*, New Delhi: Gandhi Book House, 1975.
Vora, Harshkant, *Not Submergence But Emergence*, Rangpur: Anand Niketan Publishers, 1991.

Sources in Hindi

Bahuguna, Sunderlal, *Chipko Ka Sandesh*, Teri: Chipko Information Center, Navajivan Ashram, (no date).
Bang Thakurdas, *Bharat Kidhar*, Varanasi: Sarva Seva Sangh Prakashan, 1988.
Bang Thakurdas, *Mahatma Gandhi*, Varanasi: Sarva Seva Sangh Prakashan, 1990.
Bang, Thakurdas, *Gaon Ki Satta Gaon Ke Hath*, Varanasi: Sarva Seva Sangh Prakashan, 1990.
Bang, Thakurdas, *Hindu - Muslim Manas,* Varanasi: Sarva Seva Sangh Prakashan, 1993.
Bhave, Vinoba, *Sarvodaya Vichar Aur Swaraj Shastr*, Varanasi: Sarva Seva Sangh Prakashan, 1963.
Bhave, Vinoba, *Acharyakul*, Varanasi: Sarva Seva Sangh Prakashan, 1973.
Bhave, Vinoba, *Dharma Samanvya*, Delhi: Gandhi Peace Foundation, 1977.
Bhave, Vinoba, *Sapt Shaktiyan*, Varanasi: Sarva Seva Sangh Prakashan, 1978.
Bhave, Vinoba, *Acharyakul Prashnopanishad,* Paunar: Acharyakul, 1981.
Bhave, Vinoba, *Shiksha Men Kranti Aur Acharyakul,* Paunar: Acharyakul, 1981.
Bhave, Vinoba, *Acharyon Ka Anushasan*, Varanasi: Sarva Seva Sangh Prakashan, 1981.
Bhave, Vinoba, *Jivan Drishti*, Varanasi: Sarva Seva Sangh Prakashan, 1982.
Bhave, Vinoba, *Atmagyan Aur Vigyan*, Varanasi: Sarva Seva Sangh Prakashan, 1983.
Chaudhury, Manmohan, *Azadi Ke Liye Khatre,* Varanasi: Sarva Seva Sangh Prakashan, 1983.
Deshpande, Achutya, *Goraksha Satyagraha Ki Prishtabhoomi,* Paunar: Paramdhan Prakashan, (no date).
Dhadda, Sidhraj, *Lok Swaraj - Lokniti*, Varanasi: Sarva Seva Sangh Prakashan, 1989.
Dharmadhikari, Dada, *Sarvodaya Darshan*, Varanasi: Sarva Seva Sangh Prakashan, 1979.
Dixit, Rajiv, *Bahurashtra Companiyon Ka Makarhjal*, Allahabad: Gandhi Bhawan, 1991.
Gandhi, M. K., *Hind Swaraj Ka Sandesh,* Wardha: Seva Gram Ashram, 1992 (Analysis by Kanti Shah and Vasant Palsheekar).

Kumarappa. J. C., *Gaon Andolan Kyun?*, Varanasi: Sarva Seva Sangh Prakashan, 1986.

Majumdar, Dhirendra, *Kranti Banam Swadeshi Raj*, Varanasi: Sarva Seva Sangh Prakashan, 1979.

Majumdar, Dhirendra, *Kranti Prayog Aur Chintan*, Varanasi: Sarva Seva Sangh Prakashan, 1979.

Narayan, Jaiprakash, *Meri Vichar Yatra*, Vol. I, Varanasi: Sarva Seva Sangh Prakashan, 1974, Vol. II, 1978.

Narayan, Jaiprakash, *Sampoorn Kranti Ke Liye Aawahan,* Varanasi: Sarva Seva Sangh Prakashan, 1974.

Rammurti, Acharya, *J. P. Ka Varg Sangarsh,* Varanasi: Sarva Seva Sangh Prakashan, 1977.

Rammurti, Acharya, *Kis Ore*, Varanasi: Sarva Seva Sangh Prakashan, 1983.

Rammurti, Acharya, *Kheti Ke Mazdoor Bhaiyon Se*, Varanasi: Sarva Seva Sangh Prakashan, 1983.

Rammurti, Acharya, *Lok Umeedvar*, Varanasi: Sarva Seva Sangh Prakashan, 1983.

Rammurti, Acharya, *Kranti Ki Nai Disha*, Vidchi: Sampoorn Kranti Vidyalaya, 1987.

Rammurti, Acharya, *Sampoorn Kranti: Tab Aur Ab*, Patna: Bihar Sarvodaya Mandal, 1989.

Rammurti, Acharya, *Shiksha Sanskriti Aur Samaj*, Munger: Shrambharati Khodigram, 1990.

Rammurti, Acharya, *Vartman Rashtriya Paristhiti Aur Meri Bhoomika,* Patna: Bihar Sarvodaya Mandal, 1992.

Rammurti, Acharya, *Panchayati Raj Ki Kalpna,* Jamui: Khadi Gram, 1996.

Rammurti, Acharya, *Apna Raj: Panchayati Raj Kya? Kaise?,* Jamui: Khadi Gram, 1998.

Tada, Shanti Swaroop, *Samaj Ki Chunautiyan*, Vol. I, II, Alwar, India: Anand Prakashan, (no date).

Tikekar, Indu, *Kranti Ka Samagr Darshan*, Varanasi: Sarva Seva Sangh Prakashan, 1985.

Unknown Author, *Gay Bachegi - Desh Bachega*, Wardha: Akhil Bharat Krishi Go Seva Sangh, 1981.

Unknown Author, *Sangarsh Ka Agla Kadam*, Varanasi: Sarva Seva Sangh Prakashan, 1981.

Unknown Author, *Rajniti Men Lok-niti Ka Pravesh*, Varanasi: Sarva Seva Sangh Prakashan, 1984.

Unknown Author, *Vartman Arthic Sankat Aur Vikalp Ki Disha,* Varanasi: Sarva Seva Sangh Prakashan, 1991.

Interviews

Over the years the author has conducted several interviews with several Gandhian scholars, leaders, and Sarvodaya workers in different parts of India. The following is a list of those who graciously contributed through surveys and face to face conversations.

Amarnath bhai, a leading Sarvodaya worker, past secretary, Sarva Seva Sangh, and Gandhian youth worker, Varanasi, U. P.

Bhandari, Lakshmichand, past president, Rajasthan Samagr Seva Sangh, Jaipur, Rajasthan.

Bhargava, Ram Chandra, Sarvodaya worker, Gandhi Bhavan Trust, Bhopal, Madhya Pradesh.

Damodar, Gokhale Vishnu, Nature Cure Ashram, Urli-Kanchan, Pune, Maharashtra.

Desai, Jyotibhai, a leading Sarvodaya worker in Gujarat, Surat, Gujarat.

Desai, Pravina, a member of Vinoba's Paunar Ashram, a Sarvodaya worker and youth leader.

Dev Dutt, journalist and commentator on Sarvodaya.

Dharampal, writer, thinker, and an astute observer of Sarvodaya.

Diwakar, R. R., a Gandhian thinker, writer and past president of the Gandhi Peace Foundation, New Delhi.

Dube, Narendra, a leading Sarvodaya worker and supporter of Go-Raksha Satyagraha, Indore, Madhya Pradesh.

Chandra, Avinesh, Sarva Seva Sangh, Rajghat, Varanasi.

Ganesh, Behede, Nature Cure Ashram, Urli-Kanchan, Pune, Maharashtra.

Ghallani, R. D., a leading Sarvodaya worker in Rajasthan, Jodhpur, Rajasthan.

Goyal, Chittarmal, a leading Khadi worker, Rajasthan Kadhi Sangh, Khadibag, Rajasthan.

Haldhar, Hawaldar, Sarvodaya worker, Patna, Bihar.

Hiroodkar, Eknath, Sarvodaya worker, Rajpeth, Maharashtra.

Hoshiyari Bhahin, member of the staff, Nature Cure Ashram, Urli-Kanchan, recited Ramayan to Gandhi regularly at his ashram.

Jain, Jawaherlal, associated with Kumarappa Gram Swaraj Sanstha, Jaipur, Rajasthan.

Jana, Chittranjan, associated with the Sarvodaya Mandal, Calcutta, W. Bengal.

Kelekar, Ravindra, Sarvodaya worker, Mardol, Goa.

Kothari, Rajini, writer, thinker, activist, and a committed Gandhian.

Kumar, Nirmal, past editor of "Gandhi Marg" (Hindi Edition), The Gandhi Peace Foundation, New Delhi.

Kumar, Prashant, Sarvodaya worker and youth leader, Bombay Sarvodaya Mandal, Bombay, Maharashtra.

Lavanam, one of the secretaries of Sarva Seva Sangh, an atheist Gandhian and Sarvodaya worker, Vijayvada, Andhra Pradesh.

Narayan, Surya, Sarvodaya worker, Patna, Bihar.

Padmanabhan, V., managing trustee, Gandhi Gram Trust, Gandhi Gram, Tamil Nadu.

Pandya, Kirtibhai, Sarvodaya worker, Bhavnagar, Gujarat.

Perumal, N. M., Sarvodaya worker associated with LAFTI (an organization headed by Krishnammal), Kilrelur, Tamil Nadu.

Pyarelal Nayar, the late junior secretary of Gandhi, writer, thinker in the Gandhian movement.

Ragini Bahin, currently directs the Varanasi Seva Ashram. A committed Sarvodaya worker.

Roychowdhury, K., one of the leading Sarvodaya workers in Bengal, Abhoy Ashram, Balrampur, W. Bengal.

Roy, Lila, Gandhi Peace Foundation, Calcutta, W. Bengal.

Saran, Tripurari, leading Sarvodaya activist, past president of Bihar Sarvodaya Mandal, a member of Sarva Seva Sangh, Patna, Bihar.

Satchidanand, Gandhian thinker-worker, Aligarh, U. P.

Sharma, Ramesh, Gandhian Youth Activist, the Gandhi Peace Foundation, New Delhi.

Sharma, Vichitra Narayan, past leader in the Khadi movement, member Sarva Seva Sangh, Lucknow, U. P.

Singh, Ramjee, Gandhian scholar, professor, and vice chancellor of universities in Bihar and Rajasthan.

Sundarani, Swarko, a leading Sarvoadaya worker, director Samanvya Ashram, Bodh-Gaya, Bihar.

Menon, E. P., a leading Sarvodaya worker, Bangalore, Karnataka.

Misra, Anupam, coordinator, The Ecology and Environment Cell, the Gandhi Peace Foundation, New Delhi.

Mukerjee, Gopal Das, Gandhi Peace Foundation, Calcutta, W. Bengal.

Muniandi, K., chairman, Gandhiniketan Ashram, Madurai Distr., Tamil Nadu.

Tandon, Vishwanath, a Gandhian scholar-writer, a follower of Vinoba, and an associate of the Gandhi Smarak Nidhi, New Delhi.

Tapeshwar Bhai, Sarvodaya worker, Madhubani, Bihar.

Thakkar, Vimla, a Gandhian mystic, youth leader, writer-thinker, Mt. Abu, Rajasthan.

Upadhyaya, Rabindra Nath, past president of Sarva Seva Sangh, and a leading Sarvodaya worker in Assam.

Vargiya, Shyam Narayan Vijay, writer, thinker, one time member of Sarva Seva Sangh, Guna, Madhya Pradesh.

Varma, Ravindra, Director, Gandhi Vichar Parishad, president, The Gandhi Peace Foundation, a leading Gandhian thinker, Wardha, Maharashtra.

Vidrohi, Mahadev, Director, Abhikram, Ahmedabad, Gujarat.

Vijayam, an atheist Gandhian and Sarvodaya worker, Vijayvoda, Andhra Pradesh.

Vinaya Bhai, member, Sarva Seva Sangh, Varanasi, U. P.

[31] Nageshwar Prasad, ed., HindSwaraj: A Fresh Look (New Delhi: Gandhi Peace Foundation), 1985, p.21.

[32] M. L. Handa, Manifesto for a Peaceful World Order: A Gandhian Perspective (Delhi: Gandhi Bhawan), 1983, p.134.

[33] Ignatius Jesudasan, "Behavioral Patterns and Social Structures in the Gandhian Perspective," in Mercy Kappen, ed., Gandhi and Social Action Today (New Delhi: Sterling Publishers), 1990, p.2.

[34] Rajni Kothari, Transformation and Survival (New Delhi: Ajanta Publications), 1988, p.15.

[35] Shashi Sharma, "Technology and Man - Gandhian Perspective," in R. P. Misra, ed., Gandhian Model of Development and World Peace (New Delhi: Concept Publishing Co.), 1990, p.79.

[36] J. D. Sethi, op.cit., p.104.

[37] M. V. Naidu, "The Modern Industrial-Military State: A Gandhian Analysis" in Gandhi Marg (Special Issue on non-violence), April-June 1992, pp. 253-257.

[38] Amlan Dutta, The Gandhian Way (Shillong: North-Eastern Hill University Publications, 1986), p.4.

[39] Rajni Kothari, op.cit., p.89.

[40] Based on a conversation with Prof. Desai, retired professor of Economics, Gujarat Vidya Pittha, Ahmedabad, 1993.

[41] Sudhir J. George, "Gandhian Economics and its Relevance Today: Points to Ponder in Mishra, op.cit., p. 73.

[42] See Anil Dutta Mishra, Gandhian Approach to Contemporary Problems (Mittal Pub., 1996) p. 84-85.

[43] K. J. Charles, "The New Economic Policy or the Recolonisation of India" in Anil D. Mishra, op.c.t., p. 85-86.

[44] Jai Narayan, "Technology and Dispersal of Economy: A Gandhian Perspective" in R. P. Misra, ed., Gandhian Model of Development and World Peace, op.c.t., p.86.

[45] Ibid., p.86.

[46] J. D. Sethi, op.c.t., p.131.

[47] S. Venkatachalam, "The Relevance of Swadeshi in Contemporary India", in Mishra, op.c.t., p. 128.

[48] M. Vinaik, "Kumarappa the forgotten Deity", in Gandhi Vigyan (A quarterly journal of the Gandhi Vigyan Trust, Bangalore, vol. IV, #3, Jan. 1993, p.47.

[49] Banwari Lal Sharma, "Dava Ke Naam Par Zahar Aur Loot" (Poison and Robbery in the name of Medicine) in Nai Azadi (new Freedom), Published by Gandhi Bhawan, Allahabad, U.P., India, # 11-12, Nov.-Dec. 1992, p.3.

[50] According to L. C. Thanu, "Most of the drugs banned in developed countries are marketed in the third world countries." In fact, developed countries are using India as a guinea pig to "experiment their dangerous medicine through MNCs (Multinational Companies). Due to these malpractices, India appointed the Hathi Foundation, which found that out of 15,000 medicines produced, only 116 were essential. The rest of the medicines circulated in the India market are "unnecessary as well as dangerous." (L. C. Thanu, in Gandhian Approach to Contemporary Problems (Mittal Pub., 1996) p. 92-93.

[51] Meera Shiva, "Dava Niti Aur Nai Gulami" (The Medicine Policy and New Slavery), op.c.t., p.6.

[52] Narendra Nath Mahrotra, op.cit., p.16.

[53] Chandrakant Rohtagi, op.cit., p.18.

[54] Manoj Tyagi, op.cit., p.30.

[55] K. M. Prasad, Sarvodaya of Gandhi (New Delhi: Raj Hans Pub. 1984), p.56.

[56] Hitesranjan Sanyal, "Modern Development and the Gandhian Alternative," in Nageshwar Prasad, ed., Hind Swaraj: A Fresh Look (New Delhi: Gandhi Peace Foundation,1985), p.171.

Appendix

The following is the list of addresses of the Gandhian constructive workers profiled in this book:

Acharya Rammurti
Shram Bharti
Post Khadi Gram
Dist. Munghyer, Bihar

Achyut Deshpande
Goraksha Satyagraha
Sarvodaya Hospital
Ghatkopar 400086
Mumbai

Chunibhai Vaidya
Gujarat Loksamiti
Lal Darwaja
Ahmedabad 380001
Gujarat

Devendra Kumar
Centre for Science for Villages
Magan Sangrahalaya
Wardha 442001
Maharashtra

Govind Rao Deshpande
20, Juthica, 4th floor
22 N. Bharucha Road
Mumbai 400007
Maharashtra

Harivallabh Parikh
Anand Niketan Ashram
Rangpur (Kawant)
Via Kosindhara
Dist. Varodhara
Gujarat

Jagannathan
Vinoba Ashram
Kuthur 611105
Nagai Quaid-E-Millath Dist.
Tamil Nadu

Krisnammal
c/o LAFTI
Vinoba Ashram
Kuthur 611105
Nagai Quaid-E-Millath Dist.
Tamil Nadu

Narayan Desai
Institute of Total Revolution
Veddchi
Dist. Surat
Gujarat

Nirmala Deshpande
Harijan Sewak Sangh
Kingsway Camp
Delhi 110009

353

V. Ramachandran
Bharatiya Khadi Gramodyog
Coimbatore
Tamil Nadu

Shobana Ranade
Gandhi National Memorial Society
Agakhan Palace
Pune 411014
Maharastra

S.N. Subba Rao
Gandhi Peace Foundation
221-223 D.D. Upadhyaya Marg
New Delhi 110002

Sunderlal Bahuguna
Ganga Himalaya Kuti
Tehri, 249001
Garhwal

Thakurdas Bang
Sarva Seva Sangh
Gopuri
Wardha Dist. 442001
Maharastra

Index

355

358